UNION COUNTY, SOUTH CAROLINA

DEED ABSTRACTS

VOLUME V: DEED BOOKS T-W

1828-1835 [1778-1835]

BY

BRENT H. HOLCOMB

SCMAR
COLUMBIA, SOUTH CAROLINA
2007

SCMAR
Columbia, South Carolina

ISBN: 978-0-913363-57-X
Library of Congress Catalog Card Number: 98-61136

Copies may be ordered from
Brent H. Holcomb
Box 21766
Columbia, SC 29221.

INTRODUCTION

Union County was formed in 1785 as a county of Ninety Six District. It was included in Pinckney District 1791-1799. In the year 1800 with the end of the county court system, it became Union District. In the colonial period the area of Union County was considered part of Craven County or Berkeley County in South Carolina. Prior to the border surveys of 1764 and 1772, the area was included in the North Carolina counties of Anson, Mecklenburg, and Tryon. For this reason many grants and deeds from North Carolina are referenced in the Union County deeds, and such grants from North Carolina are frequently referred to as "north patents." The South Carolina deeds prior to 1785 were recorded in Charleston and in some cases a few years later. The Charleston deeds have been abstracted and published through the year 1788, those from 1773-1788 by the writer. The deeds of the aforementioned North Carolina counties have also been abstracted and published. The deeds in this volume were recorded 1828-1835. As is common, there arc deeds recorded from a much earlier time period. The earliest instrument included in this work dates from 15 May 1778 (Deed Book T, pages 420-421). Therefore, with this volume, the deed abstracts for the Union County area are now in print from the beginning through the year 1835. The deeds in this volume have been abstracted from South Carolina Archives microfilm, Rolls C2211 and C2212. Some unusual records found in this volume (Deed Book W, page 207 and others) are the divisions of Union District into militia companies, the boundaries of which are indicated.

Union County bordered on the counties of Spartanburg, Laurens, Newberry, Fairfield, York, and Chester. Few changes in its boundaries occurred until 1897 when a portion of Union County was taken, with portions of Spartanburg and York counties, to form Cherokee County. As already stated, Union County became a district in the year 1800, at which time Pinckney Judicial District, of which Union County had been a part, was discontinued. Some people were reluctant to change to the term *district* for several years and there are usually deeds recorded years after their execution. For those reasons we find the term *county* in some of the deeds included in this volume. The term *county* was resumed in 1868.

My thanks to Mr. James D. McKain for preparing the excellent indices.

Brent H. Holcomb
August 10, 2006

UNION COUNTY SOUTH CAROLINA
DEED ABSTRACTS VOLUME V

T, 1: South Carolina. James Duncan son of Alexander, of District of Union, to Edward M. Bobo & Elizabeth Bobo his wife, my grand daughter, tract of 100 acres on the south side of Tyger River adj. corner of William B. Murphy, granted to William Wofford 10 May 1770, to line where David Johnson's line crosses it, 12 March 1818. James Duncan son of Alexr. (LS), Wit: Thos Oneall, Richard H. Hughes, Jesse Jackson. Proved by the oath of Thos Oneall 12 March 1818 before Bird Murphey, J.Q. Elizabeth Duncan (X), wife of James Duncan, relinquished dower. Recorded 21 April 1828.

T, 2-3: John Anderson, Sheriff of Union District, by virtue of a writ of fieri facias from the court of common pleas tested 15 Dec 1827 at the suit of Thomas Saunders commanding me to levy of the goods and chattles, lands and tenements of Suprey Anderson, $25.23, sells tract of 79 acres on waters of Tinker Creek whereon Thomas Saunders now lives adj. Daniel Peak, R. Edwards, Randolph Peak, and Wm. Townson, sold for $36 to Thomas Anderson, 23 April 1828. John Anderson S. U. D. (LS), Wit: B. J. Gregory, Isaac Whitton. Proved by the oath of Isaac Whitton 23 April 1828. Recorded 23 April 1828.

T, 3-4: John Anderson, Sheriff of Union District, by virtue of a writ of fieri facias from the court of common pleas tested 17 Jan 1828 at the suit of John Gage Sr. and Z. P. Herndon commanding me to levy of the goods and chattles, lands and tenements of John Bates, Late Sheriff, $1132.12, sells tract of 400 acres adj. Mrs. Bates, James Foote[?], Thomas Sortor, being a tract formerly owned by John McNeale, sold for $307 to Dr. E. M. Bobo, 22 April 1828. John Anderson S. U. D. (LS), Wit: B. J. Gregory, Wm. M. Thomson. Proved by the oath of Wm M Thomson 23 April 1828 before J. Rogers, Q. U. Recorded 23 April 1828.

T, 4-5: John Anderson, Sheriff of Union District, by virtue of a writ of fieri facias from the court of common pleas tested 5 Apr 1828 at the suit of Z. Hooker commanding me to levy of the goods and chattles, lands and tenements of James Turner $54.22, sells tract of 200 acres on branches of Brown Creek adj. Porter, lands formerly owned by Wm Giles deceast, Rhoda Gregory, Ellender Wilson, purchased by Dr. Edward M. Bobo, sold for $50, 22 April 1828. John Anderson S. U. D. (LS), Wit: B. J. Gregory, Wm. M. Thomson. Proved by the oath of Wm M Thomson 23 April 1828 before J. Rogers, Q. U. Recorded 23 April 1828.

T, 5-6: John Anderson, Sheriff of Union District, by virtue of a writ of fieri facias from the court of common pleas tested 17 Jan 1828 at the suit of John Gage Senr & Z. P. Herndon commanding me to levy of the goods and chattles, lands and tenements of John Bates, Esqr., late Sheriff, $1132.12, tract of 237 acres on the north east side of Fair Forest adj. widow Malone, heirs of Hezekiah Rice decd, tract whereon David Spiva lately lived, purchased by Dr. Edward M. Bobo, sold for $350, 22 April 1828. John Anderson S. U.

D. (LS), Wit: B. J. Gregory, Wm. M. Thomson. Proved by the oath of Wm M Thomson 23 April 1828 before J. Rogers, Q. U. Recorded 23 April 1828.

T, 6-7: South Carolina, Union District. Ellis Palmer for $250 to William Palmer, both of said state, part of tract granted to Daniel Hughger, 18 March 1823. Ellis Palmer (Seal), Wit: James Rountree, Lemick Ezell. Proved by the oath of James Rountree Esqr 26 April 1828 before J. Rogers, Q. U. Nancy Palmer (X) relinquished dower 6 Sept 1824 before Isaac Gowing, Q. U. Recorded 26 April 1828.

T, 7-8: John Anderson, Sheriff of Union District, for $1800 to Edward Stevens, eleven negro slaves, to wit, Abram, Phillips, Majina[?], Violett, Buck, James, Sawney, Harriott, Barry, Sicily and Amelia, sold by me as sheriff to satisfy the execution of Jincy J. Glenn & others against Col. Reuben Sims, 14 Sept 1827. John Anderson S. U. D. (LS), Wit: John Giles, Silas Baker. Proved by the oath of Silas Baker 5 May 1828 before J. Rogers, Q. U. Recorded 5 April 1828.

T, 8-9: Articles of agreement between John Palmer and Hanner Cole, widow, that they have agreed to live together after the holy order of marriage and each one shall keep his and her property, and the said widows children shall be intitled to all her property as she sees fit the names of the children are as follows, John Cole & Richard Cole & Rebecca Cole [not dated]. John Palmer (LS), Hannah Cole (X) (LS), Wit: James Lane, S. Cole. Proved by the oath of James Lane and that he saw Samuel Cole sign, 19 Oct 1813 before I. J. Foster, J. P. Recorded 28 April 1828.

T, 9-10: $232.75 By the 1st of Jany next, I promise to pay Z. Reid or order $232.75 for value recd, 20 Feb 1828. Wm. J. Burnes. Test: J. Moreland.

South Carolina, Union District. Wm. J. Burnes of Union District in order to secure payment of a note given to Z. Reid for $232.75, mortgage 73 acres on Fannens Creek, waters of Broad River, also one sorrel mare and colt, 20 Feb 1828. W. J. Burnes (LS), Wit: J. Moreland, J. A. Stephenson. Proved by the oath of J. Moreland 7 March 1828 before Lott Whitlock, J.P. Recorded 5 May 1828.

T, 10: James Harrington of Union District do lease[?] unto Drury Harrington of same, the plantation on which he now lives unto a cross fence on the south side of his house to be his own property as long as he lives and what he is a mind to clear, also bound in the penal sum of $200 if I sell this land in the said term of time or dispossess him of the same, 27 Oct 1825. James T. Harrington (LS), Wit: Wm. H. Steen, Joseph A. Darby. Proved by the oath of Wm. H. Steen 26 March 1828 before Wm. H. Cotter, J.P. Recorded 21 March 1828.

T, 10-11: South Carolina, Union District. Wm. Spears of District aforesaid for natural love and affection to my daughter Delilah Steen, independent of the control of her husband James Steen, a negro girl named Zenuly supposed to be about five or six years old, and appraise to $175, also a certain boy named Right aged about four years, appraised to $150, 3 May 1828. Wm. Spears (X) (LS), Wit: J. F. Walker, Thomas Jenkins, L. B. Murray. Proved by the oath of James F. Walker 5 May 1828 before J. Rogers, Q. U. Recorded 5 May 1828.

T, 11-12: John Anderson, by a writ of fieri facias from the court of common pleas for the district of Union tested 13 Oct 1827 at the suit of Jno Oland indorsee to me directed to levy of the goods and chattles, lands and tenements of Olias Norman the sum of $300, sells tract of three lots in the village of Union, numbers 36, 24, and 10, and a small quantity of land lying directly back of Lott #10, adj. McBeths line, purchased by John Oland of the District of Spartanburgh for $565, 17 Jan 1828. John Anderson, S. U. D. (LS), Wit: Isaac Whitton, Silas Baker. Proved by the oath of Silas Baker 5 May 1828 before J. Rogers, Q. U. Recorded 5 May 1828.

T, 12-13: South Carolina, Union District. Nathan Glenn of district aforesaid have granted and quit claimed unto William W. Glenn, all of the interest I have in a tract of land called the Otterson tract, on Tigar River, adj. Nathan Glenn, bought of Lewis Fant and adj. George Fant, Samuel Gordon, James Dugan, and others, also one tract formerly belonging to Lewis Fant, said to contain 137½ acres, on east side Tigar River adj. John Lewis decd, George Smith, and the Otterson tract, 28 Feb 1828. Nathan Glenn (LS), Wit: t. A. Carlisle, Thos Walker. Proved by the oaths of both wit 28 Feb 1828 before E. McGraw, Q. U. Recorded 3 March 1828.

T, 13: South Carolina, Union District. Each of us acknowledge ourselves satisfied at the sale of the property of the estate of Sijasmond Stribling, agreeable to the sale made by Daniel White, admr., 29 Jan 1827. Nancy Stribling (X) (LS), Sijasmond Stribling (LS), Frances Stribling (LS), Wit: Wm. Rice, James Savage. Proved by the oath of Wm Rice 10 March 1828 before Daniel White, Q. U. Recorded 10 March 1828.

T, 13-14: South Carolina, Union District. B. J. Gregory of district aforesaid for $275 to John V. Johnson of same, 116 acres adj. Levy Gregory's land, Savages, John Porter, B. Stork[?], 26 Jan 1826. B. J. Gregory (Seal), Wit: John Rochester, Jesse Turner, James Turner Senr. Elizabeth Gregory (X) relinquished dower 28 April 1828 before E. McGraw, Q.U. Proved by the oath of John Rochester 5 May 1828 before E. McGraw, Q.U. Recorded 5 May 1828.

T, 14-15: South Carolina, Union District. Henry Smith of York District for $210 to John Jeffries Senr of said district, tract in Union district on both sides Gilkies Creek, adj. John Jeffries corner, 10 March 1828. Henry Smith (LS), Wit: W. Graham, Cyntha Graham, Seborn Dill. Proved by the oath of Sebern Dill 25 April 1828 before Danl Thomas, Q. U. Ann Smith, wife of Henry Smith, relinquished dower 28 April 1828 before Daniel Smith, J. Q. Recorded 5 May 1828.

T, 16: South Carolina, Union District. John Jeffries Senr of Union District for $1000 to William Jeffries of same, tract on waters of Gilkeys and Thickety Creeks, waters of Broad River, near above Northerss's tan yard, Mabry's old corner, but be it property understood that this $1000 worth of land is part of William Jeffries legacy of John Jeffries estate, 1 May 1828. John Jeffries Senr (LS), Wit: James Jeffries, John V. Steen. Proved by the oath of James Jeffries 5 May 1828 before Saml Davis, J. P. Recorded 5 May 1828.

T, 16-17: South Carolina, Union District. John Mullings of district aforesaid to John Haney G a certain tract of land of 100 acres adj. Wm Reid, Jno Carothers, Hez. Spears, and John Howell, for $251, 1 March 1828. John Mullings (LS), Wit: Joseph S. Wair, John Massy (X). Proved by the oath of Joseph S. Wear 26 April 1828 before Wm. H. Cotter, J.P. Recorded 5 April 1828.

T, 17-18: James Turner of Union District for $151 to Landlott Porter of same, tract on a branch of Browns Creek, 50 acres, adj. Roady Porter, James Turner, __ May 1828. James Turner Senr (LS), Wit: John Porter, John V. Johnson, George A. Brandon. Proved by the oath of George D. A. Brandon 5 May 1828 before J. Rogers, Q.U. Recorded 5 May 1828.

T, 18-19: John Anderson, Sheriff of Union District, by virtue of several writs of fieri facias from the court of common pleas, tested 24 Oct 1827 at the suit of Walker & Lowery, A Wallace Thomas & others, to levy of the goods and chattles, lands and tenements of James Malcomson, $200, sells 350 acres being the tract whereon he now lives, on waters of Abatons Creek adj. John Jeffries, John Wilkins, Potter[?], sold for $153.50, 5 May 1828. John Anderson S. U. D. (Seal), Wit: B. S. Gregory, James Jeffries, M. B. Harrington. Proved by the oath of M. B. Harrington 5 May 1828 before J. Rogers, Q.U. Recorded 5 May 1828.

T, 19-20: Banks Meacham of District of Union for 43200 to James Meacham, all the plantation whereon I now live conveyed to me by Thomas Bowker 25 Dec 1820, and also all that adjoining plantation conveyed to me by Dred Jones on 26 Sept 1825, in the whole 661 acres on north side of Enoree River adj. Baram Bobo, Noah Garrett, John Beard, Widow Bishop, David Spiva, Thomas G. Danner, 5 Jan 1828. Banks Meacham (LS), Wit: Thomas Bowker, Noah Garret. Proved by the oath of Thomas Bowker 5 Jan 1828 before Jno Norman, J.P. Recorded 12 May 1828.

T, 20-22: Whereas John Thomas and John McIver stand indebted to John Kirkpatrick in the sum of $152,000 by their bond condition for the payment of $76,000 on or before 20 June 1838, with interest, mortgage of 53 negro slaves [named] which slaves are attached to the plantation belonging to Hall & Thomas on Broad River and also the 105 slaves [named] attached to the plantation on Sandy River belonging to Hall & Thomas, also 44 slaves attached to the plantation on Tygar River formerly belonging to said Hall and Thomas, 20 June 1828. John Thomas (LS), John McIver (LS), Wit: A.

Blanding, Wilmot R. Gibbes. Proved in Richland District by the oath of Wilmot R. Gibbes 23 June 1828 before John N. Barrillon, Not. Pub. & Q. U. Ex off. Recorded 25 June 1828.

T, 22-24: 20 June 1828, John Thomas & John McIver to John Kirkpatrick, whereas said John Thomas & John McIver stand indebted to said John Kirkpatrick by bond in the penal sum of $152,000, mortgage of tract of 474 acres in Fairfield district on Broad River near the mouth of Terrable Creek adj. Burnet Ashford, James Ashford, Philip Pearson, John Hutchenson; tract of 1027 acres in Chester district on waters of Sandy River purchased by Ainsley Hall from Anderson Thomas; tract in the district of Chester on waters of Broad and Sandy River, called the Mulberry Run, originally granted to James Young by resurvey made 6 April 1815 167 acres; tract of 315 acres in Chester District on Broad River near Sandy Run; also tract in Union District in the angle of Broad & Tyger Rivers, 400 acres; also tract purchased by Ainsley Hall, Aramanus Lyles called the Lehre tract, 200 acres. John Thomas (LS), John McIver (LS), Wit: A. Blanding, Wilmot R. Gibbes. Proved in Union District by the oath of Wilmot R. Gibbes 25 June 1828 before J. Rogers, Q. U. Recorded 25 June 1828.

T, 24-25: John Anderson, Sheriff of Union District, by virtue of several writs of fieri facias from the court of common pleas tested 25 Oct 1826 at the suit of John Robinson & others, to levy of the goods & chattles, lands and tenements of Z. Reid $4000, sells tract of 1820 acres in Union District on waters of Broad River adj. Joseph Gist, Black, Rueben Lindsey, Aron Davis, Smith and Darby, Thomas C. Taylor, 7 May 1828. John Anderson S. U. D. (LS), Wit: B. J. Gregory, M. B. Harrington. Proved by the oath of B. J. Gregory 7 May 1828 before Lem B. Askew, J. Q. Recorded 20 June 1828.

T, 25-26: John Anderson, Sheriff of Union District, by virtue of several writs of fieri facias from the court of common pleas held 25 Oct 1826 at the suit of John Robinson and others commanding me to levy of the goods & Chattles of Z. Reid, $4000, sell thirty slaves Caleb, George, Aron, Jack, Jesse, Zeck, Sam, Anderson, Bill, Sucky, Leah, Jane, Nelson, Rochell, Tanty, Peggy, Anna, Betsy, Elbert, Eliza, Any, Mille, Margaret, Zeday, Malinda, Mary, Joseph, William, Isaac, Randal, sold for $5429 to Joseph Reid, 7 May 1828. John Anderson S. U. D. (LS), Wit: Leml B. Askew. Proved by the oath of Lem B. Askew 10 July 1828 before J. Rogers, Q.U. Recorded 10 July 1828.

T, 27-28: Joseph Reid of York District bound to John Robinson of Charleston in the sum of $40,000, 20 May 1828, whereas the above bound Joseph Reid is indebted to the said John Robinson in the sum of $13,092.13 by three several promissory notes. Jos Reid (LS), Wit: B. F. Whitner, Wm. Miller. Proved in Charleston District by the oath of Wm. Miller 28 May 1828 before Thos Simons Jones, Notary Public. Recorded 20 June 1828.

T, 28-30: Joseph Reid of York District is indebted to John Robinson of Charleston in the sum of $40,000, mortgage of tract of 1820 acres on waters of Broad River and Fannens Creek in Union District, adj. Reuben Lindsey, Aron Davis, George Smith, Darby & Smith, Thomas C. Taylor, Col. Joseph Gist, as the same was conveyed to said Joseph Reid 7 May 1828 by John Anderson, Sheriff of Union District, also thirty slaves per bill of sale 7 May 1828 from John Anderson Sheriff [see Deed Book T, pages 26-27, preceding page], 20 May 1828. Jos Reid (LS), Wit: B. F. Whitner, Wm. Miller. Proved in Charleston District by the oath of Wm. Miller 28 May 1828 before Thos Simons Jones, Notary Public. Nancy T. Reid, wife of Joseph Reid, relinquished dower 20 June 1828 before J. Rogers, Q.U. Recorded 20 June 1828.

T, 30-31: South Carolina, Union District. James McWhirter & Treasey his wife of district aforesaid for natural love and affection to Reuben Coleman in trust for said Treasey McWhirter, 127 acres on waters of Mill Creek adj. Bartly Coleman, Charles Jones, Absalom Coleman & Treasey Coleman, also one negro boy named Peter about 9 years old, one feather bed & Furniture, one loom & all the household furniture which was left under the care of said Reuben by said Treasey at her marriage, 21 May 1828. James McWhirter (X) (LS), Treasey McWhirter (mark) (LS), Wit: Wormack Fowler, William Gibson. Proved by the oath of William Gibson 24 May 1828 before Wm Littlejohn, J. P. Recorded 2 June 1828.

T, 31-32: South Carolina, Union District. Kindred Bobo of district aforesaid for $100 to Dr. Edward M. Bobo of same, piece of land on Tygar River on both sides of Woffords Creek, Dr. Bobo's old line, 31 Jan 1828. Kindred Bobo (LS), Wit: Z. Hooker, Hosey Ray. Mary Bobo (X), wife of Kindred, relinquished dower 1 March 1828 before Robert Martin J.Q. Proved by the oath of Z. Hooker 6 June 1828 before J. Rogers, Q.U. Recorded 6 June 1828.

T, 32-33: South Carolina, Union District. William B. Murphey of district aforesaid for $75 to Dr. E. M. Bobo, tract on waters of Tyger River adj. Wm. B. Murphy, said Dr. E. M. Bobo, R. Martin, 10 or 15 acres, 25 Aug 1826. Wm. B. Murphy (LS), Wit: Z. Hooker, Foster Golding. Henrietta Murphy, wife of William B. Murphy, relinquished dower 31 March 1828 before Robert Martin, J. Q. Proved by the oath of Z. Hooker 6 June 1828 before J. Rogers, Q.U. Recorded 6 June 1828.

T, 34: Isaac Peeler of Union District bound to James Malcomson for $30, sells tract on waters of Gilkies Creek adj. James Malcomson, Davis Whelchel, 27 Sept 1819. Isaac Peeler (LS), Wit: John Whelchell, Anthony Peeler. Proved by the oath of John Whelchel 23 May 1828 before Nicholas Corry, J.P. Recorded 9 June 1828.

T, 34-35: John Parham, exr. to the will of John Parham decd, for $140 to Thomas Craven of Union District, tract on south side of Mitchells Creek, a water course of Fairforest, 253 acres on north side Sallys branch, adj. heirs of Thomas Brooks decd, Thomas Craven, 22 May 1828. John Parham (Seal), Wit: R. G. H. Farr, Joseph Harlan. Proved by oath of both wit. 22 May 1828 before

Wm. Rice, Q. U. Mary Parham, wife of John Parham decd, relinquished dower 30 May 1828 before Hiram Gibbs, Q. U. Recorded 2 June 1828.

T, 36: South Carolina, Union District. John White Jr. for $60 to Jas M. Whitten, both of said district, small piece of land on Sholy Creek ad. said Whitton, John Anderson, 29 March 1828. John White Jr. (LS), Wit: Wm. White, Isaac Clark. Proved by the oath of Isaac Clark 3 June 1828 before Robt Stokes, J.P. Recorded 20 June 1828.

T, 36-38: South Carolina, Union District. 7 July 1828, William K. Clowney, Esquire, Commissioner of the Court of Equity for Union District, to Charles Humphries, whereas the heirs at law of William Gibbs decd on or about 16 Oct did exhibit their bill of Complaint in the Court of Equity against Charles Humphries & the heirs at law of William Williams decd, concerning a tract of land containing 371 acres, part of tract of 1173 acres granted to William Giles decd in which the said William Giles decd & William Williams decd in their life time were jointly interested, the cause being at issue before the honorable court at June term, the said court did decree that the said land be partitioned and divided between Charles Humphries and John Giles, now sold to Charles Humphries 194 acres, being a part of said tract. Wm. K. Clowney (LS): Wit: R. G. H. Farr, I. T. Gregory, Thos Humphries. Proved by the oath of Isaac T. Gregory 7 July 1828 before J.Rogers, Q. U. Recorded 7 July 1828.

T, 38-39: Charles Humphries of Union District for $524 to Gasaway Hames of same, tract on waters of Packolett, 194 acres, designated on a plat from the court of equity by No. 1, granted to William Giles decd, 7 July 1828. Charles Humphries (mark), Wit: I. T. Gregory, W. K. Clowney, Lemuel Hames. Proved by the oath of Isaac T. Gregory 7 July 1828 before J.Rogers, Q. U. Recorded 7 July 1828.

T, 39: 20 Feb 1828, David R. Burns to William Black, for $40, tract in the district of Union and Spartanburg, on both sides of Harrises Creek, part of tract granted to Hugh Donaldson adj. Mrs. Sarah Thomson, 13 acres. David R. Burns (LS), Wit: William D. Thomson, Isabella Black, A. W. T. McBride. Proved by the oath of Wm. D. Thomson 18 April 1828 before J. P. Thomason, Q.U. Recorded 7 July 1828.

T, 39-40: South Carolina, Union District. George B. Alexander of said district, do acknowledge myself to occupy and possess the land whereon I now live as the tenant of Joseph M. J. Alexander, said tract is between Tinker & Brushy Creek adj. George Gregory, James Tate, Thos Sartor, and which tract was given about the year 1814 to said Jas M. J. Alexander by his grandfather Maj. Joseph McJunkin, and in consideration of his the said Jas M. J. Alexander permitting me live there, I will pay at the expiration of each and every year, the sum of $200, and I will not sell any part of the crop until that sum be satisfied, 15 June 1828. George B. Alexander (LS),Wit: John Gage Junr, John Keisler. Proved by the oath of John Keisler 25 June 1828 before J. Rogers, Q. U. Recorded 25 June 1828.

T, 41: 10 Jan 1828, John George Senr to Thomas Pridmore for $500, part of tract laid out for John Portman on north side Packolett River supposed to be 80 acres, another tract of 100 acres laid out for John George. John George (LS), Wit: Saml M. Gowdey, Saml Otterson. Proved by the oath of Saml M. Gowdey 2 Feb 1828 before W. H. Cotter, J.P. Recorded 7 July 1828.

T, 41-42: South Carolina, Union District. 10 March 1828, John C. Volentine to John F. Smith, both of district aforesaid, for $158, 79 acres on a branch of Browns Creek, 10 March 1828. John C. Volentine (LS), Wit: Daniel Coomer (X), B. J. Gregory. Proved by the oath of Benj. J. Gregory 10 July 1828 before J. Rogers, Q.U. Recorded in Book O, No. 8, 10 July 1828.

T, 42-43: John White Senr of Union District for $800 to John Saunders of same, tract on north side Tyger River adj. C. Greer, Steen's corner, Fairforest Creek, 1 March 1828. Jno White (Seal), Wit: John H. Skelton, Silas Baker. Proved by the oath of John H. Skelton 2 June 1828 before J. Rogers, Q.U. Recorded 2 June 1828.

T, 43-44: Catherine Cotter of Union District for natural love and affection to my son in law William Palmer of same, and towards the better support & maintenance of himself and his wife after my decease, a negro girl named Seely[?], 12 years of age, 22 March 1828. Catharine Cotter (X) (LS), Wit: Samuel M. Gowdey, E. J. Cotter. Proved by the oath of Samuel M. Gowdey 3 June 1828 before Wm. H. Cotter, J.P. Recorded 7 July 1828.

T, 44-45: George Malcomson for $10 to James Malcomson, tract on head of Abbingtons Creek, part of tract of 373 acres granted to me ___ 1803, 128 acres, 15 July 1821. George Malcomson (X) (LS), Wit: Joseph Camp, George Makamson. Proved by the oath of Malcomson 31 May 1828 before Nicholas Corry, J.Q. Recorded 9 June 1828.

T, 45-46: William Palmer of Union District for £30 to Thomas Kennedy, 100 acres on waters of Buffalow Creek, waters of Fairforest, part of tract granted to John Martin, the dividing line to begin at a post oak near the fork of the branch adj. Daniel Huger's line, Joseph Jones, 9 Aug 1823. William Palmer (LS), Wit: W. P. Kennedy, John P. Kennedy. Permelia Palmer (X), wife of William Palmer, relinquished dower 19 Jan 1825 before George Brandon, J.Q. Proved by the oath of John P. Kennedy 5 March 1825 before J. Rogers, Q.U. Recorded 28 July 1828.

T, 46-48: South Carolina, Union District. Thomas Kennedy of Union District for $1000 to Isaac Going, Bird Murphy, John Steen, Henry Stevens & James Gage, Commissioners of the Poor of the District of Union, 189 acres on waters of Browns Creek and Fairforest Creek, part of 500 acres granted to Jesse Low[?], also a tract on waters of Buffalow , waters of Fairforest adj. to the above tract, 61 acres, adj. Hugers line, Joseph Jones, 5 Nov 1827. Thos Kennedy (LS), Wit: Wm. White, Wm. K. Clowney. Proved by the oath of Wm.

K. Clowney 5 Nov 1827 before James Rountree, J.P. Elizabeth Kennedy, wife of Thomas Kennedy, relinquished dower 28 July 1828 before J. Rogers, Q.U.

T, 48-49: Ruth Hail, John & Samuel Hail, George McKnight, James Foster, John Thomson, Thomas Stribling & Fanny Haile, all of Union District excepting Thomas Stribling of the District of Pendleton, for $135 acres, to John Gibson of Union District, 625 acres on branches of Fairforest Creek, part of tract granted to Daniel Huger Esqr., adj. Saml Clowney, Sumeral, 3 Feb 1817. Saml Hail (LS), J. I. Foster (LS), J. Haile (LS), John Thomson (LS), Geo McKnight (LS), Fanny Haile (X), Thos Stribling (LS), Wit: Jesse Lyles, John Lyles, Nicholas Cavenah, James Reans. Proved by the oath of John Lyles 31 May 1828 before Wm. K. Clowney, Q.U. Recorded 4 Aug 1828.

T, 49-50: John Gibson of Union District for $130 to Herod Gibson of same, 125 acres on branches of Fairforest, part of tract granted to Daniel Huger & conveyed to John Gibson by the legal representatives of John Haile Senr decd, adj. Col. Clowney's corner, Summerall's line, also 19 acres granted to me John Gibson on south west side of Rocky Creek, adj. land surveyed for Saml Clowney, W. P.Pool, _____ 1827. John Gibson (LS), Wit: W. W. White, Alexander Gibson. Proved by the oath of Alexander Gibson 19 March 1827 before J. P. Thomson, Q.U. Recorded 4 Aug 1828.

T, 50: South Carolina, Union District. Thomas & Jas Goodrum of district aforesaid for $600 to Henry Gault of same, tract on each side of Pinckney Road, 270 acres on a branch of Sandy Run, adj. Daniel White, Aron McCollum, J. H. Galman, Johnson's, Fanny Fowler, 12 April 1828. Thos Goodrum (LS), James Goodrum (X), Joseph Goodrum (X) (LS), Wit: Andrew Park, Davidson Gault, William Harwick. Proved by the oath of Davison Gault 4 Aug 1828 before J. Rogers, Q.U. Recorded 4 Aug 1828.

T, 51: South Carolina, Union District. John H. Galman, Daniel Galman & John Galman of district aforesaid for natural love and affection to my son John, in trust to be held by him and at his death to his lawful heirs, tract of land in Union District on the Pinckney Road, 161 acres per plat made by Giles N. Smith, 24 March 1828. John H. Galman (LS), Daniel Galman (LS), John Galman (LS), Wit: John Stribling, Thomas Fowler. Proved by the oath of John Stribling 21 March 1828 before Daniel White, J. Q. Recorded 4 Aug 1828.

T, 51-52: John H. Galman of Union District for $1353 to Henry Gallman of Newberry District, tract of 600 acres in different surveys in Union District on the north fork of Browns Creek adj. Elisabeth Long, Aron McCollum, John Gallman, Widow Bevis, Saml Smith, Isaac Hany, Nancy Shell, 230 acres, also 230 acres on north fork of Browns Creek adj. lands of David Eigner, Aquilla Powers, Samuel Harris, Thomas Pall, also four negroes a fellow named Joe about 20 years of age, Will a fellow about 58 years of age, Hilliard a boy about 9 years old, and Hannah a woman about 22 years of age, 28 Feb 1828. John H. Gallman (LS), Wit: Wm Rutherford, Jno B. Oneall. Proved in

Newberry District by the oath of John B. Oneall 4 Aug 1828 before James Kellard, J.P. Recorded 4 Aug 1828.

T, 53: John Anderson, Sheriff of union District, by virtue of several writs of fieri facias from the court of common pleas tested 22 March 1828 at the suit of Tilman Stone and the State for taxes dated 12 June 1828 to levy of the goods & chattles, lands & tenements of Zephaniah Holmes $35.85, sells 180 acres to Samuel M. Gowdey & Co., for $11, 4 Aug 1828. John Anderson S. U. D. (LS), Wit: B. J. Gregory, Robt McDaniel. Proved by the oath of B. J. Gregory 7 Aug 1828 before J. Rogers, Q.U. Recorded 7 Aug 1828.

T, 54: South Carolina, Union District. Richard C. Jeter do acknowledge myself guardian for Jim Russel a free man of colour, which said free man Jim I believe to be of good Character & correct habits, 18 Aug 1828, R. C. Jeter.

South Carolina, Union District. Edward Mays of district aforesaid for $300 to Josiah McDaniel of same, tract on waters of Beaver dam Creek, a branch of Fairforest, part of tract granted to John Powell adj. Mary Means, Edward Mays, Mary Riley, 85 acres, 30 March 1827. Edward Mays (LS), Wit: D. A. Mitchell, Charles M. Murphy. Proved by the oath of D. A. Mitchell 16 Aug 1828 before J. Rogers, Q.U. Recorded 16 Aug 1828.

T, 55: South Carolina, Union District. William Wright Esqr. of Union District, farmer, for #75 to James Dugan of same, 170 acres agreeable to the grant dated 2 Aug 1813 on south side Tyger River adj. Richard Pellum, John Hall, Henry Addington, C. Shellaw Sims, 26 Feb 1828. Wm. Wright (LS), Wit: Wm. Davis, John Chambl'd [Chamberland] (X). Proved by the oath of Wm. Davis 3 Aug 1828 before J. Rogers, Q.U. Recorded 4 Aug 1828.

T, 55-56: South Carolina, Union District. Ephraim A. Crenshaw of York District for $600 to James Dugan Esqr., of Union District, tract on Tinker Creek, waters of Tyger River adj. McDaniel, Burgess old corner, Nathan Hawkins, 6 Feb 1826. Ephraim A. Crenshaw (LS), Wit: Jas McJunkin Jr., Wm. Davis. Proved by the oath of Wm. Davis 3 Aug 1828 before J. Rogers, Q.U. Recorded 4 Aug 1828.

T, 56-57: South Carolina, Union District. James Barry of district aforesaid for $86 to Robert Martin, 50 acres adj. William Rountree, Polly Gibbs, David Holcomb, A. Hays, conveyed to me by Isaiah Whitlock & since sold by the sheriff vs J. Whitlock for bastardy & purchased by me, on waters of Sugar Creek, waters of Fairforest, 28 Feb 1828. James Barry (LS), Wit: Elisa Bobo, Samuel Martin. Proved by the oath of Samuel L. Martin 27 Aug 1828 before Jno Norman, J. P. Recorded 27 Aug 1828.

T, 57: John Stokes of Union District for natural love and affection to my grandson John B. F. Stokes of same, a negro boy named John, dated 20 Aug 1828. John Stokes (X), Wit: Benjamin Saunders, Levy Gregory. Proved by the oath of Capt. Benj. Saunders 22 Aug 1828 before J. Rogers, Q.U. Recorded 23 Aug 1828.

T, 58-59: John Anderson, Sheriff of Union District, by virtue of several writs of fieri facias from the court of common pleas, held the ___ Monday of March 1826 at the suit of the ordinary to me to levy of the goods & chattels, lands, and tenements of Thomas McJunkin, $476.40, sells tract of 230 acres on Tinker Creek, waters of Tygar River whereon John T. McJunkin now lives, adj. Abram McJunkin, Thos Sartor & others, sold to William M. Thomson for $84, 4 March 1828. John Anderson S. U. D. (LS), Wit: A. B. Hall, John T. Murrell. Proved by the oath of A. B. Hall 23 April 1828 before J. Rogers, Q.U.

T, 59-60: Whereas the undersigned John A. Edwards is indebted to James Farnandis by a sealed note $648.88 due ten days after 25 Feb 1828, John A. Edwards sells 606 acres on Padgets Creek, waters of Tyger River, adj. lands of George Mayers, David Myers, Joseph Phillips, William Fant, Jerry Phillips, Charles King & others, being the tract of land whereon Edward Edwards formerly lived, also the following slaves Scipio aged about 33 years, Sarah aged about 30 years, Sarah aged about 8 years, Dinah aged about 40 years dark complexion, Cuffy aged about 50 years light complexion, John aged about 30 years dark complexion, Caty aged about 30 years dark complexion, Sally aged about 12 years dark complexion, Tom aged about 16 years dark complexion, Andrew aged about 6 years dark complexion, Pender aged about 30 years dark complexion, Priscilla aged about 16 years dark complexion, Ferguson aged about 18 years dark complexion, Bob aged about 14 years dark complexion, Peter aged about 30 years dark complexion, Hester aged about 30 years dark complexion, Marcus aged about 15 years dark complexion, Auba aged about 30 years dark complexion, Eve aged about 14, Adam 10, Phoeba 30, Rachel 12, Ned about 4, Sophy 6, Monday 60, Quasaba aged about 60 years dark complexion, Peggy aged about 50 years dark complexion, March aged about 70 years dark complexion, Auga aged about 30 years dark complexion, Eve aged about 14 years, dark complexion, Adam aged about ten years dark complexion, Phoebe aged about 30 years dark complexion, Rachel aged about 12 years dark complexion, Ned aged about four years dark complexion, Sophy aged about 6 years dark complexion, Monday aged about 60 years dark complexion, Quasaba aged about 40 years. John A. Edwards (Seal), Wit: James Foree, John T. Young. Proved by the oath of John T. Young in Newberry District 8 May 1828 before Y. J. Harrington, Q. U.

T, 60-61: John Coleman of District of Union for $300 to Treacey Coleman of same, tract on waters of Mill Creek adj. Bartley Coleman, 127 acres, __ March 1828. John Coleman (LS), Isabel Coleman (LS), Wit: Reuben Coleman, Absalom Coleman, William Gibbson. Proved by the oath of Reuben Coleman 4 Aug 1828 before J. Rogers, Q. U.

T, 61: To Philip Edward Pearson, Esquire, whereas the Senate and House of representatives did by their Joint Ballot in the Chambers on 30 Nov 1824 elect you Solicitor of the Middle Circuit, issue this commission, 30 Nov 1824. John L. Williams by the Governor; William Laval, Secretary of State.

T, 62-63: South Carolina, Union District. 15 Sept 1828, John B. Baley of district aforesaid to Logan & McEntire of same, whereas by two certain bonds dated as follows, one note on 1 Jan 1827 and on dated 15 Sept 1828, mortgage, my plantation on Little Browns Creek adj. James Savage, Daniel Runnels, James Ennis, 124 acres, one sorrel stud horse, a younger sorrel mare known by the name of Bedford. John Baile (Seal), Wit: Thos C. Taylor,E. G. Logan. Proved by the oath of Elbert G. Logan 20 Sept 1828 before R. Lipsey, J.P. Recorded 24 Sept 1828.

T, 64: South Carolina, Union District. James Petty for $130 to James Makamson, both of said state, tract beginning at his own fence, line made by Joseph Kemp, 1 Jan 1822. James Petty (Seal), Wit: William Malcomson, John Waters. Proved in Hall County Georgia by the oath of John Waters 13 Aug 1828 before John Whelchel, J.P. Recorded 30 Sept 1828.

T, 64-65: Daniel Thomas of District of Union for $100 to James Sandlin of same, plantation whereon the said James Sandlin now lives adj. John Cook's spring, de Graffenreid, James Gassaway Jr., Pressley Williams, granted to said Daniel Thomas in 1817, 40 acres, 7 Feb 1828. Danl Thomas (LS), Wit: William B. Johns, James V. Thomas. Mary B. Thomas, wife of Daniel Thomas, relinquished dower 23 Aug 1828 before E. McGraw, Q. U. Proved by the oath of James V. Thomas 13 Aug 1828 before E. McGraw, Q.U. Recorded 27 Sept 1828.

T, 65-66: South Carolina, Union District. Peter Tucker of union District for $300 to Hill & Scaife, one negro girl slave named Jean about 12 years of age, 1 Jan 1828. Peter Tucker (X) (Seal), Wit: T. A. Carlisle, William Fewell. Proved by the oath of Thomas A. Carlisle 27 Sept 1828 before E. McGraw, Q. U. Recorded 27 Sept 1828.

T, 66-67: 16 Aug 1828 Rich'd Sharp of the first part, Lucretia Sharp, wife of said Richard, of the second part, and Lot Whitlock, trustee, of the third part, whereas some unhappy differences have arisen between said Richard Sharp and his wife Lucretia, and they have agreed to live separate and apart, said Richard hath consent to allow her to use the following property: three negroes called Riter & her two children Daniel and Mary, one bed and furniture and other household articles, one pied cow. Richard Sharp (Seal), Wit: John Arnett, George Smith. Proved by the oath of George Smith 27 Sept 1828 before E. McGraw, J.P.

T, 67-68: Margaret Spencer, George Spencer, Eliza Hancock, Thuruton Hancock, Louisa Kyle & James Kyle of Union District to James Dawkins of same, tract on south side of Gilkeys Creek, waters of Broad River, 222 acres adj. lands of said James Dawkins, Francis Whelchell, the joint heirs of Annas Davis, Nancy Davis, Genl Walton & the joint heirs of Maj. Spencer Morgan,

5 July 1828. Margaret Spencer (X) (LS), George Spencer (LS), Eliza Hancock (X) (LS), T. B. Hancock (LS), Luesa A. Kyle (LS), James Kyle (LS), Wit: Aron Wilkins, Hobson Thomson (X), Wm. H. Neal. Proved by the oath of Aron Wilkins 20 Aug 1828 before Nicholas Corry, J. Q. Eliza R. Hancock (X), wife of Thomson B. Hancock, relinquished dower before Daniel Smith, J. Q. of York District. Louisa A. Kyle, wife of James Kyle, relinquished dower before Daniel Smith, J. Q. of York District. Recorded 4 Feb 1829.

T, 68-69: Union District, So Car. James McWhorter Senr of district aforesaid do appoint Robert McWhorter, Charles McWhorter, James McWhorter Jr. and John McWhorter, my heirs at law, to manage and transact the concerns of my estate whether personal or real during the term of my natural life and at the expiration of which time the above named heirs at law do agreed to make an equal dividend with the other heirs of my deceased wife (Wineford), also that we the above named heirs at law do bind ourselves to give the said James McWhorter (our father) a decent support during his life, 9 April 1828. James McWhorter (LS), Jas McWhorter (LS), Robert McWhorter (LS), Charles McWhorter (LS), John McWhorter (X), Wit: Isaac Kimberly, Ellis B. Fowler. Proved by the oath of I. S. Kimberly 4 July 1828 before A. Foster, J.P. Recorded 1 Sept 1828.

T, 69: South Carolina, Union District. John B. Bailey of district aforesaid for love and good will for John Inman, tract between Fannans Creek and Packolett River, 41¼ acres, adj. land surveyed for George Bailey, land surveyed John McCracken, S. McGuire & lands surveyed John Cunningham, 15 Sept 1828. John Baile (LS), Wit: Samuel Swearengame, Ruth Fielder (X). Proved by the oath of Samuel Swearingam 15 Sept 1828 before Isaac Going, Q. U. Recorded 27 Sept 1828.

T, 69-70: South Carolina, Union District. 22 Sept 1---, Sally Ingman of state aforesaid to John B. Bailey, whereas said John Bailey by a bond or note executed bearing equal dates herewith doth stand bound to Sally Ingman in the penal sum of $1600 whenever demanded, mortgage of property real and personal: plantation whereon I now live joining John Black, James Baley, Reuben Lindsey, 135 acres, a sorrel horse & three cows & calves, 70 head of hogs, 1 still & 21 vessels, four feather beds & furniture, 22 Sept 1828. John Baily (LS), Wit: Griffin Dupree (X), Judy Dupree (X). Proved by the oath of Griffin Dupree 27 Sept 1828 before Isaac Going. Q. U. Recorded 27 Sept 1828. Satisfied in full June 1st 1829. Salley Inman (X).

T, 71: South Carolina, Union District. Anne Woodson, widow of James Woodson, late of said district, decd, for love, good will, and affection to my son Goodwin Woodson of said district, part of my tract of land whereon I now live, including all the western part adj. Harlan's corner, part of two tracts of land, one granted to some person now know, the other to John Little, 90 acres, adj. Robert & James Woodson, by Fairforest, Thomas Woodson, 24 March 1828. Anne Woodson (mark) (LS), Wit: Wm. White, Thos Woodson,

Thomas Wilbourn. Proved by the oath of Thos Woodson 18 Sept 1828 before J. Rogers, Q. U. Recorded 18 Sept 1828.

T, 71-72: South Carolina, Union District. Anne woodson, widow of James Woodson, late of said district, decd, for love, good will, and affection to my daughter Nancy Woodson of said district, the balance of the money that is coming to me from my father's estate, 24 March 1828. Anne Woodson (mark) (LS), Wit: Wm. White, Thos Woodson, Thos Wilbourn. Proved by the oath of Thos Woodson 18 Sept 1828 before J. Rogers, Q. U. Recorded 18 Sept 1828.

T, 72-73: South Carolina, Union County. William Lockhart and Cresey his wife for £30 to Owny Ownsby of same place, 100 acres on waters of Gilkies Creek adj. Wm Wheler, Simeon Watson, William Lockhart, Jane[?] Gilky, being the lower end of a tract now occupied by the said William Lockhart, originally granted to Isaac Chapman, on south side Gilkies Creek, with the houses, plantations & improvements whereon the said William Lockhart now lives, 4 Sept 1797. William Lockhart (LS), Cresey Lockhart (X) (LS), Wit: John Nuckolls, Jno Blanton. Proved in Murry County, Tennessee, by the oath of John Blanton 1 March 1819 before Wm. Polk, J.P. Recorded 1 Sept 1818.

T, 73: Moses Wright of Adair County, Kentucky, for divers cuases have appointed my son Isaac Wright of county & state aforesaid my lawful attorney in fact to take possession of allm y land in the state of South Caorlina, and to bring any suit or suits to recoever or obtain possession and to rent, lease or sell any of all of my said lands, 5 Oct 1820. Moses Wright (Seal), Wit: Henry Antle, Zachariah Collins. Proved by the oath of Henry Autle 1 Jan 1821 before Wm.Caldwell, Clerk of County Court of Adair County, Kentucyl. Daavid Traben[?], presiding Judge of the county court, certifies that the certificate of William Caldwell is in due form of law, 13 Jan 1821. Recorded 1 Sept 1828.

T, 74: South Carolina, Union District. Moses Wright Senr & Isaac Wright his lawful atorney in fact, of Adair County, KY, for $1000 to Powerl Ownsby of Union District, pat of two tracts of land being150 acres on north side of Packoeltt River, being the plantation whereon Moses Wright formerly lived adj. Joseph Cowin, Moses Wright, to a road upon Joacb Mitchell's old original line, John Littlejohn's corner, east side of Moses Wright's spring branch, 15 Aprill 828. Isaac Wright attorney for Moses Wirght (LS), Wit: Robt Wilkins, Moses Simmons. Proved in Union District by the oath of Robert Wilkins 5 May 1828 before Wm. Goudelock, J.P. Recorded 1 Sept 1828.

T, 75-76: South Carolina, Union District. John Anderson, Esq., Sheriff of Union District, in virtue of a fifa at the suit of McAdams & David Jackson against William Hall and Geo Crotchet, exrs. of A. Hall decd, to levy $21,000 of the goods & chattles, houses and lands which were of Ainsley Hall decd at the time of his death, in the hands of William Hall & Geo Crotchett, exrs., now sells to John Kirkpatrick for $3187.50 negroe slaves Hartwell, Hester,

Sabrey, Cloe, Judy, Matilda, Solomon, Hanseal, Sam, Peter. Alsey, Mariah, Binch, Sampson, Mose, Will, Daffney, Peter (smith), Franky, Fanny, Leah, Anderson, Simon, Elisa, John, Robbin, Phebe, Hariot, George, Judy & Harry, 4 Feb 1828. John Anderson, S. U. D. (Seal), Wit: J. Rogers, Silas Baker, Thos Williams Jr.

John Kirkpatrick for $3187.50 secured to be paid to me by John Thomas & John McIver, sell the slaves named in the above, 20 June 1828. John Kirkpatrick (LS), Wit: A. Blanding, Wilmot R. Gibbes. Proved in Richland district by the oath of Abram Blanding 21 June 1828 before James S. Guignard, Clerk & Q. U. Exoff. Recorded 22 Sept 1828.

T, 76-77: Russel P. McCord & Elisa M. McCord his wife to John Thomas & John McIver, all the right title, and interest of the said Eliza both equitable and legal in the estate of Ainsley Hall deceased & in various commercial concerns & plantation copartnerships excepting any real estate which the said Ainsley Hall at the time of his death owned in England, 17 June 1828. R.P. McCord (Seal), E. M. McCord (LS), Wit: j. R. McCord, Galaway Monteith. Eliza M. McCord, wife of Russel P. McCord, relinquished dower in Orangeburgh District 26 June 1828 before Henry Caver, J. Q. Proved in Richland District 28 July 1828 by the oath of Galaway Monteith before J. S. Guignard, clk & Q. U. ex off. Recorded 2 Sept 1828.

T, 78: Whereas William Hall decd in his lifetime was indebted to John Kirkpatrick in the sum of $43,246.92 and to secure payment thereof on 1 Dec 1826, gave bond, dated Charleston Dec 20th 1827, and whereas John Thomas & John McIver have assumed the payment, said John Kirkpatrick has assigned to the said John Thomas & John McIver all the undivided third part of the said William Hall of the residuary estate of his brother Ainsley Hall decd, 20 June 1828. John Kirkpatrick (LS), Wit: A. Blanding, Wilmot R. Gibbes. Proved in Richland District by the oath of Abram Blanding 21 June 1828 before James S. Guignard, Clerk & Q. U. Exoff. Recorded 22 Sept 1828.

T, 79-80: Whereas John Thomas and John McIver have purchased from the devisees, legatees, and heirs of Ainsley Hall decd, all his estate real and personal, and all his interest in the various mercantile concerns, planting copartnerships, etc., now, it is understood and agreed that the bond of the said John Thomas payable to the said Ainsley dated 6 July 1818 for the payment of $89,0000 is hereby given up to the said John Thomas, 20 June 1828. John Thomas (Seal), John MacIver (Seal), Wit: J. M. Davis, A. Blanding. Proved in Richland District by the oath of John M. Davis 21 June 1828 before James S. Guignard, Clerk & Q. U. Exoff. Recorded 22 Sept 1828.

T, 80-82: Agreement entered into 12 June 1828 between Sarah C. Hall and John Thomas & John McIver, said Sarah C. Hall agrees to assign all her right, title and interest in the estate of Ainsley Hall, late of Town of Columbia, deceased, excepting the house and square of land in the Town of Columbia bounded by Walnut, Taylor, Picking & Henderson streets, which house and square has been sold by the Commissioner in equity and purchased by John Hopkins, also excepting a bond & mortgage given by John Howell to Ainsley Hall dated 1 May 1819 for the payment of $18,769.45. Sarah C. Hall (LS), John MacIver (Seal), John Thomas (Seal), Wit: John W. Arthur, James Gregg. Proved by the oath of John W. Arthur 26 July 1828 before James S. Guignard, Clk & Q. U. Exoff. Recorded 22 Sept 1828.

T, 83: Agreement entered into between George Cothell and John Thomas & John McIver, 12 June 1828, said John Thomas & John McIver have agreed to indemnify the said George Cothell against all claims brought against him on account of any losses which may be sustained by the concerns of A. & W. Hall & Co. or Hall, Kirkpatrick & Co., all his title and interest in the said concerns. Geo Cothrell (LS), Wit: James Patterson, A. Douglas. Proved in Charleston District by the oath of James Patterson 16 June 1828 before J. W. Mitchell, Q. U. Recorded 22 Sept 1828.

T, 83-84: South Carolina, Union District. Kindred Bobo of said district for $150 to Dr. Edward M. Bobo, tract on south side of Tygar River on south side of Wofford Creek beginning at the ford of the creek, 25 June 1822. Kindred Bobo (Seal), Wit: Wm. B. Murphy, Alvan Dean. Mary Bobo (X), wife of Kindred, relinquished dower 31 March 828 before Robt Martin, J. Q. Proved by the oath of William B. Murphy 1 Sept 1828 before J. Rogers, Q. U. Recorded 1 Sept 1828.

T, 84-85: Meriam Kershaw of Union District for $300 to Charles Kershaw of Charleston, tract upon which I now live on the north side of Fairforest Creek, adj. lands of Christopher young, Charles Humphries, Henry Anderson, John White, 27 Sept 1828. Mariam Kershaw (Seal), Wit: Hamlet Goudelock, David N. Saunders. Proved by the oath of Hamlet Goudelock 27 Sept 1828 before Saml Davis, J.P. Recorded 7 Sept 1828.

T, 85-86: John Anderson, Sheriff of Union District, by virtue of two writs of fieri facias from the court of common pleas for the district of Union tested 15 Oct 1827 at the suit of James Corry admr & Y. J. Harrington & others to levy of the goods & Chattles, lands and tenements of John Patrick Senr, to levy the sum of $333.15, sells 222 acres on a branch of Abingtons Creek adj. Gabriel Patrick, Nicholas Corry, Charles Patrick, part of which tract is known by the name of the Porters old field & part conveyed by Bert & Hezekiah Harrington to said John Patrick now sold for $201 to Nicholas Corry, 8 March 1828. John Anderson, S. U. D. (Seal), Wit: Silas Baker, F. Ison. Proved by the oath of F. Ison 18 Sept 1828 before J. Rogers, Q.U.

T, 86-88: South Carolina, Union District. Angus Alexander of district aforesaid for $400 to David Boyce of same, 188 acres on both sides of the Columbia Road leading from the Cross Keys to Columbia and on both sides of Padgets Creek on the line of said David Boyce where he now lives, the dividing corner betwixt Williamson Browning & said Angus Alexander, Alfred Wilbourns, William Malone, Wm. C. Pearson, part of tract of 150 acres granted to John

Campbell granted 19 Aug 1774 and conveyed by John Campbell to Joseph Randal and by said Joseph Randal to James Randal, Amos Hawkins by power of attorney, and through Amos Hawkins to Angus Alexander, 25 Feb 1828. Angus Alexander (Seal), Wit: W. C. Pearson, Martin Hopkins. Sarah (Sally) Alexander, wife of Angus, relinquished dower 30 Aug 1828 before Robert Martin, J. Q. Proved by the oath of Martin Hopkins 1 Sept 1828 before Robt Martin, J. Q. Recorded 1 Sept 1828.

T, 88-89: William Rice of Union District for $325 to Samuel O. Gordon of same, 162 acres agreeable to a deed from John Bates, Esqr., Sheriff, dated 5 July 1822, 26 Dec 1824. Wm Rice (Seal), Wit: Spilsby Glenn, James Hill. Proved by the oath of James Hill 7 Oct 1828 before W. K. Clowney, Q. U. ex off. Recorded 7 Oct 1828.

T, 89: Recd of Mr. John Steen $450 in full for a negro woman named Nancy and her three children Leathy, Ellen & Manrace, 15 June 1828. William Vincent, Wit: W. Wess[?], W. H. Steen. Proved by the oath of William H. Steen 14 Oct 1828 before Davis Goudelock, J.P. Recorded 15 Oct 1828.

T, 89-90: John Anderson, Sheriff of Union District, by several writs of fieri facias from the court of common pleas for Union District, tested the first Monday of March 1824 at the suit of A. W. Thomas admr. of Hall also one other tested the first Monday in March 1826 at the suit of R. Gilliam, also one other tested the second day of November 1826 at the suit of Z. Hooker, also one other tested 28 Oct 1826 at the suit of Nathan Cooper to me directed to levy of the goods & Chattels, lands & tenements of Samuel Ivey, $1220.60, sells tract of 476 acres on Tygar River and waters thereof, composed of several tracts whereon the said Samuel Ivey lately lived & those adjoining as purchased by him of John Hall now deceased, Flemming Harris & Cooper, adj. lands at present owned by James Dugan Esq., heirs of John Cook or William Smith, Jones Malone, widow Malone, Thomas Lee, purchased by Wm. K. Thomas & William Rice, Esqr., for $406, 12 Sept 1828. John Anderson, S. U. D. (Seal), Wit: B. J. Gregory, D. A. Mitchell. Proved by the oath of Benj. J. Gregory 29 Sept 1828 before J. Rogers, Q. U. Recorded 29 Sept 1828.

T, 91: South Carolina, Union District. Nicholas Corry of district aforesaid for $210.15 to Isaac Guyton of same, tract on waters of Abington Creek adj. Charles Patrick, Gabriel Patrick, Aron Wilkins, 229 acres, 21 April 1828. Nicholas Corry (LS), Wit: Wm. Corry, Nathaniel Guyton. Proved by the oath of Nathaniel Guyton 4 Oct 1828 before Henry Smith, J.P. Recorded 6 Oct 1828.

T, 91-93: South Carolina, Union District. 3 Nov 1828, Joseph S. Sims, Esqr., Commissioner of the Hon. Court of Equity for Union District, to Thomas Fowler, whereas Ruth Hail, widow of John Hail decd, Hampton Hail & others on or about 18 May 1821 did exhibit their bill of complaint in the court of equity against Sarah Hail & others, shewing that John Hail in his lifetime was possessed in his own right, and that Thomas Howard, James Means, Henry

Gault & Richard Thomson to make partition & division thereof, who made their report after assigning to the widow one third part of said land, the remainder be sold in three separate parcels, one of 250 acres, now sold to Thomas Fowler for $400, part of land conveyed by Robert Coleman to John Hail, also part of same land conveyed by Hartwell Jackson to John Hail. J. S. Sims (LS), Wit: J. Giles, William Gault. Proved by the oath of John Giles 3 Nov 1828 before J. Rogers, Q. U. Recorded 3 Nov 1828.

T, 93: John Stokes of Union District for love and affection to my daughter Dorcas Gregory, a negro girl named Mary, 20 Aug 1828. John Stokes (X), Wit: Robert Stokes, Benjamin Saunders. Proved by the oath of Benjamin Saunders 3 Nov 1828 before J. Rogers, Q.U. Recorded 2 Nov 1828.

T, 94: South Carolina, Union District. Anne Woodson, widow of James Woodson, late of said district decd, for love, good will and affection to my daughter Cassey Perkins of said district, part of my tract of land whereon I now live, being all the ballance not deeded to my son Goodwin, 90 acres, also one chest and cupboard, 24 March 1828. Anne Woodson (mark) (LS), Wit: Wm. White, Thos Woodson, Thos Wilbourn. Proved by the oath of William White 8 Oct 1828 before Saml Davis, J.P. Recorded 8 Oct 1828.

T, 94-95: 2 Sept 1828, Richard Sharp to Giles Sharp, whereas said Richard Sharp stands indebted to said Giles Sharp by his note of hand for $1500 payable 1 Oct next, mortgage of tract of 225 acres on the waters of Fannans Creek. Richard Sharp, Wit: J. Rogers, Jonathan Hampton. Proved by the oath of Jonathan Hampton 18 Nov 1828 before J. Rogers,Q.U. Recorded 18 Nov 1828. Satisfied 5 Jan 1832.

T, 95-96: John B. Glenn of Union District for $400 to John Bowles of same, 60 acres, being a tract of land I purchased of my father Robert Glenn which he purchased of Alexr McBeth & David Johnson, adj. Robert Glenn, Nelson, John Bowles, Jarret Gregory, 18 Sept 1827. J. B. Glenn (Seal), Wit: Robert Glenn, Mary B. Glenn. Proved by the oath of Robert Glenn 18 Nov 1828 before J. Rogers, Q.U. Recorded 18 Nov 1828.

T, 96-98: Absalom Davis of Union District for $1000 to Edward M. Bobo of same, tract on waters of Browns Creek, adj. George Brandon, T. Vance, Thos Young, the late James Meng, 27 Oct 1828. Absalom Davis (LS), Wit: Z. Hooker, Foster Hooker. Proved by the oath of Z. Hooker 4 Nov 1828 before J. Rogers. Jane Davis (X), wife of Absalom, relinquished dower 20 Nov 1828 before J. Rogers, Q.U. Recorded 20 Nov 1828.

T, 98-99: John Anderson of Union District, by virtue of order of court from the court of common pleas for Union District at October Term 1827 at the suit of the heirs of Clarke Thomson decd to levy of the goods & chattles, lands & tenements of Gibson Rickman, sells 100 acres on waters of Gilkies Creek adj. Reese Parker, James Dawkins, Frank Wilkins, sold for $31, 1 Sept 1828. John Anderson, S. U. D. (Seal), Wit: B. J. Gregory, John White Junr.

Proved by the oath of B. J. Gregory 3 Dec 1828 before J. Rogers, Q. U. Recorded 3 Dec 1828.

T, 99-100: South Carolina, Union District. Z. Hooker of Union District for $3000 to John Cunningham, Wm. M. Thomson, A. W. Thomson, E. M. Bobo, Daniel A. Mitchell & Daniel Thomas of Union District, one negro named Norvell a blacksmith about 28 years old, one negro man named Billy Randolph about 18 or 20 years old a cooper, two negro boys brothers named Dick & James about 15 & 18 years of age, one negro girl named Hagar about 15 years of age, one negro boy named Joseph about 18 years old, a negro girl named Mariah about 7 years old, a negro boy named Fincher about five or six years old, mortgage due 1 Dec 1827, dated 13 Nov 1826. Z. Hooker (Seal), Wit: Nathl Gist. Unionville, 25 June 1828. We release Z. Hooker on a note dated 13 Nov 1828 payable to Col. N. Gist. Jno. Cunningham, W. M. Thomson, A. W. Thomson, E. M. Bobo, D. A. Mitchell & Danl Thomas. Proved by the oath of Nathl Gist 18 Dec 1828 before J. Rogers, Q. U. Recorded 18 Dec 1828.

T, 100-101: Joshua Wilbourn of Union District for $550 to John T. Murrell, tract on Buffalow Creek, a watercourse of Fairforest, by a late survey made by William White, Esq., 274 acres, to the corner of Rice's field, Claybrook, 30 [sic] Sept 1828. Joshua Wilbourn (Seal), Wit: Robt H. Spencer, J. Rogers. Proved by the oath of Robt H. Spencer 3 Sept 1828 before J. Rogers, Clk. Recorded 3 Sept 1828.

T, 101-102: Hezekiah Palmer of Union District for $5 to Joshua Wilbourn & Robert Bullington, lot of two acres on Thomas Kennedy's line, part of tract where Hezekiah Palmer now lives, near the Duck pond, for Fairforest Baptist Church and that the congregation will build and erect a meeting house or other suitable place of public worship, 18 Aug 1814. Hezekiah Palmer (Seal), Wit: James Rountree, Daniel Holder.

T, 102: Thomas Kennedy for $2 to Joshua Wilbourn & Robert Bullington, one half acre of land including a spring convenient to the premise mentioned in the said deed, ___ Aug 1814. Thomas Kennedy (Seal), Wit: Wit: James Rountree, Daniel Holder. Proved by the oath of James Rountree, Esqr., 3 Nov 1828 before J. Rogers, Q.U. Recorded 3 Nov 1828.

T, 103: Articles of agreement between James Mays of Union District and William Smith of Randolph County, Indiana, 15 Dec 1826, the said James Mayes doth agree to repair the mils on Tiger River known by the name of Coocks Mills, to repair the grist mill and saw mill and dam, said Smith agreed to find the irons for the mills and the bolting cloth and pay the said Mayes, $500 out of the first money he or his agent receives from the rent or sale of the mills. James Mayes (LS), Wm Smith (LS), Wit: A. W. Thomson. Proved by the oath of A. W. Thomson, 21 Nov 1828 before J. Rogers, Q. U. Recorded 21 Nov 1828.

T, 103-104: John Love of Union Village for $1061 to Zacheriah P. Herndon of Union Village, lot numbers 39, 64, and 77, on Union Street, Bachelor Street, 18 March 1828. John Love (LS), Wit: Wm. M. Thomson, Silas Baker. Elizabeth Love, wife of John Love, 18 March 1828 before Lemuel B. Askew, J.Q. Proved by the oath of William M. Thomson 29 Aug 1828. Recorded 29 Aug 1828.

T, 104-105: John White of Union District for $400 to John Anderson of same, a piece of land where I now live, on Shoaly Creek, 100 acres adj. Joseph Reeder, B. Steen, Thos Willard, Bogan, J. M. Whitlow, 23 Feb 1827. John White (LS), Wit: Silas Baker, B. J. Gregory. Proved by the oath of B.J. Gregory 9 April 1828 before J. Rogers, Q.U. Recorded 29 April 1828.

T, 105-106: John Anderson, Sheriff of Union District, by virtue of a writ of partition from the court of common pleas held for Union District tested the first day of October 1827 at the suit of Benjamin Hay & Wife to levy of the goods and chattels, lands and tenements of Wm. R. Wilborn admr. of Elijah Wilbourn, decd, $775, sells 280 acres formerly owned by Elijah Wilborn deceased adj. Wm Wallace decd, Solomon Putman, Nathan Harling, Henry Smith, Hannah Brooks, purchased by Wm. R. Wilbourn for $775, 18 Nov 1828. John Anderson, S. U. D. (LS), Wit: James Smith, B. J. Gregory. Proved by the oath of B. J. Gregory 17 Dec 1828 before J. Rogers, Q. U. Recorded 17 Dec 1828.

T, 106-107: South Carolina, Union District. Jeremiah Gregory Senr for love and good will to my son Thomas B. Gregory, two negroes (viz) one woman Polly and her child Ruth and 230 acres whereon he now lives, 20 Nov 1828. Jeremiah Gregory (LS), Wit: B. J. Gregory, George Crawford. Proved by the oath of B. J. Gregory 17 Dec 1828 before J. Rogers, Q. U. Recorded 17 Dec 1828.

T, 107-108: South Carolina, Union District. Jeremiah Gregory Senr for love and good will to my daughter and son-in-law John Gregory and Lettie Gregory, three negroes (viz) one woman Dinah, man Adam and boy Billy, 200 acres whereon they now live, with all my stock of cattle, sheep, hogs, house hold & kitchen furniture, farming tools, horses, except one for my own use, 20 Nov 1828. Jeremiah Gregory (LS), Wit: B. J. Gregory, George Crawford. Proved by the oath of B. J. Gregory 17 Dec 1828 before J. Rogers, Q. U. Recorded 17 Dec 1828.

T, 108: South Carolina, Union District. Jeremiah Gregory Senr for love and good will to the lawful heirs of my son George Gregory decd, two negroes (viz) one woman Molly and her child Mariah, 20 Nov 1828. Jeremiah Gregory (LS), Wit: B. J. Gregory, George Crawford. Proved by the oath of B. J. Gregory 17 Dec 1828 before J. Rogers, Q. U. Recorded 17 Dec 1828.

T, 108-109: South Carolina, Union District. Jeremiah Gregory Senr for love and good will to my son John Gregory, two negroes (viz) one boy named Jesse and one girl Sarah and 65 acres of land formerly owned by Wm. Hawkins adj. Isaac Gregory's land, 20 Nov 1828. Jeremiah Gregory (LS), Wit: B. J. Gregory, George Crawford. Proved by the oath of B. J. Gregory 17 Dec 1828 before J. Rogers, Q. U. Recorded 17 Dec 1828.

T, 109-110: Drury Harinton of Union District for twenty shillings to Spencer Morgan of same, tract on a branch of Gilkys Creek, waters of Broad River, adj. Alexander Martin, Young, Rutherford, John Arinton, Martin, 335 acres, 25 July 1803. Drury Harrington (LS), Wit: Alexander Martin, Josep Smith. Proved in Pickens County, SC, by the oath of Joseph Smith before John A. Daily, J. P., 5 Dec 1828. Recorded 18 Dec 1828.

T, 110: South Carolina, Union District. Jeremiah Gregory Senr for love and good will to my son Jeremiah Gregory Junr, one negro man named David, 20 Nov 1828. Jeremiah Gregory (LS), Wit: B. J. Gregory, George Crawford. Proved by the oath of B. J. Gregory 17 Dec 1828 before J. Rogers, Q. U. Recorded 17 Dec 1828.

T, 110-111: South Carolina, Union District. Jeremiah Gregory Senr for love and good will to my son Isaac Gregory, two negroes Philis and Horah and 65 acres of land formerly owned by WM. Hawkins adj.said Isaac Gregory, 20 Nov 1828. Jeremiah Gregory (LS), Wit: B. J. Gregory, George Crawford. Proved by the oath of B. J. Gregory 17 Dec 1828 before J. Rogers, Q. U. Recorded 17 Dec 1828.

T, 111: Zacheriah P. Herndon of Union Village for $1061 to Thomas N. Dawkins of Union Village, three lots numbers 49, 63, and 77, on Union Street, adj. Z. P. Herndon, by the race paths, Batchelor Street, 22 April 1828. Z. P. Herndon (LS), Wit: Robt H. Spencer, John N. Herndon. Proved by the oath of Robert H. Spencer 19 Dec 1828 before J. Rogers, Q.U. Recorded 19 Dec 1828.

T, 112: South Carolina, Union District. Hannah Brooks (widow) for $300 to W. R. Wilbourn of district aforesaid, a small piece of land on the branches of Mitchells Creek, waters of Fair Forest, being the land that fell to me by division after a settlement between my former children (the heirs of Thomas Brooks decd) and myself, adj. Amos Martin for his son James Martin, Wallace, heirs of Thomas Brooks decd, Wilbourn, Henry Smith, 18 Dec 1828. Hannah Brooks (X) (LS), Wit: Sandford Wilborn, Isaac Smith. Proved by the oath of Sandford Wilborn 20 Dec 1828 before J. Rogers, Q. U. Recorded 20 Dec 1828.

T, 113: South Carolina, Union District. Wm R. Wilborn for $300 to Hannah Brooks, part of tract whereon the Rev'd John Putman decd [lived?], adj. Littlefield, Jas Palmer, Winny Brown, on the wagon road, and said M. R. Wilborn, 18 Dec 1828. W. R. Wilborn (LS), Wit: Isaac Smith, Sandford Wilborn. Proved by the oath of Sandford Wilborn 20 Dec 1828 before J. Rogers, Q. U. Recorded 20 Dec 1828.

T, 114: James Hollingsworth of Union District for $800 to James Hill of same, tract whereon Aquilla Hollingsworth now lives, 100 acres, part of tract granted to Col. William Farr adj. James Hill, Capt. Titus G. Farr, Spilsby Glenn, 23 July 1828. James Hollingsworth (X) (Seal), Wit: C. T. Scaife, Aq. Hollingsworth, Thonton S. Freeman. Proved by the oath of Charner T. Scaife 29 Dec 1828 before E. McGraw, Q.U. Recorded 29 Dec 1828.

T, 114-115: South Carolina, Union District. Wiley Nix for $196 to Elijah Wilburn, both of said district, tract on each side of Pagets Creek, waters of Tiger River, adj. William Melone, Randolph Alexander, David Boyes, William Bobo, Alfred Wilbourn, 23 Jan 1828. Wiley Nix (X) (LS), Wit: William Malone, Alexander Ray. Proved by the oath of William Malone 3 April 1828 before Robert Martin, Q. U. Sarah Nix (X), wife of Wiley Nix relinquished dower 3 April 1828 before Robert Martin. Also her name appears as Sarah Hopkins. Recorded 5 Jan 1829.

T, 116-117: South Carolina, Union District. Wiley Nix for $485 to Alfred Wilburn, both of said district, 112 acres on Hills Creek, waters of Enoree River, adj. William Melone, B. Bobo, James DeHay, Wm Bobo, 23 Jan 1828. Wiley Nix (X) (LS), Wit: William Malone, Alexander Ray. Proved by the oath of William Malone 3 April 1828 before Robert Martin, Q. U. Sarah Nix (X), wife of Wiley Nix relinquished dower 3 April 1828 before Robert Martin. Also her name appears as Sarah Hopkins. Recorded 5 Jan 1829.

T, 117-118: South Carolina, Union District. John Hart of district aforesaid for $200 to Wiley Nix, tract on branches of Hills Creek, waters of Enoree River, Turley's old field, adj. Marshal Wilbanks and James Dahay's line, 110 acres adj. Chas Turley, Judge Owens, Marshal Wilbanks, Hosea Prince, 27 Jan 1821. John Hart (LS), Wit: Baily Lawson, A. Boyce. Proved by the oath of Bailey Lawson 29 Dec 1828 before Robert Martin, J. Q. Elizabeth (X) Hart, wife of John, relinquished dower 31 Dec 1828 before Robert Martin, Q. U. Recorded 5 Jan 1829.

T, 118-119: South Carolina, Union District. John Guiner of district aforesaid for $150 to James Ward of same, 50 acres adj. Aron McCollum, Miles Bruton, Mr. Pool, 18 Nov 1828. John Guiner (X), Wit: William Smith, Nathan Ward. Proved by the oath of Nathan Ward 29 Dec 1828 before Wm. R. Clowney, Q. U. Ex. of. Recorded 5 Jan 1829.

T, 119-120: South Carolina, Union District. Edward M. Bobo of district aforesaid for $1000 to Absolam Davis of same, tract on waters of Tiger River on south side adj. Wm. B. Murphy, Kindred Bobo, 150 acres, 27 Oct 1828. E. M. Bobo (LS),Wit: Z. Hooker, Foster Hooker. Proved by the oath of Foster Hooker 2 Jan 1829 before Robert Martin, J. Q. Elizabeth Bobo, wife of E. M. Bobo, relinquished dower 30 Dec 1828 before Robert Martin, J. Q. Recorded 3 Jan 1820.

T, 120-121: South Carolina, Union District. Levi G. Danner and Robert McDaniel of district aforesaid to Jerry Phillips, tract of land between Tiger and Enoree River on Pagets Creek, being the interest of John A. Edwards adj. Joseph Philips, and formerly owned by John Hall, and bequeathed to said Philips, 8 Oct 1828. Levi G. Danner, Robert McDaniel, Wit: D. B. McCoy, Green T. Lee. Proved by the oath of Green T. Lee 3 Jan 1829 before John Norman, J.P. Recorded 5 Jan 1829.

T, 121: South Carolina, Union District. Levi G. Danner and Robert McDaniel of district aforesaid to Jerry Phillips, tract of land between Tiger and Enoree River on Pagets Creek, adj. Joseph Philips, John Hewey, Mires and Jerry Phillips, formerly owned by John Hall, and bequeathed to said Philips, 8 Oct 1828. Levi G. Danner, Robert McDaniel, Wit: D. B. McCoy, Green T. Lee. Proved by the oath of Green T. Lee 3 Jan 1829 before John Norman, J.P. Recorded 5 Jan 1829.

T, 121-122: South Carolina, Union District. Zachariah Nance Senr for $200 to Drury Sparks, both of said district, tract of land granted to Peter Renfrow in 1773, on said Nance's line, adj. Charles Bogan, Mills Sumner, 23 Nov 1827. Zacheriah Nancy (LS), Wit: William White, Merrimon Lawson (X). Proved by the oath of Merrimon Lawson 4 Dec 1828 before Robert Martin, J. Q. Mary Nance (X), wife of Zacheriah, relinquished dower 18 Jan 1828 [sic] before Robert Martin, J. Q. Recorded 5 Jan 1829.

T, 123: South Carolina, Union District. Lucy Porter for $175 to Thomas Davis, both of said district, part of tract granted to my father William Porter and conveyed by will to me on the ridge between Fair Forest & Broad River on branches of Browns Creek, adj. said Thomas Davis, Dogan, Ben Ruals[?], to the mouth of the meeting house spring branch (ten acres for the meeting house excepted), 5 Nov 1828. Lucy Porter (mark), Wit: E. M. Bobo, Absalom Barnett. Proved by the oath of E. M. Bobo before J. Rogers 6 Jan 1829. Recorded 6 Jan 1829.

T, 124: South Carolina, Union District. Lucy Kennedy $77 to Thomas Davis, both of said district, part of tract on each side of the Pinckney Road on branches of Browns Creek, adj. said Thomas Davis, Dogan, E. M. Bobo, widow Brandon, Lucy Porter, 73 acres, 11 Nov 1828. Lucy Kennedy, Wit: Thomas Kennedy, E. M. Bobo. Proved by the oath of E. M. Bobo before J. Rogers 6 Jan 1829. Recorded 6 Jan 1829.

T, 125-126: South Carolina, Union District. Thomas Davis of District of Union for $383.22 to Edward M. Bobo of same, land on east side of Union Ct. House on both sides of the Pinckney Road, it being composed of lands lately belonging to Lucy Porter, Lucy Kennedy and said Thomas Davis, on the meeting house branch (Presbiterian), 152 acres, 1 Dec 11828. Thomas B. Davis (Seal), Wit Wm. B. Murphy, F. H. Leonard. Proved by the oath of Foster H. Leonard 7 Jan 1829 before J. Rogers, Q. U. Isabel Davis (X), wife of Thomas, relinquished dower 27 Dec 1828 before Robert Martin, J. Q. Recorded 7 Jan 1829.

T, 126-127: South Carolina, Union District. A. B. Hall of Union District for $400 to Edward M. Bobo of same, tract on waters of Fair Forest adj. Charles Humphries Senior, James Steen, Mrs. Shaw or the land where Mrs. Shaw now lives, it being the tract of land which I have lately purchased of John White Senr, also bounded by lands of Henry Anderson, Jno Saunders, 250 acres, known by the name of the Steen Tract of land, 24 Nov 1828. A. B. Hall (LS), Wit: F. H. Leonard, Z. Hooker. Proved by the oath of F. H. Leonard 7 Jan 1829 before J. Rogers, Q.U. Recorded 7 Jan 1829.

T, 127-128: South Carolina, Union District. Aron Guyton of Pendleton District for $300 to Daniel Smith of York District, tract of 185 acres on head waters of John Moor's spring branch, adj. John and Gordon Moore, Daniel Smith, Rutherford, Patsy Guyton, 8 Sept 1828. Aron Guyton (LS), Wit: J. E. Guyton, John Parker, J. W. Guyton. Proved by the oath of John E. Guyton 4 Dec 1828 before Henry Smith, J. P. Recorded 5 Jan 1829.

T, 128-129: South Carolina, Union District. Dabney Becknal of district aforesaid for $150 to James A. Becknal of same place, tract in District of Union on waters of Browns Creek adj. Talkings, George Brandon, 100 acres, 10 Dec 1828. Dabney Becknell, Wit: J. Cunningham, J. P., John McLure. Proved by the oath of John Cunningham 19 Dec 1828 before J. Rogers, Q.U. Recorded 5 Jan 1829.

T, 129-130: Anthanasius Thomas of Union District for $1100 to George Perry of Fairfield District, tract whereon I now live, 140 acres adj. Lucy Johnson, Daniel Glenn (deceased), Farr Posey, and on Broad River, said land conveyed by Nathan Hawkins & Peter Tucker, exrs., of Ashford (deceased) to Thomas Hardy and by him conveyed to me, 13 Feb 1827. Athan's Thomas (LS), Wit: James McGraw, Drury T. McClowney [sic], William P. Ragsdale. Proved in Fairfield District by the oath of Drury T. McCully 13 Feb 1827 before James McCraw, J. P. Sarah Thomas (X), wife of Athenathius Thomas, relinquished dower 17 Jan 1828 before David R. Coleman, J. Qu. Recorded 30 Dec 1828.

T, 130-131: South Carolina, Union District. John Morgan of said district to John B. Shelton of same, part of tract on Bogans Creek, waters of Cane Creek for $282, 50 acres adj. Nathan Sims, Samuel Hardy, 1 March 1823. John Morgan (LS), Wit: George P. Smith, William Kelly. Proved by the oath of William Kelly 28 March 1826 before Titus G. Farr, Q. U. Jenny Morgan (X), wife of John Morgan, 28 March 1826 before Titus G. Farr, Q. U. Recorded 5 Jan 1829.

T, 131-133: John Anderson, Sheriff of Union District, by virtue of a writ of fieri facias from the court of common pleas held 25 Oct 1828 at the suit of Hartwell Jackson plaintiff to me directed to levy of the goods and chattels, lands and tenements of James Somerville $100, sells tract of 162 acres, sold for $201 to David Jones, 5 Jan 1829. John Anderson S. U. D. (LS), wit: J. Palmer, B. J. Gregory. Proved by the oath of B. J. Gregory 5 Jan 1829 before J. Palmer, J. P. Recorded 5 Jan 1829.

T, 133: Thomas Anderson of Union District for $110 to Bennet Edwards of same, 76 acres on waters of Tinker Creek adj. Wm. Townson, Daniel Peak, R. Edwards, 6 Jan 1829. Thos Anderson (LS), Wit: B. J. Gregory, Thos Sanders. Proved by the oath of Thomas Saunders 6 Jan 1829 before J. Rogers, Q.U.

T, 134-135: South Carolina, Union District. John Whelchel Sr. and Francis Whelchel Jr. for $732 to John Jeffries of district aforesaid, 488 acres on London Bridge Creek, waters of Broad River adj. John Whelchel Jr., Pealer, 15 July 1828. John Whelchel (LS), Francis Whelchel (LS), Wit: Samuel Jeffries, Daniel McAdams (X), David Johnson. Proved by the oath of S. Jeffries 22 Dec 1828 before W. Hotten, Q. U. Nancy Whelchel (X), wife of Francis Whelchel, 30 July 1828 before Nicholas Corry, J. Q. Recorded 5 Jan 1829.

T, 135-137: Whereas Ainsley Hall in his lifetime made his will and departed this life in the year 1823 leaving the said will in force and wherein he made the following devise, I will that as soon as my debts and the legacies herein specified are paid that my estate real and personal be divided by my executors or the personal whom a majority of my executors may appoint into three equal parts, one of the said parts to be divided among the persons following, to wit,to George Cotchell one half of the said third, and should George Cotchell think property to give one half of his one half to Sarah Ann Cotchell his sister he can do so, but if not then she in the mean time be supported till married, and whereas the said George Cotchell afterwards on 23 Nov 1823 by declaration of trust one moiety thereof was made in trust for the said Sarah Ann Cotchell, who has since married Thomas Robson; and such proceedings have been had in the court of Equity at Columbia, that John McIver has been appointed the receiver thereof, and said John Mciver was come to a compromise and final settlement with the said George Cotchell, Thomas Robson & Sarah Ann Robson for the shore or twelfth part of the estate of said Ainsley Hall, and has paid the said George Cotchell, 18 June 1828. Thos Robson (LS), Sarah Ann Robson (LS), John MacIver (LS), George Cotchell (LS), Wit: S. Doolittle, Wilmot R. Gibbes, A. Douglass. Sarah Ann Robson relinquished dower in Richland District 1 Dec 1828 before James S. Guignard, Clerk & Q. U. ex off. Proved by the oath of A. Douglass 28 June 1828 before Saml Alexander, Not Pub. & Q. U. Recorded 20 Jan 1829.

T, 137-138: John Thomas & John McIver have paid to John Cotchell $5000 and have agreed to indemnify him against all debts and legacies which may be brought against him on account of any share of the estate of Ainsley Hall deceased, 20 June 1828. John Cotchell (LS), Wit: William Thomas, Danl T. Ryan. Proved in Chester District by the oath of William Thomas and Daniel T. Ryan 28 June 1828 before Ferdinand Hopkins, J. P. Sarah Cotchell, wife of John, relinquished dower in Chester District 20 Jan 1829 before Richard Elam, J. Q. Recorded 20 Jan 1829.

T, 138-139: George Fant of Union District for $25 to Edward McGraw of same, 15 acres, part of tract sold by the exrs. of James Webb decd to said George Fant, by corner of Spray's grant, dividing line made by John P. Sartor, Cain Creek, 29 May 1828. George Fant (LS), Wit: Thos H. Word, James Fant. Proved by the oath of Thos H. Word 12 July 1828 before Saml O. Johnson, J. P. Recorded 17 Jan 1829.

T, 139-140: Titus G. Farr of Union District for $1000 to James B. Glenn of same, tract whereon I now live on branches of Cane Creek of Tyger River and according to a survey made by Richard Thomson 26 Nov 1828, 365 acres, 26 Dec 1828. T. G. Farr (Seal), Wit: Thos Bowker, Geo Douglass. Proved by the oath of Thomas Bowker 26 Dec 1828 before E. McGraw, J.P. Mary H. Farr, wife of Titus G. Farr, relinquished dower 16 Jan 1829 before E. McGraw, Q. U. Plat included showing 364 acres adj. John Evans, Wm. Sartor, Jas Hill. Recorded 17 Jan 1829.

T, 140-141: South Carolina, Union District. Elijah Dawkins of Union District for $3400 to John McEntire of Rutherford County, North Carolina, tract on north side of Thickety Creek, 345 acres, 16 April 1828. Elijah Dawkins (LS), Wit: Thos N. Dawkins, Joseph Collins. Nancy Dawkins, wife of Elijah Dawkins, relinquished dower 19 Dec 1828 before J. S. Sims, Q. U. Proved by the oath of Thos N. Dawkins 28 Jan 1829 before J. Rogers, Q.U. Recorded 18 Jan 1829.

T, 142: South Carolina, Union District. Erastus Giddings of Union District for $300 to James S. Brooks & Co. of same, mortgage of one negro woman named Ville or Vilot about 26 years of age, one bay horse about 14 hands high & seven years old, four red and pided steers or two pair of oxen about five years old, one cart, one saddle and bridle, 28 Jan 1829. Erastus Giddings (LS), Wit: W. E. Churchill. Proved by the oath of William E. Churchill 31 Jan 1829 before J. Rogers, Q.U. Recorded 31 Jan 1829.

T, 142: Union Court House, July 22, 1828. Mr. John Anderson, Sheriff of Union District. Sir, you will please make titles to the land of Mr. John H. Farnandis on Packolett on the north side to Z. Hooker, he having purchased the said tract at my sale as sheriff and being the highest bidder, made sale day in Jany 1827. J. Bates.

T, 143: John Anderson, Sheriff of Union District, by virtue of several writs of fieri facias from the court of common pleas tested 24 March 1824 at the suit of Saml Green & the executors of E. Fowler to levy of the goods & chattels, lands and tenements of John H. Farnandis, $636.81, 700 acres on north side of Packolett adj. Lemuel Farnandis, E. Dawkins, John Littlejohn, and Laurence & Packolett River, purchased by Dr. E. M. Bobo, 16 Jan 1829. John Anderson, S. U. D. (LS), Wit: B. J. Gregory, W. P. Murphy, Z. P. Herndon.

Proved by the oath of Z. P. Herndon 18 Jan 1829 before J. Rogers, Q. U. Recorded 18 Jan 1829.

T, 144: South Carolina, Union District. Joseph Quinn of District of Union for $100 to Alsa Tampertin of same, 50 acres on Mill Creek adj. Saml Quinn, Bartly Coleman, 8 Jan 1829. Joseph Quinn (LS), Wit: Giles N. Smith, John Smith (X). Proved by the oath of John Smith 10 Jan 1829 before J. Rogers, Q.U. Recorded 10 Jan 1829.

T, 144-145: Geo Fant of Union District for $150 to David Harris of same, tract on Cane Creek, waters of Tyger River, part of tract that the executors of James Webb granted to the said George Fant, adj. Williams, William Sartor, Boyd, 29 May 1828. Geo Fant (LS), Wit: Thomas H. Word, James Fant. Elizabeth Fant (X), wife of George Fant, relinquished dower 28 ___ before E. McGraw, Q. U. Proved by the oath of Thomas H. Word 29 May 1828 before E. McGraw, Q. U. Recorded 29 Jan 1829.

T, 145-146: South Carolina, Union District. Saml. O. Gordon of district aforesaid for $150 to Wiley Webster of same, 50 acres, a part of tract granted to Patrick H. Sims adj. Jeremiah Gregory, Gilliam, Jehu Gregory, Wm. R. Sims, 5 Jan 1825. Saml O. Gordon (LS), Wit: E. P. Porter, Jehu Gregory. Proved by the oath of E. P. Porter 12 Jan 1829 before J. Rogers, Q.U. Recorded 12 Jan 1829.

T, 146-147: B. J. Gregory of Union District for $1200 to Garrett Gregory Junr of same, tract on waters of Browns Creek, 258 acres per plat, 4 May 1825. B. J. Gregory (Seal), Wit: B. G. Davis, Geo Crawford. Proved by the oath of B. G. Davis 4 Fe 1828 before E. McGraw, Q. U. Elisabeth Gregory, wife of B. J. Gregory ,relinquished dower 28 Jan 1828 before E. McGraw. Recorded 2 Feb 1829.

T, 147-148: William Sartor of Union District for $100 to John P. Sartor of same, tract adj. land formerly belonging to William Glenn decd now John P. Sartor, John Evans, land formerly belonging to Richard Cox now James Hill, land formerly belonging to William Hemingway now Jas Hill said land including the Cross Road & plantation whereon the said John P. Sartor now lives, 118 acres, part of tract granted to William Farr in 1786, dated 10 Jan 1829. Wm Sartor (LS), Wit: Cn. T. Scaife, T. A. Carlisle. Proved by the oath of Charner T. Scaife 20 Jan 1829 before E. McGraw, Q. U. Recorded 29 Jan 1829.

T, 148-149: South Carolina, Union District. John Anderson of said district for $400 to Charner Humphries, 120 acres taken out of the present tract of land whereon Joseph Reeder lives on Shoaly Creek, adj. Joseph Reeder, Benj. Steen, Thomas Willard, J. M. Whitlow, 9 Sept 1828. John Anderson (Seal), Wit: D. A. Mitchell, W. P. Murphy. Proved by the oath of D. A. Mitchell 7 Feb 1829 before J. Rogers, Q.U. Recorded 7 Feb 1829.

T, 149-150: William R. Wilbourn of Union District for #1624 to Elisabeth W. Farrow of Spartanburgh District, two tracts of land on Union District, by estimation 400 acres, one tract whereon Elijah Wilbourn formerly lived adj. William Wallace, Amos Martin & his son James, Nathan Harlan, Solomon Putman; the other tract, part of tract of the estate of Thomas Brooks deceased, adj. Amos Martin and son James, Brooks, Blasingame, 98 acres, conveyed to me by Hannah Brooks, 31 Jan 1829. W. R. Wilbourn (Seal), Wit: Wm. Rice, H. W. W. Rice. Proved by the oath of Wm Rice 13 Fe 1829 before J. Rogers, Q. U. Recorded 13 Feb 1829.

T, 150-151: Henry Farnandis of Union District for $1000 to Joseph S. Sims of same, tract assigned to me by the Commissioners in Partition appointed by the Court of Equity, composed of two plats deposited in the Commissioners Office adj. Joseph S. Sims, and the orad leading to Spartanburgh, Giles Smith, Mr. Little, Mill Creek, William Henderson, Warmack Fowler, 397 acres, 7 Feb 1829. H. Farnandis (Seal), Wit: W. K. Clowney, Clough S. Sims. Proved by the oath of William K. Clowney 7 Feb 1829 before J. Rogers, Q. U. Recorded 7 Feb 1829.

T, 151-152: South Carolina, Union District. Wiley Webster of district aforesaid for $110 to John Gregory of same, 50 acres, part of tract granted to Patrick H. Sims adj. Jeremiah Gregory, Gilliam, 5 July 1825. Wiley Webster (X) (Seal), Wit: B. J. Gregory, William S. Savage, John Savage. Proved by the oath of Benj. J. Gregory 7 Aug 1826 before Titus G. Farr, Q. U. Recorded 12 Jan 1829.

T, 152: On the 24 Dec next I promise to pay John Parham exr. of the wil of John Parham decd or bearer $252.50, for a negro woman Vile, 7 April 1828. Erastus Giddings (LS), Wit: Hugh Greer. Proved by the oath of Hugh Greer 21 Feb 1829 before James Rountree, J.P. Recorded 21 Feb 1829.

T, 153: South Carolina, Union District. Saml O. Gordan of district aforesaid to Jehu Gregory of same, 150 acres, part of tract granted to Patrick H. Sims at Gilliams corner, Reid, William Sims, 5 Jan 1825. Saml. O. Gordon (seal), Wit: Proved by the oath of Jeremiah Gregory 7 Aug 1826 before T. G. Farr, Q. U. Anna C. Gordon, wife of Saml O. Gordon, relinquished dower 17 April 1828. Recorded 12 Jan 1829.

T, 154: South Carolina, Union District. Mrs. Nancy Gregory, wife of Jeremiah Gregory Senr, relinquished dower to Jehu Gregory for 200 acres, being the tract whereon Jehu Gregory now lives and conveyed by deed to him 20 Nov 1828, dated 7 Jan 1829, before E. McGraw, Q. U. Recorded 19 Jan 1829.

Freelove Gregory of Union District for love, good will and affection to my son Gerard Gregory of same, tract of land on east side of Browns Creek, 28¼ acres, 3 June 1828. Freelove Gregory (LS), Wit: Geo. P. Smith, Uriah Porter. Proved by the oath of Geo. P. Smith 21 Feb 1829 before J. Rogers, Q. U. Recorded 21 Feb 1829.

T, 155: South Carolina, Union District. Lydia Petty, wife of Robert Petty, relinquished dower to Joshua Petty, 9 Feb 1829. Lidy Petty (X), before Nicholas Corry, J. Q. Recorded 2 March 1829.

Elizabeth Petty, wife of James Petty, relinquished dower 9 Feb 1829 before Nicholas Corry, J. Q. Signed Lizzy Petty (mark). Recorded 2 March 1829.

T, 155-156: South Carolina, Union District. Mary Wilbourn (widow) for an obligation given my by my two sons William & Sandford Wilbourn (which binds them to purchase a place for me and look to my support and maintenance) do give them one negro boy named Bob worth $388, one woman Lydia worth $200, one negro girl Julia & her future increase worth $250, one horse Charley worth $100, thee feather beds with $75, the amount of the sale $150, two cows & Calves & 2 heifers worth $36, my part of the cotton 1800 lbs @$2-36, my interest in the land worth $300, 12 Dec 1827. Mary Wilbourn (X) (LS), Wit: Hiram Gibbs, James Wilbourn, Elijah Wilbourn. Proved by the oath of Hiram Gibbs 2 March 1829 before J. Rogers, Q. U. Recorded 2 March 1829.

T, 156-157: John Bates, Sheriff of Union District, by virtue of several writs of fieri facias from the court of common pleas for Union District tested the first Monday in Oct 1823 and the first Monday in March 1824 at the suits of Silas M. Wilbourn, Gist & Coleman, and John Gage Senr, to levy of the goods and chattels, lands and tenements of Aaron Pruitt, to levy $112.25, sells tract of 87 acres on a ranch, waters of Sugar Creek adj. estate of Thos Palmer decd, Thos Smith, Elias Pruett, sold to William R. Wilbourn, for $80, 26 Jan 1827. J. Bates (LS), Wit: William C. Pearson, Z. Hooker. Proved by the oath of Wm C. Pearson 2 March 1829 before J. Rogers, Q. U. Recorded 2 March 1829.

T, 157-159: South Carolina, Union District. John Turner of Union District for $189 to David Turner of same, tract on south side of Tyger River on a branch of said River, part of tract granted to James Addington and from him by will to his son John Addington, and from him to Wm. C. Pearson and from him to John Stuard from him to John Turner, 189 acres adj. Robt McDaniel, James Dugin, David Myers, Susan Turner, 16 May 1828. John Turner (X) (LS), Wit: Robert McDaniel, John Chamblin (X), Mildred Fant. Proved by the oath of Robert McDaniel 16 May 1828 before Wm. Fant, J. P. Nancy Turner (X), wife of John Turner, relinquished dower 29 May 1828 before Thomas Stribling, Q. U. Recorded 3 March 1829.

T, 159-160: John Anderson, sheriff of Union District, by virtue of a writ of fieri facias from the court of common pleas tested 30 May 1807 at the suit of Wm. R. Wilbern to levy of the goods and chattles, land and tenements of John P. Patterson $100, sell tract of 125 acres adj. Samuel Hays, Thomas Nance, James Smith, Sarah Putman; sold to William R. Wilburn for $20, 10 May 1827. John Anderson, S. U. D. (Seal), Wit: Wm. Rice, B. J. Gregory. Proved by the oath of Wm Rice 3 March 1829 before J. Rogers, Q. U. Recorded 2 March 1829.

T, 160-161: John Anderson, sheriff of Union District, by virtue of a writ of fieri facias from the court of common pleas tested 1 January 1828 at the suit of Silas M. Wilbern to levy of the goods and chattles, land and tenements of John Norrell $196, sell tract of 300 acres adj. Samuel Hays, Widow Putman, James Palmer, Smith, Lucy Littlefield, Benjamin Bettington, known by the name of the Putman tract; sold to William R. Wilbern for $200, 6 Feb 1828. John Anderson, S. U. D. (Seal), Wit: B. J. Gregory, John Harrington. Proved by the oath of B. J.Gregory 3 March 1829 before J. Rogers, Q. U. Recorded 2 March 1829.

T, 161-163: South Carolina, Union District. John Turner of Union District for $50 to Susan Turner of same, tract on south side of Tyger River on a branch of said River, 55 acres, part of tract granted to James Addington and from him by will to his son John Addington, and from him to Wm. C. Pearson and from him to Henry R. Stuard from him to John Turner, on west side of Tyger River or branch of said river, 16 May 1828. John Turner (X) (LS), Wit: Robert McDaniel, John Chamblin (X), Mildred Fant. Proved by the oath of Robert McDaniel 16 May 1828 before Wm. Fant, J. P. Nancy Turner (X), wife of John Turner, relinquished dower 29 May 1828 before Thomas Stribling, J. P. Recorded 2 March 1829.

T, 163-164: South Carolina, Union District. John Petty of district aforesaid for $507 to John Jeffries Senr of same, tract of land where the said Joshua Petty now lives, on waters of Gilkeys and Abitons Creeks, waters of Broad River adj. James Petty, William Lockhart, said Jeffries, 30 Jan 1829. Joshua Petty (LS), Wit: James Jeffries, Samuel Jeffries. Proved by the oath of James Jeffries 7 Feb 1829 before Wm. C. Cotter, J.P. Rebeca Petty (mark), wife of Joshua Petty, relinquished dower 9 Feb 1829 before Nicholas Corry, J.P. Recorded 2 March 1829.

T, 164: South Carolina, Union District. Mary Davis, wife of Samuel Davis, relinquished dower to Samuel P. Baley 9 Sept 1828 before Lem. B. Askew, J. Q.

T, 165: Plat of Union Village sowing the distance from each wall and the distance on each cross street from Union Street, 28 June 1827 by Richard Thomson, D. S. Recorded 4 March 1829. Shows Tushes branch.

T, 166: Mary Ann Moorman of Union District for $500 to William Rice, Esquire, of same, all right, title, interest and estate to two tracts of land on both sides Cane Creek adjoining at present James Hill, James Meacham, said William Rice, Robert Underwood, which said lands were purchased by James A. Moorman of William Lucas & William Jeter, by estimation 550½ acres, 2 March 1829. Mary A. Moorman (LS), Wit: Joseph H. Dogan, J. W. Fletcher. Proved by the oath of John W. Fletcher 4 March 1829 before J. Rogers, Q.U. Recorded 4 March 1829.

T, 167-168: Daniel Thomas of Union District for $296 to Richard G. Hobson of same, tract on branches of Neals big Creek, 74 acres, 15 Jan 1829. Daniel Thomas (LS), Wit: Adam Thomson, L. B. Jeter. Proved by the oath of Capt. Little B. Jeter stating that he saw Col. Daniel Thomas sign the within, 5 Jan 1829, before Titus G. Farr, Q.U. Mary B. Thomas, wife of Daniel Thomas, relinquished dower 21 Jan 1829 before Titus G. Farr, Q.U. Recorded 2 March 1829.

T, 168: James B. Thomas of Union District for $1000 to Christopher De graffenried of same, one negro man named Daniel, a blacksmith by trade, 20 Feb 1829. James B. Thomas (LS), Wit: Ferd'd Hopkins Sr., Titus G. Farr. Proved by the oath of Ferdinand Hopkins Senr 20 Feb 1829 before Titus G. Farr, Q.U. Recorded 2 March 1829.

T, 169-171: South Carolina, Union District. Whereas on 18 July 1825, I, Christopher de Graffenried of district aforesaid, executed a deed by which I conveyed the whole of my estate real and personal to my two sons Doctor John de Graffenried and Tresvant de Graffenried and my daughter Mrs. Thomas, with a condition that I should be paid the sum of $500 during my and my wife's lifetime and that upon the death of either of us the survivor should be paid the sum of $250 during life and upon failure of paying the said sum of money, I retained the power or revoking the deed. Now, that I having requested my said sons John and Tresvant to accept and receive the said property under the conditions and restrictions in the said deed mentioned and they having utterly refused to have any thing to do with said property or to pay the said sum of money, I do revoke and annul the said deed; now for natural love and affection towards my three children John de Graffenreid, Tresvant de Graffenreid, Mary Thomas, wife of James V. Thomas, and for one dollar, do give them the following property as tenants in common and not as joint tenants, one tract of land in Union District 66½ acres adj. lands of T. G. Farr, Thos G. B. Degraffenreid & James Gazaway, being the same I purchased of Samuel P. Johnson, all my stock of hogs, horses cattle & sheep, three feather beds, and all other household and kitchen furniture, with my waggon and harness, my corner, fodder, oats, rye & Wheat now growing, all the money due me as coming from my fathers estate in the state of Virginia, with negroes Rollin, Watt, Matt, Peter, ____, Silla, Amber, Robbin, Banda, Dover, Nance, ___, Esther, Mariah, Abba, Joe, Daniel, Henry, Abram, ____ Minerva, Patt, Keziah, Anderson, , ____ Claiborn, Catharine, Bill & a child at breast not named and Eliza with their future increase, and my children are to pay all debts by me now due and owing out of the above property; and one debt due by me to my son Trezvant Degraffenreid of $605.27 is to be paid out of the above property to be valued and appraised by Ferdinand Hopkins Senr, Richd Wilks, both of Chester District, and William Sorter Senior of Union District, 20 Feb 1829. Christopher Degraffenreid (Seal), Wit: Ferd'd Hopkins Senr, Richard Wilks, Titus G. Farr. Proved by the oath of Ferdinand Hopkins Senr 20 Feb 1829 before Titus G. Farr, Q.U. Recorded 2 March 1829.

T, 171-172: South Carolina, Union District. Christopher DeGraffenreid for natural love and affection for the children of my daughter Mary Thomas, wife of James V. Thomas, one negro man named Daniel, a Black smith, 20 Feb 1829. Christopher Degraffenreid (Seal), Wit: Trezvant de Graffenried, Titus G. Farr, Ferd'd Hopkins Senr,. Proved by the oath of Ferdinand Hopkins Senr 20 Feb 1829 before Titus G. Farr, Q.U. Recorded 2 March 1829.

T, 172-173: Starling Baker of Union District for $1236 to Little B. Jeter of Union District, tract on Neals little creek, 309 acres, 5 Feb 1829. Starling Baker (Seal), Wit: Wm. Hobson, D. A. Thomas. Alsey Baker (X), wife of Starling Baker, relinquished dower 5 Feb 1829 before Titus G. Farr, Q. U. Proved by the oath of David A. Thomas 5 Feb 1829 before Titus G. Farr, Q. U. Recorded 2 March 1829.

T, 173-174: South Carolina, Union District. William Williams of Union District for $400 to Sarah Owins of Fairfield District, two tables, six chairs, two feather beds and furniture, all my live stock, two cows & calves, on black horse, all my present crop of corn, cotton & fodder, one negro man named Will, if said William Williams does not pay to said Sarah Owins $400 before 1 Jan 1833, dated 27 Aug 1828. Wm Williams (LS), Wit Wm. R. Clowney. Proved by the oath of Col. W. R. Clowney, 20 Dec 1828 before J. Rogers, Q.U. Recorded 20 Dec 1828.

T, 174-175: John Boyce of Union District for $150 to Matthew H. Boyd of same, 135 acres on the south side of Cane Creek, branches of Tyger River adj. Pruett, Wm. Hobson, Peter Sorter, ____ 1828. John Boyce (X) (Seal), Wit: Wm. Jeter, Samuel Harriss. Proved by the oath of William Jeter and Samuel Harriss 8 May 1838 before W. McGraw, Q. U. Recorded 2 March 1829.

T, 175-176: South Carolina, Union District. George Fant of district aforesaid to Zachariah Johnson of same, all his interest in a tract of land of 160 acres on Beverdam Creek, waters of Tyger River adj. Philip R. Pearson, James Johnson, Samuel Fant decd, 100 acres of said land originally granted to John Coulter 15 March 1771 conveyed by said Coulter to Marshall Lewallen 13 Aug 1771 and by Shadrick Lewallen heir at law to Meshack Lewallen deceased 1 Sept 1789 to Wm Mitchell and conveyed by said Mitchell to Isaac Cook Senr decd, 17 March 1790, and by Dinah Cook, William Cook and Rebekah Cook, heirs at law to the estate of Isaac Cook decd to Isaac Cook and conveyed by Isaac Cook to Samuel Crumpton 7 Feb 1798; one other tract of 60 acres granted to Daniel Tolleson and by said Tolleson to Isaac Cook 13 May 1797, and conveyed by said Cook to Samuel Crumpton 17 Feb 1798 and by him to Isaac Cook 17 Aug 1803, conveyed by Isaac Cook to Samuel O. Johnson and John C. Valentine 13 Jan 1805 and sold by John Bates, late Sheriff, by John Anderson, successor of said Bate, to George Fant and by Gant to Zachariah Johnson, 22 March 1828, now for $117.. dated 23 July 1828. George Fant, Wit: Sintha Fant, James Fant. Proved by the oath of James Fant 28 Feb 1829 before James O. Johnson, J.P. Recorded 2 March 1829.

T, 175-176: South Carolina, Union District. George Fant of district aforesaid to Zacheriah Johnson of same, all his interest in a tract of land of 160 acres on Beverdam Creek, waters of Tyger River, adj. Philip R. Pearson, James Johnson, Samuel Fant decd, 100 acres granted to John Coulter 15 March 1771 and conveyed by him to Meshack Lewallen 13 Aug 1771 conveyed by Shadrick Lewallen heir at law to Meshack Lewallen deceased 1 Sept 1789 to Wm Mitchell and by said Mitchell to Isaac Cook Senr 17 March 1790 by Dinah Cook, William Cook and Rebekah Cook, heirs of Isaac Cook to Isaac Cook and by Isaac Cook to Samuel Crumpton 7 Feb 1798; one other tract of 60 acres granted to Daniel Tolleson and conveyed to Isaac Cook 13 May 1797 and by said Cook to Samuel Cumpton 17 Feb 1798 and by Samuel Cumpton to Isaac Cook 17 Aug 1803 conveyed by Isaac Cook to Samuel O. Johnson and John C. Valentine, and sold by John Bates, late Sheriff of said district conveyed by John Anderson, Successor of said Bates to George Fant, 22 March 1828, now conveyed 23 July 1828. George Fant, Wit: Sintha Fant, James Fant. Proved by the oath of James Fant 28 Feb 1829 before Samuel O. Johnson, J.P. Recorded 2 March 1829.

T, 176-178: John Anderson, Sheriff of Union District, by virtue of a writ of fieri facias from the court of Common pleas tested the first Monday of October 1825 at the suit of Zedoc Hooker to me directed, to levy of the goods and chattels, lands and tenements of Samuel O. Johnson, 4536.31, sells tract of 160 acres on Beaverdam Creek, waters of Tyger River adj. Philip R. Pearson, James Johnson, Samuel Fant, sold to John Bates for $102, 22 March 1828. John Anderson, S. U. D. (LS), Wit: Silas Baker, Wm. Skelton. Proved by the oath of William Skelton 2 March 1829 before E. McGraw, J. Q. Recorded 2 March 1829.

T, 178-179: South Carolina, Union District. A. B. Hall of district aforesaid for $300 to Christopher Young (Senr) of same, 184 acres near Sardis Meeting house, in the fork Authers branch, 6 Feb 1829. A. B. Hall (LS), Wit: John Joiner, Michael Lee. Proved by the oath of John Joiner 10 March 1829 before Wm. Skelton, J.P. Recorded 10 March 1829.

T, 179-180: South Carolina, Spartanburg District. William Wofford of said district for $300 to William West of Union District, 200 acres on waters of McClures Creek, part of tract granted to said William Wofford, 425 acres Sarcom Lancaster's corner, 14 Aug 1824. Wm. Wofford (LS), Wit: George Sparks, Hosea Wofford. Proved by the oath of Hosea Wofford 5 Feb 1825 before James Smith, J.P. Recorded 9 March 1829.

T, 180: Martha Saunders of Union District for natural love and affection for my two grandsons Reuben S. and John D. Saunders of said district for $1, three negroes Violet, Lin & Thomas, 21 Jan 1829. Martha Saunders (X) (Seal), Wit: J. W. Williams, Thos Hays. Proved by the oath of Thomas Hayes 10 March 1829 before J. Rogers, Q. U. Recorded 10 March 1829.

T, 181: Henry Parr of Union District for $1515 to John Harris of same, 142 acres on waters of Browns Creek, adj. Thomas Powers, Vaughan, Widow Woods, Galman, 20 Feb 1829. Henry Parr (LS), Wit: Thomas Parr (X), Samuel P. Harris, Flemin M. Harris, James C. K. Harris. Proved by the oath of Thomas Parr 10 March 1829 before R. Lipsey, J.P. Recorded 10 March 1829.

T, 182: South Carolina, Union District. William Cole of said district for $600 to Vinson Davis, tracts of land on waters of Tramels Creek adj. said Davis, Isaac Young, William Hamey, Thomas Glass, 170 acres, 8 Dec 1828. William Cole (W) (LS), Wit I. J. Foster, J. S. Weir. Proved by the oath of Joseph S. Weir 27 Dec 1828 before Isaac Going, Q.U. Recorded 10 March 1829.

T, 182-183: Martha Saunders of Union District for love and affection to my daughter Chloe M. Saunders of same, six negroes Marky a woman about 29 years of age, and her five children Jonas, Fanny, Juliett, Prince, Eadon, 21 Jan 1829. Martha Saunders (X), Wit: J. W. Williams, Thomas Hays. Proved by the oath of Thomas Hays 10 March 1829. Recorded 10 March 1829.

T, 183-184: Martha Saunders of Union District for love and affection to my daughter Charlotte C. Harlan, wife of Joseph Harlan, of same, six negroes Jessy[?] a woman about 30 years of age, and her five children Enoch, Thomas, Sally, Jane and Mary[?], 21 Jan 1829. Martha Saunders (X), Wit: J. W. Williams, Thomas Hays. Proved by the oath of Thomas Hays 10 March 1829. Recorded 10 March 1829.

T, 184-185: South Carolina, Union District. James Dugan of district aforesaid for $600 to Farr Bates of same, 200 acres, 10 Oct 1825. James Dugan (Seal), Wit: George Young, William Steen. Frances Dugan, wife of James Dugan, relinquished dower 18 Dec 1828 before J. Rogers, Q.U. Proved by the oath of George Young 18 March 1829. Recorded 18 March 1829.

T, 185-186: Daniel Chandler of Union District for $521.96 to Delilah Langston of same, all my plantation whereon I now live, a mair, five head of cattle, nine head of hogs, eighteen head of sheep, one waggon, and all furniture, 24 May 1828. Daniel Chandler (LS), Wit: Jeremiah Kingsley, James Tate (X). Proved by the oath of Jeremiah Kingsley 12 March 1829 before Wm Skelton, J.P. Recorded 9 Jan 1829.

T, 186-187: Recd of John Steen $150 in full payment of a negro boy named Orange about 5 years old, 9 Jan 1829. W. H. Steen, Wit: Jepthah Harrington James Jeffries. Proved by the oath of Jepthah Harrington 14 March 1829 before Wm. R. Clowney, Qu. ex off. Recorded 14 March 1829.

T, 187: Polly Powel of Union District for $50 to Frazer Chandler of same, lot of ten acres, part of tract being formerly the property of Wm. Tomblin on waters of Morris[?] branch, adj. Repps Edwards, Doc. G. D. Phillips, 6 Nov 1828. Mary Powel (LS), Wit: Jeremiah Kingsley, James Tate (X). Proved by the oath of Jeremiah Kingsley 12 March 1829 before J. Rogers, Q.U. Recorded 12 March 1829.

T, 188-189: South Carolina, Union District. William Dillard of Laurens District for $3000 to David Boyce of Union District, 671 acres, part of four tracts of land originally granted to Henry Clark, John Price, Jeremiah Cooper, David Smith, just above where the columbia road crosses Padgets Creek near Spencer Bobo's, 1 Jan 1827. William Dillard (X) (LS), Wit: Nathan Fowler, Asa Dodd. Susannah Dillard (X), wife of William Dillard, relinquished dower 31 Dec 1828 before Robert Martin, J.Q. Proved by the oath of Asa Dodd 21 Jan 1827 before Jno Norman, J.P. Recorded 11 March 1829.

T, 189-191: Frederick Nance, one of the exrs. of Col. Robert Rutherford of Newberry District, for $250 to Nathaniel Guiton of Union District, 608½ acres by a plat made by Marmaduke Coat, Esq., 21 July 1825, on waters of Gilkeys Creek, a branch of Thickety Creek, being a tract originally granted to Charles Harrington for 500 acres 3 Nov 1788, dated 10 March 1829. F. Nance (Seal), Wit: R. R. Nance, P. C. Caldwell. Proved in Newberry District by the oath of Patrick C. Caldwell 10 March 1829 before Henry Oneall, Q.U. Elizabeth Nance, wife of Frederick Nance, relinquished dower 10 March 1829 before Henry Oneall, Q.U. Plat included showing adj. land owner John Jeffreys Esqr. The part included by gum lines is claimed by Josiah Martin, containing 81 acres and is said to be an older grant.

T, 191-192: John Bates, Sheriff of Union District, by virtue of a writ of fieri facias from the court of common pleas tested the first Monday of October 1823 at the suit of Porter & Miller to levy of the goods & Chattels, lands and tenements of Amos Northrop $89.21, sells 57 acres adj. John Jeffries, Drury Harrington, John Steen, for $115 to Jepthah Harrington, 2 March 1824. J. Bates, S. U. D. (LS), Wit: M. B. Harrington, Wm. H. Neal. Proved by the oath of Wm. H. Neal 10 March 1829 before Lot Whitlock, J.P. Recorded 11 March 1829.

T, 192-193: Samuel M. Gowdey and Company of Union District for $300 to William Brown of Union District, tract sold as the property of T. Holmes by the Sheriff of Union District on 23 March last, 108 acres, 30 Jan 1829. Samuel M. Gowdey, Timothy Levet (LS), Thad. Sneed (LS), Wit: C. L. West, George Gibbon. Proved by the oath of Charles L. West 5 Feb 1829 before Jeremiah Condy, N. P. and Q. U. exofficio. Recorded 12 March 1829.

T, 193-196: State of Tennessee, Maury County. Jeremiah Tranum heir at law of Obediah Tranum deceased of Union District, for $98 to James Meacham, all my claim and interest in that tract of 139 acres on waters of Cane Creek originally granted to Thomas Shockley and from him conveyed to James Ringet and from said James Ringet to Obediah Tranum, 30 April 1828. Ack. Jeremiah Tranum (Seal), Wit: Thos. B. Craighead, John H. Linam, George G. Farrar. Acknowledged in Maury County Court, April Term 1828 before Joseph B. Porter, Parry W. Porter, D. Clk. James Walker, county clerk of

Maury County, certified that Parry W. Porter was Deputy Clerk, 1 May 1828. Recorded 11 March 1829. Elizabeth Tranum, wife of Jeremiah Tranum, relinquished dower before 30 April 1828 before Thos B. Craighead, Maury County, Tenn.

T, 196-197: William R. Wilbourn of Union District for $1000 to William Rice of Union District, tract on both sides of Mitchells Creek, a water course of Fairforest, adj. Joseph Harlan, Stephen McPherson, John Hays, and the heirs of John Parham decd, it being the tract whereon the said John Parham lately lived, and sold at sheriffs sale by John Bates, late Sheriff, 7 May 1828. W. R. Wilbourn (LS), Wit: Jno Nance, John Anderson. Proved by the oath of John Anderson 4 April 1829 before J. Rogers, Q. U. Recorded 4 April 1829.

T, 197-198: South Carolina, Union District. James Richardson of said district for $10 to Mark Murphy, Bird Murphey, and Angus Alexander, trustees appointed by the Paget Creek Church, a small piece of land including the graveyard near the said Meeting House, to the corner of the meeting house tract as conveyed by John Alexander Sr., 19 March 1827. James Richardson (X) (LS), Wit: Spencer A. Bobo, C. F. Grimke, John Ray. Proved by the oath of Charles F. Grimke 28 March 1827 before John Norman, J.P. Recorded 4 June 1827.

T, 198-199: South Carolina, Union District. James Harrington of district aforesaid for $500 to James Jeffries of same, tract on waters of Thickety Creek and Gilkeys Creek, part of tract granted to J. McNit Alexander, 100 acres adj. land granted to Drury Harrington, 15 Dec 1828. James Harrington (LS), Wit: Jepthah Harrington, John Harrington. Proved by the oath of Jepthah Harrington 9 March 1828 before J. S. Sims, Q.U. Sarah Harrington, wife of James Harrington, relinquished dower 21 Jan 1829 before John Giles, Q. U. Recorded 9 March 1829.

T, 200: Robert White Sr. of District of Spartanburg for $91 to Johnson Coggin of Union District, part of tract granted to Patrick McGarity, near William Baley's, near Elias Whites, 61 acres adj. William Bailey, Robert Boatman, Jesse Boatman, Ambrose[?] Yarborough, Elias White, 4 April 1829. Robt White (X) (Seal), Wit: Robt White Junr, James White. Proved by the oath of Robert White 4 April 1829 before J. Q. Cooper, J.P. Recorded 6 April 1829.

T, 201: South Carolina, Union District. William White for $93 to Johnson Coggin, both of said district, part of tract granted to Ambrose Yarborough adj. Jesse Boatman, Frederick Jackson, Wm White, on the Ninety Six Road, 62 acres, 4 April 1829. Wm White (Seal), Wit: John Gibbs, James White. Proved by the oath of James White 6 Apr 1829 before H. Gibbs, J.Q. Recorded 6 April 1829.

T, 201-203: John Anderson, Sheriff of Union District, by virtue of a writ of fieri facias from the court of common pleas tested 30 March 1825 at the suit of James Norris to levy of the goods and chattels, lands and tenements of

George McKnight $143.25, sells 241 acres adj. John Harris, Ruth Hall, Godfrey Fowler, Charles Jones, Charles Cunningham, sold for $143.25 to Andrew Park for John Hames, 20 Sept 1828. John Anderson S. U. D. (Seal), Wit: B. J. Gregory, Elijah Gossett. Proved by the oath of Benjamin J. Gregory 6 April 1829 before H. H. Means, J.P. Recorded 6 April 1829.

T, 203-204: South Carolina, Union District. George McKnight for $600 to John hames, tract whereon I now live on branches of Sandy River and Mill Creek, 240 acres, 10 March 1828. Geo McKnight (LS), Wit: Chas Jones, Joseph Quinn. Proved by the oath of Charles Jones 18 March 1828 before Danl Thomas, Q.U. Ruth Mcknight, wife of George McKnight, relinquished dower 18 March 1828 before Danl Thomas, Q.U.

T, 204-205: Richard Bullock of Warren County, North Carolina, exr. of the will of Len Henly Bullock of said place, by which I am authorized to sell his lands in South Carolina, for $575 to Henry Farnandis of Union District, tract on Packolett River including the shoals known by the name of Easterwoods, 862 acres, adj. Thomas Sparks, Norton, Hames, and others, 27 Oct 1810. Richard Bullock (LS), Wit: Womac Fowler, John Henderson. Proved by the oath of Womack Fowler in Union District before John Saunders, Jr., J.P. Recorded 6 April 1829.

T, 205-206: Henry Farnandis of Union District, for $1035 to James Norris, tract on north side Packolet River which Henry Farnandis purchased of Richard Bullock, adj. Giffon, Greer, Sparks, 764 acres and 100 acres purchased of Matthew Sparks, 10 Feb 1823. H. Farnandis (LS), Wit: J. A. Farnandis, Saml Moseley. Proved by the oath of Capt. Samuel Moseley 6 April 1829 before J. Rogers, Q. U. Recorded 6 April 1829.

T, 206-208: John Anderson, Sheriff of Union District, by virtue of a writ of fieri facias from the court of common pleas tested the first Monday of October 1825 at the suit of Christopher Brandon against Lucinda Frey & David Eigner to levy of the goods and chattels, lands and tenements of the said Lucinda and David $42.80, sells 360 acres on Little Browns Creek, waters of Broad River, in the fork of Broad River and Packolet, adj. Isaac White, R. Lipsey, John H. Galman, Samuel Smith, Isaac Haney, conveyed by John Bates, formerly Sheriff to Lucinda Fry, sold to William Norris for $200, 3 Oct 1827. John Anderson, S. U. D. (LS), Wit: Thos Anderson, Silas Baker. Proved by the oath of Thos Anderson 6 April 1829 before J. Rogers, Q.U.

T, 208-209: Thomas C. Taylor of Union District for $455 to Benjamin F. Logan of Pinckneyville, Union District, and John McEntire of Rutherford County, NC, copartners in trade at Pinckneyville, lot in Pinckneyville beginning at the lower end of Logan & McEntire's cotton house on the main street, to the line of Gallant's lott, adj. Daniel McMahan, 17 May 1828. Thomas C. Taylor (Seal), Wit: John McGowan Junr, E. S. Gilmore. Proved by the oath of John McGowan 17 June 1828 before Isaac Going, Q.U.

Elizabeth Taylor, wife of Thomas C. Taylor, relinquished dower 17 June 1828 before Isaac Going, Q.U. Recorded 6 April 1829.

T, 209-210: South Carolina, Union District. John Steen of Union District to Charles Miles, my son-in-law, for natural love and affection for my daughter Lucinda wife of said Charles, one negro girl named Sophia, one mare about the value of $100, two beds and furniture of the value of $40 each, and two cows & calves, 5 Feb 1828. John Steen (LS), Wit: Wm. K. Clowney. Proved by the oath of Wm. K. Clowney, Esq., 7 April 1829 before J. Rogers, Q.U. Recorded 7 April 1829.

T, 210-211: South Carolina, Union District. Solomon West of district aforesaid for $103.25 to Elias High of same, tract on Mitchells Creek, waters of Fairforest, 59 acres adj. Elias High's line, John Hughes old corner, 13 Feb 1829. Solomon West (LS), Wit: Caswell Bogan, Larkan Lancaster, Wm. West. Proved by the oath of Caswell Bogan 2 March 1829 before J. Palmer, J.P. Elender West (X), wife of Solomon West, relinquished dower 5 March 1829 before Hiram Gibbs, Q.U. Recorded 7 April 1829.

T, 211-212: South Carolina, Union District. Randolph Alexander of district aforesaid for $250 to John S. Grissel of same, 60 acres, part of tract granted to John Prince, conveyed by said John Prince to Daniel Prince, on Holans Creek, waters of Tyger River, adj. Caleb Smith, Thomas Ray, Sion Murphey, Edward Prince, Absolam Bishop, 8 Nov 1827. Randolph Alexander (Seal), Wit: S. W. Alexander, Roley Alexander. Proved by the oath of Rolley Alexander 12 March 1829 before J. Rogers, Q.U. Recorded 12 March 1829.

T, 213: South Carolina, Union District. Zachariah Belew Senr for love, good will and affection to the citizens of Union District and the community at large, to Mr. John Rogers, Clerk of the Court in said district, a small piece of land for a burying ground lying between 2 & 3 hundred yards nearly north from my house where I now live, on Capt. B. Saunders line, one car of land adj. Capt. Benjamin Saunders, Z. Belue's land, __ March 1826. Zacheriah Belew (LS), Wit: Wm. White, Mial Ezell. Proved by the oath of William White 7 April 1829 before Daniel White, Q. U. Recorded 7 April 1829.

T, 214-215: South Carolina, Union District. 25 Nov 1828, Barney Oneel of district aforesaid to Logan & McEntire of same, mortgage for $101.64, tract on waters of Fannans Creek adj. James Millwood, James Vinson & others, the tract on which said Barney Oneal now lives, 50 acres. Barney Oneal (+) (Seal), Wit: E. G. Logan. Proved by the oath of Elbert G. Logan 13 March 1829 before Isaac Going, Q.U. Recorded 20 April 1829.

T, 215: Daniel Thomas of Union District for $100 to William J. Thomas of same, tract on waters of Neals Creek whereon the said William J. Thomas now lives, adj. Jesse Leach, William hobson, 50 acres, 12 Feb 1828. Daniel Thomas (LS), Wit: Titus G. Farr, W. B. Johns. Proved by the oath of Titus G. Farr, Esqr., 18 April 1829 before J. Rogers, Q.U. Recorded 19 April 1829.

T, 216: South Carolina, Union District. James V. Thomas of district aforesaid for natural love and affection to my children to wit Christopher, Mary Sarahan, & Daniel, and all the rest of my children that I may have by my now wife Mary Thomas, 13 negroes Nat, Old Robbin, Matt, Old Mary, Sillar, Amber, Young Robbin, Bander, Rose, Dover, Nance, Patience & one man Daniel a Blacksmith, 19 April 1829. James V. Thomas (Seal), Wit: Richd Thomson, T. B. Mitchell. Proved by the oath of Richard Thomson 19 April 1829 before Titus G. Farr, Q.U. Recorded 20 April 1829.

T, 217-218: South Carolina, Union District. 17 Feb 1829, Charles Humphries of the first part, Elizabeth Holland of the second part, and Robert Martin & Saml Martin of the third part, whereas a marriage is intended between the said Charles Humphries and said Elisabeth Holland, and said Elisabeth Holland is seized in fee simple of a certain tract of land on waters of Enoree River, 2250 acres whereon the said Elisabeth Holland now lives, and one negro man named Noah,one negro woman named Juna and her for children Lewis, Allen, Tom & Davy, one sorrel horse & one bay horse, nine head of cattle, etc., it is agreed that the property of said Charles shall not be liable for the payment of any debts which may be contracted by said Elisabeth Holland and no property of her be liable for his debts. Charles Humphries (mark) (LS), Elisabeth Holland (LS), Robt Martin (LS), Saml L. Martin (LS), Wit: Thomas Young, Carry Ray. Proved by the oath of Carry Ray 23 March 1829 before John Norman, J.P. Recorded 25 April 1829.

T, 219: South Carolina, Union District. Thomas White of said district for a tract of land which I consider to be equal and exchange with Clifton Mitchell of same, tract lying adjoining him, 19½ acres, 6 July 1818. Thomas White (LS), Wit: Edward Anderson, James C. Mayhew. Proved by the oath of Jas C. Mayhew 6 July 1818 before William Mitchell, J.P. Recorded 28 April 1829.

T, 219-220: South Carolina, Union District. Jesse Spencer of district aforesaid for $300 to James C. Mayhew, tract on waters of Fairforest, 80 acres, part of tract conveyed by John Parham to said Jesse Spencer, now in possession of James Mitchell, 25 Aug 1820. Jesse Spencer (Seal), Wit: t. c. Means, Joseph R. Howard. Proved by the oath of Joseph R. Howard 24 Aug 1820 before H. Means, Q. U. Elizabeth Spencer, wife of Jesse Spencer, relinquished dower 25 Aug 1820. Recorded 28 April 1829.

T, 220-221: Mary Howard of Union District, SC, for natural love and affection to my son Clemmons Howard of said state, a negro boy named Jim, 5 Jan 1829. Mary Howard (X) (LS), Wit: Robt Stokes, Nathan Harlan. Proved by the oath of Nathan Harlan 25 April 1829 before J. Rogers, Clk. Recorded 25 April 1829.

T, 221: To Mr. Jacob Stroup. Dear Sir, you may rely upon it that at the expiration of my bargain with Mr. McKown if I should live that long, you shall have my mill and farm at thirty five dollars a year during my lifetime. Therefore you may begin to make what improvements you please. 9 Dec 1826.

Elizabeth Smith (X), Wit: Nicholas Corry, William Terry. Proved by the oath of Nicholas Corry 25 April 1829 before Henry Smith, J.P. Recorded 4 May 1829.

T, 222: South Carolina, Union District. Sandford Wilbourn & R. W. Wallace of district aforesaid for $4005 to Jane Wallace of same, tract of 100 acres adj. Wm. R. Wilbourn, Thos Smith, 3 Nov 1828. R. W.Wallace (LS), Sandford Wilbourn (LS), Wit: L. V. Nance, James Smith. Proved by the oath of L. V. Nance 9 May 1829 before J. Rogers, Q.U. Recorded 4 May 1829.

T, 222-223: South Carolina, Union District. Samuel Harland for love, good will and affection to my son George Harland, both of said district, tract of land on east side Fairforest Creek, adj. Goodwin Woodson, Wyche Goodwin, Isaac Gregory, Nathan Harland, 150 acres, 10 April 1829. Samuel Harlan (Seal), Wit: Wm. Rice, John Murrell. Proved by the oath of Wm. Rice, Esqr., 4 May 1829 before J. Rogers, Q.U. Recorded 4 May 1829.

T, 223-225: South Carolina, Union District. Gabriel Patrick Sr. for $352 to John Philips of district aforesaid, 104½ acres on waters of Abetons Creek, part of tract of which John Harrington, late of Union District, deceased, died seized and possessed, and sold upon order of the court of common pleas for Union District to make partition amongst the heirs and purchased by Ezra Cates & Hezekiah Harrington, the one half of which said Ezra Cates & Hezekiah Harrington sold Y. J. Harrington & Birt Harrington by deed 11 March 1819, adj. Wilkins & Corry, Patrick, 1 Jan 1829. Gabriel Patrick Senr (LS), Wit: Aaron Wilkins, James Philips. Proved by the oath of Aaron Wilkins 26 Jan 1829 before Nicholas Corry, J.Qu. Jane Patrick, wife of Gabriel Patrick, relinquished dower 10 Feb 1829 before Nicholas Corry, J. Q. Plat included dated 18 July 1826, by J. Jeffries. Recorded 4 May 1829.

T, 225-226: South Carolina, Union District. Jesse Dood [*sic*] of district aforesaid for $40 to Joseph Cooper of same, tract of 40 acres near the waters of Frenchman's Creek, part of tract formerly laid out for Thomas Todd adj. Wilson, 27 March 1816. Jesse Dodd (LS), Wit: Edmund Foster, Joseph Cooper. Proved by the oath of Edmond Foster 31 March 1816 before Joseph Harris, J.P. Recorded 4 May 1829.

T, 226-227: John Anderson of Union District, by virtue of a writ of fieri facias from the court of common pleas tested 12 May 1827 at the suit of Richard Starns to levy of the goods and chattels, lands and tenements of Joseph Cooper, sells 40 acres on waters of Frenchmans Creek adj. lands of Edmond Foster, Jesse Dodd, & the widow Gilliam, sold for $20.50 to Richard Starns 5 May 1829. John Anderson S. U. D. (LS), Wit: D. A. Mitchell, John H. Skelton. Proved by the oath of D. A. Mitchell before J. Rogers, Q. U., 5 May 1829. Recorded 5 May 1829.

T, 227-228: Mary Howard of Union District for natural love and affection to my son Jason Howard of same, a negro boy named Bill, 5 Jan 1829. Mary

Howard (X) (LS), Wit: Robert Stokes, Nathan Harlan. Proved by the oath of Nathan Harlan 4 May 1829 before J. Rogers, Q. U. Recorded 4 May 1829.

T, 228-229: South Carolina, Union District. James Meacham of district aforesaid for $2400 to Hezekiah Rice of Laurens District, tract conveyed to me by Banks Meacham 5 Jan 1828, and also the adjoining plantation conveyed to said Banks Meacham by Dread Jones 26 Sept 1825, in the whole 660 acres on north side Enoree River adj. Barram Bobo, Noah Garret, John Beard, Widow Bishop, David Spyva, Thomas G. Danner, 12 Jan 1829. James Meacham (LS), Wit: Bern'd Glenn, C. B. N. Rice. Proved by the oath of Charles N. Rice 6 April 1829 before J. Rogers, Q.U. Lucy C. Meacham, wife of Doct. James Meacham, relinquished dower 8 April 1829 before E. McGraw, Q.U. Recorded 4 May 1829.

T, 229-230: South Carolina, Union County. William Spears of county aforesaid for $40 to William Palmer of same, 21 acres, part of the tract on which I now live, on south side Pacolett River, part of said tract of land granted on 5 May 1769 by William Tryon, Gov. of NC, to William Sisson and again surveyed by William Gastin 3 Jan 1800, adj. Wm. Palmer, 27 Jan 1829. William Spears (W) (LS), Wit: Joshua D.Palmer, William Walker. Proved by the oath of Joshua D. Palmer 30 Jan 1829 before Wm. H. Cotter. Recorded 4 May 1829.

T, 230-231: South Carolina, Union District. John Philips of district aforesaid for $236 to Nicholas Corry, esqr., mortgage of tract on waters of Abbetons Creek adj. Aaron Wilkins, said Corry, John Patrick, 14 Feb 1829. John Philips (LS), Wit: Wm Corry, S. R. Parker, Peter Aikins. Proved by the oath of Wm Corry 25 April 1829 before Henry Smith, J.P. Recorded 4 May 1829.

T, 232: Wm. R. Wilborn for love, good will and affection, to the Baptist Society known by the name of the Union Church on the Charleston Road about three & a half miles above Wofford Shoals on Sugar Creek, to Solomon Putman & Elias High in behalf of said Society, a small piece of land for the purpose of enlarging the grave yard and pass-way to and from the spring, so as to include the Spring, 11 April 1829. Wm. R. Wilbourn (LS), Wit: Benjamin West, Goodwin Woodson, Larkin Lancaster. Proved by the oath of Goodwin Woodson 4 May 1829 before J. Rogers, Q. U. Recorded 4 May 1829.

T, 233: George Perry of Union District sells to William Smith of same [no amount given], 140 acres adj. Mrs. Lucy Johnson, Doctor James Macham, widow Posey, and on Broad River, 3 Jan 1829. George Perry (LS), Wit: M. P. Meador, Mary McGraw. Proved in Fairfield District by the oath of M. P. Meador 3 Jan 1829 before James McGraw, J.P. Ann Perry, wife of George Perry, relinquished dower in Union District before E. McGraw, Q.U. Recorded 2 June 1829.

T, 234-235: George Perry of Union District sells to William Smith of same [no amount given], 63 acres on Broad River, adj. Dr. Daniel Ryant, Thomas Henderson, part of tract granted to George Belle and by him devised to

William B. Floyd by him to John Mobly and by him to Athansius Thomas, by him to George Perry, 3 Jan 1829. George Perry (LS), Wit: M. P. Meador, Mary McGraw. Proved in Fairfield District by the oath of M. P. Meador 3 Jan 1829 before James McGraw, J.P. Ann Perry, wife of George Perry, relinquished dower in Union District before E. McGraw, Q.U. Recorded 2 June 1829.

T, 235-236: Clifton R. Mitchell of Union District for $400 to James C. Mayhew of same, 191 acres adj. John Parham, John Hays, Francis Parham, James Mitchell, on Mitchell Creek, Mayhew's line, 21 Oct 1822. Clifton R. Mitchell (LS), Wit: Casper Parham, Stephen Jones. Proved by the oath of Stephen Jones 1 June 1829 before J. Rogers, Q. U. Ruth Mitchell (X), wife of Cliften Mitchell, relinquished dower 21 Oct 1822 before H. Means, Q.U. Recorded 1 June 1829.

T, 236-237: William R. Wilbourn of Union District for $1000 to William Rice of same, tract on both sides Mitchells Creek, a water course of Fairforest, 300 acres adj. lands of Joseph Harlan, Stephen McPherson, John Hays, and the heirs of the late John Parham decd, it being the tract whereon the said John Parham lived and was sold as his property at Sheriffs Sale and conveyed to me by John Bates, Esq., late Sheriff, 17 May 1828. Wm. R. Wilbourn (LS), Wit: Jno Vance, John Anderson. Recorded 1 June 1829.

T, 237: South Carolina, Union District. John Anderson (Sheriff) for $35 to James M. Whitlow, both of said district, a strip or small piece of land on east side of Sholey Creek on a drain below the said Anderson's mill, from the creek to the lower line of the Bullington tract, it being 10 acres, 4 May 1829. John Anderson (Seal), Wit: M. Keenan, William Steen. Proved by the oath of Malechi Keenan 2 June 1829 before J. Rogers, Q. U. Recorded 2 June 1829.

T, 238: James P. Walker of Chester District for $250 to Isaac Jones of Union District & village, lot in Union Village, number 38 on Union Street and Fair Street, 7 Dec 1825. Jas P. Walker (Seal), Wit: Z. P. Herndon, A. Goss. Proved by the oath of Z. P. Herndon 3 June 1829 before J. Rogers, Q.U. Recorded 3 June 1829.

T, 239-240: Daniel A. Mitchell of Union District for $700 to Thomas C. Jeter of same, tract on waters of Broad River, 177 acres, granted to Henry Geddes and by him conveyed to Daniel Thomas and by said Daniel Thomas to Wm. B. Johnson and conveyed by John Bates, Sheriff, to said Daniel A. Mitchell, 5 Jan 1829. D. A. Mitchell (LS), Wit: Titus G. Farr, R. H. Spencer. Proved by the oath of T. Green Farr 5 Jan 1828 before J. Rogers, Q.U. Susannah A. A. Mitchell, wife of D. A. Mitchell, relinquished dower 3 June 1829 before J. Rogers, Q.U. Recorded 3 June 1829.

T, 240-241: South Carolina, Union District. Robert Livrett of district aforesaid for $168 to Elijah Anderson of same, 28 acres on north side Enoree River adj. Caldwell, Goven Gordon, land formerly Benjamin Gordon now Elijah, 15 Feb

1819. Robert Leverett (LS), Wit: Thos Gannon, James Hughey (mark). Proved by the oath of Thomas Gannon 4 July 1822 before Thos Stribling, Q.U. Margaret Leverett (mark) relinquished dower 8 June 1829 before Thomas Stribling, Q.U. Recorded 16 June 1829.

T, 241-242: Daniel A. Mitchell of Union District for $100 to John Rogers of same, tract on main road to Spartanburgh Court House from Union Court house, about one and a half [miles] from Union Ville, 160 acres resurveyed by Richard Thomson, 27 Jan 1823, adj. James Rountree, Adam little, John Gage Senr, 9 June 1829. D. A. Mitchell (LS), Wit: G. Gregory, Jasper Gibbs. Proved by the oath of Jasper Gibbs 19 June 1829 before James Rountree, J. P. Recorded 19 June 1829.

T, 242-243: Spilsby Glenn of Union District for $586.25 to John Sartor of Union District, 117 acres, part of tract on drains of Broad River near Rock Spring, on the north bank of Lower Fish Dam Creek, on Said Sorter's line, 16 April 1829. Spilsby Glenn (Seal), Wit: C. T. Scaife, James C. Posey. Proved by the oath of James C. Posey 19 June 1829 before J. Rogers, Q.U. Recorded 19 June 1829.

T, 243-244: South Carolina, Spartanburgh District. David Dauntzler of district aforesaid having been appointed by the Hon. Court of Equity for said District of Spartanburgh at the session of the said court 4th Monday in August 1827 a committee of lunacy for the person and property of Nicholas Harris of said district, and in pursuance of the decretal order of the said court, having sold the real estate of the said Nicholas harris at public auction, at which sale Ann Harris became the purchaser for $190, now conveys to said Ann Harris, 74 acres on the District of Union, 5 Jan 1829. David Dauntzler (Seal), Wit: Wm. Trimmier, Jas Norris. Proved in Spartanburgh District by the oath of Jas Norris 4 Jan 1829 before Wm. Trimmier, J.P. Recorded 20 June 1829.

T, 244-245: John Rogers of Union District for $100 to Daniel A. Mitchell of Union District, tract on west side of Broad River called the Caldwell place, 120 acres, as appears by a plat resurveyed by Richard Thomson 25 March 1827, on Browns Creek, near the Machine, 9 June 1829. J. Rogers (Seal), Wit: G. Gregory, Jasper Gibbs. Proved by the oath of Jasper Gibbs 19 June 1829 before James Rountree, J. P. Recorded 19 June 1829.

T, 246: Susannah Anderson vs John Jennings. Summons. To John Vanlew Senr, Henry Vanlew, Mary Vanlew & Eleanor Vanlew & John Vanlew. You will take that I am sued by Susannah Anderson for her dower in the lands sold by George C. Vanlew. If therefore you defendant the suit as his Heirs at law, tis well. If not I will do so and hold you liable for the value of the lands and the costs of suit & the fees of my council, 9 March 1829. Jno Jennings. We acknowledge the service of this Notice 9 March 1829. Henry D. Vanlew, Mary S. Vanlew, Eleanor Vanlew. Recorded 20 June 1829.

South Carolina, Union District. John Foster, stiller, for the natural love and affection to my son Thomas Foster of Union District, 70 acres adj. Baxter Moseley, James Moseley. The above obligation of gift to be good at my death [not dated]. John Foster (LS), Wit: Dawson Gault, James S. Foster. Proved by the oath of Dawson Gault 24 June 1829 before J. Rogers, Q.U.

T, 247: Thomas Waters of Hall County, Georgia, in the Eleventh District, for $307 to James Morrow of Union District, tract of land whereon James Mooreman now lives on waters of Gilkeys Creek, waters of Thickety Creek of Broad River, adj. William Philips, 88 acres, 29 Dec 1828. Thos Waters (Seal), Wit: William Morrow, John Jeffries Senr. Proved by the oath of William Morrow 24 June 1829 before Wm. Gowdelock, J.P. Recorded 24 June 1829.

T, 248: State of Mississippi, Pike County. Henry Ming of Pike County appoint my friend John Rogers of Union District, my true and lawful attorney, to do all things necessary for me respecting the estate of my father Col. Jas Ming, 18 July 1828. Henry Ming (LS), Wit: Proved by Jas Y. McNabb, J.P. in Pike County, Miss. Gerard C. Brandon, Gov. of Mississippi, certified that James Y. McNabb was on 18 July last a justice of the peace for Pike County. Recorded 29 June 1829.

T, 248-249: South Carolina, Union District. Thomas D. Johnson of district aforesaid for $600 to James Johnson of same, land whereon I formerly resided, formerly the property of Samuel Otterson, transferred from him to Nicholas Rochester and from him to Isaac Cook from Cook to said Thomas D. Johnson, 19 Jan 1827. Thomas D. Johnson, Wit: Isaac M. Smith, Zacheriah Johnson, George P. Smith, Saml O. Gordon. Proved by the oath of Zackeriah Johnson 1 July 1829 before Samuel O. Johnson, J. P. Martha Johnson (X), wife of Thomas D. Johnson, relinquished dower 30 Jan 1827 before Thomas Stribling, Q. U. Recorded 1 July 1829.

T, 249-251: South Carolina, Union District. John Sorter of Union District for $205 to Jas Johnson of same, 100 acres on waters of Swift Run, it being part of a tract granted to James Hall 5 Dec [no year], adj. Prock, Hedgpath, 1 March 1823. John Sorter (Seal), Wit: David Harris, Sarah Harris, Aney Harris. Proved by the oath of David Harris 25 March 1829 before E. McGraw, Q.U. Franky Sorter (X), wife of John Sorter deceased, conveyed her dower for $20, __ Dec 1826. Wit: Wm. N. McGraw, James Tate Jr., William Wilson. Proved by the oath of James Tate 21 Dec 1826 before E. McGraw, J.P. Recorded 1 July 1829.

T, 251-252: South Carolina, Union District. William R. Wilbourn for $100 to Elias High, both of said district, part of two tracts of land belonging to the estate of Revd. John Putman decd, at Putman Meeting House, Samuel Hays, Amos Lee, Elias High, spring branch, 4 May 1829. W. R. Wilbourn (Seal), Wit: Nathl Gist, Wm White. Proved by the oath of Col. Nathl Gist 4 May 1829 before J. Rogers, Q. U. Chloe M. Wilbourn, wife of William R.

Wilbourn, relinquished dower 26 May 1829 before Hiram Gibbs, Q.U. Recorded 3 July 1829.

T, 252-253: William Williams of Spartanburgh District stands indebted to Alexander Pruitt admr. of the estate of Alexander Pruitt decd, by note of hand calling for $864.50 and Larcan Lancaster security to said note, now for better securing said note, mortgage of Fillis and Miller, one bay mare, 9 July 1828. William Williams (LS), Wit: James Mays, James Lancaster. Proved in Union District by the oath of James Mays 7 July 1828 before H. H. Means, J.PO. Recorded 6 July 1829.

T, 253-254: South Carolina, Spartanburgh District. Nicholas Harris, isaac Harris, Thomas Scott, Richard Harris, Rochell Haile and Ann Harris, heirs and legatees of Nicholas Harris decd, for $370 to David Dauntzler, tract on both sides of the branch, 332 acres adj. lands of Charles Jones, Charles Cunningham, lands surveyed for Isaac & James Harris, lands of Ann Harris, Richard Thomson[?], 24 Jun 1829. N. Harris for himself & Richd Harris (LS), Thomas Scott for himself & Isaac Harris (LS), Ann Harris (LS), Rochell Hale (LS), Wit: Wm. Trimmier, Richd Thomson. Proved by the oath of Richard Thomson, 24 June 1829 before Wm. Trimmier, Q.U. Recorded 6 July 1829.

T, 254-255: Gadsden County, Florida Territory. William Wright of Union District for $4000 to Bird B. Wright of county and territory first above written, 1000 acres on Pagets Creek, adj. Lewis Pressley, Isaac Pearson, James Mayes, Enoree River, said Bird B. Wright, Mark Kennedy, Thomas Terry, 14 Feb 1829. William Wright (Seal), Wit: Joshua Davis, Banks Meacham. Proved in Gadsden County, Florida, by the oath of Banks Meacham 25 Feb 1829 before Robt C. Leaster, C. G. C. C. Recorded 9 June 1829.

T, 255-256: Tho's Bates of Union District for $120 to John Bowles of same, 26¼ acres, being a tract of land given to me by my grandfather John Gregory by deed of gift, adj. Isaac Caines, John Bowles, Edward Gregory, 14 July 1829. Thompson Bates (Seal), Wit: Jerry Gregory (X), John Giles. Proved by the oath of John Giles 16 July 1829 before J. Rogers, Q. U. Jane Bates (X), wife of Thompson Bates, relinquished dower 14 July 1829. Recorded 16 July 1829.

T, 256-257: South Carolina, Union District. James Petty of district aforesaid for $10 to Lydia Petty of same, tract on waters of Abetons Creek, waters of Broad River, 9 Feb 1829. James Petty (LS), Wit: Joshua Petty, John Whelchel. Proved by the oath of John Whelchel, M. D., 9 Feb 1829 before Nicholas Corry, J. Q. Recorded 17 July 1829.

T, 257: South Carolina, Union District. Nancy Goodrum (X) relinquished dower to Henry Gault, 15[?] July 1829 before Daniel White, Q. U. Recorded 3 July [probably should be August] 1829.

T, 257: South Carolina, Union District. Winny White (X), wife of Daniel White, relinquished dower to Joseph Goodrum, 15 July 1829 before Daniel White, Q. U. Recorded 3 July [probably should be August] 1829.

T, 258: South Carolina, Union District. Jaret Tramel of Union District to Levi Tramel of same, for $100, tract adj. William Fant, Hambleton's Road, 16 Jan 1829. Jaret Tramel (X), Wit: A. V. Jeter, Elender Tramel (X). Proved by the oath of A. V. Jeter 3 Aug 1829 before J. Rogers, Q.U. Recorded 3 Aug 1829.

T, 258-259: South Carolina, Union District. Edward Bevis of district aforesaid for $100 to James Meacham of same, the north west corner of a tract whereon Thomas Wilson is now living, which said lands Thos Wilson granted and sold to Edward Bevis, adj. James Fant, on Fant's spring branch, said Thos Wilson's fence, Jesse Gordon, 8 Feb 1828. Edward Bevis (LS), Wit: E. McGraw, Lucy Wright. Proved by the oath of E. McGraw 3 Aug 1829 before J. Rogers, Q. U. Recorded 3 Aug 1829.

T, 259-260: South Carolina, Union District. William Eavens of district aforesaid for $50 to John Eavens, tract whereon I now lie for several years past and now own and possess, part of two tracts conveyed to me: part of one tract conveyed to me by Isaac Hawkins, attorney for Benjamin Hawkins, 13 Oct 1812, also part of another plantation adjoining conveyed to me by Peter Tucker 6 Feb 1813, on a small branch of Cane Creek, adj William Rice, Robert Underwood, Vessells, 26 Jan 1829. William Eavans (X) (LS), Wit: John A. Sarter, Reuben Gilliam, James C. Posey. Proved by the oath of John P. Sarter 10 Aug 1829 before E. McGraw, Q.U. Recorded 19 Aug 1829.

T, 260: South Carolina, Union District. Jonathan Hampton came personally before me John Rogers, Clerk of the Court of common pleas, and acknowledged himself guardian for Johnson Allen, a free man of color, 28 Aug 1829. J. Hampton (LS). Recorded 28 Aug 1829.

T, 260-261: South Carolina, Union District. Titus G. Farr of district aforesaid for $600 to Stephen Jordan Ashley of same, tract on NW side of Broad River on the bank of Broad River adj. lands of C. DeGraffenreid, Titus G. Farr, Judge Johnson, 202 acres, 4 June 1829. Titus G. Farr (LS), Wit: Danl Thomas, Daniel K. Thomas, B. J. Thomas. Mary H. Farr, wife of Titus G. Farr, relinquished dower 25 Aug 1829 before E. McGraw, Q.U. Proved by the oath of Daniel Thomas 25 Aug 1829 before E. McGraw, Q.U.

T, 262-263: South Carolina, Union District. Moses L. White and Robert White of district of Union and Spartanburg, for $300 to William P. Davidson of Union District, tract in the districts of Union and Spartanburgh on both sides of McElevanes Creek, a branch of Fairforest, and on Story's Creek, 27 Jan 1829. Moses L. White (LS), Robert White (LS), Wit: Z. P. Herndon, Wm. Rice. Proved by the oath of William Rice 15 March 1829 before J. P. Thomson, Q.U. Mary White, wife of Moses L. White, relinquished dower 312 Jan 1829 before J. P. Thomson, Q.U. Recorded 31 Aug 1829.

T, 263: South Carolina, Union District. Whereas my deceased husband Zach'y Nance by his will has vested me with full power to dispose of a negro girl named Hailey and a choice negro which I say is Tom, for love, good and affection to my daughter Sarah Nance, have given them to her, 25 Aug 1829. Mary Nance (X) (LS), Wit: Wm. White, Peggy Nancy (X). Proved by the oath of Wm. White 31 Aug 1829 before J. Rogers, Q.U. Recorded 31 Aug 1829.

T, 264: $29.93. Twelve months after date I promise to pay to B. G. Davis or bearer $29.93 for value recd with interest, 14 May 1829. Elijah Dottry (mark (LS), Wit: Thomas Eubanks.

In order to secure said note, mortgage of tract of land whereon I now live, supported to be 40 acres on waters of Browns Creek adj. Wm. McBride, D. A. Mitchell, William John, 14 May 1829. Elijah Dottry (mark (LS), Wit: Thomas Eubanks, Asbury Rochester. Proved by the oath of Thomas Eubanks 22 Aug 1829 before William Skelton, J.P. Recorded 22 Aug 1829.

T, 264-265: John Anderson, Sheriff of Union District, by virtue of a case tested first day of June 2829 at the suit of William Fant, Esq., guardian ad litem for Jane, Robert & Kitty Fant, minors & Legatees of Lovell Fant decd, vs Kitty[?] R. Fant to me directed to sell the tract of land of 85 acres on Beaver Dam Creek, waters of Tyger River adj. James Johnston, James Johnson, Samuel Johnson, Thomas Word, George Fant, purchased by George Fant for $100, 6 June 1829. John Anderson S. U. D. (LS), Wit: Wm.White, Jasper Gibbs. Proved by the oath of William White 7 Sept 1829 before Danl White, J.Q. Recorded 7 Sept 1829.

T, 265-266: South Carolina, Union District. Goodwin Woodson for $300 to Saml Harlan Senr, both of said district, part of tract belonging to the estate of my father James Woodson decd, which land was given by his last will and testament to my mother Anne Woodson, to dispose of as she pleases, now she being dead and having deeded of conveyed the present piece to me lying on each side of Fairforest Creek adj. Elijah Perkins, Robert Woodson, James P. Woodson, Geo Harlan, 80 acres, 12 Sept 1829. Goodwin Woodson (LS), Wit: S. M. Wilbourn, Elijah Pirkins. Proved by the oath of S. M. Wilbourn 19 Sept 1829 before H. Gibbs, Q.U. Nancy Woodson (X), wife of Goodwin Woodson, relinquished dower 19 Sept 1829 before H. Gibbs, Q.U. Recorded 22 Sept 1829.

T, 266-267: John Anderson, Sheriff of Union District, by virtue of a writ of fieri facias from the court of common pleas tested the first Monday in October 1829 at the suit of the President & executors to levy of the lands and tenements of William Henderson $1802.14, tract of 2212 acres on Sandy River on Mill Creek adj. estate of Henry Farnandis, Foster & Hames, widow Berry[?], widow Hail, Aaron McCollum, Charles Jones, Wormack Fowler, sold to Abram Nott of Union District for !600, 7 Sept 1829. John Anderson S. U. D. (LS), Wit: Lott Whitlock, John H. Skelton. Proved by the oath of John H. Skelton 15 Sept 1829 before J. Rogers, Q.U. Recorded 15 Sept 1829.

T, 268-270: South Carolina, Union District. Plat of 3 acres showing adj. land owners Frances Morgan, John Jeffries, E. T. Mitchell, and Elisabeth T. Mitchell. Pursuant to the request of Elisabeth T. Mitchell I have admeasured unto Pleasant Grove Meeting House, A Methodist Episcopal Church, three acres of land on a ridge which divides the rains of Thickety & Gilkeys Creeks, 15 June 1829. Jno Dawkins, D. S.

30 July 1829, Elizabeth T. Mitchell of district aforesaid to James Dawkins, Jno Jeffries, R. S. Rice, John B. Goudelock, John Jeffries, William Jeffries, and Aron Wilkins, trustees in trust for the use and purposes herein after mentioned, and for $20, three acres, in trust that they shall build a place of workshop for the use of the members of the Methodist Episcopal Church. Elisabeth T. Mitchell (LS), Wit: D. Goudelock Jr., B. F. Dawkins. Proved by the oath of Davis Goudelock 11 Sept 1829 before Wm. Goudelock, J.P. Recorded 14 Sept 1829.

T, 270-271: South Carolina, Union District. Zachariah Bryant of Union District for $375 to Giles H. Bryant of same, tract on a branch of Buffalow Creek, waters of Fairforest, 65 acres, adj. Aron Harlan, David Johnson, Robert Claybrook, Wm. Rice, 1 Oct 1825. Zachariah Briant (LS), Wit: Daniel Jackson, William Little. Proved by the oath of William Little 24 Sept 1829 before J. Rogers, Q.U. Recorded 24 Sept 1829.

T, 271-272: John Anderson of Union District for $1100 to Suprey Anderson of same, tract of land on Morrises Creek, 101 acres adj. Chandler, part of 320 acres granted to William Goldsmith, also part of another tract adj. McJunkin, on the waggon road, 134 acres, 10 Sept 1829. John Anderson, Wit: John H. Skelton, Geo Ashford. Proved by the oath of John H. Skelton 15 Sept 1829 before J. Rogers, Q. U. Recorded 25 Sept 1829.

T, 272: Recd of Mrs. Patsey Clark $300 for a negro girl named Sally, 20 May 1826. Rob't Thomson (LS), Wit: Amos Northrop, William Tate. Proved by the oath of Amos Northrup 29 July 1829 before Wm. Goudelock, J.P. Recorded 5 Oct 1829.

T, 272: South Carolina, Union District. Charles Gowin acknowledged himself guardian of Jacob Green, a free man of color, 25 Oct 1829. Charles Gowin (LS), Wit: John Rogers, Clerk. Recorded 25 Oct 1829.

T, 273: South Carolina, Union District. John Jones, eldest son of David Jones decd, of Union District, for $1 to Thomas Young of same, all my right, title, and interest to all lands originally granted to Charles Jones & which by descent came into the possession of David Jones, eldest son of Charles Jones decd, to which I may be entitled as the eldest son of said David Jones decd, land on waters of Morris's branch & Fairforest, 7 Oct 1829. John Jones (Seal), wit Wm. K. Clowney, John Gage Jr. Proved by the oath of W. K. Clowney 20 Nov 1829 before J. Rogers, Q. U. Recorded 20 Nov 1829.

T, 273-274: Saml Otterson of Union District for $1200 to Leonard B. Murry of same, tract near where William Cotter's store formerly stood, 246 acres, except the lot on which Wm. H. Cotter's house stands inclosed within the fence immediately round his house on the line, 6 Nov 1829. Saml Otterson (LS), Wit: Richard Thomson, Saml O. Lay. Proved by the oath of Saml O. Lay 6 Nov 1829 before Isaac Going, J.Q. Narcissa Otterson, wife of Samuel Otterson, relinquished dower 6 Nov 1829 before Isaac Going, J.Q. Recorded 11 Nov 1829.

T, 274-275: John Brandon, Margaret Brandon, John T. McCool, William L. McCool, John Hardin & Letticia Hardin, & Andrew P. McCool, all of the District of Chester, SC, legatees of the estate of John McCool decd, appointed James A. McCool of district aforesaid, our lawfull attorney, to bring to a reckoning & to adjust and settle all matters relating to the estate of John McCool, decd, 15 Jan 1821. John Brandon (Seal), Margaret Brandon (Seal), John P. McCool (LS), Wm. L. McCool (LS), John T. Hardin (LS), Lettitia Hardin (LS), Andrew P. McCool (LS). 10th March 1822.

T, 275: Jane McCool of Chester District appoints James A. McCool lawful attorney to settle matters on the estate of John McCool, deceased, 20 Feb 1821. Jane McCool (seal), Wit: Thos McDaniel. Recorded _____.

T, 276: Jane McCool of Chester District appoints James A. McCool lawful attorney to settle matters on the estate of John McCool, deceased, 25 May 1820. Jane McCool (LS), Wit: John Brandon, William Love McCool. Recorded 25 Nov 1829.

T, 276-277: Zachariah P. Herndon of Union District for $50 to John Gage Senr of same, six lots in the Village of Unionville bounded by the Main or Union Street, on Fair Street, adj. lot of John Rogers Esqr., numbers 51, 65, 79, 52, 66, & 80, land now in possession of John Gage Senr, heirs of John McCool, as appears by a deed given by James A. McCool, attorney of Jane McCool, executrix of John Mccool, deceased, 2 July 1825, dated 11 Oct 1828. Z. P. Herndon (Seal), Wit: Samuel M. Gowdey, Richd Thomson. Proved by the oath of Richd Thomson 11 Oct 1828. Recorded 17 Nov 1829.

T, 277-278: Georgia, Franklin County. John Shelton, John Simmons, Elisabeth Simmons & Mary Shelton, appoint Garrett L. Sandridge of the aforesaid state and county, our true and lawful attorney, to recover demands indebted to us as legal representatives of Francis Lee decd, late of Union District, SC, 4 Nov 1829. Jno Shelton (LS), John Simmons (LS), Mary Shelton (I), Elizabeth Inman (mark) (LS), Wit: Jacob Strickland, J.P. Thomas King, Clerk of the Inferior Court of Franklin County, GA, certified that Jacob Strickland was a justice of the peace 5 Nov 1829. Robert Pullian, one of the justices of the inferior court, certified that Thomas King was clerk, 5 Nov 1829. Recorded 10 Nov 1829.

T, 278-279: South Carolina, Union District. Martin Hunt of said district for $54 to Hezekiah Johnson, 22 acres granted to J. W. Sartor 3 Jan 1820, 4 Sept 1829. Martin Hunt (LS), Wit: Hugh M. Hunt, Adam Cromer. Proved by the oath of Adam Cromer 27 Oct 1829 before J. T. McJunkin.

T, 279-280: Davis Goudelock of Union District for $34 to William Moorhead of same, 20 acres on south side of Thickety Creek, adj. said Moorhead's line, said Goudelock's new field, 18 Nov 1811. Davis Goudelock (LS), Wit: Robert Moorhead, Betsey Goudelock. Proved by the oath of Robert Moorhead 5 oct 1829 before Wm. H. Cotter, J.P. Recorded 5 Oct 1829.

T, 280-281: Jesse Mabry of Spartanburgh District for $9000 to Abner Benson of Union District, tract in Union District on north side Packolett River, 970 acres, dated 24 March 1828. Jess Mabry (Seal, Wit: E. Dawkins, Joshua P. Dawkins. Elisabeth Mabry, wife of Jesse Mabry, relinquished dower in Spartanburgh District 29 April 1828 before Jas Henry, J. Q. Exoff. Proved by the oath of Elijah Dawkins 8 Oct 1829 before E. McGraw, Q. U. Recorded 8 Oct 1829.

T, 281-282: South Carolina, Union District. Abraham Nott of state aforesaid for $4000 to Edward Hames of district and state aforesaid, tract on both sides Sandy River adj. Mrs. Farnandis, James Mosley, John Foster, said Edmond Hames, widow Berry, Widow Hail, Aron McCollum, Charles Jones, Wormack Fowler, 2212 acres, per plat made by Richard Thomas, Esq., 18 Sept 1829. Abm Nott (LS), Wit: William B. Nott, Lemuel Hames. Proved by the oath of Lemuel Hames 13 Oct 1829. Recorded 13 Oct 1829.

T, 282: South Carolina, Union District. Edmond Hames of district aforesaid to Lemuel Hames of same, tract on Sandy River and house branch, below the old mill, adj. Ed Hames, Aron McCollum, widow Hails, Godfrey Fowler, widow Berry, Edmond Hames, 820 acres, 13 Oct 1829. Edmond Hames (LS), Wit: Saml Mosley, John Mosley. Proved by the oath of Saml Mosley 13 Oct 1829 before Wm. H. Cotter, J.P. Recorded 10 Oct 1829.'

T, 283: South Carolina, Union District. Whereas James Park, late of the district aforesaid deceased, did by his will direct his land to be sold did appoint Joseph Quinn & Andrew Leeper, exrs., and whereas the said Joseph Quinn only has taken upon himself the burthen of said will, now sells for $1400 to Mrs. Sophonesba Golding of state aforesaid, tract on both sides of the Beaver dam Creek adj. Joseph Mayes, John Wright, Abraham Nott, Mrs. McBride, 280 acres, 22 Sept 1829. Joseph Quinn (LS), Wit: Abm Nott, Tilman Gregory. Proved by the oath of Ab'm Nott 15 Oct 1829 before J. Rogers, Q.U. Recorded 15 Oct 1829.

T, 284: South Carolina, Union District. Thomas Linam of said district for $2000 to John C. Jeter of same, tract originally granted to different persons & by them to Thos Linam, on waters of Bever Dam Creek, a branch of Tyger River adj. John P. Farr, John C. Jeter, Geo Fant, Nathan Coleman Johnson,

Thos H. Wood, Thos Wilson, 1000 acres, 28 July 1829. Thos Linam (LS), Wit: Thos C. Jeter, Nathan Coleman, P. R. Pearson. Proved by the oath of Thos C. Jeter 29 July 1829 before Saml O. Johnson, J.P. Recorded 7 Sept 1829.

T, 284-285: Saml P. Baley of Union District for $100 to John J. Pratt of same, lot in the village of Union on west side of Grog Street where Pratt's line intersects the street, on Pratt's lott, back of his smoke house, 28 May 1829. Saml P. Baley (LS), Wit: Jesse Rountree, A. M. Adickes. Proved by the oath of A. M. Adickes 27 Nov 1829 before J. Rogers, Q.U. Recorded 27 Nov 1829.

T, 285-286: South Carolina, Union District. William J. Bobo of Union District for $7726.65 to Barrum Bobo Senr of same, 390 acres where my plantation now is, it being the land given to me by the said Barrum Bobo, also a tract of land that I purchased at Marshal Wilbanks sale, 350 acres, described by the title made to me by William Rice, Ordinary of said district, also my negroes Nancy, Sally, Harry, Prince, Patty & her child and Adaline, all my sock of horses, cattle, hogs, goats, sheep & geese, farming tools, all the medicine and furniture of my medical shop, all my notes and books of accounts, 1 May 1829. Wm. J. Bobo, M. D. (LS), Wit: B. Bobo Jr., Robert Martin. Proved by the oath of Col. R. Martin 10 Oct 1829. Recorded 10 Oct 1829.

T, 286-287: John P. Farr of Union District for $858 to James Hill of same, part of different grants which by succession of title has been conveyed to William Hobson who has conveyed to Presley Williams & by said Presley Williams to said John P. Farr, on east side of Cane Creek and adj. the same, adj. said James Hill, 12 Aug 1829. J. P. Farr (LS), Wit: [Dr.] James Glenn, R. Sims, T. A. Carlisle. Proved by the oath of Reuben Sims 12 Aug 1829 before E. McGraw, J.Q. Mary Farr, wife of John P. Farr, relinquished dower 20 Aug 1829 before E. McGraw, Q.U. Recorded 22 Oct 1829.

T, 288: South Carolina, Union District. Jeremiah Gregory of district aforesaid for $200 to James Leach of same, 200 acres adj. David Stewart, on Cane Creek, Nathan Sandridge, 22 Sept 1829. Jeremiah Gregory (LS), Wit: James C. Thomas, John Cook. Proved by the oath of both wit. 22 Sept 1829 before E. McGraw, Q.U. Recorded 31 Oct 1829.

T, 288-289: Jesse Leach of Union District for $210 to Richard G. Hobson of same, 52 acres on the drains of Neals big Creek, 27 Oct 1829. Jesse Leach (Seal), Wit: James Hamilton, Josiah Leach. Proved by the oath of James Hamilton 28 Oct 1829 before T. G. Farr, Q. U. Rachel Leach (X), wife of Jesse Leach, relinquished dower 28 Oct 1829 before Titus G. Farr, Q. U. Recorded 30 Oct 1829.

T, 289-290: South Carolina, Union District. John Man & Gerard Gregory of said district have entered into agreement, Gerard Gregory has sold 58 acres of land to said John Man, the title of which is executed, it being the land whereon John Man now lives, & the said John Man is indebted to the said Gerard Gregory for the sum of $134 by note, 1 Dec 1829. John Man (LS),

Wit: David A. Thomas, Levy Gregory. Proved by the oath of David A. Thomas and Levy Gregory 1 Def 1829 before E. McGraw, Q.U. Recorded 4 Dec 1829.

T, 290-291: John Bates, Sheriff of Union District, by virtue of several writs of fieri facias from the court of common pleas, at the suits of Wm. Ducket, admr. of Hall, and other writs against Charles A. King, to levy of the lands and tenements goods and chattels of said Charles A. King $200, sells tract of 151 acres between Enoree & Tyger River on the main road about which is called Jane's Hill, adj. Peter Davis, John Lee, Philip Whitton, said King, purchased by Nathan Cooper for $84, 14 Nov 1826. J. Bates (Seal), Wit: Wm. C. Pearson, J. Rogers. Proved by the oath of William C. Pearson 14 Nov 1826 before J. Rogers, Q. U. Recorded 6 Oct 1829.

T, 291-292: South Carolina, Union District. John Whelchell Senr of district aforesaid for $1000 to John Jeffries Junr of same, land whereon said John Whelchel Senr now lives, on the bank of London Bridge Creek, waters of Broad River, adj. Charles Patrick, 256 acres, 12 May 1829. John Whelchel (Seal), Wit: S. Jeffries, Singleton Page. Abigail Whelchel (X), wife of John Whelchel, relinquished dower 21 May 1829 before Nicholas Corry, J. Q. Proved by the oath of Samuel Jeffries 19 May 1829 before Isaac Going, J. Q. Recorded 7 Dec 1829.

T, 293: South Carolina, Union District. R. Lipsey, exr. of James Johnson decd, and Robert Johnson of Union District, for $448 to James Vinson of same, 112 acres on waters of Fannans Creek, adj. Johnson's land, 31 Dec 1828. R. Lipsey, Exor of Jas Johnson decd (Seal), Robert Johnson (Seal), Wit: Saml Harris, Francis Logan. Proved by the oath of Saml Harris 31 Dec 1828 before Isaac Going, J. Q. Recorded 7 Dec 1829.

T, 294-295: 7 Sept 1829, William K. Clowney, Esqr., Commissioner of the Court of Equity for Union District, to Charner T. Scaife of the other part, whereas Thomas McMakin & wife on or about 7 Sept did exhibit their Bill of Complain against Susannah Brummit, Sarah A.Lewis & Daniel B. Lewis, Robert L.Lewis & William J. Lewis, shewing that Daniel Brummit of district aforesaid, departed this life intestate, leaving a tract of land on Tyger River of 460 acres, conveyed to said Daniel Brummit by Bird Beuford 29 Sept 1808, praying that said land be partitioned & Divided among the lawful heirs of said Daniel Brummit decd, also another tract of land on Tyger River adj. the aforesaid tract, 155 acres, part of lands originally granted to John Lindsey & John Hughey, and said case heard at June them when said court decreed that the said tracts should be sold at publick auction, now sold for $850 to Charner T. Scaife, said land adj. Crook, Glenn, also one acre on the west side of Tyger River opposite Mill seat to secure a mill dam, also the privilege of a road from the premises conveyed. Wm. K. Clowney (LS), Wit: John Murphey, N. Glenn. Proved by the oath of John Murphy 7 Dec 1829 before J. Rogers, Q. U. Recorded 7 Dec 1829.

T, 296-297: South Carolina, Union District. 28 Dec 1829, Suckey Prisock otherwise & more properly called Sucky Russel, daughter of James Russel Senr, about eleven years of age, both of her own free will and accord planned and bound herself apprentice unto Rich'd C. Jeter, farmer or planter, to lead and be instructed in the said calling or occupation of a farmeress such as spinning, weaving & kitchen work, cooking & C., continuing from the date hereof for the term of seven years and six months or untill she shall arrive at the age of eighteen years. Sucky Russel (X) (Seal), Jas Russel (X) (Seal), Rich'd C. Jeter (Seal), Wit: N. Eaves, Alfred Adams (X). Certified by Titus G. Farr, Q. U. Recorded 20 Dec 1829.

T, 297-298: South Carolina, Union District. Gordon Gregory for $850 to James McCright of Union District, 222 acres in Union District on the waters of Browns & Neals Creek, 28 Jan 1829. G. Gregory (Seal), Wit: Isaac Gregory, John Giles. Susannah Gregory (X), wife of Gordon Gregory, relinquished dower 28 Jan 1839 before John Giles, Q. U. Proved by the oath of John Giles Esqr 21 Dec 1829 before J. Rogers, Q. U. Recorded 21 Dec 1829.

T, 298-300: South Carolina, Union District. Daniel Palmer of District of Union for natural love and affection and in consideration for his services rendered in adjusting and settling my business and debts which at this time is in a critical condition, to my son Jeffrey Palmer of same, tract of land whereon I now live, consisting of several grants or conveyances purchased by me of sundry persons, 600 acres, this being all my real estate adj. Mills Sumner, Mary Pruett, William Wallace, Elisabeth Palmer, also one negro man named Isaac thirty years old, one negro man named Abram 30 years old, one by named Solomon 20 years old, one boy named Sam sixteen years old, one negro woman named Susa aged 60 years old, one negro woman named Dinah aged forty years old, Charles about nine years old & Milly about two years old, also a negro girl named Nelly about forty five years of age, one negro girl named Mariah about eighteen years old, 20 Oct 1829. Daniel Palmer (Seal), Wit: Muckel Bogan, Elias Smith. Proved by the oath of Elias Smith 28 Dec 1829 before Jas. Smith, J.P. Recorded 31 Dec 1829.

T, 300-301: South Carolina, Union District. Whereas on or about ___ December 1829, Elizabeth Hollander, the daughter of the undersigned was married to George Miller of said district, and upon the marriage of said Elizabeth, I did give to the said Elizabeth the following property, two feather beds & the furniture belonging thereto, one mare, one woman's saddle & all the other property consisting of sundry articles, and that upon the death of the said Elisabeth the property above given is to descend to the lawful begotten heirs of the said George upon the body of said Elisabeth, and the said property is not to be liable for any of the debts of said George previous to his intermarriage with said Elisabeth, 31 Dec 1829. John Hollander (X) (Seal) Wit: R. G. H. Farr. Proved by the oath of Robt G. H. Farr, 1 Jan 1830 before Saml Davis, J.P. Recorded 1 Jan 1830.

T, 301-302: South Carolina, Union District. John Beard of said district for $33 to Spencer A. Bobo, tract on both sides of Hills Creek, waters of Enoree River adj. said Spencer A. Bobo, John Beard, Noah Garrett, Dr. Rice, 12 acres, 12 Nov 1829. John Beard (Seal), Wit: Robt Martin, Joshua Wilborn. Proved by the oath of Joshua Wilbourn 27 Nov 1829 before Robert Martin, J. Q. Lettice Beard (X), wife of John Beard, relinquished dower __ Nov 1829 before Robert Martin, J. Q. Recorded 31 Dec 1829.

T, 302-303: South Carolina, Union District. Noah Garrett of district aforesaid for $708 to Hezekiah Rice of Laurens District, 177 acres upon a resurvey, granted to James Hughes on each side of Hills Creek, waters of Enoree River, adj. said Hezekiah Rice, Estate of B. Bobo decd, John Beard, 12 Nov 1829. Noah Garrett (Seal), Wit: William White, William Malone. Proved by the oath of Wm White 22 Nov 1839 before Robert Martin, J. Q. Elisabeth Garrett, wife of Noah Garrett, relinquished dower 28 Nov 1839 before Robert Martin, J. Q. Recorded 31 Dec 1829.

T, 303-304: South Carolina, Union District. Spencer A. Bobo of district aforesaid for $200 to Hezekiah Rice of Laurens District, tract on each side of Hills Creek, waters of Enoree River, 61 acres, adj. said Rice, Spiva, Jas Goswick, John Beard, 12 Nov 1829. Spencer A. Bobo (Seal), Wit: William White, William Malone. Proved by the oath of Wm White 22 Nov 1839 before Robert Martin, J. Q. Louisa Bobo, wife of Spencer A. Bobo, relinquished dower 28 Nov 1839 before Robert Martin, J. Q. Recorded 31 Dec 1829.

T, 304-305: Jeremiah Gregory Senr of Union District bound in the sum of $198 by John Porter, tract of 99 acres, part of larger tract of land granted to Patrick H. Sims and given by said Patrick to his son William Sims and conveyed by William Sims to Jeremiah Gregory, adj. John Gregory, de Graffenreid, 7 March 1827. Jeremiah Gregory (Seal),Wit: John Van Lew, Israel Teague. Proved by the oath of John Van Lew 3 Dec 1827 before J. Rogers, Q. U. Recorded 8 Jan 1830.

T, 305-306: South Carolina, Union District. George young for $33 to Solomon Clark of district aforesaid, 11 acres, being a part of a tract now owned by George young on Morrises branch, 14 Oct 1829. George Young (Seal), Wit: Thomas Sartor, L. B. Musgrove. Proved by the oath of Thomas Sartor 4 Jan 1830 before J. Rogers, Q.U. Recorded 4 Jan 1830.

T, 306: South Carolina, Union District. Joshua Petty of district aforesaid for $15 to John Jeffries Senr of same, tract on Abetons Creek, waters of Broad River, five acres on the branch of said John Jeffries, adj. said Joshua Petty, 28 Dec 1829. Joshua Petty (Seal), Wit: Joseph Ashworth, John Steen. Proved by the oath of John Steen 1 Jan 1830 before Wm. N. Cotter, J.P.

T, 307-308: Gideon Steen of Union District, whereas the said Gideon Steen is indebted to Joseph H. Dogan by two several notes for $500, one for $250 due 1 Jan next and one for $250 due 1 Jan 1832 with interest from 1 Jan 1831, mortgage of one negro fellow named Jack about 21 years of age, 2 Jan 1830. Gideon Steen (Seal), Wit: John Parham. Proved by the oath of John Parham 2 Jan 1830 before J. Rogers, Q. U. Recorded 2 Jan 1830.

T, 308-309: South Carolina, Union District. 15 Jan 1830, contract between Lucinda Free and Abram Free; said Lucinda does agree to sell to said Abram the following negroes Fanny, Lott, Tener, Amy, Betty & Daniel; Fanny for $100, Lott for $3500, Tener for $250, Daniel for $100, Amy for $175, Betty for $150 (payment schedule and notes included). Lucinda Free (mark), Abram Free (LS), Wit: John H. Galman. Proved by the oath of John H. Galman 16 Jan 1830 before J. Rogers, Q. U. Recorded 16 Jan 1830.

T, 310: South Carolina, Union District. Whereas I, Lucinda Free, own and possess a tract of land in Union District, 360 acres adj. Isaac White, R. Lipsey, John H. Galman, Saml Smith, Isaac Haney, signed by John Bates, late Sheriff of Union District, 13 Sept 1826 and tested by Gordon Gregory and Wm. C. Pearson. I give this to Abram Free on the following terms, that said Abraham is to pay off the balance of a mortgage which William Norris holds in said land, not being more than $100. Lucinda Free (mark), Abram Free (LS), Wit: John H. Galman. Proved by the oath of John H. Galman 16 Jan 1830 before J. Rogers, Q. U. Recorded 16 Jan 1830.

T, 310-311: South Carolina, Union District. Lucinda Free in consideration of Abraham Free paying the mortgage on a tract of land, by above contract 15 Jan 1830, sells tract sold by John Bates, Esqr., late Sheriff, recorded in Book N. No. 7, page 356, dated 16 Jan 1830. Lucinda Free (mark), Wit: Robt G. H. Farr, John H. Galman. Proved by the oath of John H. Galman 16 Jan 1830 before J. Rogers, Q. U. Recorded 16 Jan 1830.

T, 311-312: South Carolina, Union District. James Harlan of district aforesaid for $300 to Robert Woodson, 87 acres on Fairforest Creek adj. Green Woodson, Elisabeth Woodson, 3 Sept 1827. James Harlan (LS), Wit: Green Woodson, James Woodson. Elisabeth Harlan (X), wife of John Harland, relinquished dower 2 Nov 1829 before Lem. B. Askew, J.P. Proved by the oath of Green Woodson 2 Jan 1830 before J. Rogers, Q. U. Recorded 2 Jan 1830.

T, 313-315: Whereas Capt. B. Bobo, late of the District of Union, died on or about 20 Sept 1829, leaving his last will and testament in writing duly executed 12 Sept in the same year, which said will was duly proved 2 October in the same year and recorded in the Ordinaries Office, by which he named his wife Frances Bobo executrix and Robert Martin & John F. Murrell executors, and they having taken upon themselves the execution of said will in which he has authorized them to sell part of his real or personal estate at their judgment & discretion in order to pay the debts and they have determined that for the benefit of the estate of the said Barrum Bobo decd, sell a tract of six separate pieces on Enoree River, 300.4 acres known as the Garrett Mill tracts & the three others purchased by the said B. Bobo decd of Banks Meacham, John Beard and John Norman and whereas Docr. Hezekiah Rice hath by contract with the said executors purchased the said land, now for $500 paid by said Doctr. Hez'h Rice, sell the six pieces of land, two plats containing 235½ acres granted to Jacob Earnest made out by William C. Pearson, dated 10 Sept 1825, also a tract of 28 acres conveyed from John Beard to said B. Bobo decd, 19 acres on Judges Branch, waters of Enoree River, part of tract granted to John Martindale conveyed by John Norman to said B. Bobo decd, adj. Boyce, Norman, another of 9.4 acres conveyed by Banks Meachem to said B. Bobo decd., and one tract in Laurens District originally lying in Union District, and part of tract granted to Joseph Earnest but thrown into Laurens by the changing of the River, adj. land owned by Dr. H. Rice, dated 14 Jan 1830. Frances Bobo (Seal), Robt Martin (LS), John T. Murrell (LS), Wit: F. H. Leonard, H. W. Foote. Frances Bobo, wife of Barrum Bobo decd, relinquished dower 14 Jan 1830 before Hiram Gibbs, Q. U. Proved by the oath of H. W. Foote 16 Jan 1830 before J. Rogers, Q. U. Recorded 16 Jan 1830.

T, 315-316: John Malcomson of Union District for $1000 to John McKee of Chester District, tract in Union District on the south of Broad River adj.lands of the estate of John Leek[?], Jeffers, Geo & Daniel Malcomson & Moses Durr [Deen?], 768 acres, 18 Sept 1829. John Malcomson (LS), Wit: Thomas Carroll, David Malcomson. Mary Malcomson (X), wife of John Malcomson, relinquished dower before Nicholas Corry, J. Q. Proved by the oath of Daniel Malcomson 30 Oct 1839 before Nicholas Corry, J. Q. Recorded 20 Jan 1830.

T, 316-317: South Carolina, Union District. Thomas Kennedy for $950 to Mathias Hilburn of same, 173 acres, part of tract laid out for George Gabriel Barnet[?], adj. John Gage, 22 May 1822. Thos Kennedy (LS), Wit: Jas Hilburn, William P. Kennedy. Proved by the oath of James Hilburn 21 Jan 1830 before J. Rogers, Q. U. Recorded 21 Jan 1830.

T, 317-318: Isaac L. Whitten of Union by bond dated 13 Aug 1839 for the payment of $300 bearing interest from the date to David Hendricks of Pickens District, to be paid in one month from this day, mortgage of 560 acres adj. Mathew Sims, William Turpin, Henry Rogers, also one negro woman & child named Malinda & Mima, with all stock and household furniture, 13 Aug 1829. Isaac L. Whitten, Wit: Moses Hendricks. Proved in Union District by the oath of Moses Hendricks before Edward Norton, J.P. Recorded 3 Jan 1830.

T, 318-319: South Carolina, Union District. Hiram Wood, James Haney & Elisabeth Haney legatees of John Haney (Goodfellow dec'd) for $550 to George Garner of same, 100 acres adj. lands of Robert Foster, Isaac J. Foster, Timothy Haney, 24 Nov 1828. Hiram Wood (mark), James Haney (LS), Elisabeth Haney (X) (LS), Wit: James Moorland, I. J. Foster. Proved by the oath of James Moorland 26 Nov 1838 before Isaac Going, Q. U. Eady Haney, wife of Jas Haney, and Sebby [?] Wood, wife of Hiram Wood, relinquished dower 16 Dec 1838 before Isaac Going, J. Q. Recorded 30 Oct 1829.

T, 320: Winney Porter & Lucy Porter, both of Union District, being legally possessed of a certain tract of land made to us jointly by our father William

Porter in his lifetime bearing date 19 Sept 1815, 400 acres, and also another deed for divers goods & Chattles dated 21 March 1817 which vested in us jointly, but since the date of the above deeds we have sold off to Thomas Davis 72 acres of the above tract and also another small piece sold off to George Crawford, we do agree to make a partition and division; the said Winny Porter to take the south part of said tract adj. E. Porter, Davis, and personal property one bay mare, one bed and furniture, bed stead & Pots, one spinning wheel, one trunk and with the consent of said Lucy Porter, and said Lucy agrees to take the north part of said tract, 14 Jan 1830. Winny Porter (X) (Seal), Lucy Porter (X) (Seal), Wit: E. M. Bobo, James H. Becknell. Proved by the oath of James H. Becknell 25 Jan 1830 before J. Rogers, Q. U. Recorded 25 Jan 1830.

T, 321-322: Suprey Anderson of Union District for $418 to John Gage Senr of Union District, tract whereon I now live near Union Court House, consisting of two tracts, near a spring along side of 18¼ acres purchased by said John Gage prior to the date hereof and 90 acres, and tract of 119 acres adj. John Gage Senr. M. Hilburn, E. Bearden, Henl[?] Davis, Johnson Woodson and Isaac Pollard, being a parcel of land formerly owned by Sheldon Swift and sold by John Bates, Sheriff, to A. W. Thomson, Esqr., and signed by John Anderson, the s'd Bates' successor in office, conveyed by said A. W. to said Suprey, 15 July 1829. Suprey Anderson (X) (LS), Wit: Jasper Gibbs, Powell W. Skelton. Proved by the oath of Powell W. Skelton 26 Jan 1830 before J. Rogers, Q. U. Elisabeth Anderson (X), wife of Suprey Anderson, relinquished dower 23 De 1829 before J. Rogers, Q.U. Recorded 26 Jan 1830.

T, 321-322: South Carolina, Union District. William Johnson, Ellis Johnson & R. Lipsey, exr., for $301 to John Gault of same, tract of land sold by us as legatees of the estate of Zacheriah Johnson decd, 125 acres adj. said John Gault, Tansey[?] Fowler, Joseph Goodrum, John Galman Jr., John H. Galman, 1 Jan 1829. William Johnson (X) (LS), Ellis Johnson (X) (LS), R. Lipsey Esqr (LS), Wit: W. E. Morland, Jas Vinson. Louisa Johnson (X), wife of William Johnson; Mary Johnson (X), wife of Ellis Johnson; and Elizabeth Lipsey (X), wife of R. Lipsey, exr., relinquished dower 2 Jan 1830 before Isaac Going, J. Q. Proved by the oath of W. W. E. Moreland 1 Jan 1830 before Isaac Going, J. Q. Recorded 26 Jan 1830.

T, 322-323: South Carolina, Union District. William Whitfield of district aforesaid to Thomas Wood, tract whereon said Whitfield now lives on waters of Browns Creek, 76½ acres, on the main road adj. William Mitchell, Robert Walker, Jas Newton, 22 Oct 1826. William Whitfield (LS), Wit: Randolph W. Vaughan, John M. Davis. Proved by the oath of John M. Davis 25 Oct 1829 before J. Rogers, Q.U. Recorded 25 Oct 1829.

T, 323-324: John J. Pratt of Union District for $100 to Samuel P. Baley of same, tract adj. the village of Union adj. John Gage Jr., Kennedy, J. J. Pratt, 8 acres, 28 May 1829. J. J. Pratt (Seal), Wit: Alexd M. Adickes, Jesse

Rountree. Proved by the oath of Alexr M. Adickes 26 Jan 1830 before J. Rogers, Q.U. Recorded 26 Jan 1830.

T, 324-325: John Anderson, Sheriff of Union District, by several writs of fieri facias from the court of common pleas tested 3 March 1829 at the suit of Mitchell Sparks and John McLure to levy of the goods & chattels, lands and tenements of Jesse Greer the sum of $85, sells 40 acres on the waters of Fairforest adj. lands of Thomas Greer, Jacob Greer and Thomson White, sold for $56 to Mitchell Sparks, 4 Jan 1829. John Anderson S. U. D. (LS), Wit: Thos Anderson, John H. Skelton. Proved by the oath of John H. Skelton 26 Jan 1830 before J. Rogers, Q.U. Recorded 26 Jan 1830.

T, 326-327: John Anderson, Sheriff of Union District, by a writ of fieri facias from the court of common pleas tested 18 March 1828 at the suit of Alexander Boyce to levy of the goods & chattels, lands and tenements of Mathew Hobkins, $380, sells tract of 300 acres on waters of Tyger River adj. Isaac Prince Gist, Jasper Saunders, whereon said Mathew Hopkins now lives, sold to William Prince Senr for $300, 4 Feb 1828. John Anderson S. U. D. (LS), Wit: B. J. Gregory, B. M. Pearson. Proved by the oath of Bird M. Pearson 26 Jan 1830 before J. Rogers, Q. U. Recorded 26 Jan 1830.

T, 327-328: Isaac N. Pollard of Union District for $1500 to John Anderson of same, 429 acres on branches of Shoal Creek adj. Widow Howard, Jacob Paulk, John Gage Senr, John Gage Junr, Cary Woodson, and said John Anderson, __ Oct 1829. Isaac N. Pollard (LS), Wit: John H. Skelton, John White. Anne Pollard, wife of Isaac N. Pollard, relinquished dower 2 Dec 1829 before J. Rogers, Q. U. Proved by the oath of John H. Skelton 26 Jan 1830 before J. Rogers, Q.U. Recorded 26 Jan 1830.

T, 328: South Carolina, Union District. David R. Burns acknowledged himself guardian for Alfred Hardy a free man of colour, 1 July 1830, before J. Rogers, Clk. Recorded 1 Feb 1830.

T, 329-330: South Carolina, Union District. Agreement dated 26 Jan 1830 between William Rountree and Mrs. Elisabeth Bryant, and Adam Little; whereas a marriage is intended to be had and solemnized between said William Rountree and said Elisabeth Bryant, and said Elisabeth Bryant is seized of a tract of land on Buffalow Creek, a water course of Fairforest, 65 ares adj. John Anderson, Aron Harlan, Wm Rice, Robert Claybrooks, Cary Woodson, and also some personal property, and said William Rountree is seized of four tracts of land in the whole 700 acres on Buffalo and Fairforest, and sundry negroes to wit Lewis, Jonas, Daniel Mitchell, Sarah & her children Washington, Robert, Simpson, Andrew, Jeffrey, Alec, Charlotte, Jasper, Anna; & Martha & her children John, Aron, Hannah, lucy, Polly, Vile & child Hampton, now it is agreed that no part of the property above mentioned shall be liable for the debts of either, Adam Little is trustee. William Rountree (LS), Elisabeth Briant (LS), Adam Little (X) (LS), Wit: Willis Walker,

William Little, Joshua Little. Proved by the oath of the Rev. Willis Walker, 1 Feb 1830 before J. Rogers, Q. U. Recorded 1 Feb 1830.

T, 330-331: John Anderson, Sheriff of Union District, tested 6 Oct 1829 at the suit of Thomas howard vs Job Hammond & Evans Williams, guardian for the minor heirs and legatees of John Coomer Junr decd, commanding me to sell the lands of s'd decd in said district containing 30 acres adj. Joseph Greer, Hammond, Mary Howard & Thos Howard, John Coomer Senr, sold to Job Hammond for $75, 6 Oct 1829. John Anderson S. U. D. (LS), Wit: Henry Stevens, John McGarity. Proved by the oath of John H. McGarity 1 Feb 1830 before J. Rogers, Q.U. Recorded 1 Feb 1830.

T, 331-332: South Carolina, Union District. Daniel A. Mitchell of Union District for $238.50 to William Rice Esqr of same, one acre adj. Union Village, part of tract formerly belonging to George McKnight adj. R. P. Taylor, John Wright, fronting the main road leading into Union Village, being the lott where Dr. Geo McCrary now lives, 28 Dec 1822. D. A. Mitchell (LS), Wit: David Johnson, Z. Reid. Proved by the oath of Z. Reid 2 July 1830 before R. Rogers, Q.U. Recorded 2 Feb 1830.

T, 332-333: Hannah Brooks of Union District, widow of Thos Brooks, late of said district, deceased, for $600, to Magness Brooks of State of Georgia, Sarah Brooks of the State of North Carolina, William Mayhew of the state of N. C. in right of his wife Anna, & John Pool of the District of Laurence, SC, in right of his wife Susannah, legatees of the estate of Thomas Brooks, part of tract granted to Thomas Blasingame in the year 1785 for 400 acres on Sally's branch, waters of Fairforest, recorded in grant book AAAA, page 380, 180 acres adj. John Parham, Bullington, Littlefield, Levi Smith, Wallace, Wilbourn, Hannah Brooks, 28 Nov 1823. Hannah Brooks (X) (LS), Wit: Wm. White, Joseph Harlan. Proved by the oath of Joseph Harlan before Jas. Smith, J.P. Recorded 1 Feb 1830.

T, 333-335: South Carolina, Union District. Richard Wilks, William Sartor, and Ferdinand Hopkins Senr, having been chosen by Christopher de Graffenreid to appraise and divide his property to his children, do aware to his son John de Graffenreid the one third part of the property as mention in his deed to his children, and its prices as follows Kassy $50, Anderson $450, Malinda $375, D--- $350, Claiborn $300, Catharine $200, Billy $150, Suckling child without a name $100, 243 1/3 bushels of corn at 25 cents per bushel, 25 sheep, 11 hogs, one sorrel bald horse called Tate, one cow Calf, two yearlings, 1 walnut cupboard, earthen plates, etc; to Mary Thomas wife of James V. Thomas, Sellah and Dover $437.50, Amber $250, Robin younger $225, Bander $1215, Robin, $20, Watt $100, Mate, $300, Nancy $200, Patience $#115, Mary $50, 243 1/3 bushels corn, sheep, hogs, furniture, etc; To Tresvant de Graffenreid, Ester & Infant child Mahala $300, Mariah $200, Jo $150, Abby $150, Daniel $150, Henry $150, Abram $115, Clary & infant child called Paul[?] #350, Manerva $115, 243 1/3 bushells corner, sheep, hogs, etc., date 20 Feb 1829. Richard Wilks (L)s, Fer'd Hopkins Senr (LS), Wm Sartor (LS),

Wit: Jas McJunkin Junr. Proved by the oath of Joseph McJunkin Jr. 21 Jan 1830 before E. McGraw, Q. U. Recorded 5 Feb 1830.

T, 335-336: South Carolina, Union District. Whereas Benjamin Bullington is indebted to W. H. Gist in the sum of $110 by sealed note dated 1 Feb 1830 due 23 1 Jan 1832, mortgage of 90 acres near Tyger River adj. Widow Greer, John Saunders, Estate of Duncan. Benjamin Bullington (LS), Wit: Ann Fincher, T. D. Burns. Proved by the oath of T. D. Burns 3 Feb 1840 before Robt Stokes, J.P.

T, 336-337: South Carolina, Union District. John Anderson for $930 to Dr. Christopher Young, both of said district, part of tract known by the name of Andersons land place where Joiner has his shop adj. Thomas Anderson, Jas Smith, Week & Tampetion[?], Christopher Young Senr, Saml Martin, Jared Young, 310 acres, 9 Nov 1829. John Anderson, Wit: Wm. White, John H. Skelton. Proved by the oath of John H. Skelton 19 Jan 1830 before J. Rogers, Q.U. Susannah Anderson, wife of John Anderson, relinquished dower 12 Feb 1830 before J. Rogers, Q.U. Recorded 12 Feb 1830.

T, 337-338: South Carolina, Union District. John Anderson for $450 to Jerard Young, both of said district, part of tract known as Anderson's lower place adj. John Joiner now has a machine shop, adj. Jas Willard, Crawford, William Humphries, Jared Young, John Crawford, Dr. Young, Saml Martin, 150 acres, 9 Nov 1829. John Anderson (LS), Wit: William White, John H. Skelton. Proved by the oath of John H. Skelton 19 Jan 1830 before J. Rogers, Q.U. Susannah Anderson, wife of John Anderson, relinquished dower 12 Feb 1830 before J. Rogers, Q.U. Recorded 12 Feb 1830.

T, 338-339: South Carolina, Union District. John Anderson for $465 to Saml Martin, both of said district, part of tract known as Anderson's lower place where John Joiner has a machine shop, 155 acres, adj. William Humphries, Jared Young, Dr. C. Young, Saml Martin, 9 Nov 1829. John Anderson (LS), Wit: Wm White, John H. Skelton. Proved by the oath of John H. Skelton 19 Jan 1830 before J. Rogers, Q.U. Susannah Anderson, wife of John Anderson, relinquished dower 12 Feb 1830 before J. Rogers, Q.U. Recorded 12 Feb 1830.

T, 339-340: South Carolina, Union District. Winny Porter of district aforesaid for $100 to James H. Becknell, tract on waters of Browns Creek adj. Bobo, 50 acres, 14 Jan 1830. Winey Porter (X) (LS), Wit: E. M. Bobo, Letty Becknell (X). Proved by the oath of Dr. E. M. Bobo 16 Feb 1830 before J. Rogers, Q.U. Recorded 16 Feb 1830.

T, 340-341: South Carolina, Union District. Jesse Gordon of district aforesaid to William Gordon of same, 190 acres, part of tract of 796 acres on the waters of Ottersons Creek, waters of Tyger River, 20 Jan 1829. Jesse Gordon (LS), Wit: Saml O. Gordon, Jeremiah Kingsley. Proved by the oath of Saml O. Gordon 18 Feb 1830 before J. Rogers, Q. U. Recorded 18 Feb 1820.

T, 341-342: South Carolina, Union District. Thomas Wood for $300 to James Harlan, tract whereon the said Thos wood now lives on waters of Browns Creek, 76½ acres on the main road adj. William Mitchell's land, Robert Walker, James Newton, 24 Aug 1827. Thos Wood (LS), Wit: Green Woodson, Robert Woodson. Proved by the oath of Robert Walker 20 Feb 1820 before J. Rogers, Q. U. Recorded 20 Feb 1830.

T, 342-343: South Carolina, Union District. James Harlan of district aforesaid for $275 to William Bentley, tract where said James Harlan now lives on waters of Browns Creek, 76½ acres, adj. William Mitchell, Robert Walker, James Newton, 26 Oct 1829. James Harland (Seal), Wit: John Parham, J. Rogers. Mrs. Elizabeth B. Harland (X) relinquished dower 25 Oct 1829 before J. Rogers. Q.U. Proved by the oath of John Parham 24 Feb 1830 before J. Rogers, Q. U. Recorded 243 Feb 1830.

T, 343-344: South Carolina, Union District. 26 Aug 1828, Gabriel Lockhart and wife Catharine, James Lockhart & wife Keziah, of district aforesaid, to John Dunn of same, for $325, 272 acres, part of 328 acres on both sides of Hoopers Creek, waters of Broad River, the remaining 56 acres on the north side of Smiths ford road. Gabriel Lockhart (LS), Katharine Lockhart (LS), Jas Lockhart (LS), Wit: Josiah Martin, Morgan Martin. Katherine Lockhart, wife of Gabriel, and Keziah Lockhart, wife of James, relinquished dower 29 Dec 1829 before Nicholas Corry, J. Q. Proved by the oath of Josiah L. Martin 26 Aug 1828 before Nicholas Corry, J. Q.

T, 344: South Carolina, Union District. The wife of John U. Koon relinquished dower to Christian F. Cromer her dower 23 Feb 1830. Christian Koon (X), 23 Feb 1830 before Edward McGraw, J. Q. Recorded 2 March 1830.

T, 345: South Carolina, Union District. Christian F. Cromer of Union District for $200 to John Cunningham of same, tract on Swift Run Creek, 96 acres, 6 Feb 1730. Christian F. Cromer (X) (LS), wit: A. T. Burns, Gideon Steen. Proved by the oath of Gideon Steen 27 July 1830 before J. Rogers, Q.U. Recorded 2 March 1830.

T, 345-346: South Carolina, Union District. Jehu Gregory bound to Jeremiah Gregory Senr for $1000, said Jehu has received a deed of gift from said Jeremiah Gregory Senr of three negroes, 200 acres of land, with all stock, waggon, farming tools etc., and said Jehu is bound to take the said Jeremiah Gregory Senr as one of his family, clothe him decently & keep him comfortably in sickness & health during his life, 20 Nov 1828. Jehu Gregory (LS), Wit: B. J. Gregory, George Crawford. Proved by the oath of Benj. J. Gregory 3 March 1830 before J. Rogers, Q.U. Recorded 3 March 1830.

T, 346-347: South Carolina, Union District. Geo Fant of said district for $496 to Philip R. Pearson, sold to the said children of P. R. Pearson namely Francis Marion Pearson, Christian Grace Pearson, John Jefferson Pearson, Solomon Strother Pearson, Philip Layfayette Pearson, Pleasant Willingham Pearson &

Martisia Ann H. Pearson, and all other children that the said P. R. Pearson may hereafter lawfully beget, tract of land in Union District, 100 acres, part of a tract deeded by William Turpin Junr to said George Fant, 3 Oct 1829. George Fant (LS), Wit: Thos Linam, Thos Stribling, Nath Glenn. Elisabeth Fant (mark), wife of George Fant, relinquished dower 23 Feb 1830 before E. McGraw, J. Q. Proved by the oath of Nathan Glenn 23 Feb 1830 before E. McGraw, Q.U. Recorded 3 March 1830.

T, 347-348: South Carolina, Union District. Lemuel Farnandis of district aforesaid for $60 to William Cook of same, 59 acres on the waters of Packolette, adj. John Giles, William Cook, Abner Benson, said Lemuel Farnandis, 1 Feb 1830. Lemuel Farnandis (LS), Wit: John Rogers, Allen Foster Jr. Proved by the oath of John Rogers 8 March 1830 before E. McGraw, Q. U. Recorded 8 March 1830.

T, 348-349: Whereas by articles of agreement entered into by John Bruce, David Johnson, James A. Black and Enmer[?] Graham, dated 15 June 1829, among other things it is agreed that upon the part & behalf of said James A. Black, that he will furnish $2500 on his part in order that the agreement so entered into may be carried into effect, and in order to enable the said James A. Black to comply with is part of the said agreement some time in May 1829, John G. Brown, J.as H. Irby, John McLean, Richard Oneal & R. & S. Purvis became indorsers for the said James A. Black to the bank of South Carolina for $2500, assigns to them his part of the agreement, 6 March 1830. James A. Black, Wit: Thomas Williams Jr., H. H. Thomson. Proved by the oath of Thos Williams Jr. 9 March 1830 before J. Rogers, Q.U. Recorded 9 March 1830.

T, 349-350: South Carolina, Union District. James Palmer of district aforesaid for $240 to Elisha Palmer of same, tract granted to John Little on the south branch of Anesworths branch, adj. Palmer, with the exception of ten acres of land sold to Sally Johnson, 22 Feb 1830. James Palmer (LS), Wit: Wm. Smith, Aron Pruett. Proved by the oath of Aron Pruett 5 March 1830. Recorded 10 March 1830.

T, 350-351: John Whelchel of district aforesaid for $425 to John Jeffries Junr of same, tract on the head of Gilkies Creek adj. said Whelchell's old corner, Isaac Peeler, Davis Whelchel, John Whelchel, 230 acres, 26 Jan 1835. John Whelchel (LS), Wit: Jepthah Harrington, John W. Davis, Jeptha Neal. Abagail Whelchel (X), wife of John, relinquished dower, 6 Feb 1830 before Nicholas Corry, J. Q. Proved by the oath of Jephthah Harrington 6 Feb 1830 before Jas Dawkins, J.P. Recorded 9 March 1830.

T, 351-352: Christian Frederick Cromer of Union District for natural love and affection to the heirs of my son Simon Cromer of Union District, 130 acres, 29 Sept 1829. Christian F. Cromer (mark), (LS), Wit: A. f.Burns, Geo. C. Vance, John D. Word. Proved by the oath of Geo C. Vance 27 March 1830 before J. T. McJunkin, J.P. Recorded 27 March 1830.

T, 352-353: South Carolina, Union District. George Garner of district aforesaid for $250 to Israel Fowler of same, tract of land whereon Thomas wood formerly lived and conveyed by him to said Garner, 200 acres adj. Charles Hames, James Golding, Coleman Fowler, to the head of Walkers Spring branch, 27 Jan 1816. Geo Garner (LS), Wit: Charles Gault, William Gault. Proved by the oath of Charles Gault 27 Jan 1816 before W. Henderson, Q.U. Sally Garner (X), wife of George, relinquished dower 7 Feb 1816 before W. Henderson, Q. U. Recorded 6 April 1830.

T, 354-355: John Anderson, Sheriff of Union District, by virtue of several writs of fieri facias from the court of common pleas for Union District tested 13 March 1828 at the suit of William M. Thomson, John Wilbanks & others to levy of the goods & chattels lands & tenaments of Enoch Bearden $74.65, sells 150 acres on Buffalow Creek, part of two tracts, one granted to Richardson Rountree and the other to Humphrey Mills, adj. Jonas Little, Joshua Wilbourn, sold for $300 to John McLure, 3 March 1830. John Anderson, S. U. D. (LS), Wit: A. M. Adicks, John H. Skelton. Proved by the oath of John H. Skelton 7 April 1830. Recorded 7 April 1830.

T, 355: South Carolina, Union District. James McCollum of district aforesaid for $300 to Aaron Stephen McCollum of same, 125 acres on Browns Creek adj. James Goodrum, 26 Dec 1829. James McCollum (LS), Wit: Thos Goodrum, Jas Orr. Proved by the oath of Thomas Goodrum 5 April 1830 before Daniel White, J. Q. Recorded 5 April 1830.

T, 356: South Carolina, Union District. Baley Lawson of district aforesaid for $150 to Navel G. Holcomb of same, tract on Dining Creek, a branch of Fairforest, at the mouth of a branch leading from the fairforrest Meeting House to Dining Creek, adj. Kindred Bobo, widow Holcomb, 50 acres, 5 Dec 1828. Bailey Lawson (LS), Wit: H. H. Holcomb, Wm. Baley. Proved by the oath of H. H. Holcomb 5 April 1830 before J. Rogers, Q. U. Recorded 5 April 1830.

T, 356-357: South Carolina, Union District. Kindred Bobo for $450 to Navel G. Holcomb, land on each side of Dining Creek, waters of Fairforest adj. Fed Jackson, said N. G. Holcomb, heirs of Philip Holcomb, Alex'r Hays, Fredk Jackson, __ Dec 1828. Kindred Bobo (LS), Wit: Jesse Holcomb, H. H. Holcomb. Proved by the oath of H. H. Holcomb 5 April 1830 before J. Rogers, Q. U. Recorded 5 April 1830.

T, 357-358: South Carolina, Union District. Christopher Young of Union District for natural love and affection to my son Thomas Young, a negro boy about 13 years old named Bill, 3 Feb 1830. Christopher Young (LS), Wit: Wm. K. Clowney. Proved by the oath of William K. Clowney 12 April 1830 before J. Rogers, Q. U. Recorded 12 April 1830.

T, 358-359: South Carolina, Union District. Thomas Wilson of district aforesaid for $200 to Jesse Gordon of same, 100 acres, part of tract formerly owned by Presley Williams, Esqr., on waters of Cane Creek, waters of Tyger River, on the west side of the road leading to Gordons Ferry on Tyger River, 19 May 1829. Thos Wilson (LS), Wit: Thos H. Wood [Word?], John F. Edwards. Proved by the oath of John F. Edwards 21 Jan 1830 before E. McGraw, Q. U. Recorded 5 April 1830.

T, 359-360: South Carolina, Union District. South Carolina, Union District. Thomas Wilson of district aforesaid for $200 to Jesse Gordon of same, 100 acres, part of tract formerly owned by Presley Williams, Esqr., on waters of Cane Creek, waters of Tyger River, on the west side of the road leading to Gordons Ferry on Tyger River, 19 May 1829. Thos Wilson (LS), Wit: Thos H. Wood [Word?], John F. Edwards. Proved by the oath of John F. Edwards 21 Jan 1830 before E. McGraw, Q. U. Recorded 5 April 1830.

T, 359-361: South Carolina, Union District. Elisabeth Fant, wife of James B. Fant, and James B. Fant, lawful husband of said Elisabeth, of Union District, for $600 to Jesse Gordon of same, 320 acres, part of tract granted to Jean Brown on a branch of Cane Creek, waters of Tyger River, adj. Thomas Brodwick, Edward McGraw, William Sartor, Jas Johnson, 14 March 1829. J. B. Fant (LS), Elisabeth Fant (LS), Wit: Thos Wilson, Robt Wilson. George Fant relinquished all of his right to said plan and this deed executed to supply the place or in lieu of a deed made by me to Elisabeth McCan near Elisabeth Fant, wife of James. B. Fant, 13 March 1829. Proved by the oath of Thomas Wilson 21 Jan 1830 before E. McGraw, Q. U. Elisabeth Fant, wife of James B. Fant, relinquished dower 21 Jan 1830 before E. McGraw, Q. U. Recorded 5 April 1830.

T, 361: South Carolina, Union District. Volentine Martin of said district for $300 to William Mullinax, 120 acres on waters of Guilkies Creek, adj. Daniel McAdams, Lowrey, and adj. to another tract of said William Mullinax and by Jeffries, 3 Oct 1826. Voluntine Martin (LS), Wit: G. W. Suttle, John Massey (X). Proved by the oath of John Massey 13 Feb 1830 before Jas Dawkins, J.P. Recorded 5 April 1830.

T, 362-363: South Carolina, Union District. Daniel McAdams for $450 to Claybourn D. Lawrence of same, tract adj. Thomas Lantrip, part of a tract granted to Drury Harrington and conveyed from said Harrington to Joseph Dawson and from Dawson to Peter Club and from Club to Jacob Peeler and from him to G. Penix and from Penix to said Daniel McAdams, 5 Dec 1818. Daniel McAdams (X) (LS), Wit: Gabriel Patrick Senr, James Lockhart. Judah McAdams, wife of Daniel McAdams, relinquished dower 29 Jan 1830 before Nicholas Corry, J.Q. Proved by the oath of Jas Lockhart 28 Jan 1830 before Nicholas Corry, J. Q. Recorded 9 March 1830.

T, 363: South Carolina, Union District. William Mullenax of district aforesaid to Clabourn D. Lawrence for $138, 92 acres on waters of Guilkies Creek, waters of Broad River, adj. Jeffries, 13 March 1829. William Mullinax (LS),

Wit: Joseph Guthrie, Drury Byers. Proved by the oath of Drury Byers 26 Feb 1830 before Jas. Adkins, J.P. Recorded 9 April 1830.

T, 363-364: South Carolina, Union District. William Mullinax of said district for $300 to John McKown of same, tract on Gilkies Creek adj. C. Laurence, 120 acres [not dated]. William Mullinax (LS), Wit: Saml J. Hoey, Hezekiah Mullinax. Martha Mullinax, wife of William, relinquished dower 8 March 1830 before Nicholas Corry, J.Q. Proved by the oath of Hezekiah Mullinax 13 Feb 1830 before Jas Dawkins, J.P. Recorded 13 March 1830.

T, 365-366: South Carolina, Union District. Thomas Lantrip of Spartanburgh District for $130 to William Hendricks of Union District, tract on Wolf branch, a branch of Abington Creek, 196 acres, adj. Petty, Jas Lockhart, Joshlin, 7 Aug 1829. Thos Lantrip (X) (LS), Wit: Aron Wilkins, Gabriel Patrick Jr. Rebecca Lantrip, wife of Thomas, relinquished dower 6 Feb 1830 in Spartanburgh District before Robert Wilkins, J. Q. Proved in Union District by the oath of Gabriel Patrick Jr., 13 Feb 1830 before Nicholas Corry, J.Q. Recorded 12 March 1830.

T, 366-367: William Wright, Esqr., of Union District for $300 to George Myers of same, 92 acres in Union District adj. Edward Edwards, Mabrick, 8 Jan 1830. Wm Wright (LS), Wit: David J. Raiford, Jesse Whitmire, Wm. Whitmire. Proved in Newberry District by the oath of William Whitmire 8 Jan 1830 before Wm. Epps, J. Q. Mary Wright, wife of William Wright, relinquished dower 8 Jan 1830 in Newberry District before Wm. Epps, J. Q. Recorded 7 April 1830.

T, 367: South Carolina, Union District. James P. Walker of State of Tennessee for $100 to Joseph H. Dogan and Z. P. Herndon of Union District, SC ,tract on waters of Buffalow Creek, 53 acres, 24 Jan 1829. Jas. P. Walker (LS), Wit: John Parham, Robt H. Spencer. Proved by the oath of John Parham 14 April 1830 before J. Rogers, Q. U. Recorded 14 April 1830.

T, 368-369: R. S. Rice & Stephen McCollum of Union District for $500 to James Jackson of Union District, 126 acres, part of 2000 acres conveyed to us by Maj. Pierce Butler, adj. Hilery Guy's corner, 1 Jan 1827. R. S. Rice (LS), S. McCollum (LS), Wit: Wm. Rice, Joseph H. Dogan, Nancy McCollum (X), wife of Stephen McCollum, relinquished dower 24 March 1829, before Daniel White, J. Q. Agness B. Rice, wife of Reuben S. Rice, relinquished dower, 11 March 1830 before Isaac Going, J. Q. Proved by the oath of Joseph H. Dogan 2 April 1830 before J. Rogers, Q. U. Recorded 1 April 1830.

T, 369-370: South Carolina, Union District. John Anderson, Sheriff of Union district, by several writs of fieri facias from the court of common pleas tested 20 Oct 1827 at the suit of Hiram Hutchinson to levy of the goods of Amos Northrup $110.80, 90 acres between Thickety and Guilkies Creek adj. Alexander, sold to Jeptha Harrington for $25, 10 March 1830. John Anderson, S. U. D. (LS), Wit: John H. Skelton, Thos Anderson. Proved by the oath of

Thomas Anderson 11 March 1830 before Wm. H. Cotter, J.P. Recorded 13 March 1830.

T, 370-371: South Carolina, Union District. D. A. Mitchell of district aforesaid for $200 to Titus G. Farr of Union District, tract on waters of Broad River on the road near the Gage and Titus G. Farr line, 18 acres, 11 July 1828. D. A. Mitchell (LS), Wit: William B. Johns, William A. Sims. Proved by the oath of William B. Johns 11 March 1830 before Wm Mitchell, J.P. Recorded 11 March 1830.

T, 371-372: South Carolina. Hugh Davit of Union District for $1000 to Joseph H. Dogan of state aforesaid, lot formerly in the possession of Dr. Geo McCreary adj. land of Peter P. Taylor, John Wright, a square acre, 5 Feb 1827. Hugh Davitt (LS), Wit: J. Rogers, John Greer. Mary M. Davitt, wife of Hugh, relinquished dower 6 Feb 1827 before Danl White, J. Q. Proved by the oath of John Rogers before Lem B. Askew, J. Q. Recorded 21 Apr 1830.

T, 372-373: South Carolina. Henry Van Lew of Union District, whereas said Henry Van Lew by bond to A. Y. Walton of Charleston in the penal sum of $1520 for the payment of $1260 before 1 January 1831, mortgage of negro slaves Toney aged about 50 years, Dick aged about 21 years, Nelson aged about 18 years and Robin aged about 12 years, 28 Aug 1829. H. D. VanLew, Wit: William Maybin. Proved in Charleston District by William Maybin 26 March 1830 before Geo. W. Egleston. Satisfied by agent Thomas[?] Pratt of Newberry District, 19 May 1834. Recorded 29 April 1830.

T, 374-375: South Carolina. James Davis of Richland District for $ ___, to Arthur Lipsey of Union District, 145 acres in Union District adj. Handcock Porter, John Smith, Arthur Lipsey, John McCool, Jas McKibbin, Jas McBride, on waters of Tinker Creek, a branch of Tyger River, for $253.75, 24 March 1830. Jas Davis (LS), Wit: W. A. Branthwaite, Jeremiah Morris. Proved in Richland District by the oath of William A. Branthwaite 26 March 1830 before Benj Rawls, Q. U. Catharine Davis, wife of Jas Davis, relinquished dower 26 March 1830 before Benj. Rawls, Q. U. Recorded 3 May 1830.

T, 375-376: South Carolina. Joseph Gist and William B. Farr of Union District for $850 paid by Spilsby Glenn of Union District, tract on south side of Broad River conveyed by Wm. Beckham to Richard Farr, 218 acres, adj. Bird Bowker, 25 Feb 1812. W. B. Farr (LS), Jos Gist (LS), Wit: Jas Moorman, Jas Dugan. Proved by the oath of Jas Dugan 16 Nov 1827 before Aq. Hollingsworth, J. P. Recorded 3 May 1830.

T, 376: South Carolina. Joseph Gist and William B. Farr of Union District for $150 paid by Spilsby Glenn of Union District, tract of 10 acres, the hill whereon Richard Far did build a store house and including said store house, adj. Gasaway, 25 Feb 1812. W. B. Farr (LS), Jos Gist (LS), Wit: Jas Moorman, Jas Dugan. Proved by the oath of Jas Dugan 16 Nov 1827 before Aq. Hollingsworth, J. P. Recorded 3 May 1830.

T, 377-378: South Carolina. 1st Monday in September 1803, William Rice, Esquire, Sheriff of Union District, to William B. Farr, whereas Richard Farr was seized of a tract of 210 acres and the executors of Thos McDaniel decd, Robert Crenshaw Jr. & others, on 15 April 1803 before the Justices of the Court of Common Pleas held at Union Court House, and obtained judgment against the said Richard Farr for $1253.29 and $23.78 cost & charges, sold for $820 to William B. Farr, said 210 acres on Broad River adj. Spilsby Glenn, Bird Bowker, James Glenn. Wm Rice S. U. D. (LS), Wit: Edward Stevens, Jeremiah Stevens. Proved by the oath of Edward Stevens 8 Jan 1828 before Aq Hollingsworth, J. P. Recorded 3 May 1830.

T, 379: September 26 1825. Then received of Spilsby Glenn $6.00 in part payment for a tract in Union District granted to David Hopkins and gave to me by my father for which said Spilsby Glenn is to pay me $2000. Alexr Glenn (LS), Wit: Eli Odell, Bern'd Glenn. Proved by the oath of Bernard Glenn 3 May 1830 before Thos A. Glenn, J.P.

August 10th 1826. We recd of Spilsby Glenn $2000 in full for the purchase of a tract of land sold by Alexander Glenn to Spilsby Glenn in Union District near the fish dam, Broad River adj. Wm. Glenn, Spilsby Glenn, Cooper, Johnston, & Meacham. Hez Rice (LS), Nancy Rice (LS), Wit: Daniel Coleman, Susannah Anderson. Proved by the oath of Daniel Coleman 3 May 1830 before T.A.Glenn, J. P. Recorded 3 May 1830.

T, 379-380: South Carolina, Union District. Jesse Gordon of said district for $200 to Reuben Gilliam of same, part of tract formerly owned by Presley Williams, Esqr., on waters of Cain Creek, waters of Tyger River on the west side of the Road leading to Gordon's Ferry on Tyger River, 29 Dec 1829. Jesse Gordon (LS), Wit: John V. Johnson, Saml O. Gordon. Elizabeth Gordon (X), wife of Jesse Gordon, relinquished dower 21 Jan 1830 before E. McGraw, Q. U. Proved by the oath of Saml. O. Gordon 3 May 1830 before J. Rogers, Q. U. Recorded 3 May 1830.

T, 380-381: South Carolina, Union District. Jesse Gordon of said district for $1725 to Reuben Gilliam of same, 600 acres adj. William Gordon, George L. Smith, part of several tracts surveyed by John Smith 23 Jan 1816, recorded in Grant book No. 8, page 292 on Ottersons Creek, waters of Tyger River, 29 Dec 1829. Jesse Gordon (LS), Wit: John V. Johnson, Saml O. Gordon. Elizabeth Gordon (X), wife of Jesse Gordon, relinquished dower 21 Jan 1830 before E. McGraw, Q. U. Proved by the oath of Saml. O. Gordon 3 May 1830 before J. Rogers, Q. U. Recorded 3 May 1830.

T, 382-383: South Carolina, Union District. Jesse Gordon of said district for $1725 to Reuben Gilliam of same, tract granted to Jean Brown on a branch of Cain Creek, waters of Tyger River, adj. Thos Browrick, Thos Wilson, Edward McGraw, Jas Johnson, Jesse Gordon, 29 Dec 1829. Jesse Gordon (LS), Wit: John V. Johnson, Saml O. Gordon. Elizabeth Gordon (X), wife of Jesse Gordon, relinquished dower 21 Jan 1830 before E. McGraw, Q. U.

Proved by the oath of Saml. O. Gordon 3 May 1830 before J. Rogers, Q. U. Recorded 3 May 1830.

T, 383: South Carolina, Union District. William Ezell for love and good will to my son Thomas Ezell, tract where he now lives, 143 acres on south side of Browns Creek adj. Wm. Mitchell, Jas Newton, D. Hancock, widow Nancy Shell, 20 March 1830. Wm Ezell (X) (LS), Wit: Ellis Palmer, James Newton (X). Proved by the oath of Ellis Palmer 1 April 1830 before Wm Mitchell, J.P. Recorded 10 May 1830.

T, 383-384: Thos Harris and Anna Harris of Union District for $300 to Giles Sharp of same, 83 acres it being the lott of land laid off to Anna Harris, wife of Thomas Harris, as one of the heirs of William Sharp Senr decd, 26 Jan 1830. Thos Harris (X) (Seal), Anna Harris (X) (Seal), Wit: Wm Sharp, John Giles. Anna Harris, wife of Thomas Harris, relinquished dower 28 April 1830 before John Giles, Q. U. Proved by the oath of John Giles 3 May 1830 before J. Rogers, Q. U.

T, 385: South Carolina, Union District. Thomas H. Word for $800 to be paid annually $2300 per year by Reuben Clifton of Newberry District, mortgage of tract whereon he now lives, 16 Jan 1830. Reuben Clifton (Seal), Wit: John F. Edwards, Thos Wilson Jr. Proved by the oath of Thos Wilson Junr 3 April 1830 before Reuben Gilliam, J. P. Recorded 3 May 1830.

T, 385-386: South Carolina, Union District. Henry D. VanLew of district aforesaid to John VanLew, Sr., for $500, 200 acres, the boundary described in the deed from Thomas Gordon Otterson to myself, 7 Dec 1820, 5 Feb 1830. H. D. VanLew (LS), Wit: John Porter, Wm. H. Gregory. Proved by the oath of John Porter 8 May 1830 before J. Rogers, Q.U. Recorded 8 May 1830.

T, 386: Nevil G. Holcomb of Union District for natural love and affection to my son Hampton H. Holcomb of same, two tracts of land on the waters of Dining Creek, 132 acres and 50 acres, __ May 1830. Nevil G. Holcomb (LS), Wit: David Holcomb, Clemons Howard. Proved by the oath of David Holcomb 8 May 1830 before J. Rogers, Q. U. Recorded 8 May 1830.

T, 386-387: South Carolina, Union District. B. Bobo Senr for $1002 to John Norman, both of said district, tract on each side of the Ninety Six Road south of the Cross Keys, adj. Lawson, B. Bobo, Jas Batty, Jacob Lawson, Archer Kennedy, Thos Norman, Thos Ray Jr., 8 Aug 1829. B. Bobo (Seal), Wit: Martin Hopkins, Spencer A. Bobo. Frances Bobo, wife of B. Bobo, relinquished dower 8 Aug 1829 before Robert Martin J. Q. Proved by the oath of Spencer A. Bobo 8 Aug 1829 before Robert Martin J. Q. Recorded 8 May 1830.

T, 388-389: Daniel A. Mitchell of Union District for $1000 to David Johnson of Town of Columbia, tract at Neals Shoal on Broad River, below the mill, adj. S. S. Ashby, 235 acres, 25 July 1828. D. A. Mitchell (Seal), Wit: Gordon

Gregory, Edward Johnson. Proved by the oath of Edward C. Johnson 2 March 1830 before J. Rogers, Q. U. Susannah A. A. Mitchell, wife of D. A. Mitchell, relinquished dower 20 Nov 1828 before J. Rogers, Q. U. Recorded 2 March 1830.

T, 389: Andrew Hampton of Rutherford County, North Carolina, for $200 to Jonathan Hampton of Union District, SC, tract on north fork of Browns Creek, 58 acres adj. land of Saml Sharp, Jonathan Hampton, Robert Savage, and the land whereon Z. Ivey now lives, the same being the land allotted to my wife from the estate of Wm. Sharp decd, 6 Nov 1829. And'w Hampton (Seal), Wit: J. Rogers, Robt Walker Senr (X). Proved in Union District by the oath of John Rogers 15 May 1830 before Saml Davis, J.P. Recorded 18 May 1830.

T, 390: S. J. Ashley of Union District for $140 to Henry Gibbes of same, all my interest in the tract of land belonging to the estate of John Ashley [Ashby?] decd, not yet divided to the legatees but the said S. J. Ashley and Dempsey Hill being two of the heirs, the said Dempsey Hill having sold his interest and his part of the land to S. J. Ashley, 29 Dec 1827. S. J. Ashley (LS), Wit: E. McGraw, Sarah McGraw (X). Proved by the oath of Sarah McGraw 19 May 830 before E. McGraw, J. Q. Recorded in Book O No. 8, 19 May 1830.

T, 390-391: South Carolina, Chester District. John Thomas of district aforesaid do give to a certain negro man named Robin his freedom with permission from me to pass to the state of Indiania unmolested, said negro man Robin is about 65 years old, has a remarkable stout frame and speaks with a loud voice, 18 May 1830. John Thomas, Wit: Thomas Morris, Joseph Crosby, Atha Thomas. Proved in Union District by the oath of Atha Thomas 19 May 1830 before Saml Davis, J.P. Recorded 19 May 1830.

T, 391-392: Sarah Putman, Solomon Putman, and Nathan Harlan, all of said district, exrs. of the will of Rev. John Putman, late of Union District, deceased, for $100 to Bicey Bullington of same, tract on branches of Mitchells Creek, waters of Fairforest, known by the name of the Jacob Martin piece, 111½ acres originally granted to John Little adj. Brooks, Parham, Stephen McPherson, Putman now Silas & Caleb Wilburn, Littlefield & Brooks, 13 Aug 1821. Sally Putman (X) (LS), Nathan Harlan (LS), Solomon Putman (LS), Wit: William Hays, Benjamin Hays. Proved by the oath of Benjamin Hays 22 Oct 1825 before Jas. Smith, J. P. Recorded 22 May 1830.

T, 392-393: South Carolina, Union District. Bicy Bullington for $150 to James White, both of said district, a piece of land whereon I now live on branches of Mitchells Creek, waters of Fairforest, formerly belonged to the estate of Rev. John Putman decd, known by the name of the Jacob Martin piece, adj. Stephen McPherson, Wilbourn, Littlefield, Farrow, 111½ acres, 19 Oct 1829. Bicey Bullington (LS), Wit: Wm White, Elias White. Proved by the oath of Elias White 8 April 1830 before Hiram Gibbs, J. Q. Recorded 22 May 1830.

T, 393-394: John Anderson, Sheriff of Union District, by virtue of a writ of fieri facias from the court of common pleas held for the district of Union, 23 March 1829, at the suit of James Mayes to levy of the goods & chattles, lands and tenements of William Smith $450, 180 acres on the north side of Tyger Fiver adj. James Dugan, Wm. Rice, William M. Thomson, Robert McDaniel, sold to Ely Cooper for $499, 24 May 1830. John Anderson (LS), Wit: John H. Skelton, Robert Mayes. Proved by the oath of Robert Mayes, 24 May 1830 before J. Rogers, Q. U. Recorded 23 May 1830.

T, 394: South Carolina, Union District. Elisabeth Glenn to my son Robert Glenn, having boarded & otherwise attended to & Maintained myself & my negro woman Siller since 1 February 1827, I give to him all my personal estate namely one promissary note given by my son James Glenn to me for $815 dated 2 Dec 1828 payable to me or bearer 25 Dec 1829, also my negro man Tarlton now in the possession of my son John B. Glenn in the state of Georgia, also the amt of all that property sold by Spilsby Glenn exrs of the estate of James Glenn decd, 20 Dec 1827, but which was & is justly & lawfully my own, 6 May 1830. Elisabeth Glenn (X) (LS), Wit: Gideon Glenn, Thomas N. Glenn. Proved by the oath of Thomas N. Glenn 26 May 1830 before J. Rogers, Q. U. Recorded 26 May 1830.

T, 395: Francis Edrington of Union District for natural love and affection to my sister Mildred Fant, all my goods and chattels, leases & personal estate, 9 Feb 1830. Francis Edrington (LS), Wit: Peter Davis, John Mulky. Proved by the oath of Peter Davis 18 May 1830 before Thos Stribling, Q. U. Recorded 27 May 1830.

T, 395-396: Geo Young of Union District for $600 to Jas Willard of same, tract on the main road leading from Union Court House to Cook bridge on Tyger River, 325 acres adj. John Clark, Solomon Clark, Caleb Frazer, Joseph McJunkin, Chesley Conant, Charles Humphries, Saml Boyd, 18 Jan 1830. George Young (LS), Wit: J. Rogers, Thos H. Bankhead. Proved by the oath of John Rogers 15 May 1830 before Saml Davis, J.P. Agness Young (X), wife of George Young, relinquished dower 25 Jan 1830 before J. Rogers, Q. U. Recorded 15 May 1830.

T, 396-397: James Gasaway of Union District for $60 to John Cook of same, tract whereon I now live, 45 acres, 27 Nov 1829. James Gassaway Junr (LS), Wit: David A. Thomas, Isaac Cain (X), Titus G. Farr. Sarah Gasaway, wife of James Gasaway, relinquished dower 27 Nov 1829 before Titus G. Farr, Q. U. Proved by the oath of David A. Thomas 27 Nov 1829 before Titus G. Farr, Q. U. Recorded 18 May 1830.

T, 398: Jesse McKinney of Monroe County, Mississippi, appoint John Gallant of York District, my attorney in face to sell my interest in the real estate of Daniel Gallant of State of North Carolina, Macclenburgh County, decd, of whose estate he is administrator, 5 April 1830. Jesse McKinney (Seal), W. A. Tucker, an acting J. P. in Monroe County, Mississippi, made oath that Jesse

McKinney acknowledged the power of attorney 5 April 1830. Stephen Cocke, clerk of the county court, certifies that W. A. Tucker was a J. P., by his deputy J. B. Sims 5 April 1830. William Coates, Chief Justices of the County Court certified that Stephen Cook is the clerk of the court. Recorded 8 June 1830.

T, 399: John Whelchell Senr, planter, of Union District, to John McKee, merchant of Chester District, tract whereon my son John Whelchell now lives, 367 acres, adj. Gastney, 23 Jan 1830. John Whelchel (Seal), Wit: Jas. Service, William Logan. Abigail Whelchel (mark), wife of John Whelchel, relinquished dower 1 Feb 1830 before Nicholas Corry, J.Q. Proved by the oath of James Service 1 Feb 1830 before Nicholas Corry, J.Q. Recorded 22 June 1830.

T, 400: South Carolina, Union District. Elisabeth Duncan, wife of James Duncan son of Alexr, in lieu of 200 acres of land he bought of Ambros Ray which has been conveyed to me & four negroes (viz) Aley and three children Dennis, Sandy & Fanny, and $300 in cash, all my right of dower to all the remainder of his estate, real and personal, 22 April 1819. Elisabeth Duncan (mark) (LS), Wit: Wm. B. Murphy, Jesse D. Murphy, Wm. Prater. Proved by the oath of Capt. Jesse D. Murphy 25 June 1830 before J. Rogers, Q. U. Recorded 25 June 1830.

T, 400-401: Charles Humphries of Union District for $116 to Thomas Humphries, tract whereon he now lives, on a branch of Fairforest, 86 acres on Mulkies branch, adj. Charles Humphries line of house tract, Anderson, 28 June 1820. Charles Humphries (mark) (LS), Wit: Muckle Bogan, J. Rogers. Proved by the oath of M. B. Bogan 28 June 1830 before J. Rogers, Q. U. Recorded 28 June 1830.

T, 401-402: John Murry of Spartanburgh for $360 to Nathaniel Jeffries of Union District, tract on north side of Thicketty Creek granted to Sion Clanton, 360 acres on waters of Thickety, granted to Sion Clanton relapsed in office to John Murry then to his son John Murry by heirship, 16 Jan 1830. John Murry (Seal), Wit: Saml Littlejohn, Benj. F. Dawkins, Joshua P. Dawkins. Proved by the oath of Saml Littlejohn 25 June 1830 before Wm. Goudelock, J.P. Recorded 5 June 1830.

T, 402: Joshua Floyd of Union District for $250 to Mathias Hilburn of State of Georgia, Dekalb County, tract on Rocky Creek, a branch of Fairforest, being a tract conveyed from Stephen McCollum to Mathias Hilburn and from said Hilburn to Joshua Floyd, and from said Floyd to said hilburn, adj. David Floyd, Rolly Henton[?], Wm. Hammond, Nathl Gist, Jno Jackson, Sarah Hilburn, 65 acres, 12 March 1830. Joshua Floyd (LS), Wit: Jas. Hilburn, Levy Clark (mark). Proved by the oath of Jas Hilburn 5 July 1830 before J. Rogers, Q. U. Recorded 4 July 1830.

T, 403: Georgia, DeKalb County. M. Hilburn of county aforesaid appoints James Hilburn attorney to sell tract on Rocky Creek in Union District known by the name of the Belew tract with the addition of the piece reserved from the Gist tract, adj. Wm Hammond, David Floyd, Robt Hilburn & Nathaniel Gist, also one small lot bound all round by N. Gist, 8 May 1830. M. Hilburn (Seal), Wit: Jephthah V. Gurge, A. Corry, J.P. Charles Murphy, Clerk of the Inferior Court of Dekalb County, certified that A. Corry was a justice of the piece 8 May 1830. James Lemon, one of the Justices of the Inferior Court certified that Charles Murphy was an acting clerk. Recorded 5 July 1830.

T, 403-404: South Carolina, Union District. William Wright of Union District for $246.57½ to Lewis Presley of same, 98 3/4 acres adj. Isaac Pearson[?], Lewis Presley, heirs of Charles Presley decd, heirs of Hopkins decd, James Mayes, 7 Jan 1830. Wm Wright (LS), Wit: Michael Troutman, Amos L. Jinkins. Proved by the oath of Amos L. Jenkins 26 June 1830 before Robt Stokes, J.P. Recorded 28 June 1830.

T, 404-405: South Carolina, Union District. Edward McGraw of district aforesaid for $25 to John Smith of same, three acres, part of a tract of 150 acres granted to John Hawkins 19 Aug 1775, from said Hawkins sold to Edward McGraw adj. Ashby, 29 Jan 1823. E. McGraw (LS), Wit: W. N. McGraw, Isaac M. Smith. Proved by the oath of both witnesses 29 Jan 1823 before Saml O. Johnson, J.P. Recorded 12 July 1830.

T, 405-406: South Carolina, Union District. Presley Williams of district aforesaid for $290 to John Smith Jr. of same, 100 acres on waters of Cain Creek, a branch of Tyger River, part of tract granted to William Sims, 3 Oct 1818. Presley Williams, Wit: Jas T. Williams, Geo L. Smith (mark), Nancy T. Williams. Proved by the oath of James T. Williams 6 Nov 1818 before Reuben Sims, J. Q. Rebecca Williams, wife of Presley Williams, relinquished dower 6 Nov 1818 before Reuben Sims, J.Q. Recorded 12 July 1830.

T, 406-407: South Carolina, Union District. John Smith of district aforesaid for $200 to Thomas Brodrick, tract, being part of two different tracts, one granted to William Sims the other to John Hawkins adj. McGraw, Ashley, 103 acres. John Smith (LS), Wit: John Morgan, W. N. McGraw, Proved by the oath of John Morgan and William N. Graw 28 Dec 1827 before E. McGraw, Q. U. Elisabeth Smith (X), wife of John Smith, relinquished dower 28 Dec 1827 before E. McGraw, Q. U. Recorded 12 July 1830.

T, 407: South Carolina, Union District. 11 Nov 1829, Thos Hollis and Anna Pearson to be married, and possessed of consideration real and personal estate, after their deaths what property is to be equally divided betwixt each of their children. Thos Hollis (LS), Anna Pearson (LS), Wit: Jason Norman, Jno Norman. Proved by the oath of Jason Norman 7 June 1830 before J. Rogers, Q. U. Recorded 7 June 1830.

T, 408-409: 31 March 1830, Edw'd M. Bobo to William Gist, whereas said Edw'd M. Bobo stands indebted to said W. H. Gist by note of hand in the sum of $3000 secured by John Cunningham and Z. Hooker at six months from the date, now mortgage for $1, tract on Tyger River on the north side known by the name of the Parham lands, formerly owned by John Parham deceased, adj. estate of Barrum Bobo, Thomas Layton, 400 acres. E. M. Bobo (LS), Wit: Jno Cunningham, F. H. Leonard[?]. Proved by the oath of ___ 19 July 1830 before J. Rogers, Q. U. Recorded 19 July 1830.

T, 409-410: John Anderson, Sheriff, pursuant to an order from the Court of Ordinary signed by John J. Pratt, Ordinary of Union District, 3 May 1830 at the suit of John Gee & Wife vs Martha Wilbright et al to sell two tracts of land belonging to the estate of Barnabas Wilbright, decd, on the west side of Broad River a little before the mouth of Thickety Creek, 110 acres, adj. Henry Good, originally granted to Ichabod Clark in 1766 and conveyed by him to Neal McKissick and from his heirs to Richard Brook and from him to Barnabas Wilbright 13 Jan 1796, sold to Richard Thomson for $266, 22 May 1830. John Anderson S. U. D. (LS), Wit: Thos N. Dawkins, H. H. Thomson. Proved by the oath of Thos N. Dawkins 17 July 1830 before J. Rogers, Q. U. Recorded 17 July 1830.

T, 410-411: South Carolina, Union District. James Foote of district aforesaid for $100 to Thomas Sartor of same, tract on a branch of Tinker Creek, on said Foot's spring, adj. Rice, which formerly belong to Caleb Frazier, and conveyed to James Foote by Caleb Frazier decd, also a tract adj. said Foote, 14 Jan 1830. James Foote (Seal), Wit: Thos Bates, John T. McJunkin. Proved by the oath of Thos Bates 6 July 1830 before J. Rogers, Q.U. Recoreed 6 Feb 1830.

T, 411: South Carolina, Union District. James Smith, Esqr., came before John Rogers, Clerk of the court of Sessions & Common pleas, and with consent of Aggy Baley, a free woman of color, acknowledged himself her guardian, 19 July 1830. Jas Smith (LS), J. Rogers, Clk. Recorded 19 July 1830.

T, 411-412: John Anderson, Sheriff of Union District, by a writ of fieri facias from the court of common pleas held for the District of Union tested 2 April 1827 at the suit of Jeremiah Chandler to levy of the goods & chattels, lands & tenements of Catharine Harris $1109.53, sells tract of 122 acres on Enoree River adj. Burwell Chick, Saml Shelton, Robert Leverett, purchased by P. Chick for $187, dated 5 Aug 1830. John Anderson, S. U. D. (LS), Wit: John H. Skelton, J. Rogers. Proved by the oath of John Rogers 11 Aug 1830 before J. Palmer, J.P. Recorded 11 Aug 1830.

T, 412-413: Peter & John W. C. Tucker purchased form James Meacham a tract of land whereon we now live in Union District on waters of Cain Creek, 234 acres adj. T. G. Farr, William Sartor, John Jennings, Edward McGraw, Ashby, for which tract we have this day jointly signed & give unto James Meacham five notes of hand dated this day, and drawn each for $225, in the whole $1125... 7 Dec 1827. Peter Tucker (X) J. C. Tucker. Wit: John S. Sims, E. McGraw. Proved by the oath of John S. Sims and E. McGraw 10 Aug 1830 before F. A. Glenn, J.P. Recorded 11 Aug 1830. Satisfied 18 Oct 1833, signed by Jas Meacham, Wit: Stith Hardy.

T, 413-414: South Carolina, Union District. Josiah Foster Senr for $175 to Edward T. Hendley, part of tract of land which I now live [on] supposed to be 32 acres adj. William Hendley, said Edward, on the south side of Reedy branch, 9 April 1830. Josiah Foster (X) (LS), Wit: Herod Hendley, Richard Palmer. Proved by the oath of Richard Palmer 17 April 1830. Polly Foster (X), wife of Josiah Foster, relinquished dower 17 April 1830 before Isaac Going, Q. U. Recorded 1 Sept 1830.

T, 414-415: South Carolina, Union District. M. B. Harrington of said district for $45 to John Patrick Jr. for the benefit of the heirs of Charles Patrick, decd, 30 acres on Abington Creek, 3 Oct 1830. M. B. Harrington (LS), Wit: Singleton Page, W. D. Robinson. Proved by the oath W. D. Robertson 4 Sept 1830 before Jas. Dawkins, J.P. Recorded 6 Sept 1830.

T, 415: South Carolina, Union District. John Bird of said district for $300 to James C. Bird of same, tract between Thickety & Gilkies Creek, 170 acres, 9 June 1830. Jno Bird (LS), Wit: Jepthah Harrington, M. B. Harrington. Proved by the oath of Jepthah Harrington before Wm. H. Cotter, J. P. Recorded 6 Sept 1830.

T, 416: South Carolina, Union District. David Adams of district aforesaid for $157.50 to Isom Vaughan of said district, 63 acres on waters of Hughes Creek, 14 Jan 1825. David Adams (LS), Wit: Sherw'd W. Nance, Rich'd Nance. Proved by the oath of Richard Nance 14 March 1826 before Lot Whitlock, J.P. Recorded 17 Aug 1830.

T, 416-417: John Beard of Union District for $310 to Hezekiah Rice of Laurens District, tract on branches of Hills Creek, 40 acres of the north part of which being a part of 280 acres granted to Walter Roberts and 100 acres granted to William Edmondson adj. Barnett, Esqr. John Norman, said Hez. Rice, Joseph Goswick, 150 acres, dated 13 July 1830. John Beard (LS), Wit: Wm. C. Pearson, Thos Mitchell. Proved by the oath of William C. Pearson 30 July 1830 before John Norman, J. Q. Lettice Beard (X), wife of John Beard, relinquished dower 7 Aug 1830 before John Norman, J. Q.

T, 417-418: South Carolina, Union District. Danl Palmer of district aforesaid for $300 to Henry Smith of same, tract whereon said Henry Smith now lives, 139 acres adj. Nathan Harlan, 4 June 1826. Daniel Palmer (LS), Wit: John Jones (X), Aron Pruett. Proved by the oath of Aron Pruett 15 Jan 1826 before Jas Smith, J.P. Recorded 5 Sept 1830.

T, 418-419: South Carolina, Union District. Mrs. Ann Norvell, wife of John Norvell, relinquished dower to tract whereon said Clough S. Meng now lives, about 417 acres, also another from Hon. Abram Nott as atty for Sarah C. Huger, executor of Danl Huger decd, also a grant of 31 acres all of the same on waters of Browns Creek, sold at Sheriffs sale as the property of John Norvell and purchased by Col. Z. P. Herndon, 30 Aug 1830 before J. Rogers, Q. U. Recorded 30 Aug 1830.

T, 419-420: John Ramsay, Thomas Fraser & David Campbell, acting assignees of Dr. James Clitherall deceased, appointed by him 25 Feb 1799, the said David Campbell at present of the Parish of St. Bartholomews and said John Ramsay and Thomas Fraser of City of Charleston, for $700 to William Simms of _____, tract on west bank of Broad River, 844 acres by resurvey granted to Phillip Henry 15 Sept 1775, then taken to measure 700 acres conveyed by deed 14 & 15 May 1778 by said Philip Henry & Sarah Maria his wife to said James Clitherall and by said James Clitherall conveyed by deed of assignment above to us, 11 Feb 1819. John Ramsay (LS), Thos Fraser (LS), D. Campbell (LS), Wit: Isaac Motte Campbell, William Lance. Proved in Charleston District by the oath of William Lance before Lawrence Ryan, J.P., 13 Feb 1819. Recorded 10 Aug 1830.

T, 420-423: 14 & 15 May 1778, Philip Henry of Charlestown, South Carolina, and Sarah Mariah his wife, to James Clitherall of the same place, for £3300 current money, 1000 acres in Orangeburgh District granted to Thomas Warburton Powell 21 April 1775, also tract of 700 acres in Craven County, the west side of Broad River adj. John Steen, Benjamin Farrar, Esquire, granted to Phillip Henry 15 Sept 1775. Phillip Henry (LS), S. M. Henry (LS), Wit: John Moncrieffe, Will Currie. Proved 22 Aug 1786 by the oath of John Moncrieffe before Daniel Mazyck, J. P. in Charleston District. Recorded 10 Sept 1830.

T, 423-430: 25 Feb 1799, James Clitheral of City of Charleston, Doctor of Physic, and Elizabeth his wife, to John Ramsay, David Campbell, Thomas Fraser and William Robertson, of same place, esquires, whereas said James Clitherall is justly indebted to the said James Ramsay, David Campbell, Thomas Fraser and William Robertson, in the sum of £9855, and he is unable to make payment, assigns tract on both sides of Horseshoe Creek in St. Bartholomews Parish, and divided into two plantations, one call Horseshoe and the other Round O, 1961 acres, in one parcel and 933 acres in the other parcel on the public road from the Fishpond to the northward adj. Mr. Cunningham, William Elliott, Esqr., deceased, Dickard Woodcraft, Peter Smith, Esqr., Charles Elliott decd, Estate of Tobias Ford, and 1010 acres in St. Bartholomews Parish; 2400 acres of land near big Brown Creek, 700 acres on Broad River near Fish Dam Ford, 1176 acres in Orangeburgh District, also negroes, stock cattle, horses, etc., in the second schedule. James Clitherall (LS), Eliza Clitherall (LS). Schedule of debts No. 1. Debt due the estate of Thomas Loughton Smith & which is to be divided amongst the heirs of that estate after the death of Mrs. Clitherall, debts due Doctor John Ramsay in right of his wife, William Smith, Rawlins Lowndes, Doctor Robert Wilson Junr, Mrs. Harriett Poaug, John Potter, Miss Mary Inglis, McWhann & McWhann Naples, Tunno & Coe, James Gregorie & Son, Mrs. Bell, William Greenwood, William Robertson, Thomas Fraser, Alexander Rose, David Denoon, The Vestry of St. James Goose Creek, William McLeod & Co., James Fisher, James Mathews. Schedule 2 is a list of negroes the property of James Clitherall, 1 Jan 1799. Includes 15 men, 11 girls, 26, women, and 20 boys [named]. Schedule three includes furniture. Proved by the oath of George

C. Clitherall 7 March 1799 before Isaac Motte Dart, J. Q. Wm Robertson, one of the trustees, relinquished to the other trustees, all his authority and power, interest & Benefit, 1 Feb 1801. Wit: J. Horne. Recorded 10 Aug 1830.

T, 430: South Carolina, Union District. Hardy Dick of said district for love and affection to William Dick of same, one sorrel horse colt, two years old, 29 Sept 1830. Hardy Dick (LS), Wit: Isaac Going, Isaac M. Going. Proved by the oath of Isaac Going 30 Sept 1830 before A. Foster, J.P. Recorded 30 Sept 1830.

T, 431: South Carolina, Union District. James Woodson, formerly of said district decd, did by his will give all his real estate to his wife Anne Woodson, with a right to dispose of the same, and said Anne Woodson did on 24 March 1828 dispose of about one half by deed of gift to her daughter Cassey Dickins, including the houses where she then lived, being all the land not deeded to her son Goodwin Woodson, now for $330 to John P. Woodson, Cassey and her husband Elijah Perkins convey 100 acres adj. James Greer, Wyche Goodwin, Elizabeth Woodson, 5 Nov 1829. Cassey Perkins (X) (LS), Elijah Perkins (LS), Wit: Wm. Rountree, James Greer. Proved by the oath of James Greer 2 Aug 1830 before J. Rogers, Q. U. Recorded 2 Aug 1830.

T, 431-432: South Carolina, Union District. James Malcomson for $72.28½ to John Jeffries Senr, tract on waters of Abbingtons Creek adj. George Malcomson, 11 Jan 1830. James Makamson (LS), Wit: Jepthah Harrington, Saml J. Hoey. Proved by the oath of Saml J. Hoey 25 Feb 1830 before Nicholas Corry, J. Q. Recoreed 2 Aug 1830.

T, 432-433: John Anderson, Sheriff, pursuant to an order from the court of ordinary, directed to me as sheriff, signed by William White, Ordinary of Union District, tested 1 June 1829, at the suit of Reuben S. Rice guardian & others, to sell tract of the estate of John Derboro[?] decd, on the north side of Thickety Creek, 252 acres adj. lands of Widow mitchell, said Reuben S. Rice, purchased by Reuben S. Rice for $600, 15 Jan 1830. John Anderson, S. U. D. (LS), Wit: John H. Skelton, Thos Anderson. Proved by the oath of John H. Skelton 23 Aug 1830 before J. Rogers, Q. U. Recorded 23 Aug 1830.

T, 433-434: William Hammond & William R. Powell of Union District for $560 to Hobson Thomson of same, 150 acres on Rocky Creek, a water course of Fairforest, part of tract originally the property of William Morgan decd, and sold by an order of the court of common pleas to make partition among the heirs of said William Morgan, purchased by Jonathan Morgan and by him conveyed to Elizabeth Powell, the present wife of said William Hammond, 4 May 1813, and part of said tract was sold to said William P. Powell by William Hammond and Elizabeth Hammond 5 Jan 1827, 29 July 1829. Wm Hammond (LS)l ,Wm. R. Powell (LS), Wit: Wm Rice, Wm. R. Wilbourn. Martha L. Powell, wife of William Powell, and Elizabeth Hammond wife of Wm. Hammond, relinquished dower 28 Aug 1830 before Daniel White, Q. U.

Proved by the oath of Wm R. Wilbourn 6 Sept 1830 before J. Rogers, Q. U. Recorded 6 Sept 1830.

T, 434-435: South Carolina, Union District. Henry Stevens of district aforesaid, attorney for James Glover, for $60.47, and the one sixth part of 46½ acres, assigned to Mary Boyd as her third of the real estate of William Hamilton decd, relinquish all the right, claim or title which James Glover has to the whole lands of William Hamilton decd., 13 Sept 1830. Henry Stevens (Seal), Wit: Nathan Coleman, T. A. Glenn. Proved by the oath of Thomas Glenn 13 Sept 1830 before Wm. K. Clowney, Q. U. Recorded 16 Sept 1830.

T, 435: Maria Whitlock alias Barnhill of Jefferson County, Tennessee, appoint Samuel Sellars of same county and state, my lawful attorney, to receive from Bethel Kent of Union District, SC, all sums of money deposited in the hands by John Kent for my use, 5 June 1823. Maria Barnhill (X) (LS). Acknowledged before John Cate, H. Collier, Justices of the Peace in Jefferson County, TN. Joseph Hamilton, clerk of court, certifies that John Cate and Henry Collier were justices of the peace 8 June 1823.

T, 436-437: John Bates, Sheriff of Union District, by virtue of a writ of fieri facias issued out of the court of common pleas 18 August 1826 at the suit of Wm. R. Wilbourn to levy of the goods & chattels lands & tenements of James Whitlock, $245.40 with costs, 50 acres on waters of Sugar Creek adj. Alexander Hay, David Holcombe, Wm Rountree, purchased by Wm. R. Wilbourn for $10, 26 Jan 1827. J. Bates S. U. D. (LS), Wit: Z. Hooker, Wm. C. Pearson. Proved by the oath of Wm. C. Pearson 14 Aug 1830 before H. Gibbs, J. Q. Recorded 14 Aug 1830.

T, 437: South Carolina, Union District. William Gault of district aforesaid for $300 to Gazawa Hames of same, 75 acres adj. Wm. Gault, C. Hames, 14 Aug 1830. William Gault (LS), Wit: James Briggs, Thomas Kelly. Proved by the oath of James Briggs 14 Aug 1830 before A. Foster, J. P. Recorded 6 Sept 1830.

T, 438: South Carolina, Union District. Charles Hames for $500 to Gazawa Hames of same, 100 acres on the east side of Portmans Creek adj. Kelly, William Gault, Thomas Hames, 14 Aug 1830. Charles Hames (mark) (Seal), Wit: James Briggs, William Gault. Proved by the oath of William Gault 14 Aug 1830 before A. Foster, J.P. Recorded 6 Sept 1830.

T, 439: South Carolina, Union District. E. M. Bobo of district aforesaid for $525 to Thomas Sartor of same, tract on waters of Fairforest Creek adj. Rice, E. M. Bobo, Malone, Langston, B. M. Jenkins, Thomas Sartor, James Foote, Bates, 417 acres according to a survey made by John T. McJunkin 13 Sept 1828, dated 5 Feb 1829. E.M. Bobo (LS), Wit: Jno Cunningham, Thomas Bates. Proved by the oath of Thomas Bates 5 Feb 1829 before J. Rogers, Q. U. Recorded 5 Feb 1829.

T, 439-441: 7 Sept 1830, William K. Clowney, Esquire, Commissioner of the Court of Equity for Union District, to Jonathan Hawkins, whereas John Gage Junr and others exparte 28 June did exhibited their bill of complaint shewing that Col. James McKibbin died intestate and was possessed of a tract of land of 195½ acres of which partition yet remains to be made, said tract to be sold at public auction, sold 7 Sept to $600 to Jonathan Hawkins. Wm. K. Clowney, C. E. U. D. (LS), Wit: H. W. Foote, A. W. Thomson. Proved by the oath of H. W. Foote 7 Sept 1830 before J. Rogers, Q. U. Recorded 7 Sept 1830.

T, 441: South Carolina, Union District. William Smith Senr of district aforesaid for $80.50 to John Liles of same, 26 acres on waters of the forest Creek, adj. Butler[?], John Liles, 9 Sept 1829. William Smith (LS), Wit: W. Smith Senr, S. McCollum. Proved by the oath of Stephen McCollum 6 Sept 1830 before J. Rogers, Q. U.

T, 441-442: Morgan A. Spencer, George Spencer, Eliza Hancock, T. B. Hancock, Louisa Kyle, and James H. Kyle of Union District to James Dawkins, two tracts separated from said Dawkins by Gilkeys Creek adj.Heirs of Spencer Morgan, Nancy Davis, Heirs of Esquire Amos decd, 221 acres, 10 Feb 1827. Margaret Spencer (X) (LS), George A. Spencer (LS), Eliza Hancock (X) (LS), T. B. Hancock (LS), James Kyle (LS), Louisa A. Kyle (LS). Wit: Peter Spencer, Hopson Thomson (X). Proved by the oath of Peter Spencer 11 July 1837 before Wm. H. Cotter, J. P. Recorded 28 July 1827.

T, 442-443: James Foote of Union District for $786 to William Rice of same, 313 acres on the north east side of Fairforest Creek adj. land originally surveyed for Joseph Bates, Daniel Huger, heirs of Hezk. Rice decd, per plat annexed to a deed from John Saunders now decd to said James Foote dated 5 Feb 1812, dated 11 Jan 1830. James Foote (Seal), Wit: Thomas Sartor, Thomas Bates. Jane M. Foote (X), wife of James Foote, relinquished dower 20 March 1830 before Jno Norman, J. Q. Proved by the oath of Thomas Bates 2 Oct 1830 before J. Rogers, Q. U. Recorded 2 Oct 1830.

T, 444: Rody Gregory of Union District for $50 to Obadiah Whitlock of Union District, tract on Browns Little Creek adj. John Gregory, Freelove Gregory, Benj. Gregory, Rhody Gregory, it being a part of a larger tract of land belonging to the estate of John Gregory decd, sold by order of court to make division and partition among the heirs of said deceased and purchased by the said Rhody Gregory for $670, 50 acres to be laid off of the lower end of said tract but the deed of conveyance is to be so understood that Jemimah Whitlock, mother of said Obediah is to enjoy a life estate in the said land above mentioned and the said Obadiah is not to have the disposing right of said land until the death of the said Rhody Gregory, 4 June 1822. Rhody Gregory (X) (LS), Wit: Jas Leach, Jas Gasaway. Proved by the oath of James Gassaway Senr 5 June 1822 before Danl Thomas, Q. U. Recorded 19 Oct 1830.

T, 444-445: South Carolina, Union District. Robert Thomson of district aforesaid for $500 to William Goudelock of same, negro woman named Beckey aged 30 years and two of her children one named Franky a girl aged five years, one boy named James aged two years, 28 Jan 1829. Robt Thomson (LS), Wit: James Goudelock, William Thomson. Proved by the oath of James Goudelock 18 Sept 1830 before Jas Dawkins, J.P. Recorded 13 Oct 1830.

T, 445-446: We whose names are here under written for $20 to Davis Whelchel have conveyed a tract of land in Union District on the dry fork of Gilkies Creek, adj. John Whelchel, 30 Aug 1820. John Whelchel (LS), William Morrow (LS), Thos Waters (LS), Fr. Whelchel (LS), Wm. Ownsby (LS), Wit: Joseph Camp, Powell Ownsby. Proved by the oath of Joseph Camp Esqr., 10 Jan 1828 before Wm. Goudelock, J.P. Recorded 13 Oct 1830.

T, 446-447: Daniel Lipham, John Lipham, Henry Lipham, Zachariah Rentfrow, William Benton and Wm Ray appoint Martin D. Jenkins our lawful attorney to receive from the executor of Daniel Lipham decd, late of Union District, SC, such legacies as my have been bequeathed to us by the said Daniel Lipham in his last will and testament, 11 Jan 1830. Danl Lipham (X) (LS), John Lipham (LS), Wm. Ray (X) (LS), Zach Rentfrow (X) (LS), William Benton (LS), Geo H. Lipham (X) (LS), Wit: Wm. J. Echols, Gresham Scogin (Georgia, Troup County), Wm Benton, Saml Lipham (X), Marcus A. Sears, J.P. Clark County, Georgia: Robert Ligon, Clerk of the Inferior Court certifies that Marcus A. Sears was a justice of the peace 29 Jan 1830. William Dickens, one of the justices of the inferior court certifies that Robert Ligon was clerk of the court, 29 Jan 1830. Recorded 27 Oct 1830.

T, 447-448: Adam Little of district aforesaid for $35 to Benjamin Little of same, 100 acres adj. Benj. Little, Dr. Askew, Mitchell, Herndon, Dogan, McLure, 14 Oct 1830. Adam Little (X) (Seal), Wit: Benjamin H. Rice, E. M. Glenn. Proved by the oath of E. M. Glenn 15 Oct 1830 before J. Rogers, Q. U. Recorded 15 Oct 1830.

T, 448-449: James Willard of Union District for $118 to John Rogers of same, tract on a small branch of Shoal Creek adj. Joseph Howard, on Poplar Spring branch, adj. Willard, Bogan, Wm. Coomer. adj. Joseph Reeder, on a branch on which Thos McCafferty lives, to John Willard's branch, 25 Jan 1830. Jas Willard (X) (LS), Wit: John F. Murrell, Robt Lee. Proved by the oath of John T. Murrell 22 Jan 1830 before Daniel White, Q. U. Recorded 22 Jan 1830.

T, 449-450: Adam Little of district aforesaid for $900 to Jemima Reid of same, tract where I now live, on waters of Buffalow Creek, 240 acres adj. James Rountree, L. B. Askew, Benjamin Little, Daniel A. Mitchell, 3 July 1830. Adam Little (X) (Seal), Wit: James Rountree, Mary Johnson. Susannah Little (X), wife of Adam Little, relinquished dower __ Oct 1830 before Leml B. Askew. Proved by the oath of James Rountree before Lem B. Askew, J. Q. Recorded 2 Nov 1830.

T, 450-451: South Carolina, Union District. William P. Sartor of district aforesaid for $150 to John P. Sartor Senr of same, tract of 60 acres, part of a tract of 100 acres granted to Thomas Smith 23 June 1774, recorded in Book RRR, page 34, on Becks Branch, waters of Tyger River, adj. Hawkins, the differend transfers from Thomas Smith and others up to Geo Linam deceased by whom Thomas Linam son of said George Linam was advised as appears by the will of said George Linam, 16 Feb 1830. Wm. P. Sartor (LS), Wit: G. W. Sartor, Thomas Sartor, Solomon Evans. Proved by the oath of Thomas Sartor Junr 11 Oct 830 before Titus G. Farr, Q. U. Recorded 1 Nov 1830.

T, 451-452: South Carolina, Union District. John Anderson, Sheriff of Union District, by virtue of a writ of fieri facias from the court of common pleas tested third Monday in March 1823 at the suit of Reid & Hooker to John Bates, Esqr., late Sheriff of the District aforesaid, to levy of the goods & chattels, lands & tenements of Joseph McJunkin Senr $60.19, 200 acres between Capt. Bates & Wm Young adj. Mordecai Chandler, Thomas Sartor[?], sold to William R. Wilbourn for $81, 21 July 1829. John Anderson, S. U. D. (LS), Wit: Jasper Gibbs, Powell W. Skelton.

To John Anderson, Esq., Sheriff. You are hereby authorized to make titles to Mr. Thomas Sartor for the Land I purchased at Sheriff Sale while John Bates was Sheriff, as the property of Thos Okeefe for $81, 1 June 1829. W. R. Wilbourn. Proved by the oath of Powell W. Skelton 5 Nov 1830 before J. Rogers, Q. U. Recorded 4 Nov 1830.

T, 453-454: 29 July 1830, Hobson Thomson to William Hammond & William R. Powell, whereas said Hobson Thomson by his four notes of hand dated 29 July 1830 stands indebted to said William Hammond and William R. Powell in the sum of $460, mortgage of 140 acres on Rocky Creek, a water course of Fairforest, it being the tract of land this day sold and conveyed by said Wm Hammond and W. R. Powell. Hobson Thomson (X) (LS), Wm Hammond (LS), W. R. Powell (LS), Wit: Wm Rice, W. R. Wilbourn. Proved by the oath of William Rice 15 Nov 1830 before J. Rogers, Q. U. Recorded 15 Nov 1830.

T, 454-455: South Carolina, Union District. McNeal Bevel of district of Union for $120 to William Bevil of same, 30 acres on both sides of Johnsons branch of Browns Creek, waters of Broad River, 15 Sept 1830. McNeil Bevill (Seal), Wit: Greenberry Tracey, James Tracey. Proved by the oath of Greenberry Tracey 5 Oct 1830 before John Giles, Q. U. Recorded 5 Oct 1830.

T, 455-456: South Carolina, Union District. Indenture of three parts, between Dennis Miller, Francis Miller his wife, and John B. Baley, trustee, whereas said Dennis Miller has been unfortunate in trade & deeming it his duty to secure to his said wife for her separate benefit all the proceeds of her future industry & economy free from the control of said Dennis Miller, makes her a feme sole, 6 Dec 1830. Dennis Miller (Seal), Frances Miller (X) (Seal), John Baley (seal), Wit: R. Lipsey, Arthur Lipsey. Proved by the oath of R. Lipsey Esqr 6 Dec 1830 before J. Rogers, Q. U. Recorded 6 Dec 1830.

T, 456-458: South Carolina, Union District. Indenture of three parts, 9 Dec 1830, between McNeal Veil, Jane Bevil and Greenberry Tracey, trustee, whereas Jane Bevil hath heretofore given the notice required by law of her intention to trade as a free sole trader or free dealer, said Mac Bevil makes her a feme sole trader. McNeil Bevil (LS), Jane Bevil (X) (LS), Greenberry Tracey (LS), Wit: Robt G. H. Farr, G. Page. Proved by the oath of Robt G. H. Farr 9 Dec 1830 before J. Rogers, Q. U. Recorded 9 Dec 1830.

T, 458-459: South Carolina, Union District. Jeremiah Dawson of district aforesaid for $300 to Isaac Guyton of same, tract granted to Manos Dawson, 159 acres, 9 Aug 1830. Jeremiah Dawson (LS), Wit: John Phillips Sen., Saml B. Dawson, Nathaniel Guyton. Margaret Dawson, wife of Jeremiah Dawson, relinquished dower 1 Dec 1830 before Nicholas Corry, J.Q. Proved by the oath of Nathaniel Guyton 1 Dec 1830 before Nicholas Corry, Q. U. Recorded 6 Dec 1830.

T, 459-461: Reuben Gilliam and Frances P. Farr of Union district have decided to join in matrimony, and each being possession of certain properties, said Reuben Gilliam agrees to return to her heirs at her death all such property as belongs to her, 11 Nov 1830. Reuben Gilliam (LS), Frances Farr (LS), Wit: Saml O. Gordon, Charner T. Scaife, John Thomas. Proved by the oath of Samuel O. Gordon 2 Dec 1830 before J. Rogers, Q. U. Recorded 2 Dec 1830.

T, 461-462: Raney Belew of Union District for $700 to Robert Walker Junr of same, tract on waters of Buffalow Creek, 147 acres whereon said Raney Belew now lives, adj. John Coomer, Daniel Coomer, John Williams, Dr. Lem B. Askew, near Nazareth Meeting house, 25 Oct 1819. Reaney Belew (X) (LS), Wit: James Rountree, John Walker. Proved by the oath of James Rountree 6 Dec 1830 before J. Rogers, Q. U. Recorded 6 Dec 1830.

T, 462-463: South Carolina, Union District. 30 Aug 1830, Elijah Dotery to Benjamin G. Davis, for $113, 50 acres on waters of Browns Creek adj. Widow Porter, part of tract formerly belonging to Isaiah Johns decd. Elijah Dotery (mark) (LS), Wit: Jas Bell, Reuben Cox J. P., Anderson W. Bell. Georgia, Franklin County. James Morris, clerk of said court, certifies that Reuben Cox was a Justice of the peace for said county, 11 Sept 1830. Elisabeth Dotery (X), wife of Elijah Dotery, relinquished dower in Union District 17 Sept 1830 before J. Rogers, Q. U. Recorded 17 Sept 1830.

T, 463-464: South Carolina, Union District. Drury Harrington and Jepthah Harrington of district aforesaid for $200 to John Jeffries Senr of same, tract on waters of Gilkies Creek, a branch of Broad River, near the school house branch, 103 acres, 8 Nov 1830. Drury Harrington (LS), Jepthah Harrington (LS), Wit: Wm. Gee, James Jeffries, S. Jeffries. Nancy Harrington, wife of Jepthah Harrington, relinquished dower 25 Nov 1830 before Nicholas Corry, J. Q. Proved by the oath of James Jeffries 20 Nov 1830 before Jas Dawkins, J.P. Recorded 3 Jan 1831.

T, 464-465: George Malcomson of Pickens County, Alabama, for $195 to John McKee of Chester District, tract in Union District on both sides of London Bridge Creek adj. John McKee, David Makomsom Johnson & James Makamson, 245 acres, 10 Nov 1830. George Makeomson (G) (LS), Wit: James Service, Thomas Carroll. Proved in Union District by the oath of James Service 17 Nov 1830 before Nicholas Corry, J. Q. Recorded 1 Jan 1831.

T, 465-466: South Carolina, Union District. Elisabeth Woodson of said district for the love, good will & affection to my three children namely Elisabeth, Delila, and James Woodson of said district, 50 acres of land between fairforest & Buffalow creek adj. Aron Harlan, William Rountree, Robert Woodson, Jas Greer, 1 Jan 1831. Elisabeth Woodson (X) (LS), Wit: James Greer, Anna L. Greer. Proved by the oath of Jas Greer 3 Jan 1831 before J. Rogers, Q. U. Recorded 3 Jan 1831.

T, 466-467: John Cherry, Robert Cherry, John P. Sartor, Thos Sartor & Geo W. Sartor, of Union District for $228.53 to Henry Hardy of same, 70 acres on north side of Tygar River adj. Linam, 17 Nov 1829. John Cherry (X), Robt Cherry (LS), John P. Sartor (LS) Thos Sartor (LS), G. W. Sartor (LS), Wit: Jacob Hawkins, Charles McKenzie. Proved by the oath of Charles McKenzie 3 Jan 1831 before E. McGraw, J. Q. Recorded 3 Jan 1831.

T, 467-468: Peter Tucker & John C. Tucker of Union District for $400 to James N. Hardy of same, tract on the waters of Cain Creek between Broad and Tyger River, being a part of two tracts of land originally granted to James Hawkins 1 Aug 1785 and conveyed from John Hawkins to Edward McGraw and from Edward McGraw to Dr. James Meachan & from James Meachan to Peter & John C. Tucker, 18 Oct 1830. Peter Tucker (X) (LS), John C. Tucker (X) (LS), Wit: Charner T. Scaife, James Johnson. Mary Tucker (X), wife of Peter Tucker, relinquished dower 25 Nov 1830 before E. McGraw, J. Q. Proved by the oath of Charner T. Scaife 24 Nov 1830 before E. McGraw, J. Q. Recorded 6 Dec 1830.

T, 468-469: Aquilla Parsons of Union District for $180 to Allen Foster Jr. of same, tract on waters of Johnsons Branch adj. Bevil, 72 acres, 5 Nov 1830. Aquilla Parsons (LS), Wit: John Neighbor, Thomas Nance. Proved by the oath of Thos Nance 6 Dec 1830 before J. Rogers, Q. U. Recorded 6 Dec 1830.

T, 469-470: South Carolina, Union District. Aron McCollum of district aforesaid for $1120 to William Rice, Esqr., of same, 280 acres on both sides of big Sandy run opposite the mouth of Beckhams spring branch, 6 Oct 1830.Aron McCollum (LS), Wit: Patrick Williams, R. H. Spencer. Sarah McCollum relinquished dower 14 Oct 1830 before Daniel White, J. Q. Proved by the oath of R. H. Spencer [no date].

T, 470-471: John Bates, Sheriff of Union District, by virtue of a writ of fieri facias held first Monday in October 1825 at the suit of Nicholas Corry to levy of the goods & chattels, lands and tenements of Abner Patterson $50.70 and

$7.87 costs, tract on McKowns Creek adj. Nicholas Corry, William McKown, Jeremiah Dawson, being part of a tract granted to Manos[?] Dawson, sold for $55 to Nicholas Corry, 6 Nov 1826. J. Bates, S. U. D. (LS), Wit: John Saunders, Benj. G. Davis. Proved by the oath of Benjamin G. Davis 16 Dec 1830 before J. Rogers, Q. U. Recorded 16 Dec 1830.

T, 471-472: South Carolina, Union District. Angus Alexander of district aforesaid for $250 to Elijah Wilbourn of same, 157 acres on branches of Putman Creek, waters of Tyger River, adj. Randolph Alexander, David Bayns, Sion Murphy, 11 Dec 1830. Angus Alexander (LS), Wit: James Gibbs, Geo Gordon. Sarah Alexander (X), wife of Angus Alexander, relinquished dower 28 Dec 1830 before H. Gibbs, Q.U. Proved by the oath of James Gibbs 5 Jan 1831 before Jno Norman, J. Q. Recorded 7 Jan 1831.

T, 472-473: South Carolina, Union District. James Johnson Senr of district aforesaid for $54 to Elijah Wilbourn of same, two small pieces of land on waters of Tyger River, 27 acres adj. James Johnson, Jesse Browning, Elijah Wilbourn, and 10 acres adj. James Johnson, Elijah Wilbourn, R. Alexander, 18 Dec 1830. James Johnson (LS), Wit: John Gibbs, James Johnson Jr. Proved by the oath of John Gibbs 5 Jan 1831 before John Norman, Q.U. Recorded 7 Jan 1831.

T, 472-473: John D. A. Murphy of Orangeburgh District for $50 to Aquilla Powers of Union District, 29 acres (excepting as much as may lay within John Galmans lines which is supposed to be in or about four acres leaving a residue of 25 acres) near Browns Creek adj. Clayborn Pair, Aquilla Powers, John Galman, tract originally surveyed for John Blain 12 Dec 1822 and granted to John D. A. Murphy, 14 April 1830. John D. A. Murphy (LS), Wit: Willis Fowler (X), John H. Galman. Proved in Union District by the oath of John H. Galman 31 Dec 1830 before R. Lipsey, J. P. Recorded 17 Jan 1831.

T, 474-476: State of Tennessee, Laurence County. James Glover of state and county aforesaid appoints Henry Stevens of Union District, SC, lawful attorney general & special to receive from the estate of James Glover, the former estate of Mary Ann Hamilton, 17 May 1830. James Glover (Seal), Wit: Nathan McClendon, J. Peace; George Lucas, J. Peace. Recorded 1 Nov 1830.

State of Tennessee, Lawrence County. Marriage license for James Glover and Mary Ann Hamilton, 20 Dec 1829, M. H. Buchanan, clk. Solemnized Dec 29 1829, Elias Tidwell.

B. Halford, Chairman of the court of pleas and quarter session for Lawrence County, Tennessee, certified that M. H. Buchanan was clerk. M. H. Buchanan, clerk, certificate that Nathan McClendon and George Lucas, were justices of the peace.

James Glover swore that he was over the age of 21 years, 17 May 1830 before Nathan McClendon, J. Peace.

T, 477: Nedom George of Iredell County ,North Carolina, for $100 to Elisabeth W. Farrow of Union District, all the right, title, interest & claims which I have in right of my wife late Sarah Brooks to a certain tract of land on Union District on Sallys branch, a watercourse of Fairforest Creek, 180 acres, part of an original tract of 400 acres granted to Thomas Blasingame, Esqr., in the year 1785, 1 Feb 1830. Needom George (LS), Wit: J. Rogers, Nathan Harlan. Proved by the oath of Nathan Harlan in Union District 1 Feb 1830 before J. Rogers, Q. U. Recorded 7 Jan 1831.

T, 478-479: South Carolina, Union District. Solomon Putman of district aforesaid for $550 to Mrs. Elisabeth Farrow of same, a tract whereon I now live, 148 acres near the road on the land at present owned by Mrs. Farrow, adj. heirs of William Wallace decd, on Sugar Creek adj. Browning, Thomas Woodson, also all the right and title which Harriet Woodson one of the heirs of John Woodson hath or can have to a tract of land adj. the above tract which was purchased by said decd of Joshua Thomas, the interest intended to be conveyed is one fifth part of said tract after deducting the widow's dower, 13½ acres, 22 Oct 1830. Solomon Putman (LS), Wit: H. W. W. Rice, Wm. Rice. Harriott Putman (X), wife of Solomon Putman, relinquished dower 27 Oct 1830 before Hiram Gibbs, J. Q. Proved by the oath of Wm. Rice, Esqr., 7 Jan 1831 before J. Rogers, Q. U.

T, 479-480: South Carolina, Union District. Johnson Coggins, for $111.58 to Jason Boatman, both of said district, part of tract originally granted to Patrick McGarity, on the Bailey Branch near William Baley, Robt Boatman's corner, Elias White, 61 acres adj. on Tyger River adj. Jesse Boatman, and adj. laid out to Ambrose Yarborough adj. Elias White, 27 Dec 1830. Johnson Coggins (LS), Wit: Robt Boatman Jr., Charlotte Jackson. Jane Coggins, wife of Johnson Coggins, relinquished dower 8 Jan 1831 before Hiram Gibbs, J.Q. Proved by the oath of Robt Boatman Jr. 27 Dec 1830 before Fredk Jackson, J.P. Recorded 8 Jan 1831.

T, 480-481: South Carolina, Union District. Johnson Coggins, for $111.58 to Jason Boatman, both of said district, part of tract originally granted to Ambrose Yarborough adj. McGarity, Jesse Boatman, Fred Jackson, William White, 27 Dec 1830. Johnson Coggins (LS), Wit: Robt Boatman Jr., Charlotte Jackson. Jane Coggins, wife of Johnson Coggins, relinquished dower 8 Jan 1831 before Hiram Gibbs, J.Q. Proved by the oath of Robt Boatman Jr. 27 Dec 1830 before Fredk Jackson, J.P. Recorded 8 Jan 1831.

T, 481-482: South Carolina, Union District. William Wilbanks Senr of District of Spartanburgh for $250 to Ambrose Gibbs of Union District, 100 acres on branches of Johns Creek, waters of Enoree River adj. Jabel Putman, Barrum Bobo, Thomas Norman, John Ray, Hosea Holcomb, said Gibbs, 6 March 1811. Wm Wilbanks (LS), Wit: John Ray, Hosea Holcomb. Phebe Wilbanks, wife of William Wilbanks, relinquished dower 16 Nov 1812 before Burwell Bobo, Q.U. Proved by the oath of John Ray 16 Nov 1812 before Burrel Bobo, Q. U. Recorded 8 Jan 1831.

T, 482-483: South Carolina, Union District. Hosea Holcomb of district aforesaid for $90 to Ambrose Gibbs of same, 30 acres, part of tract originally granted to E. Holcomb adj. Ray, 20 Dec 18__. H. Holcomb (LS), Wit: Thos Ray, Wm. Ray. Casse Holcomb, wife of Hosea Holcomb, relinquished dower 10 March 1810 before Thos B. Hunt, Q. U. Proved by the oath of William Ray 5 Jan 1831 before John Norman, Q. U. Recorded 8 Jan 1831.

T, 483-484: South Carolina, Union District. Simpson Alexander for $900 to Ambrose Gibbs, both of district aforesaid, tract on the head branches of Lawsons Creek, waters of Tyger River, on still house branch, adj. Mary Bobo, Frances Bobo, Carry Ray, 229 acres, 3 Dec 1830. Simpson Alexander (LS), Wit: Jason Norman, William Norman. Delila M. Alexander, wife of Simpson Alexander, relinquished dower 11 Dec 1830 before H. Gibbs, Q. U. Proved by the oath of William Norman 5 Jan 1831 before Jno Norman. Recorded 8 Jan 1831.

T, 485-486: Ezekial Hunnicutt and Aimy his late wife late Aimy Boyd of Pendleton District, for $200 to Henry Keesler of Union District, tract of land which John Boyd of Union District lately gave to his grand daughter the said Aimy Hunnicutt, the daughter of David L. Boyd, 113 acres on Brushy Creek, a fork of Tinker Creek, a branch of Tyger River, adj. Ely Cook, John Wilson, part of 215 acres granted to Moses Winder[?] 5 Nov 1786, recorded in Book PPPP, page 174, conveyed by said Welden to Mordecai Spray 3 Aug 1796, conveyed by Mordecai Spray 28 Sept 1807, and by Samuel Spray to the said John Boyd 23 Nov 1807, and by said John Boyd to Aimy Boyd 26 Sept 1809, dated 26 Nov 1830. Ezekiel J. Hunnicutt (LS), Aimy Hunnicutt (mark), Wit: Joseph Grisham, Madison Hunnicutt. Proved in Pendleton District by the oath of Madison Hunnicutt 26 Nov 1830 before Joseph Grisham, Not. Pub & ex off Q. U. Aimy Hunnicutt, wife of Ezekiel Hunnicutt, relinquished dower in Pendleton District 26 Nov 1830 before Joseph Grisham, Not. Pub & ex off Q. U. Recorded 24 Jan 1831.

T, 486-487: State of Alabama, Pickens County. Mary Smith, widow and relict of Abram Smith, formerly of Union District, appoints her brother Joseph Guyton of Union District, lawful attorney to sell tract of land on the waters of Gilkies Creek & Thickety, adj. John Jeffries, 336 acres, willed to me by my deceased husband Abraham Smith, including the brick house and improvements, 16 Sept 1830. Mary Smith (Seal), Wit: W. K. Brown, Alexr Martin. Proved by the oath of W. K. Brown (X) 6 Sept 1830 before James T. Burdine, Justice of the Peace in Pickens County, Alabama. Francis W. Bostick, clerk of the county court of Pickens County, AL certified that James T. Burdine was a J. P., 6 Sept 1830. Charles M. Holland, Judge of the county Court, certified that Francis W. Bostick was the clerk of court, 6 Sept 1830. Recorded 24 Jan 1831.

T, 488: South Carolina, Union District. Joseph Guyton, attorney for Mrs. Mary Smith of Pickens County, Alabama, for $70 annually to be paid during the late of Mrs. Mary Smith, quit claim to John Jeffries Senr, all right, title and interest in a tract of land on both sides of Gilkes Creek and Thickety Creek, 336 acres [see preceding power of attorney], ____ 1830. Joseph Guyton Senr atty for M. Smith (LS), Wit: Aron Willkins, Saml J. Hoey, Noah Pennington. Proved by the oath of Aron Wilkins in Union District 20 Nov 1830 before Jas Dawkins, J.P. Recorded 24 Jan 1831.

T, 489-490: John Anderson, Sheriff of Union District, by virtue of a writ of fieri facias issued out of the court of Chancery held for the district of Union, tested 9 Aug 1830 at the suit of Silas Anderson, executor of the will of Elijah Anderson decd, against William Phillips, to levy of the goods and chattels, lands and tenements of Wm. Phillips, $1235.92 & costs, tract of 374 acres by resurvey made by Thomas Stribling, on waters of Enoree adj. William Selby, Sarah Huson, Mary E. Prewett, on the public road leading to Thomas Henderson's Ferry on Enoree adj. Thomas Clark, Patience Burell, estate of Reuben Flanningan decd, composed of three original grants and sold by Elijah Anderson in his life time to William Phillips and conveyed to said William Phillips by order of the court of chancery, purchased by Thomas Clark of Union District for $465, 21 Jan 1831. John Anderson (LS), Wit: Wm. K. Clowney, J. H. Skelton. Proved by the oath of Wm. K. Clowney 26 Jan 1831 before J. Rogers, Q. U. Recorded 26 Jan 1831.

T, 490: Union District, So Carolina. Spilsby Glenn for $240 to Adam Cooper, all my claim to a tract in Johnston's and Bell's grants, 10 Sept 1830. Spilsby Glenn (LS), Wit: Thos Booker, John S. Sims, J. N. Hardy. Proved by the oath of John S. Sims 25 Jan 1831 before James Meacham, J. Q. Recorded 1 Feb 1831.

T, 491: Ann Foster of Union District for natural love and affection to Sarah J. B. Foster of same, one negro woman named Rachel, one boy named Elo and one bay named John, one bed and furniture, 8 Jan 1831. Ann Foster (LS), Wit: Thomas Clark, Elizabeth M. Clark. Proved by the oath of Thomas Clark 21 Jan 1831. Recorded 31 Jan 1831.

T, 491-492: John Anderson, Sheriff of Union District, by virtue of two writs of fieri facias issued out of the court of common pleas held for the district of Union, tested the first Monday in October 1822 and the first Monday in March 1823 at the several suits of D. W. Blakely & Sheldon Swift to John Bates Esqr., late Sheriff of Union District, to levy of the goods and chattels, lands and tenements of Thomas OKeefe, $204.48, sold three lots in the village of Union on Main Street and Batchelor Street, known by numbers 9, 33, and 35, adj. Judge Johnson, John Oland, sold to John Rogers for $177, 31 Jan 1830. John Anderson (LS), Wit: J. J. Pratt, Samuel Davis. Proved by the oath of J. J. Pratt before Samuel Davis, J. P. Recorded 31 Jan 1831.

T, 493: Joseph and Elizabeth Brown of Chester District for $200 to Hez'k Rice of Union District, all our interest and claim to a tract of land in Union District, Fairforest Creek, 28 Sept 1824. J. Brown, Elizabeth Brown (LS), Wit: Margaret S. K. Foote, D. Julia A. Rice. Proved in Chester District by the oath of Margaret S. K. Foote 38 Sept 1824 before John S. Rice, J. Q. Recoreed 29 Jan 1831.

T, 493: South Carolina, Union District. Jane M. Foote, wife of James Foote, relinquished dower to Hezekiah Rice 20 Oct 1830 before Jno Norman, J. Q. Recorded 29 Jan 1831.

T, 494: State of Tennessee, Giles County. Abel Ezell and Sarah Ezell for $86.66, all our right, title or claim to Isaac Going to a tract in Union District on waters of Browns Creek adj. Wm. Palmer, William Ezell, John Stribling, Robert Harris, David Nicholas, said tract belonging to the estate of John Palmer decd, 9 Aug 1830. Abel Ezell (LS), Sarah Ezell (Seal), Wit: John Porter, Nathaniel Rochester. Proved in Union District by the oath of John Porter 7 Feb 1831 before R. Lipsey, J.P. Recorded 6 Feb 1831.

T, 494-495: Georgia, Walton County. Hezekiah Palmer of County of Walton appoint my son Elijah Palmer of same, my attorney to receive and grant sufficient receipts for any moneys due me as legatee of the estate of John Palmer of Union District, SC, decd, 20 Jan 1831. Hezekiah Palmer (Seal), Wit: Egbert J. Beall, J. J. C. and acknowledged before T. Pittman, J. I. C., 20 Jan 1831. Vincent Haralson, clerk of the inferior court of Walton County. certified that Egbert B. Beall and Timothy Pittman were justices of the inferior court, 20 Jan 1831. Robert M. Echols, a justice of the inferior Court certified that Vincent Haralson was clerk, 20 Jan 1831. Recorded 6 Feb 1831.

T, 495-497: Spencer A. Bobo of Union District for $300 to Edward Stevens of same, tract on which I now live called Shady grove and formerly the property of John Rochell in Union District on waters of Pages Creek, 1000 acres adj. James Mays, Smith, Thomas G. Danner, Spivy's spring branch, Isaac Pearson, Call and Smith, Dodd, Danner, Garret, & Mays, 19 July 1830. Spencer A. Bobo (LS), Wit: Wm. C. Pearson, P. W. Pearson. Louisa A. Bobo, wife of Spencer A. Bobo, relinquished dower 29 Dec 1830 before Jno Norman, J. Q. Proved by the oath of Wm. C. Pearson 31 Dec 1830 before John Norman, J. Q. Recorded 21 Feb 1831.

T, 497-498: Isaac T. Gregory of Union District for $300 to D. A. Mitchell of same, tract on west side of Fair forest, 137 acres, 22 Nov 1830. Isaac T. Gregory (LS), Wit: Thomas Humphries, William M. B. Stribling. Martha Gregory, wife of I. T. Gregory, relinquished dower 30 Nov 1830 before H. Gibbs, Q. U. Proved by the oath of Thomas Humphries 16 Feb 1831 before J. Rogers, Q. U. Plat included by Richard Thomson, D. S., 16 Sept 1830, showing adj. land owners Thompson White, Thomas Hart, Robt Baty, William Gregory, Sanders. Recorded 2 March 1831.

T, 498-500: 7 Sept 1830, Wm. K. Clowney, Esqr., commissioner in equity for Union District at Union Ct. House, and John Rogers, whereas John Gage Junr and others exparte on or about 28 June did exhibit their bill of complaint at the court of equity shewing that James McKibben Esqr., departed this life intestate, seized and possessed of a tract on waters of Browns Creek, 40 acres and that partition remains to be made, said court did decree that the land by sold at public auction, sold for $100 to John Rogers, 50 acres adj. John Rogers, Robert Davis, widow Lucy Kennedy. Wm. K. Clowney C. C. U. D. (Seal), Wit: John K. B. Sims, H. Goudelock. Proved by the oath of H. Goudelock 23 Feb 1831 before Isaac Gregory, J.P. Recorded 2 March 1831.

T, 500-501: D. A. Mitchell, Sheriff of Union District, by virtue of several writs of fieri facias from the court of common pleas held the third Monday in October 1820 at the suit of Austin Wright and Hiram Coleman to levy of the goods & Chattels, lands & tenements of John Hodge $98.17, tract of 143 acres, part of two tracts originally granted to Joab Mitchell on the south side of Pacolett River adj. Thomas Little, Wm. Hodge, sold to John Rogers for $202, 9 July 1822. D. A. Mitchell (LS), Wit: Robt G. H. Farr, George McCrary. Proved by the oath of R. G. H. Farr 19 Feb 1831 before James Rountree, J.P. Recorded 5 March 1831.

T, 501-502: D. A. Mitchell for $550 John Rogers, 160 acres on the road leading from Union to pinckney Vill about one mile from Union Vill, adj. D. A. Mitchell, Federick Eison, John Rogers, Miss Lucy Porter, 10 Jan 1829. D. A. Mitchell (LS), Wit: Wm M. Thomson, John Murphey. Proved by the oath of William M. Thomson 19 Feb 1831 before James Rountree, J.P. Recorded 4 March 1831.

T, 502-503: South Carolina, Union District. John Hart for $15 to Susannah Hart, all of said district, five acres on waters of fair forest, part of tract said Hart sold to Jincy Brandon adj. Thomas Hart, 12 Feb 1831. John Hart (LS), Wit: F. Eison, Amy Hart (X). Proved by the oath of Frederick Ison 14 Feb 1831 before J. Rogers, Q. U. Recorded 14 Feb 1831.

T, 503-504: Shadrick Vessels of Union District for $240 to Hill & Scaife of same, tract whereon I now live on waters of Cain Creek, waters of Tiger River adj. Wm Rice, William Evans, John C. Jeter, George B. Tucker, 75 acres, 18 Dec 1830. Shadrick Vessels (X) (Seal), Wit: T. A. Carlisle, Ephraim Night. Proved by the oath of T. A. Carlisle 12 Feb 1831 before Thos Stribling, Q. U.

T, 504-505: John Anderson, Sheriff of Union District, by virtue of a writ of fieri facias from the court of common pleas held 25 Nov 1825 at the suit of Febian Parham admx. vs Robert W. Sanders commanding me to levy of the goods & chattels, lands & tenements of Robert W. Sanders $31.37, 730 acres on Tiger River adj. James Brandon, sold to William R. Wilborn for $10, 15 Feb 1831. John Anderson, S. U. D. (LS), Wit: W. M. Thomson, John H. Skelton. Proved by the oath of John H. Skelton 16 Feb 1831 before J. Rogers, Q. U. Recorded 16 Feb 1831.

T, 505-506: South Carolina, Union District. Henry Stevens & Elizabeth his wife for $1400 to Nathan Glenn of same, tract of land whereon we now live on the south side of Tiger River, 300½ acres, 5 Oct 1830. Henry Stevens (LS),

Elizabeth Stevens (LS), Wit: Wm. G. Wright, T. A. Glenn. Elizabeth Stevens relinquished dower 29 Nov 1830 before Thomas Stribling, Q.U. Proved by the oath of Wm. G. Wright 23 Dec 1830 before Thomas Stribling, Q.U. Recorded 3 March 1831.

T, 506-507: John Anderson, Sheriff of Union District, pursuant to an order from the court of ordinary signed by John J. Pratt, 15 Nov 1830, at the suit of Mary Boyd & James Pruett to sell a tract of land belonging to the estate of Daniel Prewett decd, 140 acres adj. Henry Stevens, Louis Burell, James Hughey, estate of Wm. Glenn, sold for $70 to Nathan Glenn, 4 March 1831. John Anderson, S. U. D. (LS), Wit: John H. Skelton, B. J. Gregory. Proved by the oath of John H. Skelton 5 March 1831 before Samuel Davis, J.P. Recorded 5 March 1831.

T, 508: John Anderson, Sheriff of Union District, pursuant to an order from the court of ordinary signed by John J. Pratt, 15 Nov 1830, at the suit of Wm. Rountree & wife guardian, to sell a tract belonging to the estate of Giles Brian decd, on Buffalow Creek, 65 acres adj. Ann Harlan, John Anderson, Cary Woodson, Robert A. Claybrooks, Wm. Rice, sold to Robert A. Claybrooks for $265, 19 Feb 1831. John Anderson S. U. D. (LS), Wit: John H. Skelton, Robert Young. Proved by the oath of John H. Skelton 26 Feb 1831 before J. Rogers, Q. U. Recorded 26 Feb 1831.

T, 509: South Carolina, Union District. William Evans of district aforesaid to Solomon Evans, part of tract of 127 acres granted to Benjamin Hawkins 26 July 1774, and conveyed by Isaac Hawkins agent for Benjamin Hawkins to William Evans, conveyed by William Evans to Solomon Evans 7 March 1831 for $300. William Evans (X) (LS), Wit: Zacheriah Johnson, Peter Skain, Saml O. Johnson. Proved by the oath of Samuel O. Johnson 8 March 1831 before Reuben Gilliam, J.P. Recorded 8 March 1831.

END OF DEED BOOK T

V, 1-2: South Carolina, Union District. Indenture tripartite, 1 Jan 1831, Richard Burchett, Elizabeth T. Mitchell, and Elijah Dawkins, whereas a marriage is intended shortly to be had between said Richard & Elizabeth T. and said Elizabeth is seized of a considerable personal estate consisting of negroes Ned, Jack, Eddy, Ellen, Hiram, Kitty, James, Mandavill, Chany, Jesse, Abraham, Celia, and Milly, Rachel, Hannah, Jerry, Simon, Julia and Hilliard, deeded in trust to Elijah Dawkins. Richard Birchett (LS), Elizabeth T. Mitchell (LS), Elijah Dawkins (LS), Wit: R. S. Rice, Agness B. Rice, Frances S. Dawkins. Proved by the oath of Reuben S. Rice 6 March 1831 before J. Rogers. Recorded 7 March 1831.

V, 2-4: Robert Underwood of District of Union for $1400 to William Rice of same, tract whereon I now live, 349 acres, composed of part of three tracts, two of which are described in a deed of conveyance from Isaac Hollingsworth 7 March 1817, and the other by deed by Daniel Hollingsworth 5 Oct 1822, these lands are joining at present owned by land conveyed by Edward Stephens to George Tucker and land conveyed by Shadrack Vessels to Charner Scaife, and by land conveyed by William Evans to John Evans, and said Rice, 5 Jan 1831. Robt Underwood (LS), Wit: R. Sims, William K. Sims. Martha Underwood (X), wife of Robert Underwood relinquished dower 5 Jan 1831 before E. McGraw, Q. U. Proved by the oath of Reuben Sims and William H. Sims 5 Jan 1831 before E. McGraw, J. Q. Recorded 7 March 1831.

V, 5-6: South Carolina, Union District. William Evans of district aforesaid for $175 to John C. Jeter of same, part of a tract granted to different persons, and from Peter Tucker granted to William Evans on waters of Cain Creek adj. John P. Farr (Vessels), on the Ninety Six Road, 150 acres per plat made by Thomas Stribling, D.S., 26 Jan 1831, dated 23 Feb 1831. William Evans (X) (LS), Wit: Saml Gorden, T. A. Carlisle, Solomon Evans. Proved by the oath of Samuel Gorden 26 Feb 1831 before Reuben Gilliam, J.P. Recorded 7 March 1831.

V, 6-9: South Carolina, Union District. Whereas Alexander Glenn of said district in his life time did sell to Spilsby Glenn of same a tract granted to David Hopkins and given to said Alexander Glenn by the said Alexander Glenn's father, and said Alexander Glenn departed this life without having received but a small part of the purchase money for said land and without having executed a deed,and said Alexander Glenn died leaving Nancy Rice wife of Dr. Hezekiah Rice, his soul heir and legatee, now said Hezekiah Rice and wife Nancy of Laurens District for $2000 to Spilsby Glenn, tract granted to David Hopkins, 450 acres adj. Spilsby Glenn, Wm. Glenn, Cooper, Johnson and Meacham, 7 Sept 1830. Hez. Rice (LS), Nancy S. Rice (LS), Wit: Thomas Bishop (X), Thomas Mitchell. Nancy Rice, wife of Hezekiah Rice, relinquished dower 15 Sept 1830 before Jno Norman, J.Q. Proved by the oath of Thos Mitchell 15 Sept 1830 before Jno Norman, J.Q. Recorded 7 March 1831.

V, 9-11: 7 Jan 1830, John McIlwane to John Rogers, whereas said John McIlwane stands indebted to the said John Rogers by his note in the sum of

$329.88, now mortgages for $1, lot in Union Village whereon the said John McIlwane now lives, number 38 on Main Street adj. land No. 37 belonging to John Gage Jr. John McIlwane (LS), Wit: Richd Thomson, John Murphy. Proved by the oath of John Murphy 26 Jan 1830 before Wm Skelton, J.P. Recorded 26 Jan 1830.

V, 11-13: John Anderson, Sheriff of Union District, pursuant to an order from the court of ordinary signed by John J. Pratt, Ordinary, 20 Dec 1830 at the suit of Elias Call, to sell the tract belonging to the estate of John Taylor on the waters of Enoree River, 50 acres adj. Wm Malone, John Jackson, David Spivey, Wm. C. Pearson, sold to Foster Hooker for $75.50, 21 Feb 1831. John Anderson S. U. D., Wit: L. B. Askew, J. Q., John H. Skelton. Proved by the oath of John H. Skelton 11 March 1831 before J. Rogers, Q. U. Recorded 11 March 1831.

V, 13-15: John Anderson, Sheriff of Union District, by virtue of several writs of fieri facias from the court of common pleas, 30 Oct 1826, at the suit of John Boyce admr., to levy of the estate of Allen Malone, to levy the sum of $400 damages and costs, tract of 100 acres on waters of Padgets Creek adj. Alfred Wilborn, John Norman, William Malone, purchased by John Boyce admr., for $50, 31 Feb 1831. John Anderson S. U. D., Wit: John H. Skelton, James Rountree. Proved by the oath of John H. Skelton 11 March 1831 before J. Rogers, Q. U. Recorded 11 March 1831.

V, 15-17: John Anderson, Sheriff of Union District, by virtue of an order from the court of ordinary, signed by John J. Pratt, ordinary, 15 Dec 1830 at the suit of Thomas M. D. Coln to sell a tract belonging to the estate of James Done decd, 153 acres adj. Margaret McDaniel, Edward Mays, purchased by Thomas M. D. Coln for $122, 26 Feb 1831. John Anderson, S. U. D., Wit John H. Skelton, Thomas Bates. Proved by the oath of John H. Skelton 11 March 1831 before J. Rogers, Q. U. Recorded 11 March 1831.

V, 17-19: John Anderson, Sheriff of Union District, by virtue of an order from the court of ordinary, signed by John J. Pratt, ordinary, 15 Dec 1830 at the suit of Thomas M. D. Coln to sell a tract belonging to the estate of James Done decd, 72 acres adj. James Mays, purchased by James Rogers for $115, 26 Feb 1831. John Anderson, S. U. D., Wit John H. Skelton, Thomas Bates. Proved by the oath of John H. Skelton 11 March 1831 before J. Rogers, Q. U. Recorded 11 March 1831.

V, 19-21: South Carolina, Union District. Wm. Adams of York District for $1355 to Richard Thomson of Spartanburgh District, tract of land adj. John Corethers, 209 acres at Henry Goods old corner, 59 acres originally to Richard Winn, part of a tract, 4 Nov 1830. Wm. Adams (LS), Wit: Saml Davidson, J. Madison Thomson. Proved in Union District by the oath of J. Madison Thomson 6 Nov 1830 before J. Carothers, Q. U. Recorded 15 March 1831.

V, 21-22: South Carolina, Union District. Drury Harrington of district aforesaid for $70 to Joseph Guyton of same, 45 acres on Rocky branch, waters of Abitons Creek, 3 Dec 1830. Drury Harrington (LS), Wit: A. P. Guyton, John L. Guyton. Proved by the oath of Abraham P. Guyton 3 Dec 1830 before Jas Dawkins, J. P. Recorded 18 March 831.

V, 23-24: South Carolina, Union District. John McCulloch and wife Agness of said district for $500 to Hannah McCulloch of same, and the heirs of Wm McCulloch decd, all that tract where on they now live on waters of Gilkeys Creek, 4 Sept 1830. John McCulloch (LS), Agnes McCulloch (X) (LS), Wit:W. C. Brown, J. B. Goudelock. Proved by the oath of William C. Brown 1 Jan 1831 before J. Carothers, Q. U. Agnes McCulloch, wife of John McCulloch, relinquished dower 12 March 1831 before J. Carothers, Q. U. Recorded 17 March 1831.

V, 25-26: South Carolina, Union District. Daniel Mabry for $250 to Edward J. Cotter of said district, 71 acres on the waters of Thickety Creek on the south side of said Creek, being part of a tract that formerly belonged to Zechariah Mabry decd, and by a division of the same fell to said Danl Mabry, one of his lawful heirs, adj. Edward J. Cotter, 23 Sept 1830. Daniel Mabry (LS), Wit: Wm. H. Steen, Z. Massey. Proved by the oath of W. H. Steen 15 March 1831 before J. P. Thomson, Q. U. Recorded 15 March 1831.

V, 26-28: South Carolina, Union District. Herod Gibson of district aforesaid for $115 to Absolem Ward of same, 92½ acres adj. Benjamin Culp, on the NE side of the Union Road [not dated], Herod Gibson (X) (LS), Wit: Abner McCollum, Aaron McCollum. Proved by the oath of Aaron McCollum 12 March 1831 before Daniel White, Q. U. Martha Gibson (X), wife of Herod Gibson, relinquished dower 12 March 1831 before Daniel White, Q. U. Recorded 15 March 1831.

V, 28-30: South Carolina, Union District. Allen Foster of the district aforesaid for $275 to Charles Gantt, 150 acres near the head of the bush branch on the Spartanburg Road adj. J. B. Going, Lucy Farr, near said Farr's spring, Haney, 19 Nov 1830. Allen Foster (LS), Wit: Wm. B. Hames, Edmund Hames Jr. Proved by the oath of Edmund Hames 19 Nov 1830 before Isaac Going, Q. U. Sarah Foster, wife of Allen Foster, relinquished dower 19 Nov 1830 before Isaac Going, Q. U. Recorded 22 March 1831.

V, 30-32: South Carolina, Union District. Edward Cotter for $800 to William D. Corry, tract on waters of Thickety Creek on the south side of said creek, being left by will to John V. Cotter and conveyed by him to William H. Cotter, the ballance being a part of William H. Cotter's part of the estate, adj. William Baley Junr, William Sisson, R. Lusk, 175 acres, 3 Nov 1830. E. J. Cotter (LS), Wit: A. Lancaster, Davis Goudelock. Proved by the oath of Davis Goudelock 22 March 1831 before J. Carothers, Q. U. Clarinda G. Cotter, wife of E. J. Cotter, relinquished dower 22 March 1831 before J. Carothers, Q. U. Recorded 25 March 1831.

V, 32-33: Peter P. Taylor of Union District for $45.25 to Joseph H. Dogan of same, all my interest in a tract about two miles east of Union Court House on the main road leading to Pinkney adj. Becknell, Kennedy, Miss Porter, being my half of said tract, 40 acres conveyed to myself and M. Keenan by Thomas Davis, 29 Feb 1828. P. P. Taylor (LS), Wit: Robert H. Spencer, Silas Baker. Proved by the oath of Robert H. Spencer 26 March 1831 before J. Rogers, Q. U. Elizabeth Taylor (X), wife of Peter P. Taylor, relinquished dower 1 June 1831 before J. Rogers, Q. U. Recorded 30 March 1831.

V, 34-35: John Anderson, Sheriff of Union District, by virtue of a writ of fieri facias from the court of common pleas tested 30 March 1829 at the suit of Brans & Birdsey to levy of the lands & tenements of Levi Stokes $321.43, sells 181 acres on waters of Tiger & Fairforest adj. C. B. A. Rice, Robt Lain, Jesse Fincher, Rachael Stokes, 100 acres of said land known by the name of Stedum tract and 81 acres of the same lying between said Stedum tract and Rachel Stokes' land, sold to Robert Stokes for $103, 22 March 1821. John Anderson S. U. D. (LS), Wit: John H. Skelton, P. M. Huson. Proved by the oath of John H. Skelton 22 March 1831 before Wm. Skelton, J.P.

V, 36: South Carolina, Union District. Sarah Savage of district aforesaid for natural love and affection to my daughter Margaret McJunkin, wife of Abram McJunkin, one negro boy named Sam, 11 Jan 1826. Sarah Savage (X) (LS), Wit: Robt G. H. Farr. Proved by the oath of Robt G. H. Farr 18 March 1831 before J. T. McJunkin, J.P. Recorded 18 March 1831.

V, 37-38: South Carolina, Union District. Alfred Guilkey of said district for $500 to Isaac Peeler of same, 100 acres adj. Corry, and adj. to 100 acres on which I live, by survey made by J. Camp D. S., 17 July 1830... deed dated 4 Nov 1830. Alford Gilkey (LS), Wit: Lawson Adams, Manos D. Coyle. Proved by the oath of Manos D. Coyle 29 Jan 1831 before Jas Dawkins, J.P. Milley Gilkie (X), wife of Alford Gilkie, relinquished dower 5 Nov 1830 before Nicholas Corry, Q. U. Recorded 15 March 1831.

V, 38-40: South Carolina, Union District. Whereas Samuel Gilkie by his will did bequeath the land where on he resided at the time of his death to his wife Elizabeth during her natural life and at her death to be divided between his sons William and Alford, which said land was situated on Guilkies Creek the part up the creek was to go to Wm and the part down the creek as to go to Alford, now Alford Gilkie for and in consideration of several covenants have sold all right and title to 100 acres coming at the death of my mother to Isaac Peeler, one undivided tenth part to James Peeler, one undivided tenth part to my sisters Nancy, Rebecca, Elizabeth & Jane Gilkie, the remaining undivided eight tenths of said 100 acres on which my mother now lives, adj. Henry Tate, William Philips, 4 Oct 1830. Alfred Gilkie (LS), Wit: Jas. Philips, William Philips (X). Milley Gilkie (X), wife of Alford Gilkie, relinquished dower 5 Nov 1830 before Nicholas Corry, Q. U. Proved by the oath of Jas Phillips before Jas Dawkins, J. P., 5 Feb 1831. Recorded 15 March 1831.

V, 40-42: South Carolina, Union District. South Carolina, Union District. Whereas my husband Samuel Gilkie by his will did bequeath a tract of land on Gilkies Creek, waters of Broad River, 200 acres, on which at the time of his death his family resided and on which I now reside unto me during my life and at my death to be divided between his two sons William and Alfred, and whereas William his son is now dead without issue, I, Elizabeth Gilkie, widow of Samuel Gilkie, in consideration of a deed made by Alford Gilkie of his share of his father's land willed as before said in part to him at my death and in part to Isaac & James Peeler and the balance to my daughters Nancy, Elizabeth, Rebecca, and Jane Gilkie, I do sell my life estate in 100 acres willed by Samuel Gilkie to my son William Gilkie now decd at my death, and one tenth part which I may be intitled to as heir at law to my son William Gilkie decd, surveyed made by J. Camp D. S. 17 July 1830, dated 4 Oct 1830. Elizabeth Gilkie (X) (LS), Wit: James Philips, William Philips (X). Proved by the oath of James Phillips before Jas Dawkins, J. P., 5 Feb 1831. Recorded 15 March 1831.

V, 42-44: John Saunders of Union District for good will towards the inhabitants that lives in the fork between Tyger River and Fair Forest, to James Steen, William Gregory, Thompson White, and Jason Greer, all of the district aforesaid, a tract of land on Caleb Greer's still house branch, for the purpose of building a school house for the tuition of children, 20 Jan 1831. John Saunders (LS), Wit: Caleb Greer, Jesse Greer, R. H. Hughes. Proved by the oath of Caleb Greer 8 Feb 1831 before Jno Norman, Q. U. Recorded 2 April 1831.

V, 44-45: South Carolina, Union District. Samuel Martin for $33 to Christopher Young, both of said district, part of the land lately conveyed from John Anderson to the said Martin adj. Docr. Christopher Young, said C. Young, on the east side of the road running by Sardis Meeting House, 8¼ acres, 10 Dec 1830. Samuel L. Martin (LS), Wit: John Joiner, C. T. Murphey. Proved by the oath of John Joiner 4 April 1831 before J. Rogers, Q. U. Recorded 4 April 1831.

V, 45-46: James Rogers of Union District for $1080 to James Means of same, 6 3/4 acres in Union District adj. John Parks, Jas Means, 10 March 1831. James Rogers (LS), Wit: J. Rogers, Green Woodson. Proved by the oath of Green Woodson 4 April 1831 before J. Rogers, Q. U. Recorded 4 April 1831.

V, 47-48: John Anderson, Sheriff of Union District, by virtue of several writs of fieri facias from the court of common pleas tested 23 Oct 1830 at the suit of Wm. M. Thomson & others to levy of the goods and chattels, lands and tenements of John Hughy $128.25, sells tract of 96 acres on Padgets Creek adj. William Fant, Aaron Fincher,, purchased by William Fant for $125, 21 March 1831. John Anderson S. U. D. (LS), Wit: John H. Skelton, Aquilla Powers. Proved by the oath of Aquilla Powers 21 March 1831 before Isaac Going, Q. U. Recorded 21 March 1831.

V, 49: Mr. Bartholomew Johnston. Sir please make to Mr. John Rogers titles to the lots I purchased at Sheriff sale sold as the property of John McCool decd being No. 27, 39, 53, 54, 67, 68, 81 and 82 at the suit of Margaret Monroe admx on his paying you my bid, April 54, 1831. John Anderson (LS), Test: P. P. Taylor, Daniel White.

V, 49-51: Bartholomew Johnston, Sheriff of Union District, by virtue of a writ of fieri facias from the court of common pleas held for Union District 30 Aug 1830 at the suit of Margaret Monroe admx. of the estate of Henry Lanchester decd, to levy of the goods and chattles, lands and tenements of John McCool, $167.23, sells eight lots in Union village whereon John Rogers now lives, Nos. 37,39, on the north side of the main street and Farr street, adj. L. B. Askew, Dr. E. M. Bobo, and six lots on the south side of main street, 53, 64, 67, 68, 81 and 82, adj. Col. Z. P. Herndon, sold for $1 to John Rogers, 4 April 1831. Bartholomew Johnson S. U. D. (LS), Wit: P. P. Taylor, Wm. M. Thomson. Proved by the oath of Wm. M. Thomson 4 april 1831 before Daniel White, Q. U.

V, 51-53: Bartholomew Johnson, Sheriff of union District, by virtue of a writ of fieri facias from the court of common pleas held 6 April 1827 at the suit of Wm Rice, Ordinary, to levy of the goods & chattels, lands and tenements of Sheldon Swift $2026.29, sells tract of 200 acres near Union Village adj. Cary Woodson, Daniel A. Mitchell, John Gage Sr., sold to John Gage Sr for $5.25, 4 April 1831. Bartholomew Johnson S. U. D. (LS), Wit: J. H. Skelton, William Abanathy. Proved by the oath of John H. Skelton 6 April 1831 before J. Rogers, Q. U.

V, 53-54: South Carolina, Union District. Christopher Young Jr. for $35 to Christopher Young Sr, both of said district, part of tract conveyed to said C. Young Jr. by John Anderson, adj. Joseph Tomberlind, said C. Young, Capt. Samuel Martin, 3 acres, 1 April 1831. Christopher Young Jr (LS), Wit: George Spencer, John Joiner. Proved by the oath of John Joiner 4 April 1831 before J. Rogers, Q. U. Recorded 4 April 1831.

V, 54-55: South Carolina, Union District. Christopher Degraffenreid of said district for valuable considerations to Spilsby Glenn on or about the latter end of 1812 a tract of 50 acres on Adam Skain's branch where Thomas Miles' line crosses said spring branch, to lower Fishdam Creek, adj. Magness Simonson, Wm. Farr, 9 March 1831. Christopher Degraffenreid (LS), Wit: Thomas Bowker, Daniel R. Thomas, B. G. Thomas. Proved by the oath of Daniel R. Thomas 19 March 1831 before John Giles, Q. U. Recorded 19 March 1831.

V, 56-57: South Carolina, Union District. Absolem Baley & Nancy his wife for $25 to Isaac J. Foster, tract whereon we now live, pat of the undivided land of John & Mary Cole decd and also part of 100 acres deed to said Nancy Baley by Mary & John Cole, supposed to be about 7 acres near s'd Isaac's old store house, George Garner, I. J. Foster, on the north bank of Redy branch, 23 Oct 1826. Absolem Bailey (X) (LS), Nancy Baily (X) (LS), Wit: Pattsey C.

Bailey, Joshua Foster. Proved by the oath of Joshua Foster 25 Oct 1826 before Isaac Going. Q. U. Nancy Bailey (X), wife of Absolem Bailey, relinquished dower 28 Oct 1826 before Isaac Going, Q. U. Recorded 14 March 1831.

V, 57-59: South Carolina, Union District. Anguis Alexander of district aforesaid for $500 to Littleton B. Clark of Union District, 200 acres, part of which as granted to John McGarity, which 200 acres now conveyed is on the south side of Tiger River adj. Jeremiah Murphey, Mark Murphey, on the road leading to Putman's old Mill, adj. James Putman now Steed's line, 21 Dec 1830. Angus Alexander (LS), Wit: William Norman, Robert Ray. Proved by the oath of William Norman 21 Dec 1830 before Fred'k Jackson. Sarah Alexander (X), wife of Angus Alexander, relinquished dower 1 Jan 1831 before Jno Norman, Q.U. Recorded 7 April 1831.

V, 59-61: John T. Murrell of Union District for $550 to Cary Woodson, tract on Buffalow Creek, a watercourse of Fairforest containing by a late survey (made by William White, Esqr.) 275 acres at Bearden's fence, Rice's field, 20 Oct 1830. John T. Murrell (LS), Wit: Wm. M. Thomson, H. W. Foote. Sarah Murrell, wife of John T. Murrell, relinquished dower 20 Oct 1830. Proved by the oath of H. W. Foote 4 April 1831. Recorded 4 April 1831.

V, 62-64: Bird M. Pearson of Union District for $3500 to Dr. Hezekiah Rice of Laurens District, to said Hezekiah by virtue of the power and authority of my being administrator with the will annexed to Isaac Pearson decd, tract on Padget's Creek in Union District adj. Wm. H. Gist, Independence Pearson, Mays, Edward Stevens, 677 acres, 11 March 1831. Bird M. Pearson (LS), Wit: Wm. C. Pearson, Jesse Briggs. Proved by the oath of Jesse Briggs 11 March 1831 before B. M. Pearson, Q. U. Ex off. Recorded 22 March 1831. Plat included surveyed 12 Feb 1831 by Richd Thomson, D. S. P. W. Pearson, ___ Pearson, Ch. C. Recorded same day.

V, 65: Commission from James Hamilton, Junr Esqr., Governor of SC, to Bartholomew Johnson, sheriff of Union District for four years from 1 April 1831, dated 3 Feb 1831. John Giles Jr. and John Rogers, both justices of the quorum, certified that Maj'r Bartholomew Johnson took the oath of office, 2 April 1831.

V, 66-67: Commission from James Hamilton, Junr Esqr., Governor of SC, to John Rogers, Esqr, clerk of court of general sessions and common pleas for Union District for four years from the 2nd Monday in February instant, dated 3 Feb 1831. Daniel White and John Giles, both justices of the quorum, certified that John Rogers took the oath of office for clerk of court of general sessions and common pleas and register of mesne conveyance and also for the drawing or balloting or empanneling of jurors, 25 February 1831.

V, 67-69: Zadock Hooker of Union District is indebted to Edward M. Bobo in the sum of $10,00 by bond, 14 March 1831, mortgage of one negro girl Hagar about 17 years of age, one negro boy Dick about 20 years of age, one negro boy Jim about 16 years of age, one sorrel horse and two bay horses, one bay mare mule, 22 head of cattle, 20 head of hogs, Z. Hooker (LS), Wit: Thomas N. Dawkins, E. M. Glenn. Proved by the oath of Edward M. Glenn 14 March 1831 before J. Rogers, Q. U.

V, 69-71: John Anderson, Sheriff of Union District, by virtue of several writs of fieri facias from the court of common pleas held 30 April 1829, also 22 Jan 1830, at the suit of Bird M. Pearson to levy of the goods and chattels, lands & tenements of Edward Morgan $75.72, sell tract of 97 acres on the Wild Cat Branch, waters of Enoree adj. Solomon Bobo Jr., James Alexander, Wm. J. Bobo, Hozea Ray, being the land whereon the said Edward Morgan now lives, purchased by John Rogers for $16, 22 Feb 1831. John Anderson S. U. D. (LS), Wit: Isaac Whitten, Ledford Rogers. Proved by the oath of Isaac Whitton 24 Feb 1831 before B. M. Pearson, Q. U. Ex. off. Recorded 24 Feb 1831.

V, 71-73: Charles M. Murphy of Union District for $600 to William K. Clowney of same, 257 acres on both sides of Beverdam Creek, conveyed by deed by Samuel Clowney to said Charles M. Murphy, 16 April 1831. Charles M. Murphy (LS), Wit: John Gage Jr., John Murphy. Proved by the oath of John Murphy 18 April 1831 before J. Rogers, Q. U. Recorded 18 April 1831. Plat surveyed 4 Nov 1820 by Rich'd Thomson, D. S., showing adj. land owners John White, Saml Clowney, Capt. Mays.

V, 74: William Jackson and Ann Jackson my wife sign over to Ruthy Jackson, all right or title that we have to a tract of land of 50 acres that belonged to James Jackson decd, 11 June 1825. William Jackson (X), Ann Jackson (X), Wit: James Orr, Zacheriah Reevs.

V, 74-75: Ruth Jackson of Union District for $50 to William K. Clowney of same, tract of 50 acres, part of tract granted to William Pool & conveyed by him to John McKee and by John McKee to James Jackson and by parol will of said James Jackson bequeathed to his daughter Ruth Jackson, on the waters of fair forest adj. Danl Huger, John McKee, Harod Gibson, 24 Oct 1828. Ruth Jackson (X) (LS), Wit: Thomas N. Dawkins, John Murphy. Proved by the oath of Thomas N. Dawkins, 18 April 1831 before J. Rogers, Q. U. Recorded 18 April 1831.

V, 76-77: South Carolina, Union District. John Mabry of district aforesaid for $1400 to Thomas N. Dawkins, tract on south side of Packolet River in Union District adj. Giles Smith, Caroline Farnandis, Samuel Hodges, 17 Jan 1831. John Mabry (LS), Wit: Joshua P. Dawkins, Nancy H. Dawkins. Proved by the oath of Joshua P. Dawkins 5 Feb 1831 before Samuel Mosley, Q. U. Sarah Mabry, wife of John Mabry, relinquished dower 5 Feb 1831 before Samuel Mosley, Q. U. Recorded 25 April 1831.

V, 78-79: James Glenn of Union District for $1000 to James Hill of same, tract whereon I now live on branches of Cain Creek, waters of Tyger River, which I purchased of Titus G. Farr 26 Dec 1828 and for which I have a grant 2

March 1827, per plat made by Richard Thomson 26 Nov 1828, 364½ acres, dated 4 March 1831. James Glenn (LS), Wit: Charner T. Scaife, J. B. Glenn, J. F. Glenn. Proved by the oath of Charner T. Scaife 4 March 1831 before E. McGraw, Q. U. Recorded 28 April 1831.

V, 79-81: Plat of 23 acres showing adj. land owners J. P. Farr, James Hill.

John P. Farr of Union District for $115 to James Hill of same, 23 acres, part of the land which by succession of title has been conveyed to Hobson who has conveyed to Presley Williams and by said Presley Williams to said John P. Farr on west side of Cain Creek, waters of Tiger River, 23 Feb 1831. J. P. Farr (LS), Wit: George Douglass, C. T. Scaife, T. A. Carlisle. Proved by the oath of Charner T. Scaife 4 March 1831 before E. McGraw, Q. U. Mary Farr, wife of John P. Farr, relinquished dower 12 April 1831 before E. McGraw, Q. U. Recorded 28 April 1831.

V, 81-83: William B. Farr of Union District for $600 to James Hill of same, tract on branches of lower Fishdam Creek and on both sides of Pinckney Road, part of a larger tract of 640 acres granted to William Farr 15 Oct 1784, and the same fell to me at a division of the estate of said William Farr, according to a survey made by Richard Thomson 17 Nov 1829, 126 acres, 11 March 1831. W. B. Farr (Seal), Wit: Charner T. Scaife, John Smith J., Edward A. Jackson. Proved by the oath of Charner T. Scaife 12 March 1831 before T. A. Glenn, J.P. Recorded 28 April 1831. Plat included shows adj. land owners Spilsby Glenn, James Hill, Thomas Bowker, John Evans; Allen & James Morgain, Chn Carriers.

V, 83-85: Gerred Gregory of Union District for $600 to Joseph Tate of same, tract in Union District on waters of Browns Creek, 227 acres adj. Isaac Gregory, Jeremiah Gregory, Jeter, James Man, Allen Gregory, Rody Gregory, 30 Oct 1829. Gerard Gregory (LS), Wit: Levy Gregory, J. T. McJunkin, Geo W. McJunkin. Proved by the oath of Levy Gregory 24 Nov 1829 before E. McGraw, Q. U. Margaret Gregory, wife of Gerard Gregory, relinquished dower 24 Nov 1829 before E. McGraw, Q. U. Recorded 2 May 1831.

V, 85-87: William Bevill of Union District for $130 to Jane Bevill and Greenberry Tracy (trustee) of same, tract of 30 acres on both sides of Johnsons branch of Browns Creek, waters of Broad River, adj. Clayborn Pace[?], 22 March 1831. W. A. H. Bevill (LS), Wit: M. M. Jackson, Eli L. Mitchell. Proved by the oath of Mark M. Jackson 30 April 1831 before J. Rogers, Q. U. Recorded 30 April 1831.

V, 87-88: Nicholas Corry of Union District for $1000 to James Corry of same, tract on both sides of Thickety Creek, waters of Broad River, 335 acres, 29 April 1831. Nicholas Corry (LS), Wit: Wm. Corry, Wm. Jefferies. Proved by the oath of William Jefferies 30 April 1831 before S. A. Goodman, Q. U. Recorded 2 May 1831.

V, 88-89: Nicholas Corry of Union District for $500 to James Corry of same, tract on both sides of Abbotts Creek, waters of Broad River, 479 acres, 29 April 1831. Proved by the oath of William Jefferies 30 April 1831 before S. A. Goodman, Q. U. Recorded 2 May 1831.

V, 90-91: South Carolina, Union District. Christian Frederic Cromer of Union District for natural love and affection to my son Adam Cromer of same, tract on Swift run Creek, 105 acres adj. Cromer, Thomas Burnes, 1 April 1831. Christen Cromer (X) (Seal), Wit: John D. Word, Simon Cromer. Proved by the oath of John D. Word 2 April 1831 before J. T. McJunkin, J.P. Recorded 30 April 1831.

V, 91-93: South Carolina, Union District. Allen Foster of district aforesaid for $700 to W. W. E. Moreland of same, tract on waters of Packolet River adj. Isaac Going, Charles Gault, on Spartanburg road, Lucy Farr's line, Briggs; line, Mark Wood's line, Joseph McKissick's line, T. B. Going, 27 Nov 1830. Allen Foster (LS), Wit: G. S. Nevell, Orman Moreland. Sarah Foster, wife of Allen Foster, relinquished dower 1 Dec 1830 before Daniel White, Q. U. Proved by the oath of Orman Moreland 16 March 1831 before Isaac Going, Q. U. Recorded 30 April 1831.

V, 93-94: South Carolina, Union District. Whereas a marriage is intended to be solemnized between Joshua Palmer and Rhody Porter and said Joshua Palmer is possessed of a considerable estate of land and negroes and said Rhody Porter having considerable estate of personal property, the property of the said Joshua Palmer is to go to the heirs of said Joshua at his death provided he out lives his intended wife Rhody Porter, except 100 acres of land and one negro woman Milly which my wife is to have & to hold her natural life and at the death of my wife Rhoda is to go to the heirs of said Joshua, but in the meantime my intended wife to hold the said 100 acres and negro woman Milly from all suits or debts, and the estate of Rhoda Porter to go to her heirs, the said 100 acres on the waters of Packolet and Broad River, the plantation where the said Joshua now lives adj. Daniel McMahan, Wm. W. Moreland, James Bailey, Cunningham's corner, 6 Dec 1830. Joshua Palmer (LS), Rhoda Porter (X) (LS), Wit: Isaac Going, John M. Going. Proved by the oath of Isaac Going 2 May 1831 before Daniel White, Q. U. Recorded 2 May 1831.

V, 95-96: South Carolina, Union District. William J. Hays of district aforesaid for $700 to Charles M. Murphy & John Murphy of same, tract on both sides of McLures Creek, waters of Fair Forest, 36 acres adj. land formerly of Benjamin Evans, originally granted to Charles Goodwin, adj. Haselwood, said Hayes, 26 May 1831. Wm. J. Hayes (Seal), Wit: Wm. K. Clowney, H. H. Means. Ester Hays (X), wife of William J. Hays, relinquished dower 27 May 1831 before J. P. Thompson, Q.U. Proved by the oath of Col. Wm. K. Clowney 30 May 1831 before J. Rogers, Q. U. Recorded 30 May 1831.

V, 97-98: South Carolina, Union District. Tilman Bobo of district aforesaid for $236 to John Taylor, 118 acres conveyed to me by Barham Bobo, it being land originally belonging to the estate of John F. Grimkie, adj. B. Bobo, Solomon Bobo, Lewis Bobo, Julius Howell, 8 Nov 1830. Tilman Bobo (LS), Wit: J. Devine, Saml Henderson. Proved by the oath of Saml Henderson 31 April 1831 before J. Rogers, Q. U. Recorded 30 April 1831. Plat included.

V, 98-100: Aron McCollum & Jesse McCollum of Union District for $492 to Thomas Hyatt, 164 acres originally granted to Daniel Huger adj. Belue, 15 Oct 1830. Aron McCollum (LS), Jesse McCollum (LS), Wit: Charner T. Scaife, S. McCollum. Sarah McCollum, wife of Aron McCollum, and Anney McCollum (X), wife of Jesse McCollum, relinquished dower 31 Dec 1830 before Danl White, Q. U. Proved by the oath of Stephen McCollum 31 Dec 1830 before Danl White, Q. U. Recorded 13 May 1831.

V, 100: South Carolina, Union District. John C. Voluntine with the consent of Charles Stewart, a free man, consents to become the guardian of said Charles whom he certifies to be of good character and correct habits, 28 Dec 1830 before J. Rogers, Clk. Recorded 28 Dec 1830.

V, 100-102: South Carolina, Union District. 20 Oct 1830, John Jackson of district aforesaid for $85 to Joseph Goswick of same, tract on a branch of Hill Creek, waters of Enoree River adj. said Joseph Goswick Senr, Isaac Pearson [?], originally granted to Walter Roberts, 30 acres. John Jackson (mark), Wit: Jesse Briggs, Elijah Wilbourn (X). Damaris Jackson, wife of John Jackson, relinquished dower 26 Jan 1831, before Jno Norman, J. P. Proved by the oath of Elijah Wilbourn 27 Jan 1831 before Jno Norman, J. P. Recorded 30 April 1831.

V, 102-103: South Carolina, Union District. Daniel A. Mitchell of Union District for $30 to Nancy Brown of same, 30 acres near Union Court House adj. land of Jacob Paulk, John Gage Sr, formerly belonging to Miles Hart, 6 April 1830. D.A. Mitchell (LS), Wit: Saml Brooks, Charles Gowing. Proved by the oath of Charles Gowing 18 June 1831 before J. Rogers, Q. U. Recorded 1 June 1831.

V, 103-104: South Carolina, Union District. Joseph H. Dogan of district aforesaid for $100 to E. M. Bobo of same, tract of land [acreage not stated], 26 March 1831. Joseph H. Dogan (LS), Wit: John H. Skelton, Isaac Whitton. Sarah Ann Dogan, wife of Dr. Joseph H. Dogan, relinquished dower 1 June 1831 before J. Rogers, Q. U. Proved by the oath of Isaac Whitton 1 June 1831 before J. Rogers, Q. U. Recorded 1 June 1831.

V, 105-106: John Anderson, Sheriff of Union District, by virtue of a writ of fieri facias from the court of common pleas held 14 May 1829, at the suit of A. Park to levy of the goods & chattels, lands and tenements of Jasper Tomberlin decd, $34, sells tract of 50 acres on waters of Mill Creek adj. Joseph, Nancy Little & Warmac Fowler, sold to Ailsey Tomberlin for $12, 20

March 1831. John Anderson, S.U.D. (LS), Wit: John H. Skelton, Saml Davis. Proved by the oath of Saml Davis 14 May 1831 before J. Rogers, Q. U. Recorded 14 May 1831.

V, 106-107: Samuel Leitch of Union District for $400 to John Murphy of same, tract originally granted to Charles Goodwin Esqr., 4 June 1787, about 413 acres on both sides of McClures Creek, a branch of Fairforest, at the time of the original grant adj. Joseph Park, Thomas Hazelwood, Saml Patton, 26 May 1831. S. Leitch (LS), Wit: D. A. Mitchell, Moses L. White. Proved by the oath of D. A. Mitchell 3 June 1831 before J. Rogers, Q. U. Recorded 3 June 1831.

V, 108-109: John Murphy of Union District for $300 to Saml Leitch, William B. Means, Henry Harvey Means, Abraham McCarther & William H. Clowney, all of Union District, tract originally granted to Charles Goodwin Esqr., 4 June 1787, about 413 acres on both sides of McClures Creek, a branch of Fairforest,at the time of the original grant adj. Joseph Park, Thomas Hazelwood, Saml Patton, 26 May 1831. John Murphy (LS), Wit: D. A. Mitchell, M. L. White. Proved by the oath of D. A. Mitchell 3 June 1831 before J. Rogers, Q. U. Recorded 3 June 1831.

V, 109-110: South Carolina, Union District. James Donaldson of district aforesaid bound in the sum of $430 to make good titles to 235 acres at the payment of the last note of $220 due 25 Dec 1828 to William Cowan, dated 10 Dec 1824. Jas. Donaldson, Wit: Jas Herman, Jas Cowan. Proved by the oath of Jas. Harman 6 June 1831 before J. Rogers, Q. U. Recorded 6 June 1831.

V, 110: South Carolina, Union District. For $100 I have sold to James S. McWhirter a certain negro girl named Cassada about three years old, 2 April 1831. Jas McWhorter (X) (LS), Wit: Reuben Cloeman, J. P., Robert McWhirter. Proved by the oath of Reuben Coleman Esqr., 6 June 1831. Recorded 6 June 1831.

V, 111-112: South Carolina, Union District. William West of district aforesaid to William B. Means, Henry Harvey Means, Saml Leitch, Abram McCarther and Wm. K. Clowney of district aforesaid, tract in Union District on the waters of McClures Creek adj. Lancaster, Hazelwood, estate of David Lewis decd, lands granted to Charles Goodwin, Larkin Lancaster, Sephenia Posey, 200 acres, 7 June 1831. Wm West (LS), Wm. B. Means (LS), H. H. Means (LS), S. Leitch (LS), Abram McCarthur (LS), Wm. K. Clowney (LS),Wit: Wm. J.Hayes, Benj. W. Arrawood. Proved by the oath of Benjamin W. Arrowood 8 June 1831 before J. Rogers, Q. U. Recorded 8 June 1831.

V, 113-114: South Carolina, Union District. Chamberlain L. Goodwin of District of Edgefield for $400 to Samuel Leitch of Union District, tract originally granted to Charles Goodwin Esquire, 4 June 1787, about 413 acres at the time of the grant in what was then called Ninety Six District, between Broad & Saluda Rivers on both sides of McClures Creek, a branch of

Fairforest, adj. land granted to Joseph Park, Thomas Hazelwood, Saml Patton, 7 April 1831. Chamberlain L. Goodwin (LS), Wit: J. Terry, Wm. Frazier. The wife of Chamberlain L. Goodwin relinquished dower 7 April 1831, in Edgefield District, signed E. Goodwin, before J. Terry, Q. U. Ex off. Proved in Edgefield District by the oath of James Terry 1 June 1831 before J. Richardson. C. C. P. Recorded 8 June 1831.

V, 115-116: South Carolina, Union District. John McKown of district aforesaid for $152.62½ to Samuel Lowrie of same, tract on waters of Gilkies Creek adj. C. D. Laurence, 120 acres, 28 March 1831. J. McKown (LS), Wit: C. D. Lawrence, William Mullinax. Proved by the oath of William Mullinax 5 June 1831 before Jas Dawkins, J.P. Recorded 6 June 1831.

V, 116-117: South Carolina, Union District. D. R. Burns & John A. Murray of district aforesaid for $20 to A. W. T. McBride of same, 5½ acres in Union District on the Spartanburgh Road, 20 Jan 1831. John N. Murry (Seal), D. R. Burns (LS), Wit: David Reid, Wm. J. Gordon. Proved in Spartanburgh District by the oath of David Reid 25 Jan 1831 before WM. Reid, J. Q. Recorded 6 June 1831.

V, 118-119: South Carolina, Union District. John McBeth of Union District for natural love and affection to my daughter Henrietta Murphy, wife of William B. Murphy, one negro woman named Nice and her two female children named Julia & Caroline, 28 May 1831. J. Macbeth (LS), Wit: Wm. K. Clowney, Lewis Presley. Proved by the oath of Col. W. K. Clowney 9 June 1831 before J. Rogers, Q. U. Recorded 9 June 1831.

V, 119-120: South Carolina, Union District. John McBeth of Union District for natural love and affection to my son Robert McBeth of same, negroes viz) one negro man named Solomon, one negro boy named Prudent & one negro named Dave, 28 May 1831. J. Macbeth (LS), Wit: Wm. K. Clowney, Lewis Presley. Proved by the oath of Col. W. K. Clowney 9 June 1831 before J. Rogers, Q. U. Recorded 9 June 1831.

V, 120-121: South Carolina, Union District. John McBeth of Union District for $5 to Robert McBeth of same in trust for natural love and affection for my beloved daughter Mary McBeth, one negro woman named Margaret, one female child named Parthena, and one negro boy named William in trust for the use of Mary McBeth, 28 May 1831. J. Macbeth (LS), Wit: Wm. K. Clowney, Lewis Presley. Proved by the oath of Col. W. K. Clowney 9 June 1831 before J. Rogers, Q. U. Recorded 9 June 1831.

V, 121-122: South Carolina, Union District. Humphrey Grant & Elisabeth Grant for $100 to William J. Hayes of Lincoln County, North Carolina, the plantation whereon we now live on both sides of McClures Creek, 50 acres at a dividing corner between said land and land formerly belonging to Benjamin Evans, adj. Goodwin, Hazelwood, 5 Nov 1830. Humphrey Grant (LS), Elisabeth Grant (X) (LS), Wit: H. H. Means, Henry ONeill, Wm. West.

Proved by the oath of William West 3 June 1831 before H. H. Means, J. P. as to Elisabeth Grant. Proved by the oath of H. H. Means 6 June 1831 before J. Rogers, Q. U. as to Humphrey Grant. Recorded 6 June 1831.

V, 123-124: South Carolina, Union District. Benjamin Stack of district aforesaid for $500 to John V. Johnson of same, tract on waters of Neals Creek, 200 acres, adj. Elisha Porter, Saml Alston deceast, John Porter, Charles Stewart, 26 Jan 1826. Benjamin Stack (X) (LS), Wit: Reuben Grady (X), B. J. Gregory. Proved by the oath of Benj. J. Gregory 5 June 1831 before E. P. Porter, Q. U. Recorded 6 June 1831.

V, 124-125: South Carolina, Union District. Whereas Hendley McAshan, late of the district aforesaid, died intestate leaving my self Mary McAshan his widow & relict and the following children by a formerly wife to wit Ferdinand McAshan, Elisabeth Glover Coleman wife of Nathan Coleman, Nancy Cockrell wife of Thomas Cockrell, Susan McAshan, Feaster McAshan, Judy McAshan, John McAshan and Andrew McAshan, the first four above named children only being of full age, and whereas being by the act of distribution of intestate estates, entitled to one third part of the estate both real and personal of said Hendley McAshan, and being also desirous of relinquishing all my right and interest to the above named children and their husbands of those now married, for in consideration of a negro boy known by the name of Solomon conveyed to me by the above named Ferdinand McAshan, Nathan Coleman, Thomas Cockrell, & Susan McAshan, 15 Dec 1830. Mary McShan (X) (LS), Wit: George Ashford, Redden Morgan. Proved by the oath of George Ashford 24 May 1831 before James Meacham, Q. U. Recorded 6 June 1831.

V, 125-134: Whereas a marriage is agreed upon between Mary Ann Moorman & Zadok Hooker, both of Union District, and Mary Ann Moorman is in her own right possessed of a considerable real estate and sundry slaves and other personal chattels, and said Zadok Hooker is desirous that they should be reserved and secured to the separate use of the said Mary Ann Moorman, and for $1 paid by my friend and relative William Rice, Esquire, do convey to said William Rice several tracts of land in the schedule annexed, 20 Dec 1830. Mary A. Moorman (LS), Z. Hooker (LS), Wm. Rice (LS), Wit: E. M. Bobo, Z. P. Herndon.

Schedule of property: one tract of land in the District of Chester on Broad River, 330 acres adj. C. S. Sims, William McCluney[?]; one other tract of 200 acres purchased at Sheriff Sale by Mary Ann Moorman as the property of William Foote adj. land claimed by Thomas McLure & others; 19 negroes to wit Hannibal about 45 years of age, Jinny about 30 years of age, Thomson a fellow of yellow complexion about 24 years of age, Ailsey[?] about 20 years of age & her child Christopher; George about 16 years of age; Cresy about 13 years of age, Siller about 10 years of age, Juda about 7 years of age; Louisa a girl about 3 years of age; Franklin about 1 year old, Cato a man about 30 years of age, Sally about 45 years of age and her son William about 2 years of age, Ellen a woman 22 years of age & her four children names not recollected, one horse, gig and harness, household furniture, a set of china, etc. Also notes and accounts:

Charner Scaife & Jas Hill for $54 dated 1 Jan 1830
John Lyons & Fer'd Hopkins for $230 dated 13 Jan 1830
Jeremiah Gregory for $65 due May 1831
John Stephens & Wm Wood $70 due 1 Jan 1831
C. S. Sims for $90 for the hire of Hannibal due 1 Jan 1831
Wm Kitches note for $50 for the hire of George
--- Holseys note for $25 for the hire of ____ 1830
rent for land due by Thomas Worthy for 1830 about #60
Case of Mary Ann Moorman by her next friend vs Wm Foote guardian in court of equity about $4000.

Proved by the oath of Z. P. Herndon 14 Feb 1831 before J. Rogers, Q. U. Recorded 14 Deb 1831.

V, 134-135: South Carolina, Union District. Whereas by a deed of marriage settlement made 30 Dec 1830 between Zadock Hooker and Mary Ann Hooker, wife of said Zadock Hooker, late Mary Ann Moorman, William Rice was appointed trustee, now authorize said William Rice to sell the tract of land mentioned in said schedule, 330 acres adj. C. S. Sims, Wm. McCleery [McCluny?], 1 Feb 1831. Z. Hooker (LS), Mary A. Hooker (LS), Wit: E. M. Bobo, Z. P. Herndon. Recorded 143 Feb 1831.

V, 135-136: Abner Striblin of district aforesaid for $75 paid or secured by Z. Nance, tract on the Sp'r Road formerly owned by William R. Wilbourn, 60 acres adj. Amos Lee, Hannah Brooks, S. & W. R. Wilbourn, at the meeting house spring, 13 June 1831. Abner Striplin (LS), Wit: Levi Smith, Eber Smith. Proved by the oath of Levi Smith 16 June 1831 before J. Palmer, J. P. Recorded 26 June 1831.

V, 137: South Carolina, Union District. Abner Striblin of district aforesaid for $5 paid or secured by Z. Nance, tract on the Sp'r Road formerly owned by Hannah Brooks, 15 June 1831. Abner Striplin (LS), Wit: Levi Smith, Eber Smith. Proved by the oath of Levi Smith 16 June 1831 before J. Palmer, J. P. Recorded 26 June 1831.

V, 138: Union Court House. June 12, 1831. Mr. B. Johnson, Sheriff for Union District. Please make the titles of Wm. B. Murphy land sold by you on sale day in May & bo't for me by my agent Mr. Z. Hooker to Mr. Bird Murphy & oblige your &c., L. N. Shelton.

V, 138-139: Bartholomew Johnson, Sheriff of Union District, by virtue of several writs of fieri facias from the court of common pleas for Union District tested 29 Sept 1829 at the suit of Wm. C. Pearson & Wm. P. Murphy & others to levy of the lands and tenements of William B. Murphy $328.79, sells

250 acres on waters of Tyger River adj. Col. Robert Martin, T. B. Davis, estate of Kindred Bobo, near Martin's Mills, purchased by Bird Murphy, Esqr., for $301, 13 June 1831. Bartholomew Johnson (LS), Wit: J. J. Pratt, John Gage Senr. Proved by the oath of John J. Pratt 13 June 1831 before E. P. Porter, J. P. Recorded 16 June 1831.

V, 140-141: South Carolina, Union District. John C. Tucker and Peter Tucker of Union District for $550 to Edward Stevens, James Meacham, George Fant & Elisha P. Porter of Union District, mortgage of one female slave named Silvey about 24 years of age with her two children, one a male child about 4 years old, the other a female child about 2 years old, the male named William and the female Ann, one other female slave named Jean about 13 yea of age, and a female slave named Frances about 10 years old, 1 June 1830. J. C. Tucker (LS), Peter Tucker (X) (LS), Wit: Charner T. Scaife. Proved by the oath of Charner T. Scaife 25 July 1831 before Saml Davis, J. P. Recorded 28 July 1831.

V, 141-142: South Carolina, Union District. Whereas by the last wil and testament of my father the late James Laurence decd provision was made that after the death of my mother Mrs. Frances Laurence, all the property give to her for her life should after her death be equally divided amongst all his children, now that Green Lawrence one of the sons and devisees of the said James Laurence for $70 paid by my brother Claibourn D. Lawrence, all my right, title and interest in the real and personal estate of my late father James Lawrence decd conveyed to me in h is will including $50 give=n to me drawing interest, 19 March 1831. Green Lawrence (LS), Wit :Joshua P. Dawkins, James Pearson. Proved by the oath of Jas Pearson 23 June 1831 before Wm. Goudelock, J.P. Recorded 24 June 1831.

V, 142-144: Thomas Burns of Union District for love and affection to my son Alexander Burns of same, tract of land of 100 acres adj. Lewis Fant, Jeter, Thomas Burns, dated 21 Sept 1825. Thos Burns (LS), Wit: John D. Wood, Richard Henderson, John T. McJunkin. Proved by the oath of Richard Henderson 21 Sept 1825 before J. T. McJunkin, J.,P. Recorded 8 Aug 1831.

V, 144-145: Stephen McPherson of Union District for natural love and affection to my son John McPherson of same, 207 acres on branches of Fairforest Creek, it being part of two tracts, one granted to Wood and one granted to John Putman, 22 July 1831. Stephen McPherson (X) (LS), Wit: Thomas Hays, Greenberry Hays, Nathan Harlan. Proved by the oath of Thomas Hays 26 Aug 1831 before J. Rogers, Q. U. Recorded 26 Aug 1831.

V, 145-147: Saml P. Baley of Union District for $1540 to William K. Clowney of same, parcel of land in Union Village, Lot 71 and part of lots 57 & 43, adj. John Gage Senr, on Public Square, except a small part sold to John J. Pratt, also parcel of land in Union District adj. the village of Union adj. John Gage Jr., 8 acres, adj. Kennedy, 25 July 1831. Saml P. Baley (LS), Wit: John S. Murrell, Robt J. Gage. Elisa S. Baley, wife of Saml P. Baley, relinquished dower 25 July 1831 before J. J. Pratt. Proved by the oath of John S. Murrell 30 Aug 1831 before J. Rogers, Q. U. Recorded 30 Aug 1831.

V, 147-148: South Carolina, Union District. William A. H. Bevil of the District of Union for $120 to Henry Bentley of same, 100 acres on waters of Browns Creek adj. Christopher Brandon, Nancy Brandon, Elizabeth Long & Wm. Meng, 6 July 1831. William A. H. Bevil (LS), Wit: Drury Wall, James Mitchell. Proved by the oath of James Mitchell 25 July 1831 before R. Lipsey, J. P. Recorded 1 Sept 1831.

V, 149-150: South Carolina, Union District. Abraham Nott bound to Joseph Jones Jr. in the sum of $700 to make title to tract of 385 acres adj. tract lately of George Newton, Newton's corner, 21 Aug 1806. Abm Nott (LS), Wit: John Lyle. Bond transferred to Margaret McCool however 100 acres laid off out of the tract to Thomas Howard, 2 Nov 1811. Joseph Jones Jr. (X) (LS), Wit: David Johnson, Rob Davis. Transferred by Margaret McCool to Robert Walker, except 100 acres transferred to William Bentley, 19 Dec 1822. Margaret McCool (X), Wit: James Rountree, Thomson McCluney. David Johnson testified to the handwriting of the late Hon. Abraham Nott 23 Aug 1831 before J. Rogers, Q. U. Bond transfer by Margaret McCool proved by the oath of Jas Rountree 23 Aug 1831. Recorded 31 Aug 1831.

V, 151-153: John Anderson, Sheriff of Union District, by virtue of several writs of fieri facias from the court of common pleas held 28 March 1826 at the suit of Wm Rice & others, to levy of the goods & chattels, lands & tenements of Malachi Keenan, $538, sells 40 acres on the main road leading from the village of Union to Pinckney on the SE side of the road, adj. Miss Porter, Becknell, Kennedy, sold for $40.25 to Joseph H. Dogan, 27 March 1831. John Anderson (LS), Wit: John H. Skelton, E. M. Bobo. Mrs. Rachel Keenan (X), wife of Malachi Keenan, relinquished dower 24 June 1831 before J. Rogers, Q. U. Recorded 2 Sept 1831.

V, 153-155: South Carolina, Union District. David W. Gregory, Benjamin J. Gregory, Isaac Gregory, Jehu Gregory & Jarret Gregory, part of us being of the above district and state, and part of the state of Georgia, for $100 to William Porter Jr., Melton Porter, Rhody Porter, Williamson Porter, Wm Edward Porter Jr., all being heirs of Wm Porter Senr, 100 acres on the waters of Little Browns Creek, adj. Landlot Cains, Obadiah Whitlock, John Gregory Senr, Wm Cooner Sr., Sarah Savage, Allen Gregory, George Harvey[?]. B. J. Gregory for D. W. Gregory (LS), B. J. Gregory (LS), Isaac Gregory (LS), Jehu Gregory (LS), B. J. Gregory for Gerrard Gregory (LS), Wit: Joseph Tate, John Davenport, Thos Cooner. Proved by the oath of Thos Cooner before Isaac Gregory, Esqr., 24 July 1831. Recorded 5 Sept 1831.

V, 155-156: Alex T. Burns of Union District for $250 to John Keesler and Samuel Keesler of same, 100 acres adj. Jeter, 24 Dec 1830. A. T. Burns (LS), Wit: J. T. McJunkin, Jeffries Steen. Proved by the oath of Jeffries Steen 5 Sept 1831 before E. McGraw, Q. U. Recorded 5 Sept 1831.

V, 156-159: Whereas David Johnson now of the town of Columbia became bond as indorsee of a promissory note drawn by me Daniel Thomas of Union district in the sum of $1200 which has been discounted for my accommodation at the Bank of the State of South Carolina at Columbia which is intended to be secured from time to time according to the usage of the said bank, now for the better indemnifying, tract of land whereon I now live near Neals Shoal on Broad River by resurvey 612 acres adj. Jas V. Thomas, William Hobson, A. W. Thomson, Wm. Dawkins, James Hamilton, plat by Richard Thomson, Esqr., 17 Dec 1828, dated 28 April 1830. Danl Thomas (Seal), Wit: William Dawkins, James W. Perry. Proved by the oath of William Dawkins 5 Sept 1831 before J. Rogers. Recorded 5 Sept 1831. Col. Daniel Thomas satisfied note 3 Aug 1835. Wit: Wm Dawkins, Jas Thomas.

V, 159-160: South Carolina, Union District. Saml Batey, Robert Beaty & J. Batey of Union District for $4037 to Mrs. Margaret Batey, Martha Batey & Margaret Ann Batey of same, tract on waters of Tinker Creek (known by the name of the old McJunkin tract, 807 acres) adj. Thomas Sartor, Gideon Steen, the old Jolly tract, John Cunningham, Daniel Chandler, Saml Batey, 14 Sept 1829. J. Batey (Seal), S. Batey (Seal), Robt Batey (LS), Wit: Gideon Steen, Jasper Saunders. Proved by the oath of Capt. Jasper Saunders 5 Sept 1831 before J. Rogers, Q. U. Recorded 5 April 1831.

V, 160-161: Margaret Batey & Martha Batey of Union District for $1380 to Christopher Young of same, tract on Tinker Creek, 276 acres, 1 Aug 1831. Patsey Batey (LS), Margaret Batey (X) (LS), Wit: Chesley Conant, Mary Phillips, Jasper Saunders. Proved by the oath of Jasper Saunders 5 Sept 1831 before J. Rogers, Q. U. Recorded 5 Sept 1831.

V, 161-162: South Carolina, Union District. Joseph Collins of said district for $94.16 to William Littlejohn of same, tract of 37 2/3 acres near the Grindle Shoal Road, 18 Feb 1831. Joseph Collins (LS), Wit: Miles J. Scott, John Harman. Proved by the oath of John Harman 7 July 1831 before Reuben Coleman, Esq. Recorded 5 Sept 1831.

V, 163: South Carolina, Union District. Steven Jones of district aforesaid, for $100 to Caswell Bogan of same, all my right & title and interest at law and in equity of a certain piece of land of 91 acres on the big branch, waters of Sugar Creek, adj. Caswell Bogan, 18 June 1830. Stephen Jones (Seal), Wit: John Blasingame, Chas Bogan. Proved by the oath of Charles Bogan 24 June 1831 before H. Gibbs, Q. U. Recorded 13 June 1831.

V, 164: South Carolina, Spartanburgh District. Enoch Bearden of district aforesaid for $100 to Caswell Bogan of Union District, 10 acres on Dutchmans Creek, waters of Tyger River adj. William Palmer, James Meadows, 5 March 1821. E. Bearden (LS), Wit: James Lee, Jas Smith. Proved by the oath of James Smith, J.P., 16 March 1829. Recorded 24 June 1831.

V, 165-166: South Carolina, Union District. Samuel O. Gordon of district aforesaid for $650 to Nancy M. Hamilton of same, 206 acres being a tract granted to Samuel Otterson 6 Nov 1786, 20 Nov 1830. Saml O. Gordon (LS), Wit: T. J. Glenn, P. P. Hamilton. Proved by the oath of Thomas A. Glenn 25 June 1831 before Isaac Gregory, J.P. Recorded 25 June 1831.

V, 166-169: South Carolina, Union District. 7 Sept 1831, John H. Galman of the first part, Catharine Galman his wife of the second part, and John Rogers of the third part, whereas Catharine Galman hath given notice by law required of her intention for the future to trade as a feme sole trader or free dealer, said John H. Galman does agree with said John Rogers, trustee. John H. Gallman (Seal), Catherine Gallman (Seal), J. Rogers (Seal), Wit: John Gage Jr., John T. Murrell. Proved by the oath of John Gage Jr 9 Sept 1831 before John Giles, Q. U. Recorded 9 Sept 1831.

V, 169: South Carolina, Union District. Jesse Rogers does acknowledge himself guardian for Seller Ogletree, a free woman, certified to be of good character and correct habit, 19 March 1831. Jesse Rogers, J. Rogers, Clk. Recorded 19 March 1831.

V, 170-172: South Carolina, Union District. Jane McBride, A. W. T. McBride, Robert White and Mary his wife, Isaac Cunningham and Jane his wife, and J. G. McBride, all of district aforesaid for $1000 to James Means, Joseph Mays, and Joseph Foster of said district, tract composed of sundry grants, 386 acres adj. Joseph Mays, Moses White, heirs of Hon. Abram Nott, Mrs. Goldin, 10 Sept 1831. Jane McBride (LS), A. W. T. McBride (LS), Robert White (LS), Mary N. White (LS), Isaac Cunningham (LS), Jane C. Cunningham (LS), Jane G. McBride (LS), Wit: Richd Thomson, John P. Thompson. Proved by the oath of Richd Thomson 10 Sept 1831 before J. P. Thompson, Q. U. Nancy McBride (X), wife of A. T. W. McBride relinquished dower 10 Sept 1831 before John P. Thompson, Q. U. Recorded 22 Sept 1831.

V, 172-174: South Carolina, Union District. Joseph Gist of Union District for $50 to James B. Harrison of Pinckneyville, Union District, & John Blair of York District, SC, copartners in trade at Pinckneyville, lot near Pinckneyville adj. Danl McMahan Sr's lot on the main road adj. Col. Joseph Gist, Taylor's lot, 4 May 1831. Jos Gist (Seal), Wit: J. McGowen, Albert G. Logan. Sarah Gist, wife of Joseph Gist, relinquished dower 23 July 1831 before Isaac Going, Q.U. Proved by the oath of John McGowan 1 July 1831 before L. Whitlock, J.P.

V, 174-175: South Carolina, Union District. William Bogan for mutual love and affection to my beloved mother Elizabeth Bogan and for her paying all my just debts and contracts up to this present date, all the right, title, and interest which I now have or ever may have in the estate of William Bogan decd, both real and personal, 26 March 1831. Wm. B. Bogan (Seal), Wit: W. K. Clowney. Proved by the oath of Wm. K. Clowney 16 Sept 1831 before J. Rogers, Q. U. Recorded 16 Sept 1831.

V, 175-176: South Carolina, Union District. Austin Wilson of said district for $130 to William McCafferty of same, 30 acres on waters of Little Browns Creek adj. Nancy Gregory, Moses Matthews, A. Wilson, David McCreight, part of 70 acres, 10 Sept 1831. A. Wilson (LS), Wit: Isaac Gregory, John Devenport. Proved by the oath of Isaac Gregory 22 Sept 1831 before J. Rogers, Q. U. Recorded 22 Sept 1831.

V, 176-178: John Anderson of Union District for $650 to John H. Skelton of same, tract on Morris's branch, waters of Tiger River, 150 acres 9 March 1831. John Anderson (Seal), Wit: W. M. Thomson, P. W. Skelton. Susannah Anderson, wife of John, relinquished dower 25 June 1831 before J. Rogers, Q. U. Proved by the oath of Powell W. Skelton 9 March 1831 before J. Rogers, Q. U. Recorded 9 March 1831.

V, 179-180: South Carolina, Union District. Bird B. Wright of the Territory of Florida for $1500 to Horace Lee of said district, tract on north side of Enoree River down the mill road, 400 acres adj. Mr. Maverick, Mr. Terry, Mark Kenady, Mrs. Mayes, 2 April 1831. Bird B. Wright (LS), Wit: Bird M. Pearson, J. L. Pearson. Proved by the oath of Bird M. Pearson 2 April 1831 before Thos Stribling, Q. U. Paulina C. Wright, wife of Bird B. Wright, relinquished dower 3 April 1831 before Thomas Stribling, Q. U. Recorded 5 Sept 1831.

V, 181-182: Gadsden County, Florida Territory. William Wright of county and territory aforesaid for affection and good wil for my only son Bird Booker Wright, tract whereon the said Bird Booker Wright formerly lived in Union District, SC, 500 acres on Enoree River adj. Bernard Glenn, Saml Maverick, Thomas Terry, Mark Kenady, widow Mays, 7 March 1831. Wm Wright (LS), Wit: John P. Neale, J. P. R. C. Lester, C. G. C. C. Robert C. Lester, Clerk of Court for Gadsden County certifies that Wm Wright signed the deed, 7 March 1831. Recorded 15 Sept 1831.

V, 182-183: Gadsden County, Florida Territory. Mary Wright, wife of William Wright, formerly a resident of Union District, SC, relinquished dower to land which her husband William Wright conveyed to Bird B. Wright, 7 July 1831 before R. C. Lester, C. G. C. C., John P. Neale. Proved by the oath of John P. Neale 7 July 1831. Joseph McBride, presiding Justice of the County Court of Gadsden County, certified that Robert C. Lester was clerk of court 6 July 1831. Recorded 15 Sept 1831.

V, 184-185: Bartholomew Johnson, Sheriff of Union District, by virtue of a writ of fieri facias from the court of common pleas tested 16 Jan 1829 at the suit of Spencer A. Bobo to levy of the goods &chattels, lands & tenements of Charles F. Grimke, $1800, sells tract of 468 acres on waters of Johns Creek and waters of Enoree River adj. Archy Canady, William & Edward Dodds, Jesse Briggs, Solomon Bobo & Joseph Harris, Harrison Bailey, Doct. W. J. Bobo, sod for $1 to Spencer A. Bobo, 20 Aug 1831. Bartholomew Johnson

(LS), Wit: Saml P. Bailey, J. J. Pratt. Proved by the oath of J. J. Pratt 27 Sept 1831 before J. Rogers, Q. U. Recorded 27 Sept 1831.

V, 186: So Carolina, Union District. Personally appeared Ferdinand Cain and acknowledged himself guardian for Elizabeth Prisock and her five children to wit Jane, Susannah, Saml, Ruth & Harrison, persons of colour, 27 Sept 1831. Ferdinand Cain (X), before John Rogers, Clk. Recorded 27 Sept 1831.

V, 187-188: South Carolina, Union District. 10 July 1828, Patsey Adams, the mother of Francis Marion Adams, of one part and Landlot Porter of the other part, Patsey Adams does agree to bind out her son Francis M. Adams to said Lancelot Porter until said Francis M. Adams becomes of the age of 21 years, which will be in the year 1839, to teach said Francis M. Adams the art of farming, and to teach him as far as the rule of three in arithmetic and to read and write a good legible hand, 10 July 1828. Patsey Adams (X) (LS), Wit: Robt G. H. Farr, Jonathan Hampton, William Gregory. Acknowledged by the said Patsey Adams and Landlot Porter 25 July 1828 before J. Rogers, Q. U. Recorded 25 July 1828.

V, 188-189: William Black of the District of Union for $33 to A. W. T. McBride of same, 13 acres on both sides of the Spartanburgh Road, it being part of a tract granted to John ONeil, 29 Feb 1828. Wm. Black (Seal), Wit: William D. Thompson, David R. Burns, Elisabeth Black. Proved in Spartanburg District by the oath of W. D. Thompson 4 March 1828 before William Reid, J. Q. Recorded 4 Oct 1831.

V, 190-191: South Carolina, Union District. Thomas Black & John H. Black of district aforesaid for $700 to Saml Lowry Senr of same, tract on waters of Gilkies Creek, partly on Broad River, 632 acres, 15 Aug 1831. Thos Black (LS), John H. Black (LS), Wit: Saml J. Hoey, S. Jeffries. Proved by the oath of Saml J. Hoey 4 Oct 1831 before J. Rogers, Q. U. Recorded 4 Oct 1831.

V, 191-193: South Carolina, Union District. Thomas N. Black of said district for $500 to Samuel Lowry Senr for the use & purpose of Thomas Black Senr have conveyed to said Saml Lowry Senr, tract on the waters of Gilkeys and Thicketty Creek, 150 acres, 15 Aug 1831. Thos N. Black (LS), Wit: Saml J. Hoey, S. Jeffries. Proved by the oath of Saml J. Hoey 4 Oct 1831 before J. Rogers, Q. U. Recorded 4 Oct 1831.

V, 193: South Carolina, Union District. John P. Thomson, one of the justices of the quorum, certifies that Mary N. White, wife of Robert N. White, and Jane C. Cunningham, wife of Isaac Cunningham, relinquished dower to James Means & Joseph Foster, 8 Oct 1831.

V, 193-195: South Carolina, Union District. John Keesler and Saml Keesler of Union District for $250 to Alexr T. Burns of same, mortgage 100 acres adj. Lewis Fant, Thos Burns, with reference to a plat and deed conveyed to John

& Saml Keesler, to be paid by 25 Dec 1832/3, dated 24 Dec 1830. John Keesler (Seal), Saml Keesler (Seal), Wit: J. T. McJunkin, Jeffries Steen. Proved by the oath of J. T. McJunkin 22 Oct 1831 before E. P. Porter, J. Q. Recorded 24 Oct 1831.

V, 195-197: South Carolina, Union District. William Malone of district aforesaid is justly indebted in the sum of $100 by note of hand dated 2 March 1831 and due 3rd of the same month with Jesse Fincher security to the same, said William Malone to indemnify the said Jesse Fincher, does sell to said Jesse Fincher, tract of land whereon I now live, 330 acres on the waters of Hill and Padgets Creek, waters of Enoree & Tyger Rivers adj. Joseph Goswick, on the south side of the Charleston road, Hosea Prince, Angus Alexander, Isaac Pearson. William Malone (LS), W. H. Gist, Aron F. Malone. Proved by the oath of William H. Gist 6 June 1831 before Lem B. Askew, J.P. Recorded 17 Oct 1831.

V, 197-199: South Carolina, Union District. In the Court of Equity. Whereas Elinor Cunningham & the other heirs at law of John Cunningham decd filed their Bill of Complaint in the Honorable the Court of Equity for Union District 24 June 1831 shewing that the said John Cunningham departed this life intestate seized & possessed of his own right in fee of a tract of land adj. Saml Beaty, Gideon Steen & Margaret Beaty, containing 70 acres, and that partition remain to be made of the said lands and the said cause being at issue before the said court at June Term 1831 and the said court did adjudge that the said land should be sold at publick auction by the Commissioner of the said court, now Bird M. Pearson, Commissioner of the said court, on 5 Sept 1831 at Union Court House did expose to sale, bought by Gideon Steen for $78, sells tract of 68 acres but found by resurvey to contain 74 acres on the east side of Tinkers Creek adj. Saml Batey, Gideon Steen, dated 8 Oct 1831. B. M. Pearson C. E. U. D. (LS), Wit: J. J. Pratt, A. T. Burns. Proved by the oath of A. T. Burns 8 Oct 1831 before J. Rogers, Q. U. Recorded 8 Oct 1831.

V, 199-203: South Carolina, Union District. Whereas Elenor Cunningham & others exparte heirs at law of John Cunningham decd filed their bill in the Court of Equity for Union District on 21 June 1831 shewing that the said John Cunningham departed this life intestate seized in his own right of a tract of land on Sandy branch and Tinker Creek adj. Samuel Beaty, Jonathan Hawkins, Margaret Beaty, 240 acres, sold by Commissioner 5 Sept 1831 to James S. Cunningham for $600, 8 Oct 1831. B. M. Pearson C. E. U. D. (LS), Wit: J. J. Pratt, A. T. Burns. Proved by the oath of A. T. Burns 8 Oct 1831 before J. Rogers, Q. U. Recorded 8 Oct 1831.

V, 203-205: Union Court House, 31 Oct 1831. Mr. William Rice. Dear Sir, you will do us the favour to purchase of Mr. Charles Meng a tract of land on Browns Creek, it being the land laid out for Mrs. Clough Meng, late Miss Polly Giles, 214 acres adj. Wm. Giles, Mrs. Ann Giles, Turner, Richard Faucett, according to the powers vested in you in a certain marriage contract made 30 Dec 1830 between Z. Hooker and Mary Ann Hooker, then Mary

Ann Moorman. Z. Hooker (LS), Mary A. Hooker, Wit: E. M. Bobo, J. Rogers.

South Carolina, Union District. Charles Meng of district aforesaid for $600 paid by William Rice, trustee of Mary Ann Hooker (wife of Z. Hooker), tract on waters of Browns Creek on both sides of the Sims ferry Road leading from Union Court House to the said ferry adj. William Giles, Mrs. Ann Giles, Richd Faucett, James Turner, it being land laid out for Mrs. Mary Meng, late Miss Mary Giles, 214 acres, 31 Oct 1831. Charles Meng (LS), Wit: E. M. Bobo, J. Rogers. Proved by the oath of Dr. E. M. Bobo 31 Oct 1831 before J. Rogers, Q. U. Recorded 31 Oct 1831.

V, 205-206: South Carolina, Union District. Thomas Ray for love and affection to my daughter Nancy Saunders, wife of David Saunders, two negro girls by the name of Sarah and Logina, 21 Sept 1831. Thomas Ray (LS), Wit: Wm. Ray Jr., Mary Ray. Proved by the oath of William Ray Junr 7 Nov 1831 before J. Rogers, Q. U. Recorded 7 Nov 1831.

V, 206-208: South Carolina, Union District. William Prince of district aforesaid for $950 to Thomas Ray of same, tract whereon I now live on Tyger River adj. Saunders, said Thomas Ray, Sion Murphy, 117 acres, granted to Daniel Prince, and also part of another tract granted to Daniel Prince, containing in the whole 270 acres, 17 Dec 1827. William Prince (LS), Wit: Wm. C. Pearson, Nancy Ray. Amy Prince, wife of William Prince, relinquished dower 28 Nov 1829 before Robert Martin, J. Q. Proved by the oath of William C. Pearson 7 Nov 1831 before J. Rogers, Q. U. Recorded 7 Nov 1831.

V, 208-210: South Carolina, Union District. Jepthah Harrington of aforesaid district for $200 to John Jeffries Senr, tract between Thickety and Gilkies Creek, 170 acres, part of 400 acres surveyed by Nathl Jeffries Senr, 12 Sept 1831. Jepthah Harrington (LS), Wit: Daniel S. McKee, David Goudelock. Joseph S. Weir. Proved by the oath of David Goudelock Esqr., 31 Sept 1831 before S. A. Goodman, Q. U. Nancy Harrington, wife of Jepthah, relinquished dower 17 Sept 1831 before S. A. Goodman, Q. U. Recorded 3 Oct 1831.

V, 210-211: South Carolina, Union District. Whereas Abner Stribling is indebted to John Pruett in the sum of $362 by note of hand due 25 Dec next, mortgage of one waggon & geer, one sorrel horse and one eye, one horse mule, one sorrel mare, one bay hose saddle and bridle, one red cow and calif, one pided cow & Calf, one heifer, 9 head hogs, 12 April 1831. Abner Stripling (LS), Wit: William Williams. Proved by the oath of William Williams 7 June 1831 before J. Palmer, J. P. Recorded 11 Oct 1831.

V, 211-213: South Carolina, Union District. Nathaniel Gist of district aforesaid for $350 to Andrew McBride of same, tract part in Union & in Spartanburgh Districts, 249 acres adj. James Gosset, Bullock, Benajah Thomson, Donaldson, 23 Nov 1826. Nath Gist (LS), Wit: Joseph Davidson, Weldon Perkinson. Proved in Spartanburgh District by the oath of Weldon Perkinson 19 Jan 1827 before Wm. Reid, J. Q. Elisabeth L.Gist, wife of Nathaniel Gist, relinquished dower __ Feb 1828 before William Reid, J. Q. Recorded 4 Oct 1831.

V, 213: South Carolina, Union District. Personally appeared before me Saml P. Baley & made oath that he is not the writer nor the author either directly or indirectly of a certain letter directed to Armsted Goss that the first knowledge he had of the contents of said letter he had from Z. Hooker weeks after it had passed through the post office of which he had the charge 3rd Oct 1831. Saml. P. Baley before Wm. Skelton, J. P. Recorded 4 Oct 1831.

V, 214-215: South Carolina, Union District. John Smith & Jepthah Harrington agent for Daniel Smith for $22.37 sold to John Jeffries Senr all our undivided parts of a tract of land on the south side of Gilkies Creek, part of a tract granted to Alexander Martin in 1803, supposed to be 17.9 acres adj. Jeffries, Doud, near the brick house, 15 Feb 1831. John Smith (LS), Jepthah Harrington (LS), Wit: James Jeffries, Nancy Harrington, Wm. Jeffries. Proved by the oath of James Jeffries 16 Feb 1831 before Saml A. Goodman, Q. U. Recorded 3 Oct 1831.

V, 215-216: South Carolina, Union District. James C. Bird of district aforesaid to $249 to Jepthah Harrington, tract between Thickety & Guilkies Creek whereon John Bird now lives, 170 acres, 25 Nov 1830. James C. Bird (LS), Wit: Berry Crocker, Thomas Logan. Proved by the oath of Berry Crocker 17 Sept 1831 before S. A. Goodman, Q. U. Recorded 3 Oct 1831.

V, 216-218: Wm Rice of Union District for $700 to Thomas Woodson of same, 272 acres per plat annexed to a deed dated 24 May 1811 from said Thomas Woodson & Thomas Hays to said William Rice, 7 Jan 1814. Wm Rice (LS), Wit: Robert McCollough, James Greer. Sarah P. Rice, wife of William Rice, relinquished dower 7 Feb 1817 before Bird Murphy, J. Q. Proved by the of James Greer 12 Nov 1831 before J. Rogers, Q. U. Recorded 12 Nov 1831.

V, 218-219: Fleet Smith of Union District for $15 to Thomas Woodson of same, tract of 3 acres adj. said Woodson, 7 April 1830. Fleet Smith (LS)l, Wit: Levi Smith, Cary W. Jackson. Proved by the oath of Levi Smith 11 Nov 1831 before James Greer, J.P. Recorded 12 Nov 1831.

V, 219-220: South Carolina, Union District. 23 Sept 1831 Richard C. Jeter of said district to James Russel, a free man of colour, said James Russel doth bind himself to Richard C. Jeter for the term of 21 years as a servant, for which term the said Russel puts himself under the care and protection in trust and confidence of him the said Richard, and the said Richard C. Jeter doth oblige himself to furnish said James Russel with clothes & diet and protect him from imposition & treat him well as a servant. Jas Russel (X) (LS), R. C. Jeter, Wit: E. McGraw, Gideon McGraw. Proved by the oath of Gideon McGraw 19 Oct 1831 before E. McGraw, Q. U. Recorded 20 Oct 1831.

V, 220-222: Robt Walker of Union District for $425 to Patrick Williams of same, tract on waters of Browns Creek, 185 acres, being the plantation whereon I now live, adj. Daniel Holder, William Mitchell, James Newton, 17 Feb 1831. Robt Walker (X) (Seal), Wit: J. Rogers, Thomas Goodrum. Mrs. Rebecca Walker, wife of Robert Walker, relinquished dower 24 Feb 1831 before J. Rogers, Q. U. Proved by the oath of John Rogers 15 Nov 1831 before Isaac Gregory, J. P. Recorded 15 Nov 1831.

V, 222-223: South Carolina, Union District. James Petty of district aforesaid for $10 to Joshua Petty of same, tract on the waters of Abentons Creek, waters of Broad River, 100 acres, 20 April 1829. James Petty (Seal), Wit: Francis Peterson, Berry Crocker. Proved by the oath of Berry Crocker 20 Nov 1830 before Jas Dawkins, J.P. Recorded 7 Nov 1831.

V, 223-224: South Carolina, Union District. Recd of Hezekiah Rice of district aforesaid for $150 for all the right, title and interest which I have to the land belonging to the estate of Hezekiah Rice of said district in several different tracts or surveys containing in the whole 1000 acres, the right and title to said land or so much thereof as I may be legally entitled to as one of the heirs of the estate of said decd, 16 Oct 1821. G. W. Rice (Seal), Wit: Jesse Fincher, Thos Howard. Proved by the oath of Jesse Fincher 1 Nov 1831 before J. Rogers, Q. U. Recorded 7 Nov 1831.

V, 224-225: David Jones of Union District for $400 to Alexander Akins of same, 162 acres on branches of Fair Forrest Creek, 4 Oct 1831. David Jones (Seal), Wit: Richd Thomson, Robert Davis. Sally B. Jones, wife of David Jones, relinquished dower 13 Dec 1831 before J. Rogers, Q. U. Proved by the oath of Robert Davis 4 Oct 1831 before Reuben Coleman, J.,P. Recorded 13 Oct 1831.

V, 226-227: William. R. Wilbourn of Union District for $100 to Sytha Jackson of same, tract on waters of Sugar Creek called Haynesworth branch, 87 acres adj. E. Palmer, Jas Palmer, W. R. Wilbourn, Winney Brown, being the land whereon Aron Pruett formerly lived and sold by John Bates Shff, 6 June 1831. W. R. Wilbourn (LS), Wit: J. Rogers, M. M. Jackson. Proved by the oath of John Rogers 15 Nov 1831 before Isaac Gregory. Recorded 15 Nov 1831.

V, 227-228: Robert Browning of Union District for $100 to James Browning of same, all the right, title and interest I now have ore may hereafter have at the death of my mother in the estate of Thomson Browning decd, both real and personal, the same being one ninth part of my said father's Thomson Browning's estate, 18 Aug 1831. Robt Browning (Seal), Wit: Robert Woodson, J. Rogers. Proved by the oath of John Rogers 15 Nov 1831 before Isaac Gregory, J.P. Recorded 15 Nov 1831.

V, 228-231: South Carolina, Union District. Indenture triple made 18 Aug 1831 between John Norman of the first part, Lettuce Beard of the second part, and Christopher Young and Henry Anderson of the third part, whereas a marriage is intended to be had between John Norman & Lettuce Beard and said Lettuce Beard is possessed of considerable personal estate to wit one negro boy Tilman, one negro boy Wat, one negro girl Jenny & one negro girl called Viney, one sorrel horse with a blaze face, one roan mare & one gray mare (blind), one waggon & geer, three feather beds & furniture, one bureau, with household and kitchen furniture, and it hath been agreed that the said John her intended husband shall enjoy all said property during the joint lives of the said John &* Lettuce, but the same after the death of either of them should be at the disposal of the said Lettuce notwithstanding her coverture & the said Lettuce has three children Susannah, Jane & Robert J. Franklin, it is agreed that the said John is to support and take care of the said children while they live with him or arrive at the age of 21, and send them to school sufficient to give them a common education, and as the said children arrive at the age of 21, the property or so much thereof as to give if she wishes each child their proportional part of the said estate, Christopher Young and Henry Anderson, trustees, 18 Aug 1831. John Norman (Seal), Letuce Beard (X) (LS), Christopher Young Sr (LS), Henry Anderson (LS), Wit: Thomas Humphries, John Ison. Proved by the oath of Thomas Humphries before J. J. Pratt, Q. U. Ex off. Recorded 7 Nov 1831.

V, 232: South Carolina, Laurens District. John L. Abell & Elisabeth B. his wife, James H. Abell & Sarah H. his wife, & James G. Carlisle of the district aforesaid, heirs to the state of James Glenn Senr decd of Union District, for $90 to Thomas A. Carlisle of Union District, all our right & claim to said estate either in money, goods, chattels, lands or anything else, 7 Dec 1830. J. L. Abell (LS), Elisabeth Abell (LS), Jas. H. Abell (LS), Sarah H. Abell (LS), Jas. G. Carlisle (LS), Wit: W. D. Watts, J. F. Casey, James Young. Proved in Laurens District by the oath of W. D. Watts 19 Jan 1831 before Jesse Johnson, J. P. Recorded 17 Nov 1831.

V, 233-234: John Anderson, Sheriff of Union District, tested 6 July 1829 at the suit of John Gaillard & Dr. William McGowan in right of John W. Bise[?], J. W. Binam & others, to sell the lot of land in the village of Pinckney, one acre adj. Daniel McMahan, Benj. Logan, and purchased by Dr. William MCGowan for $251.50, 5 April 1830. John Anderson, S. U. d. (LS), Wit: J. J. Pratt, Aron Wilkins. Proved by the oath of J. J. Pratt 22 Nov 1831 before J. Rogers, Q. U. Recorded 22 Nov 1831.

V, 234-235: South Carolina, Union District. Ricketson Lipsey for $480 to Moses Logan of Rutherford County, North Carolina, mortgage of Lear, a negro girl about 28 years old and four children, Joe about 8 years old, Nim about 6 years old, Glen about 4 years old and Jim about one year old, 8 Nov 1831. R. Lipsey (LS), Wit: A. G.Logan. Proved in Union District by the oath of A. G. Logan 19 Nov 1831 before J. Rogers, Q. U. Recorded 19 Nov 1831.

V, 236-237: John McLure of the village of Union for $575 to Clough S. Meng of Union District, lots # 48 and 62, in the village of Union on the south side of Main Street, formerly owned by Jesse S. Hix at the time of his death, 1 Jan

1831. John McLure (Seal), Wit: J. J. Pratt, J. Rogers. Proved by the oath of J. J. Pratt 1 Dec 1831 before J. Rogers, Q. U. Recoreed 1 Dec 1831.

V, 237-238: South Carolina, Union District. John Bowles of said district for love and affection to the children & heirs of my wife Sithe Bowles (to wit) Nathan Coleman, Daniel Coleman, Patsey Triplett, Mason Crosby, Sarah Ellis, Susan Anderson, Elizabeth Crosby, Permelia Glenn, Mary Coleman, Anna Sartor & the heirs of Lucy Hollingsworth decd, all my right, title and interest to the estate of Bernard Glenn decd, they being one eleventh of which is to be given by the above named children of my wife Sithe Bowles to the heirs of Lucy Hollingsworth, the remainder to be divided equally among themselves, 28 Nov 1831. John Bowles (LS), Wit: Thomas Bowker, Margaret K. Bowker. Proved by the oath of Thomas Bowker 5 Dec 1831 before J. Rogers, Q. U. Recorded 5 Dec 1831.

V, 238-240: South Carolina, Union District. William J. Thomas of district aforesaid for $100 to Little B. Jeter of same, tract whereon I now live on waters of Neals Creek, adj. said Jeter, deGraffenreid, Gilliam Hobson, 50 acres, 28 Nov 1831. William J. Thomas (X) (Seal), Wit: J. C. Jeter, Jas Jeter. Proved by the oath of Dr. John C. Jeter 5 Dec 1831 before J. Rogers, Q. U. Nancy Thomas (X), wife of William J. Thomas, relinquished dower 1 Dec 1831 before E. P. Porter, Q. U.

V, 240-241: South Carolina, Union District. John Gage Senr of district aforesaid for $100 to John Gault of same, tract whereon Mark Fowler Grunter[?] formerly lived, purchased by me, supposed to be 75 to 100 acres, 8 Dec 1831. John Gage Senr (Seal), Wit: Charles Gowing, A. Goss. Proved by the oath of Charles Gowing 8 Dec 1831 before J. Rogers, Q. U. Recorded 8 Dec 1831.

V, 242-243: Patrick Williams of Union District for $575 to James M. Williams of same, tract on Rocky Creek, waters of Fairforest, 103 acres, adj. Zachariah Belew, 12 Dec 1831. Patrick Williams (LS), Wit: H. W. Foote, J. Rogers. Proved by the oath of H. W. Foote 12 Dec 1831 before J. Rogers, Q. U. Recorded 12 Dec 1831.

V, 243-244: South Carolina, Union District. Abraham Smith & Sarah Davis of York District for $22.37 to John Jeffries Senr, all our undivided part of a tract on the south side of Gilkies Creek, part of a tract granted to Alexander Martin 1803, 17.9 acres, adj. David's[?] line, John Steen, near the Brick House, 29 Oct 1831. Sarah Davis (LS), Abraham Smith (LS), Wit: Aaron Wilkins, John V. Steen, John Smith. Proved by the oath of Aron Wilkins 6 Nov 1831 before S. A. Goodman, Q. U. Recorded 15 Dec 1831.

V, 244-245: South Carolina, Union District. Mary Darby of Abbeville District for $171 to James Burell of Union District, 100 acres adj. Elisabeth Glenn, John Rogers, on Tyger River, the right of which was made to me by Jas P. Darby & Elisha G. Darby, the plat made to them by Annett Underwood, 26

Nov 1831. Mary Darby (O) (LS), Wit: T. A. Carlisle, James White, Kilby T. P. Carlisle. Proved in Union District by the oath of Thomas A. Carlisle 12 Dec 1831 before Jas Meacham[?], Q. U.

V, 246: South Carolina, Union District. Elisha G. Darby for $50 to Mary Darby, 50 acres, being half of a tract divided between Jas P. Darby & Elisha G. Darby, 11 Jan 1823. Elisha G. Darby (LS), Wit: Bartholomew Johnson, Wm. Jenkins. Proved by the oath of William Jenkins 12 Dec 1831 before Thos Stribling, Q. U. Recorded 17 Dec 1831.

V, 247-248: South Carolina, Union District. James Hunter of Union District for $40.45 to Mary Darby of same, part of 100 acres the right of which was made to me by Jas P. Darby & made to said Jas P. Darby & brother Elisha G. Darby by Annett Underwood on the south side of Tyger River between Hawkins old mill, 25 Oct 1823. James Hunter (LS), Wit: William Rogers, Richard Leverett. Proved by the oath of William Rogers 12 Dec 1831. Recorded 17 Dec 1831.

V, 248: $115. Rec'd of James Duncan son of Alexr, $115, in part for two tracts of land (via) the tract called by the name of Smithwick which is 200 acres, as also the tract whereon I now live known by the name of the Duncan tract of 200 acres, which said lands have been in dispute in law between James Duncan plaintiff and Jesse D. Murphy deft, 5 Dec 1831. J. D. Murphy (LS), Wit: Jas Norris, Wm. C. Pearson. Proved by the oath of Jas Norris 2 Jan 1832 before J. Rogers, Q. U. Recorded 2 Jan 1832.

V, 249-252: South Carolina, Union District. Indenture of three parts made 27 Dec 1831 between John Coomer of the first part, Rebecca Coomer his wife of the second part, and William Coomer of the third part, whereas Rebecca Coomer hath given notice by law required to trade as a free sole trader or free dealer, said Rebecca to be a feme sole, own property, etc. Rebecca Coomer (X) (LS), John Coomer (X) (LS), William Coomer (LS), Wit: William Jolly, Wm. L. Davis, Thos Coomer. Proved by the oath of William Jolly 31 Dec 1831 before E. P. Porter, Q. U. Recorded 2 Jan 1832.

V, 252-253: South Carolina, Union District. Saml Sharp of Union District for $16 to Fleming Harris of same, 3½ acres, on waters of Browns Creek 13 Feb 1831. Saml Sharp (Seal), Wit: Robert V. Harris, J. W. L. Meng, C. A. Brandon. Proved 2 Jan 1832 before J. Rogers, Q. U. Recorded 2 Jan 1832.

V, 253-255: Elisabeth Griffin of Union District for $150 to Fleming Harris of same, 177 acres, part of a tract granted to Elisabeth Griffin including the dwelling house where Fleming Harris now lives, adj. Wm. Sharp, 21 Sept 1831. Elisabeth Griffin (X) (LS), Wit: Richard Sharp, Lott Whitlock. Proved by the oath of Richard Sharp 2 Jan 1832 before J. Rogers, Q. U. Recorded 2 Jan 1832.

V, 255-257: John Anderson of Union district for $1400 to William Rice of same, 50 acres on both sides of Shoal Creek, it being the tract of land whereon the grist mill which was built by the H on. David Johnson now stands, at the end of the mill dam above the road leading from Union Court House to McBeth's mill on Fairforest Creek, adj. Jas M. Whitton, Wm. Rountree, to the line of a small piece of land containing about three acres, conveyed to me by Jas M. Whitton by deed 4 May 1829, to include the whole of said three acres, adj. Bogan's line, estate of Wm. Bogan decd, 1 Nov 1831. John Anderson (LS), Wit: Bartholomew Johnson, P. W. Skelton. Susannah Anderson, wife of John Anderson, relinquished dower 7 Nov 1831 before Hiram Gibbs, Q. U. Proved by the oath of B. Johnson 4 Jan 1832 before J. Rogers, Q. U. Recorded 5 Jan 1832.

V, 258-260: 22 Dec 1831, Samuel P. Baley of Union Village to Joseph Rice for himself & L. B. Askew & Joseph Reed, executor of J. L. Reid, whereas said Samuel P. Baley stands indebted to the said Joseph Reid, Lemuel B. Askew & Joseph Reed, exor of J. L. Reid, by nine notes of hand, all even date with these presents, in the whole $1100, mortgage of those houses & lotts now in the possession of Maj. Jas Norris in the village of Union. Saml P. Bailey (LS), Wit: A. W. Thomson, Wm. M. Thomson. Proved by the oath of William M. Thomson 6 Jan 1832 before J. Rogers, Q. U. Recorded 6 Jan 1832.

V, 260-263: 17 Dec 1831, Clough S. Meng to Samuel Beaty, Robert Beaty, Martha Beaty, Christopher Young & Jesse Beaty, whereas the said Clough S. Meng stands indebted to the said Samuel Beaty, Robert Beaty, Martha Beaty, Christopher Young & Jesse Beaty by three notes in the sum of $500 each, payable on or before 1 Jan 1833, 1 Jan 1834 and 1 Jan 1833, mortgage of lot in the village of Union on the south side of Main Street, two acres and three roods and eleven perches, on the east end of lot No. 47 but including a part of said lott near the Piaza Post, to a stake in the race paths, by deed from Jas Reid and from Z. Reid. C. S. Meng (Seal), Wit: Robert Vaughan, Jas S. Cunningham. Proved by the oath of Robert Vaughan 17 Dec 1831 before J. Rogers, Q. U. Recorded 17 Dec 1831. Satisfied 15 July 1836, Robt Beaty (LS). Entered 19 July 1836.

V, 263-266: South Carolina, Union District. Indenture of three parts, 29 Dec 1831, between Thomas Coomer of the first part, Elisabeth Coomer his wife of the second part, and William Coomer Jr. of the third part, Elizabeth Coomer hath given notice by law required of her intention to trade as a free sole trader or free dealer, William Coomer trustee. Elizabeth Coomer (X) (LS), Thomas Coomer (X) (LS), William Coomer (LS), Wit: William L. Davis (X), John Coomer (X), Wm. Jolly. Proved by the oath of William Jolly 31 Dec 1831 before E. P. Porter, Q. U. Recorded 7 Jan 1832.

V, 266-267: Hosea Ray of Union District for natural love and affection to my beloved daughter Delilah Murphy, wife of Jesse D. Murphy, one negro girl named Rosetta, 16 Jan 1832. Hosea Ray (Seal), Wit: Elijah Ray, Carry Ray.

Proved by the oath of Elijah Ray 16 Jan 1832 before J. Rogers, Q. U. Recorded 16 Jan 1832.

V, 268-269: South Carolina, Union District. Thomas N. Dawkins of Union Village for $1200 to John T. Murrell of Union Village, three lotts in Union Village, numbers 49, 63, and 77, on Union Street, adj. Z. P. Herndon, the race paths, Batchelor, 21 Sept 1831. Thomas N. Dawkins (LS), Wit: A. W. Thomson, Robert J. Gage. Proved by the oath of Robert J. Gage 7 Jan 1832 before J. Rogers, Q. U. Recorded 7 Jan 1832.

V, 269-270: South Carolina, Union District. John M. Moore of district aforesaid for $979 to Samuel Lowry Senr of same, tract on waters of Gilkies Creek, 92 acres, 25 Dec 1832. John M. Moore (X) (Seal), Wit: Aron Wilkins, J. B. Guyton. Proved by the oath of Aron Wilkins 11 Jan 1832 before Jas. Dawkins, J. P. Recorded 23 Jan 1832.

V, 271-272: John Hart of Union District for $300 to Jinsey Brandon of same, tract on SW side Fairforest Creek, being part of divers surveys adj. Thomson White, Thomas Hart, John McBeth, Robert McBeth, Benjamin Holcombe, 12 Jan 1832. Wit: J. Rogers, M. Keenan. Elizabeth Hart (X), wife of John hart, relinquished dower 17 Jan 1832 before H. Gibbs, Q. U. Proved by the oath of M. Keenan 12 Jan 1832 before J. Rogers, Q. U. Recorded 24 Jan 1832.

V, 273-274: South Carolina, Union District. Isaac J. Foster for $250 to George Foster of said district, part of tract on the folly branch, waters of Packolett River, 72 acres, adj. Polly Hendley, 23 Feb 1829. I. J. Foster (LS), Wit: James Foster Jr., Josiah Foster Jr. Proved by the oath of Josiah Foster Jr. 17 Nov 1829 before Isaac Going, Q. U. Franky Foster, wife of Isaac J. Foster, relinquished dower 17 Nov 1829 before Isaac Going, Q. U. Recorded 24 Jan 1832.

V, 274-276: South Carolina, Union District. Hezekiah Palmer, John Palmer, Nancy Edwards, Amasa Palmer of the State of Georgia, Ellis Palmer, William Palmer, Joseph McKissick, Nancy Edward of Franklin County, Amasa Palmer of Green County, and John Palmer of Handcock County, Ellis Palmer & William Palmer, Joseph McKissick all of Union District, for $800 to Isaac Going of Union District, 300 acres reference to the plat annexed on waters of Browns Creek including the plantation on which John Palmer decd formerly lived, 27 Oct 1829. Amasa Palmer (Seal), John Palmer (Seal), Joseph McKissick (Seal), Nancy Edward (X) (Seal), Elijah Palmer (LS) agent for Hezekiah Palmer, Wit: Thos B. Going, John M. Going, John W. P. McKissick. Proved by the oath of Thomas W. P. McKissick 18 Jan 1832 before J. Carothers, Q. U. Rhoda McKissick wife of Joseph McKissick, relinquished dower 18 Jan 1832 before J. Carothers, Q. U. Recorded 23 Jan 1832.

V, 277-278: South Carolina, Union District. Benjamin Landrum of Union District for $110 to Edward M. Bobo of same, tract on north side of Tyger River on the east side of the Mill Road leading to Martin's Mills, nearly opposite Browning's house, 42 acres, 1 Oct 1828. Benjamin Landrum (LS), Wit: Thos B. Davis, Thomas Wilson. Proved by the oath of Thos B. Davis 12 Jan 1832 before J. Rogers, Q. U. Recorded 12 Jan 1832.

V, 278-280: Henry Keesler of Union District for $200 to Abram McJunkin of same, tract on Brushy Creek, 108 acres adj. Thos Burns, adj. A. Keesler, 2 Feb 1832. Henry Keesler (LS), Wit: Geo C. Vance, Robert Vaughan. Proved by the oath of George C. Vance 2 Feb 1832 before J. T. McJunkin, J.P. Elenor Keesler (X), wife of Henry Keesler, relinquished dower 2 Feb 1832 before J. Rogers, Q. U. Recorded 2 Feb 1832.

V, 280-282: South Carolina, Union District. Daniel A. Mitchell of Union District for $94.50 to E. M. Bobo of same, tract on the east side of Union Court House on the Pinckney Road, 11.84 acres, 5 Dec 1831. D. A. Mitchell (Seal), Wit: Z. Hooker, A. G. Dunn. Susannah A. Mitchell, wife of D. A. Mitchell, relinquished dower 6 Jan 1832 before J. Rogers, Q. U. Proved by the oath of Z. Hooker 9 Jan 1832 before J. Rogers, Q. U. Recorded 9 Jan 1832.

V, 282-284: Robert Tucker of Union District to Joseph Tucker for $300, tract of land that did belong to Joseph Tucker decd whilst living that fell to me the said Robert Tucker by way of legacy and purchased from Peter Tucker & Henry Beauford, the quantity of land that lies east of Duffs Creek, a branch of Tyger River adj. formerly unto John Huey & William Mays, 150 acres granted to John Hughey but laid out to James Huey the grant dated 3 July 1772, the other tract of 123 acres granted to Wm. Mays dated 5 Sept 1785, the above two tracts conveyed by said John Huey & William Mays to the above named Joseph Tucker decd, the deed from John Hughey to Joseph Tucker decd dated 12 Jan 1788, the deed from Wm. Mays to said Joseph Tucker decd dated 20 Dec 1799, dated 3 Oct 1821. Robt Tucker (X) (Seal), Wit: James A. Tucker, James C. Sims, Saml Hardy. Proved by the oath of James A. Tucker 18 Sept 1830 before Reuben Gilliam, J. P. Recorded 6 Feb 1832.

V, 284-286: William Mays Jr. & Oliver Towles of Edgefield District to Joseph Tucker of Union District for $100, part of tract that did belong to Joseph Tucker decd whilst living, that fell to me the said William Mays & Oliver Towles by way of legacy, that is all the land that lies east of Duffs Creek [same description as preceding deed], dated 3 Dec 1824. Oliver Towles (Seal), William Mays Jr. (Seal), Wit: Mary Tucker, Nancy Tucker. Proved by the oath of Nancy B. Tucker 18 Sept 1830 before Reuben Gilliam, J. P. Recorded 6 Feb 1832.

V, 286-287: Henry Hardy of Union District for $60 to Joseph Tucker of same, all the tract on the north side of Tyger River, 5 acres, part of a tract granted to John Inlow 5 Feb 1787, dated 16 July 1825. Henry Hardy, Wit: William Kelly, John Vessels. Proved by the oath of John Vessels 18 Sept 1830 before Reuben Gilliam. Recorded 6 Feb 1832.

V, 287-289: South Carolina, Union District. Fanny Tucker, Mary Tucker, Nancy Brock Tucker and George Beauford Tucker, all of district aforesaid, to James Anderson Tucker, that on account of a certain contract this day made between use, concerning a tract of land whereon the said James A. Tucker now lives, 255 acres including what was purchased from Henry Hardy, which the said James A. Tucker promises in the contract to give $8, all our interest in the said 255 acres, 23 March 1827. Fanny Tucker (Seal), Mary Tucker (Seal), Nancy B. Tucker (Seal), Wit: Elijah Hawkins, Saml Hardy. As the above George B. Tucker is a minor and not capable of acting for himself according to law, I the said Fanny Tucker do hereby bind myself for the said George B. Tucker. Proved by the oath of Elijah Hawkins 18 Sept 1830 before Reuben Gilliam. Recorded 6 Feb 1832.

V, 289-290: South Carolina, Union District. 17 June 1828, George Ashford to James A. Tucker, both of district aforesaid, for $1050, 240 acres on the north side of Tyger River in Union District originally granted to James Inlow 5 Sept 1791 and by Inlow to James Hawkins & by him to Thomas Evans and by him to his wife Martha Evans & his two daughters, adj. James A. Tucker, Henry Richard. Geo Ashford (Seal), Wit: Henry Richard, Ephraim Night, W. J. Eaves. Proved by the oath of Henry Richard 18 Sept 1830 before Reuben Gilliam, J. P. Recorded 6 Feb 1832.

V, 291-292: Bartholomew Johnson, Sheriff of Union District, by virtue of a writ of fieri facias from the court of common pleas held for Union District tested 24 Feb 1829 at the suit of ____ to levy of the goods & chattels, lands & tenements of John E. Fowler $250, sells tract of 107 acres on waters of Fanning Creek adj. John Gault, Richard White, Nancy Fowler, John Hames, and James Milwood Junr, sold for $140 to Francis Logan, 14 Feb 1832. Bartholomew Johnson (seal), Wit: John Parham, Wm. Rice. Proved by the oath of John Parham 14 Feb 1832 before J. Rogers, Q. U. Recorded 14 Feb 1832.

V, 293-294: Thomas Beauchamp of Union District for $700 to Archibald Gordon of same, 230 acres adj. Sterling Baker, heirs of Ely Jeter, Richard Jeter, David Thomas, Allen deGraffenreid, Daniel Mitchell, William Sims Senr, 15 Jan 1832. Thos Beauchamp (Seal), Wit: Clough S. Sims, W. Sims. Proved by the oath of C. S. Sims 6 Feb 1832 before J. Rogers, Q U. Recorded 6 Feb 1832.

V, 294-296: John Bates, Sheriff of Union District, by virtue of a writ of fieri facias from the court of common pleas held for the district of Union tested the first Monday of March 1824 at the suit of Mary Lockhart to levy of the goods & chattels, lands & tenements of Philip Petty $140.92, sells 100 acres on waters of Thickety Creek adj. Alexander's old Whiteoak corner, John Jeffries Junr's line, Jepthah Harrington, to the machine branch, sold to Jepthah Harrington for $100, 9 Jan 1827. J. Bates (Seal), Wit: Erastus Geddings, Thos Bates. Proved by the oath of Thos Bates 9 Feb 1832 before J. Rogers, Q. U. Recorded 9 Feb 1832.

V, 296-297: South Carolina, Union District. Edward M. Bobo of district aforesaid for $687.50 to Farr Bates of same, tract on north side of Fairforest known by the name of the Wm Ivey tract, 236 acres, 7 March 1830. E. M. Bobo (LS), Wit: Z. P. Herndon, Jas S. Shelton. Proved by the oath of Z. P. Herndon 18 Feb 1832 before J. Rogers, Q. U. Recorded 18 Feb 1832.

V, 297-299: Jonathan Hampton and Rebecca Hampton, wife of said Jonathan Hampton, of Union District, for $350 to Fleming Harris of same, 80 acres, being the lott of land laid off to Rebecca Hampton, wife of Jonathan Hampton, as one of the heirs of William Sharp Senr decd, dated 24 Sept 1831. Rebecca Hampton (X) (LS), J. Hampton (LS), Wit: W. Abernathy, J. S. Rogers. Proved by the oath of William Abernathy 2 Jan 1832 before J. Rogers, Q. U. Rebecca Hampton relinquished dower 20 Feb 1832 before J. Rogers, Q. U. Recorded 20 Feb 1832.

V, 300-303: William B. Means & Henry Harvey Means for $500 to Jesse Gordon, tract on both sides of Fairforrest Creek, part of sundry tracts containing 1140 acres, adj. heirs of Hon. Abram Nott, widow Thomson, McClure's Creek, Capt. Jas Mayes, Jas. Means, Capt. Patton, 1 Oct 1831. William B. Means (LS), Henry Harvey Means (LS), Wit: Charles Murphy, Abm McCarther, Wm. Gordon. Rachel Means, wife of Wm. B. Means, and Rebecca Means, wife of Henry Harvy Means, relinquished dower 13 Oct 1831 before John P. Thomson. Hannah Means (X), widow of Gen. Hugh Means decd, relinquished dower 12 Oct 1831 before John P. Thomson, Q. U. Proved by the oath of William Gordon before John Norman, Q. U.

V, 303-305: South Carolina, Union District. Bartholomew Johnson, Sheriff of Union District, by virtue of a writ of fieri facias from the court of common pleas tested 26 March 1830 at the suit of Mary Smith to levy of the goods and chattels, lands and tenements of John Bird $264.18, sells tract of 400 acres on both sides of Lusks branch of Thickety Creek, as Nathaniel Jeffries' plat granted in 13 Jan 1772, purchased by John Jeffries Senr for $6, 6 Feb 1832. Bartholomew Johnson S. U. D. (LS), Wit: Hezk Rice, R. Lusk. Proved by the oath of R. Lusk 6 Feb 1832 before J. Rogers, Q. U. Recorded 6 Feb 1832.

V, 305-306: Jesse Browning of Union District for $75 to James Browning of same, all the right, title and interest I now have or may hereafter have at the death of my mother in the estate of Thompson Browning decd, being one ninth part of my sd father Thomson Browning's estate, 1 Feb 1832. Jesse Browning (Seal), Wit: Robert McBeth, Caleb Greer. Proved by the oath of Robert McBeth 6 Feb 1832 before J. Rogers, Q. U. Recorded 6 Feb 1832.

V, 306-308: South Carolina, York District. Daniel Smith of district aforesaid for $1200 to John Smith Jr. of same, tract of 600 acres on the west side of Broad River in Union District at Smith's ford, adj. Nathaniel Guyton, Moore's old line, John Kennedy, James Kennedy, 12 Oct 1830. Daniel Smith (LS), Wit: Joseph G. Smith, Abraham G. Smith, Payton B. Darwin. Proved in York

District by the oath of Abraham G. Smith 3 May 1831 before Gordon Moore, J. P. Recorded 6 Feb 1832.

V, 308-310: John Gault of Union District for $1150 to John McEntire of Rutherford County, N. C. and Benjamin H. Bradley of Union, tract on Union District, 342 acres, 4 Jan 1832. John Gault (mark) (LS), Wit: A. H. Bradly, Jefferson White. Proved in Union District by the oath of Anderson H. Bradley 4 Jan 1832 before Daniel White, Q. U. Biddy Gault (X), wife of John Gault, relinquished dower 29 Jan 1832 before Daniel White, Q. U. Recorded 22 Feb 1832.

V, 310-312: Robert Glenn Senr of Union District for $132.25 to Daniel Coleman of same, all my right, title, claim or interest in a tract in Union District on the west side of Broad River, originally belonging to James Glenn Senr & now deceased and by the will of said James Glenn Senr decd he loaned the said tract to his wife Elisabeth Glenn during her life and at her death to be equally divided amongst his children, and on 18 Oct 1827 the said Elizabeth Glenn relinquished all her right & Title to said land to the heirs of said James Glenn Senr decd, and by their consent was sold 3 Jan 1831 and purchased by said Daniel Coleman, 150 acres adj. Thomas Bowker & others, 31 May 1831. Robert Glenn (LS), Wit: James N. Hardy, Nathan Coleman. Sarah W. Glenn relinquished dower 13 Dec 1831 before John Giles, Q. U. Proved by the oath of Nathan Coleman 6 Dec 1831 before T. A. Glenn, J.P. Recorded 7 Feb 1832.

V, 312-313: Union District, SC. For the sum of $20 I have mortgaged to James F. Kelly a certain sorrel horse colt two years old next spring, 11 Sept 1831. Josiah Spark (X) (LS), James Kirby. Wit: John Petty, Terry Kirby. Proved by the oath of John Petty 6 Feb 1832 before J. Rogers, Q. U. Recorded 6 Feb 1832.

V, 313-315: Rolly Horton of Union District for $354.50 to James Jackson, a tract of land in Union District, 118½ acres on Springers branch, a water course of Fairforest adj. William Hammond, Daniel Floyd, Aron Springer, John Fincher, 3 Jan 1832. Rolly Horton (Seal), Wit: Wm. Rice, John Coomer (X). Margaret Horton (X), wife of Rolly Horton, relinquished dower 3 Feb 1832 before L. B. Askew, J. Q. Proved by the oath of William Rice 10 March 1832 before J. Rogers, Q. U. Recorded 10 March 1832.

V, 316-318: 1 Feb 1832, John T. Murrell of the one part, John Gage Jr & John Rogers of the other part, whereas the said John T. Murrell stands indebted to Nathaniel Gist in the sum of $200 by three several notes for the purchase of a house & lott in Union Village, and said John Gage Jr. and John Rogers are security for the payment, mortgage of said house and lott on the north east side of Main Street at the corner of N. Gist's brick house. John T. Murrell (Seal), Wit: H. W. Foote, B. F. Bobo Jr. Proved by the oath of H. W. Foote 18 Feb 1832 before John Giles, Q. U. Recorded 18 Feb 1832. Satisfied 6 Feb 1835.

V, 318-319: James McCluney of York District for $275 to Walter Wisher of Union District, tract on waters of Broad River on the north side of Hugheses Creek, by a late survey 110 acres adj. George South, James Savage, Mr. Hughes, 1 Sept 1831. Jas McCluney (Seal), Wit: Wm Giles, Wm Jimmerson. Proved in York District by the oath of Wm Giles 26 Nov 1831 before Wm. Jimmerson, Q. U. Recorded 27 Feb 1832.

V, 320-321: Bartholomew Johnson, Sheriff of Union District, by virtue of a writ of fieri facias issued from the court of common pleas held 22 March 1828 at the suit of Z. Reid to levy of the good & chattels, lands and tenements, of Anthony Bennett $115, sells 100 acres on waters of Packolett River adj. Wm. Huckaby, Wm. Brown, Thomas Pridmore, Dr. Otterson, 29 Feb 1832. B. Johnson (Seal), Wit: John Parham, John Rogers. Proved by the oath of John Parham 29 Feb 1832 before J. Rogers, Q. U. Recorded 29 Feb 1832.

V, 322-323: South Carolina, Union District. Mary E. Pruett of district aforesaid for $31 to Thomas Clark, tract of land on the north side of Enoree River, 7 3/4 acres, 27 Aug 1831. Mary E. Pruet (X) (LS), Wit: Henry C. Martin, Elisabeth Stribling. Proved by the oath of Henry C. Martin 27 Aug 1831 before Thos Stribling, Q.U. Recorded 23 Feb 1832.

V, 323-325: John Anderson, Sheriff of Union District, by virtue of several writs of fieri facias from the court of common pleas tested 22 March 1828 at the suit of John Robinson to levy of the goods & chattels, lands and tenements of Wm. H. Cotter $461.22, sells tract adj. Wm Moorhead, Saml M. Gowdy, L. B. Murry, Wm. Huckaby, with the land reserved to William H. Cotter by Saml Otterson in his deed to Leonard B. Murry, purchased by Samuel M. Gowdy for $279.44, 25 June 1830. John Anderson (Seal), Wit: Wm. R. Wilborn, R. Lusk. Proved by the oath of R. Lusk 6 Feb 1832 before J. Rogers, Q. U.

V, 325-326: James Hill & Charner T. Scaife, being the firm of Hill & Scaife of Union District, for $205 to John C. Jeter of same, tract whereon James Visser[?] now lives, on waters of Cain Creek of Tyger River adj. Wm Rice, George B. Tucker, and said John C. Jeter, 75 acres, 13 July 1831. Hill & Scaife (LS), Wit: Geo Douglass, John T. Hill. Proved by the oath of Dr. George Douglass and John T. Hill 3 Aug 1831 before T. A. Glenn, J.P. Recorded 5 March 1832.

V, 326-328: South Carolina, Union District. Nathaniel Gist for $2000 to John S. Murrell of same, lot in Union Village bounded on Virgin & Union Street adj. Nathanl Gist, 24 Dec 1831. Nathl Gist (Seal), Wit: James McMullan, John P.Thompson. Elisabeth L. Gist, wife of Nathaniel Gist, relinquished dower 24 Dec 1831 before J. P. Thomson, Q.U. Proved by the oath of John P. Thompson Esqr., 15 Feb 1832 before J. Rogers, Q. U. Recorded 15 Feb 1832.

V, 328-329: State of Indiana, Davis County. Probate Court, January Term 1832. The court being sufficient advised & informed that there are three heirs of the estate of the late George Gregory decd to wit, Letty Gregory now the wife of Green McCoferrty, Robert Gregory & Sarah Ann Gregory, the two latter being infants under the age of 21 years, the said Robert Gregory being over the age of fourteen years, comes into court and makes choice of the said Green McCofferty for his guardian, 12 Jan 1832. John Van Truss, Clerk D. P. C. Daviess County, State of Indiana. We the undersigned judges of the circuit court certified that John Van Truss is the Clerk of the Circuit & Probate Court and the forgoing signature purporting to be his is genuine, 12 March 1832. Michael Murphy, Ephraim Thompson. Recorded 9 April 1832.

V, 330-332: South Carolina, Union District. Whereas Bernard Glenn, late of the state and district aforesaid, departed this life in the year 1831 intestate, leaving a considerable real and personal estate distributable among his heirs at law and whereas the said Bernard Glenn died without any issue and my wife Mary T. N. Sims being the daughter of the late Patience T. Herndon decd who was one of the sisters of the whole blood of the said Bernard Glenn decd is entitled as one of the heirs at law to the one half of the one seventh part of the estate real and personal, and whereas I, Reuben Sims, of the state and district aforesaid, by virtue of my marital rights as the husband of the said Mary T. N. Sims am entitled to receive the interest in said estate to which my wife may be entitled and whereas my wife is entitled to a considerable real estate by the death of her father Newton Hopkins, late of the District of Chester, who died intestate, and I am desirous of having to my said wife Mary T. N. Sims & her heirs the sole use & enjoyment of the several estates before mentioned, discharged from any liability on account of my debts, contracts or agreements, for love & affection and $500 paid by John N. Herndon of the District of Newberry, relinquish to said John N. Herndon in trust only for the sole use of my wife during her life and at her death to be divided amongst her children, 15 March 1832. R. Sims (Seal), Wit: D. A. Thomas, John Thomas, Thos Belue. Proved by the oath of D. A. Thomas 15 March 1832 before E. P. Porter, Q. U. Recorded 15 March 1832.

V, 332-333: Dorcas Thomson, Augustin P. Thomson, Nancy N. Thomson, Elisabeth H. Thomson, of the District of Union, for $602 paid by Richard Thomson and Elijah Pool of the District of Spartanburgh, tract of 200 acres granted to Joseph Park on both sides of McClures Creek, 15 Nov 1831. Dorcas Thomson (LS), Angeline [*sic*] P. Thomson (LS), Nancy N. Thomson (LS), Elisabeth H. Thomson (LS), Wit: Saml O. Gordon, W. Harris. Proved by the oath of Saml O. Gordon 2 April 1832 before J. Rogers, Q. U. Recorded 2 April 1832.

V, 334-335: South Carolina, Union District. James Dugan of district aforesaid for natural love and affection to my wife's granddaughter Sarah Ann McDaniel & my wife's grandson James Thomas McDaniel, daughter & son of Robert McDaniel, to the above named Sarah Ann my negro girl Jinny and a filly named Jennet, two heifers, a bed & furniture; to James Thomas McDaniel a tract of land called the Buncomb tract on the small branches of Tyger River, 170 acres, 3 April 1832. James Dugan (LS), Wit: Joseph H.

Dogan, Thos Sartor, John C. Jeter. Proved by the oath of Dr. Joseph H. Dogan 9 April 1832 before J. Rogers, Q. U. Recorded 9 April 1832.

V, 335-338: South Carolina, Union District. James Dugan of district aforesaid for love and affection to my wife's son Robert McDaniel and my wife's sons in law Nathanl Gist & Argulous V. Jeter of same and William Moore of the district of Laurens, all interest to all my real and personal estate herein after named, several tracts amounting to 922 acres of land and conveyed by Robert McDaniel to myself, Tho Jinkins tract lying on Swift Run adj. A. V. Jeter; the plantation called the mill tract, composed of several parcels containing in all 271¼ acres and conveyed by Thomas Skein & Nicholas Skein to Robert Crenshaw and myself & a tract in Newberry District formerly belonging to the estate of Col. Thomas Dugan decd adj. Col. Glenn, McMathis[?], Wm. Turpin, Mrs. Smith, Nathl Vance, McGunnery[?] and others, 632 acres, with the following negroes Tom, Abram, Daniel Sago, Toney, Jasper, Charles, Balaam, Will, Layfette, Grace, Letty, Rethe, Hannah, Ann, Peggy, Rode, Alex, Sally, Lucinda, Winney, Sam, Daphney, Andy & Jude; provided the above named pay all my debts & furnish myself & my wife Frances each with $200 annually, 3 April 1832. James Dugan (LS), Wit: Joseph H. Dogan, Thos Sartor, John C. Jeter. Proved by the oath of Joseph H. Dogan 9 April 1832 before J. Rogers, Q. U. Recorded 9 April 1832.

V, 338-339: South Carolina, Union District. Feby 12th 1831. Handcock Porter Senior of district aforesaid for $710 to John P. Porter, Elisa P. Porter, Hancock Porter Jr., John Gregory Senr, 314 acres, sold as the property of Jedathan [Porter] decd, on the waters of Big Browns Creek, also one tract of land on waters of Big & Little Browns Creek adj. Sarah Sharp, Absolam Ivey, & Giles Sharp, 150 acres. Hancock Porter (mark) (LS), Wit: M. M. Jackson, James Turner, James Wilson. Proved by the oath of James Turner 10 Jan 1832 before W. Skelton, J.P. Recorded 12 March 1832.

V, 340-341: South Carolina, Union District. Daniel A. Mitchell of district aforesaid for $434.91 to Titus G. Farr of same, 109 acres on waters of Neals Big Creek, waters of Broad River, 17 Feb 1832. D. A. Mitchell (Seal), Wit: S. J. Ashley, Saml Nelson, Jas. W. Perry. Proved by the oath of Stephen J. Ashley 16 March 1832 before J. T. McJunkin, J.P. Recorded 19 March 1832.

V, 341-342: South Carolina, Union District. Ann Davis, Edward S. Henly, John W. Davis & Saml J. Hughey, bound to Saml M. Gowdey admr. of Amos Davis decd in the sum of $1200, 6 April 1830, the condition of the obligation is such that whereas a Judgment having been obtained in Charleston in favour of Robert McWilliams admr. against Amos Davis decd amount at this time between six & seven hundred dollars, Saml M. Gowdey admr. of Amos Davis decd has held back money belonging to the estate for the purpose of paying said judgment should it be presented to him as admr., should the said Saml M. Gowdey admr pay the amount of money detained in his hands, the above bounden persons hold themselves bound until said judgment & Cost is satisfied, 6 April 1830. Ann Davis (LS), Edward F. Hendley (LS), John W.

Davis (LS), Saml J. Hoey (LS), Wit: Thos R. Gowdy. Proved by the oath of Joseph G. Clowney 7 Feb 1832 before J. Rogers, Q. U. Recorded 7 Feb 1832.

V, 342-344: Jonathan Hampton of Union District for $200 to Francis Logan of same, tract on north fork of Browns Creek, 85 acres adj. Samuel Sharp & Robt Savage & the land whereon Z. Ivey now lives, the same being the land allotted to Andrew Hampton's wife from the estate of William Sharp decd, 7 Feb 1832. J. Hampton (LS), Wit: J. Rogers, Henry[?] Long. Proved by the oath of John Rogers 6 March 1832 before John Giles, Q. U. Recorded 6 March 1832.

V, 344-345: South Carolina, Union District. Samuel Harlan of district aforesaid for $450 to Churchill Gibbes of same, tract on Fairforest Creek, 80 acres adj. John P. Woodson, 27 Dec 1831. Saml Harlan (LS), Wit: Samuel F. Rice, Mary Robinson. Sarah Harlan (X), wife of Samuel Harlan, relinquished dower 17 Jan 1832 before H. Gibbs, Q. U. Proved by the oath of Mary Robinson 17 Jan 1832 before H. Gibbs, Q. U. Recorded 17 Jan 1832.

V, 346-349: 5 Oct 1829, William K. Clowney, Esqr., Commissioner of the Court of Equity for Union District, to Jerry Phillips, whereas Catharine C. Edwards & Charles W. Edwards infant by his guardian Catherine Edwards on or about 26 June did exhibit their bill of complaint in the court of equity against Daniel C. Edwards, exrs., of Edward Edwards decd & others, praying that certain lands belonging to the estate of said Edward Edwards deceased be vested in a new trustee to be appointed by this Court, and on 5 Oct did sell the said land to Jerry Phillips for $500, 605 acres on both sides of Padgets Creek on the south side of Tygar River, 570 acres on the west side of Pelhams Springs branch, adj. Richd Pelham, William Turpin, Roll Jenkins, Phillips, Gage, and by the other tract conveyed in this deed & James Davis' land, the other tract of 135 acres including the dwelling house and Plantation whereon Ransom Davis formerly lived, part of a tract granted to Robert Watkins in 1772. Wm. K. Clowney (Seal), Wit: John W. Smith, John Hughey. Proved by the oath of Dr. J. W. Smith 13 March 1832 before J. Rogers, Q. U. Recorded 13 March 1832.

V, 349-350: James Quinn of the District of Spartanburgh for $62.50 to A. W. F. McBride of Union District, tract part in Spartanburgh and part in Union District adj. widow Black, Murphey, 23½ acres, 19 Feb 1832. James Quinn (LS), Wit: Wm. J. Gordon, Thos Sparks. Proved by the oath of William J. Gordon before William Reid, J. Q. 12 March 1832. Recorded 11 May 1832.

V, 350-352: South Carolina, Union District. Jane Blasingame, John Blasingame, Nancy Blasingame, Polly Blasingame, Washington Blasingame, Betsy Ann Blasingame & Benjamin West of district aforesaid & Francis Parham of Green County, Alabama, for $74 to William West of district aforesaid, tract on the waters of Sugar Creek, 197 acres, granted to Philip Blasingame, adj. Leml Lancaster, Philip Blasingame, Hembey, Isaac Bogan, 15 Sept 1831. Jane Blasingame (X) (Seal), Nancy Blasingame (X) (LS), Mary Blasingame (X)

(LS), Washington Blasingame (LS), Elizabeth A. Blasingame (LS), Benjamin West (LS), Wit: Larkin Lancaster, Lemuel Lancaster. Proved by the oath of Larkin Lancaster 24 Feb 1832 before J. Palmer, J. P. Recorded 7 May 1832.

V, 352-354: South Carolina, Union District. John Hart of said district for $375 to Robert McBeth of same, tract on the waters of Dining Creek, 120 acres adj. said John McBeth, 13 Nov 1831. John Hart (LS), Wit: Wm. B. Murphy, James Hay, Richard H. Hughey. Elisabeth Hart, wife of John Hart, relinquished dower 22 Dec 1831 before Hiram Gibbs, Q. U. Proved by the oath of James Hay 28 April 1832 before J. Rogers, Q. U. Recorded 28 April 1832.

V, 354-355: William Williams of Union District for $260 to Lemuel Lancaster of same, 119 acres, part of a tract purchased of William R. Wilbourn on both sides Ainsworth Branch, waters of Sugar Creek, 21 Sept 1831. William Williams (LS), Wit: Larkin Lancaster, Jas Lancaster. Proved by the oath of Larkin Lancaster 23 Sept 1831 before H. Gibbs, Q.U. Hannah Williams (X), wife of William Williams, relinquished dower 23 Sept 1831 before H. Gibbs, Q.U. Recorded 7 May 1832.

V, 356-357: South Carolina, Union District. William Goudelock of district aforesaid, attorney in fact for Francis Whelchel of Hall County [Georgia?], for $1600 to Samuel J. Hoey, tract on both sides of Guilkies Creek, 200 acres, adj. McCullough, 21 Nov 1831. Wm Goudelock for Francis Whelchel, Wit: Wm Tate, D. Goudelock Jr. Proved by the oath of William Tate 21 Nov 1831 before W. Goudelock, J. P. Recorded 25 May 1832.

V, 357-358: South Carolina, Union District. Joseph Gist of district aforesaid for love and affection for my son John Gist and for one dollar, tract in Union District on Broad River adj. Danl Mitchell, Widow Nelson, Bowles, John Giles, Maj. Faucett, Naugher & Judge Johnson, the same being a tract conveyed by Col. Joseph Hughes to me and represented in a plat of resurvey made 29 Oct 1824 by Richard Thomson, dated 9 Oct 1830. Jos Gist (Seal), Wit: W. N. Askew, William Reid. Proved by the oath of Dr. William N. Askew 29 May 1832 before J. Rogers, Q. U. Recorded 29 May 1832.

V, 358-359: Georgia, Hall County. F. Whelchel Junr of county aforesaid appoint William Goudelock of Union District my lawful attorney to sell a tract deeded to me by John Tindal on both sides Gilkies Creek adj. John McCollough, Thomas Black, Gibson Rickman, Widow Davis, __ Sept 1831. F. Whelchel Senr, Wit: Thos Thornton, J. P. John B. Nichols, Clerk of the inferior court of said county, certified that Thos Thornton was a justice of the peace, 20 Sept 1831. Thos S. Tate, one of the Judges of the inferior court certified that John B. Nichols was clerk, 10 Sept 1831. Recorded 25 May 1832.

V, 360: Jesse Holcomb of Union District for natural love and affection to my son Jesse Holcomb of same, tract of land on which I now live, 85 acres adj. William Sparks, Jesse Boatman, Fredk Jackson, Nevel G. Holcomb, at the death of myself and my wife, dated __ Feb 1832. Jesse Holcomb (X), Wit:

Nevel G. Holcomb, H. H. Holcomb. Proved by the oath of H. H. Holcomb 2 April 1832 before J. Rogers, Q. U. Recorded 2 April 1832.

V, 360-362: South Carolina, Union District. Saml J. Hoey for $1600 to William Goudelock atty in fact for Francis Whelchel Senr of Hall County, Georgia, mortgage of tract on both sides of Gilkies Creek, 200 acres, 21 Nov 1831. Saml J. Hoey (LS), Wit: William Tate, D. Goudelock Jr. Satisfied 13 March 1844. William Goudelock Esqr deposed that William Tate, one of the witnesses, is dead and that Davis Goudelock Jr. has left the state and that he is well acquainted with the hand write of both the witnesses, 25 May 11832 before J. Rogers, Q. U. Recorded 25 May 1832.

V, 362-363: South Carolina, Union District. Syntha Jackson of state aforesaid for $22 to M. M. [Mark] Jackson of same, all the gold, silver, brass, copper, or lead that is or can be found on a tract of land on the west side of Fairforest and on the waters of Sugar Creek, 87 acres, adj. W. R. Wilbourn, Elisha Palmer, Thomas Smith, 30 July 1831. Syntha Jackson (X) (LS), Wit: J. S. Jones, W. Morgan, Toliver Stripling. Proved by the oath of James Jones 24 March 1832 before David White, Q. U. Recorded 24 March 1832.

V, 363-365: John Anderson of Union District for $900 to George L. Smith, 199 acres on both sides of Morrises Branch adj. Maj. Thomas Young, John Clark, Jas Willard, John Anderson, Christopher Young, and the waggon road, per plat mae by Richd Thomson, D. S., 7 May 1832. John Anderson (LS), Wit: Richd Thomson, Isaac Whitton. Proved by the oath of Isaac Whitton 7 May 1832 before J. Rogers, Q. U. Susannah Anderson, wife of John Anderson, relinquished dower 31 May 1832 before J. Rogers, Q.U. Recorded 31 May 1832.

V, 365-366: Charles B. N. Rice vs Maj. Thos Young. Trespass to try titles & for Damages &c. The parties in this case agree that it shall be settled & finally disposed of in the following manner: that the lines held & claimed under by the defendant call'd and known as the Brandon lines on the plats under which he claims shall be considered & known as the dividing lines between them, 16 March 1832. C. B. N. Rice (LS), Thos Young (LS), Wit: Thos Sartor, H. W. Foote. Proved by the oath of Thomas Sartor 4 June 1832 before J. Rogers, Q. U. Recorded 4 June 1832.

V, 366-368: South Carolina, Union District. Jerome Miller of district aforesaid for love and affection to my son William Miller and for $400 which he is to account for after my decease out of my estate, 116 acres on waters of Browns Creek & Buffalow Creek, it being part of a tract I purchased of Abel Ezell on both sides of the road from Union Court House to Spartanburgh, 1 July 1831. Jerome Miller (LS), Wit: Ellis Palmer, Thos Scott (mark). Proved by the oath of Ellis Palmer 4 June 1832 before J. Rogers, Q.U. Mary Miller (X), wife of Jerome Miller, relinquished dower 10 May 1832 before J. Rogers, Q.U.

V, 368-370: John Anderson, Sheriff of Union District, by virtue of a decree from the court of ordinary tested 1 June 1829 at the suit of Jane Wear vs Thos Taylor & others to sell a tract of 120 acres on a branch of Packolet River adj. William Huckaby, William Brown, Thos Pridemore, Dr. Otterson, sold for $300 to Anthony Bennett, all the estate, right, title & interest which Thos Wear decd had in the same, 6 June 1829. John Anderson S. U. D. (LS), Wit: Wm White, Jasper Gibbs. Proved by the oath of H. Gibbs who testified to the hand write of William White & Jasper Gibbs, and that William White is dead and Jasper Gibbs has left the district, 4 June 1832, before J. Rogers, Q. U. Recorded 4 June 1832.

V, 370: South Carolina, Union District. Clough S. Meng for $100 to Jas E. Meng of same, all my right, title and interest in the real estate of Jas Meng decd, and also in the estate of my mother Sarah Meng at her death, as one of the legatees of the said James Meng decd & Sarah Meng, 23 June 1831. C. S. Meng (LS), Wit: Charles Meng, J. Rogers. Proved by the oath of John Rogers 9 June 1832 before Saml Davis, J. P. Recorded 9 June 1832.

V, 371: Recd in Feb 1831 of Jas E. Meng his note of hand for $100 which when paid will be in full of my legal claims in the estate of Jas Meng decd, 5 May 18 31. W. W. Meng, Wit: Julian Hix, Robt Macbeth, J. Rogers. Proved by the oath of John Rogers 9 June 1832 before Saml Davis, J.P. Recorded 9 June 1832.

V, 371-372: South Carolina, Union District. Jas Edward Meng of district aforesaid for in consideration of a negro boy named Albert paid by William W. Meng of same, all my right, title & interest in the real estate of James Meng decd and is also my right, title & interest I purchased of W. W. Meng & Clough S. Meng and also my right in the estate of my mother Sarah Meng at her death, as one of the legatees of the said James Meng decd, 18 July 1831. Jas. E. Meng (LS), wit: Robt McBeth, J. Rogers. Proved by the oath of John Rogers 9 June 1832 before Saml Davis, J.P. Recorded 9 June 1832.

V, 372-373: John Anderson for $200 to Charles Humphries, tract on waters of Fairforest, being part of a tract that did belong to the widow Shaw on the branch adj. Charles Humphries, 50 acres, adj. Charles Humphries, Henry Anderson, M. Kershaw, 31 Jan 1821. John Anderson (Seal), Wit: Thos Young, Thos Humphries. Proved by the oath of Thos Humphries 9 June 1832 before J. Rogers, Q.U. Recorded 9 June 1832.

V, 373-375: South Carolina, Union District. John Cole of Union District for $5 to William Cole of same, all my share, portion, or dividend of a tract of 125 acres on waters of Packolett River conveyed by my mother Mary Cole to the said William Cole at $2 per acre for her maintenance by the said William Cole as long as it will last, 22 Aug 1816. John Cole (mark) (Seal), Wit: James Foster Jr., Jordan Bailey (X). Proved by the oath of Jordan Bailey 10 June 1832 before Lott Whitlock, J.P. Recorded 11 June 1832.

V, 375-377: William Sims of Union District for love and affection to my son Clough Sims of same, 1200 acres at the mouth of the first hollow below Woods Ferry landing on Broad River, to the old fork of the road leading to McCreights, W. Sims Senr, William A. Sims, 4 Feb 1821. W. Sims (LS), Wit: J. S. Sims, Jno. K. B. Sims. Proved by the oath of Maj. Jos. S. Sims 23 June 1832 before J. Rogers, Q. U. Recorded 23 June 1832.

V, 377: South Carolina, Union District. J. Beaty of Union District for $542 to Saml Batey of same, 217 acres adj. John Cunningham decd, Daniel Chandler, William Skelton, M. Chandler, Mrs. Margaret Batey, 14 Sept 1829. J. Batey (Seal), Wit: Jasper Saunders, Gideon Steen. Proved by the oath of Gideon Steen 22 June 1832 before J. Rogers, Q. U. Recorded 22 June 1832.

V, 378: South Carolina, Union District. Saml Beaty, Martha Batey, J. Batey, Margaret Ann Batey, of aforesaid district for $1193 to Robert Batey of same, 391 acres on the waters of Neals Creek adj. Robt Batey, M. Lockhart, Jarret Young, Joseph Reeder, John Saunders, John McBeth, and Fairforest Creek, 14 Sept 1829. J. Batey (Seal), S. Beaty (LS), M. A. Beaty (LS), Patsey Beaty, Wit: Jasper Saunders, Gideon Steen. Proved by the oath of Gideon Steen 22 June 1832 before J. Rogers, Q. U. Recorded 22 June 1832.

V, 379-380: South Carolina, Union District. Hancock Porter for $50 to Sarah Porter of same, tract conveyed to me from Thos Albritton on the north side of the north branch of Browns Creek, 65 acres adj. Richard Faucett, Wm. Sharp, 13 Feb 1832. Hancock Porter (X) (Seal), Wit: Thos G. Page, Tillett Porter (X). Mary Porter (X), wife of Hancock Porter, relinquished dower 23 June 1832 before John Giles, Q.U. Proved by the oath of Tillet Porter (X) 23 June 1832 before J. Rogers, Q. U.

V, 380-382: South Carolina, Union District. George Brandon of the District of Union for $36 to E. M. Bobo of same, tract on waters of Browns Creek on the main Pinkney Road, 12 acres. 22 March 1832. George Brandon (LS), Wit: Clough S. Meng, Thos Goodrum, Proved by the oath of C. S. Meng 14 June 1832 before J. Rogers, Q.U. Frances Brandon (mark), wife of George Brandon, relinquished dower 29 June 1832 before J. Rogers, Q. U. Recorded 29 June 1832.

V, 382-384: South Carolina, Union District. James Duncan, son of Alexander, of the district aforesaid for natural love and affection to my granddaughter Elisabeth Bobo & to her husband Dr. Edward M. Bobo of same, and for $5, tract on the south west side of Tyger River adj. estate of Kindred Bobo, Bailey Lawson, Sion & Bird Murphy, Ambrose Ray, Lewis Bobo, Drury Murrell, Hosea Wilbanks, being the tract whereon I now live, 223½ acres, 2 July 1832. James Duncan, son of Alexr (LS), Wit: Z. P. Herndon, D. Wallace, E. M. Glenn. Proved by the oath of E. M. Glenn 12 July 1832 before J. Rogers, Q. U. Elisabeth Duncan, wife of Jas Duncan, relinquished dower 11 July 1832 before J. Rogers, Q. U. Recorded 12 July 1832.

V, 384-386: South Carolina, Union District. James Duncan, son of Alexander, of the district aforesaid for $500 to Edward M. Bobo of same, tract known as the Southwick Tract in Spartanburgh District on Tyger River on the north side adj Nickolls, Danl White, 200 acres, 2 June 1832. James Duncan, son of Alexr (LS), Wit: W. W. Meng, Z. Hooker, E. M. Glenn. Elisabeth Duncan, wife of Jas Duncan, relinquished dower 11 July 1832 before J. Rogers, Q. U. Proved by the oath of E. M. Glenn 12 July 1832 before J. Rogers, Q. U. Recorded 12 July 1832.

V, 386-387: South Carolina, Union District. Elizabeth Bobo & Edward M. Bobo of Unionville for natural love and affection to our Grand father James Duncan, son of Alexr, and for $5, tract whereon he now lives on the north west side of Tyger River, it being the land whereon Jesse D. Murphy formerly lived and the place which him the said James Duncan, son of Alexr, purchased of Ambros Ray and others, 2 July 1821. Elisabeth Bobo (LS), E. M. Bobo (LS), Wit: Z. P. Herndon, D. Wallace, E. M. Glenn, Proved by the oath of E. M. Glenn 12 July 1832 before J. Rogers, Q. U. Recorded 12 July 1832.

V, 387-389: South Carolina, Union District. 30 Dec 1831, William Malone to Foster Hooker, both of aforesaid district, for his being indebted to the said Foster hook by his two notes, dated 19 Nov 1831 one for $50 due 25 Dec 1832 and one for $50 due 25 Dec 1833, mortgage of tract on waters of Enoree River adj. David Spiva, W. C. Pearson, said William Malone, Joseph Goswick, 50 acres. William Malone (LS), Foster Hooker (LS), Wit: John Bates, J. B. Pearson. Proved by the oath of J. B. Pearson 16 June 1832 before John Norman, J.Q. Recorded 2 July 1832.

V, 389-390: South Carolina, Union District. Nicholas Corry of district aforesaid to Robert Corry, tract whereon the said Robt Corry now liveth, conveyed to said Nicholas Corry by deed 2 Jan 1797 from Ignatius Turley, also tract adj. the said tract conveyed by deed to said Nicholas Corry by said Ignatius Turley 18 Dec 1797, also tract on a branch of McKowns Creek, formerly belonging to Manos Dawson sold by him to Abner Potts[?] and sold by John Bates, sheriff, by virtue of a writ of fieri facias as the suit of Nicholas Corry and conveyed by said Bates in title dated 26 Nov 1826, also two tracts of land on waters of Gilkies Creek conveyed to Nicholas Corry by John Waters, his brothers & sisters 22 March 1826 & 1 Sept 1824, dated 16 Feb 1832. Nicholas Corry (LS), Wit: Saml Patrick, Gabriel Patrick Jr. Proved by the oath of Gabriel Patrick Jr., 29 March 1832 before Isaac Peeler, J.P. Recorded 2 July 1832.

V, 390-391: South Carolina, Union District. J. Batey, Rob't Batey, Martha Batey, and Margaret Ann Beaty, of aforesaid district for $685 to Saml Batey of same, tract on waters of Tinker Creek (being a part of the old Jolly survey) 137 acres adj. John Steen, Saml Beaty, John Cunningham, Mrs. Margaret Beaty, Martha Beaty & Margaret A. Beaty, 14 Sept 1829. J. Beaty (Seal), M. A. Beaty (LS), Patsey Beaty, Robt Beaty (LS), Wit: Jasper Saunders, Gideon

Steen. Proved by the oath of Gideon Steen 22 June 1832 before J. Rogers, Q. U. Recorded 22 June 1832.

V, 392-393: 2 Feb 1832, Job Hammond to John Rogers, whereas said Job Hammond stands indebted tot he said John Rogers by his note of hand for $100, mortgage of tract on Rocky Creek, 58 acres adj. Jas McDanal, Thos Howard, Joseph Greer. Job Hammond (Seal), Wit: A. W. Thomson, D. A. Mitchell. Proved by the oath of Daniel A. Mitchell 16 July 1832 before James Rountree, J.P. Recorded 16 July 1832.

V, 394-395: Hugh Milling of the District of Fairfield for $100 quit claim to James Johnson of the City of Charleston, to the tract of land of 1000 ares in the District of Ninety Six, now Union District, on the waters of London Bridge Creek adj. William McKown, John Jenkins, granted to Alexander Johnston 1 April 1793, 7 March 1832. H. Milling (LS), D. R. Evans, John L. Kernaghan. Proved in Fairfield District by the oath of David R. Evans 14 May 1832 before James Phillips, J.P. Recorded 19 July 1832.

V, 395-396: James Johnston of the City of Charleston for $100 to Hugh Milling of Fairfield District, quit claim of tract of 1000 acres on London Bridge Creek of Broad River adj. Mr. Atkinson, Robinson, Lamkin, Mr. Forsyth, Francis Bremar, Jonathan Gilkie & Isaac Chapman, granted to said Hugh Milling 3 Dec 1792, 7 March 1832. James Johnston (LS), wit: D. R. Evans, John L. Kernaghan. Proved in Fairfield District by the oath of David R. Evans 14 May 1832 before James Phillips, J.P. Recorded 19 July 1832.

V, 397-399: South Carolina, Union District. Samuel Harris of Union District for $100 to John Gregory of same, 130 acres on the waters of Swift Creek, part of a larger tract granted to James Hall 13 Oct 1784, south of the line between William Sims & said Hall, 100 acres, recorded in Grant Bok FFFF, page 157, also the part west of said line granted to William Sims, part taken of 407 acres granted to said Sims 2 June 1788, and 30 acres adj. land granted to Bartholomew Baker recorded in book WWW No. 5, page 472, 19 March 1832. Samuel Harris (LS), Wit: Isaac Gregory, Thos Y. Gregory, Levi Gregory. Proved by the oath of Thos Y. Gregory 11 June 1832 before E. P. Porter, Q. U. Amy Harris (X), wife of Samuel Harris, relinquished dower 13 June 1832 before E. P. Porter, Q. U. Recorded 25 July 1832.

V, 399-401: South Carolina, Union District. Edward M. Bobo & Zadok Hooker of said district for $2300 to Nathaniel Gist of same, tract on north side Tyger River adj. estate Capt. Barrum Bobo on Dutchman's Creek, adj. Thomas Layton, Robt Browning, Benj. Landrum, 443 acres, formerly belonging to John Parham, Benj & William Landrum, 9 Feb 1831. E. M. Bobo (LS), Z. Hooker (LS), Wit: Thos N. Dawkins, A. W. Thomson. Elisabeth Bobo, wife of E. M. Bobo, relinquished dower 15 June 1832 before J. Rogers, Q. U. Mary A. Hooker, wife of Zadok Hooker, relinquished dower 26 July 1832 before J. Rogers, Q. U. Proved by the oath of A. W. Thomson 27 July 1832 before J. Rogers, Q. U. Recorded 27 July 1832.

V, 401-402: Thomas Hart of Union District for love, good will & affection to my son Thomas Hart of same, 100 acres on Fair Forrest adj. James Groghan[?], Thomson White, John McBeth, 3 Aug 1830. Thos Hart (X) (LS), Wit: Caleb Greer, Thos S. Greer, John Hunt. Proved by the oath of Caleb Greer 6 Aug 1830 before H. Gibbs, J. Q. Recorded 9 Aug 1830.

V, 402-403: South Carolina, Union District. Elizabeth Duncan, wife of James Duncan, son of Alexr, for natural love and affection to my youngest grandson Charles T. Murphy, minor son of Bird & Charlotte Murphy, all my right and title to dowry in the estate of my present husband, little or much, as I am getting old & my grandson C. T.Murphy has not as yet had any part of his grand father's estate, 17 July 1832. Elisabeth Duncan (X) (LS), Wit: Isaac P. Murphy, Jepthah M. Murphy. Proved by the oath of Isaac P. Murphy 17 July 1832 before Fredk Jackson, J. P. Recorded 10 July 1832.

V, 403-404: South Carolina, Union District. Charles Gault of district aforesaid for $300 to Edmond Gault, 150 acres on the head of the bush branch near the Spartanburgh Road adj. Thos B. Going, Lucy Falls, David Harvey, Isaac Davis, 5 July 1832. Charles Gault (Seal), Wit: Ellis Fowler, James Gault. Proved by the oath of James Gault 27 July 1832 before Saml Mosley, J. Q. Nancy Gault (X), wife of Charles Gault, 5 July 1832 before Saml Mosley, J. Q. Recorded 6 Aug 1832.

V, 405: In Equity. Union District. Exparte. Thos Bowker, W. W. Glenn, & Lucy Ivey by her next friend. Petition. It is ordered that W. W. Glenn be appointed trustee for the within named Lucy Ivey and that he protect her property against her husband who deserted her and left her in destitute circumstances with a family. That Thomas Bowker guardian of W. G. O. Bowker now deceased be authorized and directed to deliver over the property of said W. G. O. Bowker to W. W. Glenn the trustee, 26 June 1832.

Bird M. Pearson, Commissioner and Register in Equity for Union District certify the foregoing to be a true copy of the order, 3 Sept 1832.

Schedule. Negroes David, Hempe with her two children Betsy & Bill, & an interest in the estate of Bernard Glenn, late of Union District now decd, 3 Sept 1832. Recorded 3 Sept 1832.

V, 406-408: B. Johnson, Sheriff of Union District, by virtue of an order of the court of common pleas to produce[?] a mortgage to me directed issued out of the court of common pleas held for the district of Union, first Monday in October 1831 at the suit of Henry Galman to levy of the lands & tenements of John H. Galman $1741.79, and taken off the lands of said John H. Galman, tract of 600 acres on branches of Browns Creek adj. lands of Eliz. Lang, Aron M. Collum, John Galman, Theodore Bevis, Saml Smith, Isaac Haney, Nancy Shell, purchased by Albert Hemingway of York District for $980, 3 May 1832. Bartholomew Johnson S. U. D. (Seal), Wit: Wm. M. Thomson, Titus G. Farr.

Proved by the oath of William M. Thomson 30 May 1832 before E. McGraw, Q. U. Recorded 8 Sept 1832.

V, 408-410: 2 March 1832, Richard Sharp to John Rogers, whereas said Richard Sharp stands indebted to said John Rogers in the sum of $300 by his note of hand, payable 2 March 1834, mortgage of, 225 acres on waters of Fanning Creek, also two negroes, one woman named Eave and one boy Jesse, with all stock and furniture. Richard Sharp (Seal), Wit: Robt Martin, B. Johnson. Proved by the oath of B. Johnson, Esqr., 13 Aug 1832 before James Rountree, J.P. Recorded 13 Aug 1832.

V, 410-412: B. Johnson, Sheriff of Union District, by virtue of an order from the Ordinary of Union District dated 20 Feb 1832 at the suit of David Johnson applicant against William Johnson & others defts, exparte, to sell a tract of land belonging to the estate of David Johnson decd, 103 acres on Broad River, sold to William Kelly of Union District for $400.50, 4 June 1832. B. Johnson, S. U. D. (Seal), Wit: E. Wilbourn, Wm. B. Murphy. Proved by the oath of E. Wilbourn 12 Sept 1832 before J. Rogers, Q. U. Recorded 12 Sept 1832.

V, 412-413: South Carolina, Union District. John Miller of above district for $406 to Thomas Walker of same, 101½ acres on the waters of Buffalow Creek, 23 Nov 1832. John Miller (Seal), Wit: James Rowntree, Bay Little (X). Proved by the oath of James Rountree, Esq., 3 Sept 1832 before J. Rogers, Q. U. Recorded 3 Sept 1832.

V, 414-415: Thomas Walker of Union District for $20 to Thomas Belew, 101½ acres in Union District on the main road from Union Court House to Spartanburgh C. H., and on the head of Buffalow Creek, waters of Fairforest, 3 Sept 1832. Thomas Walker (Seal), Wit: Elias Mitchell, J. Rogers. Proved by the oath of Col. Elias Mitchell 3 Sept 1832 before J. Rogers, Q. U. Recorded 3 Sept 1832.

V, 415-417: South Carolina, Union District. Isaiah Whitlock of district aforesaid for $400 to James Berry of same, tract on waters of Sugar Creek and Fairforest Creek adj. William Rountree, Polly Gibbs, 13 Nov 1826. Isaiah Whitlock (LS), Wit: J. S. Sims, John Parkins Jr. Isaiah Whitlock confirms the deed because it was signed when he was a minor, and now he is of full age, 7 Feb 1827. Isaiah Whitlock (LS), Wit: Wm. F. Clowney, A. W. Thomson, James Johnson. Proved by the oath of J. S. Sims 22 Sept 1832 before James Rountree, J.P. Proved by the oath of A. W. Thomson 22 Sept 1832 before James Rountree, J.P.

V, 417-418: South Carolina, Union District. Gideon Steen of district aforesaid for $135 to John Steen of same, 59½ acres on a branch of Tinker Creek, part of tract granted to James Tate adj. Samuel Beaty. 31 Dec 1830. Gideon Steen (LS), Wit: Stephen Johnson, Campbell Vance, Jefferies Steen. Proved by the oath of Stephen Johnson 21 Sept 1832 before J. Rogers. Recorded 21 Sept 1832.

V, 418-419: South Carolina, Union District. Sophia Golding of district aforesaid for good will and affection to Fairforest Presbyterian Church & for the better securing a burying ground for myself & friends to give to Jesse Carson, James K. Means & Washington Harris, Trustees of Fairforest Presbyterian Church, a portion of ground of 112 rods including the old grave yard, 25 Aug 1832. Sophonisba Golding (LS), Wit: John Wright, Eliza Nott. Proved by the oath of John Wright 8 Sept 1832 before John Rogers. Recorded 1 Sept 1832.

V, 419-420: A. W. Thomson of Union District for $1994 to William Rice, Esqr., tract formerly owned by Reuben Sims on Cane Creek, 727 acres, by deed of conveyance to myself 9 May 1832 from B. Johnson, Esqr., Sheriff, 11 May 1832. A. W. Thomson (LS), Wit: B. Johnson, Wm. M. Thompson. Proved by the oath of Bartholomew Johnson, 14 Sept 1832. Recorded 24 Sept 1832.

V, 420-421: South Carolina, Union District. John C. Jeter of district aforesaid for $250 to Edmund McQuaid of same, tract where John Boyd now lives and legally sold by the sheriff to John C. Jeter, 150 acres on Cane Creek, waters of Tyger River, adj. Nathan Cooper, Samuel Harris Smith & David Harris Junr, west on 25 acres called the Eaves Tract a part of the said Inman Grant adj. Bullard, Hedgespeth, sold by the sheriff as Boyd's right, 29 July 1832. John C. Jeter (LS), Wit: A. O. Jeter, Jeremiah Kingsley. Proved by the oath of A. O. Jeter 6 Aug 1832 before William Skelton, J.PO.

V, 421-422: South Carolina, Union District. John Hainy of district aforesaid for $40 to James Pair of same, 150 acres on the north fork of Browns Creek adj. Smith, 30 Jan 1832. John Hainey (LS), Wit: Andrew Pair, Joel Adams, Jesse Pair. Proved by the oath of Jesse Pair __ Sept 1832 before John Rogers. Recorded 2 Sept 1832.

V, 423-424: South Carolina, Union District. Nathaniel Rochester of Union District for $250 to Gideon Steen of same, 111 acres on a branch of Tinker Creek, part of a tract granted to James Tate, adj. John Foster, Isaac Gregory, John Cunningham, Robert Beaty, S. Beaty, 10 Jan 1827. Nathaniel Rochester, Wit: Samuel Beaty, John O. Steen. Proved by the oath of Col. S. Beaty 22 June 1832 before J. Rogers. Recorded 22 June 1832.

V, 424: South Carolina, Union District. Abram McJunkin of district aforesaid for $130.50 to Gideon Steen, 44½ acres adj. Thomas Sartor, Gideon Steen, Isaac Gregory, Joseph McJunkin, 18 Feb 1831. Abram McJunkin (Seal), Wit: John Rochester, Henry Kesler. Proved by the oath of Henry Keasler 24 Aug 1832 before J. Rogers, Q. U.

V, 424-425: South Carolina, Union District. Samuel Beaty, agent for John McJunkin, of district aforesaid for $100 to Gideon Steen, 140 acres on Tinkers Creek, waters of Tiger River, adj. Isaac Gregory, Thomas Sartor, estate of Robert Beaty, Samuel Beaty, Mrs. E. Cunningham, 15 Feb 1831. Samuel Beaty by power of attorney in fact for John McJunkin (LS), Wit: George C. Vance,

Joseph Saunders, J. S. Cunningham. Proved by the oath of James S. Cunningham 2 July 1832 before J. Rogers, Q. U. Recorded 2 July 1832.

V, 426-427: 6 Feb 1832, Stephen Fowler to William Gault, whereas said Stephen Fowler stands indebted to said WIlliam Gault in the sum of $26 by note, mortgage of tract on waters of Fanings Creek, 100 acres adj. Wm. Gault, Stephen Fowler, Jas Millwood, Mark Wood, and William Fowler. Stephen Fowler (X) (LS), Wit: Samuel Harris, Timothy Haney. Proved by the oath of Samuel Harris 5 Sept 1832 before J. Rogers. Recorded 5 Sept 1832.

V, 427-428: South Carolina, Union District. Daniel Smith of distirct aforeasid to Aaron Wilkins of same, all my right, title and interest in the real estate of Mary Smith decd, which has fallen to Hannah Alexander[?], John Smith, Mary Thompson, Catharine Richard, Sarah Davis, the heirs of Mary Smith, 2 March 1832. Daniel Smith (LS), Wit: Gabriel Patrick Senr, Jephthah Harrington. Proved by the oath of Gabriel Patrick 4 Aug 1832 before S. A. Goodman, Q.U. Recorded 6 Aug 1832.

V, 428-429: South Carolina, Union District. Lydia Petty of district aforesaid for $32.92 to Aaron Wilkins of same, tract on waters of Abatons Creek, 100 acres, 5 March 1832. Lydia Petty (X) (LS), Wit: William W. Austell, Aaron Cantell. Proved by the oath of William W. Austell 4 Aug 1832 before S. L. Gorden. Recorded 6 Aug 1832.

V, 430-431: Bartholomew Johnson, Sheriff of Union District, by virtue of a writ of fieri facias from the court of common pleas held 23 March 1829 at the suit of William B. Farr, and by virtue of a decree from the court of appearsl for this state last sitting in Columbia in a case of William B. Farr against Reuben Sims and others, to sell of the goods and chattels, lands and tenements of Reuben Sims $35.06 and $9654, sells 720 acres whreon Reuben Sims now lives and teh adjoining tract claimed by said Reuben Sims adj. land of Widow Glenn, Doct. James MEacham, John Thomas, Widow Tacker, Henry Beauford, William Rice, being the same land that was heretofore sold by John Anderson, late Sheriff of siad district, as the property of said Reubein Sims 11 May 1827, sold to A. W. Thomson for $1346, 9 May 1832. Bartholomew Johnson, S. U. D. (LS), Wit: Bird M. Pearson, John Jackson. Proved by the oath of John Jackson 25 Sept 1832 before John Rogers. Recorded 25 Sept 1832.

V, 431-433: South Carolina, Union District. John Phillips for $118[?] to Aaron Wilkins, 104 acres on waters of Abbetons Creek, part of tract which John Harrington, late of Union District deceased, died seized and possessed, sold under order of the court of common pleas of Union District for parittion among the heirs, and purchased by Ezra, Kate & Hezekiah Harrington, the one half of which said Kate Harrington, Y. J. Harrington & Robt Harrington by deed dated 11 March 1819 adj. Patrick, dated 28 Feb 1832. John Phillips (Seal), Wit: William W. Austell, Joseph Petty, Drury Byers. Proved by the oath of William W. Austell 4 Aug 1832 before S. L. Goodman. Recorded 6 Aug 1832.

V, 433-434: South Carolina, Union District. Fleming Harris of aforesaid district for $60 to Sally Porter of same, 30 acres on the waters of Browns Creek on the Pinckney Road adj. Robbin Savage, said Sally Porter, 1 Sept 1832. F. Harris (LS), Wit: James T. Porter. Rob V. Harris, Gid Porter (X). Jane Harris (X), wife of F. Harris, relinquished dower 29 Sept 1832. Proved by the oath of J. T. Porter 29 Sept 1832 before J. Rogers, Q.U. Recorded 29 Sept 1832.

V, 435-437: South Carolina, Union District. Indenture of three parts, 11 Sept 1832; John Stribling of the first part, and Hannah his wife of the second part and Francis Stribling of the third part; whereas Hannah Stribling hath heretofore given notice to act as a feme sole trader, Francis Stribling to act as trustee. John Stribling (LS), Hannah Stribling (mark) (LS), Francis Stribling (LS), Wit: Saml Stribling, Jas M. Stribling. Proved by the oath of Samuel Stribling 26 Oct 1832 before J. Rogers, Q. U. Recorded 8 Nov 1832.

V, 437-438: 11 Aug 1832, Austin Wood and Nancy Wood, daughter of Absalom Bailey, and Nancy Bailey, the heir of John Cole decd, of the District of Pickens, South Carolina, and John Bailey of the County of Franklin, Georgia, that Augustine Wood and Nancy Wood his wife for $5 paid by John Bailey, all their claim in a tract in Union District now in possession of William Cole on the Reedy branch adj. J. J. Foster, Robt Foster, Isaac McKissick and others, 574 acres, the property of John Cole, decd, being the seventh part of Nancy Bailey decd part of John Cole estate decd. Augustin Wood (X) (Seal), Nancy Wood (X) (Seal), Wit: Joel Bryan, Royal Bryan, J.P. Georgia, Franklin County. Thomas King, clerk of the inferior court certifies that Royal Bryan was a justice of the peace, 27 Oct 1832. Robert Pulliam, one of the judges of the inferior court certified that Thomas King was the clerk of court, 27 Oct 1832. Recorded 2 Nov 1832.

V, 439-440: Elisabeth Cole now Elisabeth Cannon of Habersham County, Georgia, for $20 to John Bailey of Franklin County, Georgia, all my part which is one seventh part in a tract of land which was willed to me by my father John Cole of Union District, with the rest of my brothers and sisters after the death of our mother which are the names as follows Richard Cole, John Cole, Nancy Cole now Nancy Bailey, Rody Cole now Rody Yearby, Lucy Cole now Lucy Bailey, Mary Cole now Mary Kindrick & now myself, Elizabeth Cole now Elisabeth Cannon, tract of 475 acres in possession of William Cole adj. J. J. Foster, Robert Foster, Geo Garner & others, 18 June 1832. Elizabeth Cannon (X) (LS), Wit: Hiram Potts (X), James Bryan, J. P. Andrew M. Norris, clerk of the court of Habersham County, Georgia, certifies that James Bryan was a justice of the peace. John Starritt, one of the justices of the inferior court certified that Andrew M. Norris was clerk, 23 Oct 1832. Recorded 3 Nov 1832.

V, 440-442: Edward J. Cotter of Union District for $250 to Barnabas Woolbright of same, 71 acres on the waters of Thickety Creek, part of tract formerly belonging to Zach Mabry decd, 18 May 1831. E. J. Cotter (LS), Wit: L. B. Murray, John B. Murray. Proved by the oath of John B. Murray before John Carothers, Q.U., 29 Sept 1832.

V, 442: William Ashby of Union District for $76 to James N. Hardy of same, all my part & interest as a legatee in a certain tract of land belonging to the estate of John Ashby decd on Cane Creek, 355 acres, 12 Oct 1832. Wm Ashby (LS), Wit: Charnar Stevens, Gideon McGraw. Proved by the oath of Charnar Stevens & Gideon McGraw 12 Oct 1832 before E. McGraw, Q. U. Recorded 4 Nov 1832.

V, 443-444: William Miller of Union District for $450 to Thomas Belew of same, tract on the main road leading from Union Court House to Spartanburgh C. House on the head waters of Buffalo Creek, 117 acres, 19 Oct 1832. William Miller (LS), Wit: B. H. Rice, J. Rogers. Proved by the oath of B. H. Rice 19 Oct 832 before J. Rogers, Q.U. Recorded 19 Oct 1832.

V, 444-445: South Carolina, Union District. Jesse Spencer of district aforesaid for $400 to Pascal P. Parham of same, 308 acres on a branch of Fairforest called Camp Spring, part of 500 acres granted to Daniel Jackson in 1772 and conveyed by said Daniel Jackson to John Malone and by John Malone to William Gist and from the heirs of William Gist to William F. Gist and from William F. Gist to Nathaniel Gist, adj. White's line, 11 Sept 1832. Jesse Spencer (LS), Wit: L. Leitch, M. M. High. Proved by the oath of Mitchell High 5 Nov 1832 before J. Rogers, Q. U. Recorded 5 Nov 1832.

V, 445-448: South Carolina, Union District. 1 Oct 1832, William Sisson to Samuel M. Goudy, both of district aforesaid, at the special instance and request of him the said William Sisson hath become bound with the said William Sisson unto J. J. Pratt, Esqr., Ordinary of district aforesaid, by bond dated 7 June 1830 in the penal sum of $1500 for the just administration of the estate of the late Joshua Sisson decd, father of said William Sisson, the said Samuel M. Gowdy being security, tract on which William Sisson now lives on waters of Thickety Creek adj. Mary Martin, Richard Thomson, Robert Lusk, Wm. D. Corry, Dudley Mullin, Isom Howell, 340 acres, it being three several tracts purchased of Joshua Sisson, John Carothers and one small piece taken up as being vacant, also three negroes, slaves, viz a fellow named Jerry, a wench named Priscilla (wife of said Jerry) and her child, also two horses, 11 head of neat cattle, 32 head of Swine, 17 sheep, one waggon, harness, three feather beds, two table, one cupboard, and one loom, 1 Oct 1832. Wm Sisson (LS), Wit: S. A. Goodman, A. Gordon, T. G. Farr. Proved by the oath of S. A. Goodman 1 Oct 1832 before Isaac Going, Q. U. Recorded 1 Oct 1832.

V, 448-449: South Carolina, Union District. John Carothers of district aforesaid for $445 to William Sisson of same, 125 acres between Packolett River and Thickety Creek adj. Edward Cotter, William Sisson, Richard

Thomson, Dudley Mullins, 14 Dec 1831. John Carothers (Seal), Wit: Thos G. Bankhead, William H. Robison. Proved by the oath of Thos G. Bankhead 21 July 1832 before S. A. Goodman, Q. U. Rachel N. Carothers, wife of John Carothers, relinquished dower 10 Nov 1832 before S. A. Goodman, Q. U. Recorded 17 Nov 1832.

V, 448-452: 22 June 1832, John Parham to Robert McCullough and Elisabeth McCullough his wife by a single bill in the sum of $454 payable to the said Elisabeth McCullough by 25 Dec next and dated 15 March 1831, 126 acres on the south side of Fairforest on branches of the same, waters of Tyger River adj. heirs of Parham decd, Wm Rice, Esquire, Col. N. Gist, granted to said Elizabeth McCullough 5 July 1830. John Parham (LS), Robt McCullough (LS), Elisabeth McCullough (LS), Wit: John Gage Jr., James L. Caldwell, Benj. Frazier, Wm Frazier. Proved in Edgefield District by the oath of William Frazier 11 Nov 1832 before J. Richardson, C. C. pl. Proved by the oath of John Gage Jr. 29 Nov 1832 before J. Rogers, Q. U. Recorded 20 Nov 1832.

V, 453-454: South Carolina, Union District. Charles Jones of district aforesaid for $460 to Job Hammond, 589 acres on waters of Rocky Creek, a branch of Fairforest, part of 350 acres granted to John Lyles 2 April 1773, dated 3 Jan 1831. Charles Jones (LS), Wit: J. Rogers, J. J. Foster. Proved by the oathof John Rogers 22 Nov 1832 before Jas Greer, J.P.

V, 454-455: Thomas Howard of Union District for $195 to Job Hammond of same, 60 acres on Rocky Creek adj. Jas McDonald, James Jackson, on the north side of the road leading from Unionville to Meansville, 24 Oct 1832. Thomas Howard (Seal), Wit: J. Rogers, Joseph Davidson. Proved by the oath of John Rogers 22 Nov 1832 before Jas Greer, J. P. Recorded 22 Nov 1832.

V, 456-457: Thomas Howard of Union District for $195 to James Jackson of same, 30 acres on Rocky Creek adj. said James Jackson, on the north side of the road leading from Unionville to Meansville, 24 Oct 1832. Thomas Howard (Seal), Wit: J. Rogers, Joseph Davidson. Proved by the oath of John Rogers 22 Nov 1832 before Jas Greer, J. P. Recorded 22 Nov 1832.

V, 457-459: 24 Nov 1830, Job Hammond to Thomas Howard, whereas Job Hammond stands indebted to the said Thomas Howard by his two notes one for $45 due Christmas come a year from the date of these presents, and another for $80 due Christmas come two years, mortgage of 66 acres on Rocky Creek adj. Jas McDonald, on the north side of the road leading from Union Ville to Means Ville. Job Hammond (Seal), Wit: J. Rogers, joseph Davidson. Proved by the oath of John Rogers 23 Nov 1832 before Jas Greer, J.P. Recorded 23 Nov 1832.

V, 459: Present, 13 No 1832. Maj. B. Johnson, Please be so good as to make titles to the samll tract of land which I purchased at sheriffs sale to Mr. D. A. Mitchell his paying for the same. Yours, Clough S. Sims.

V, 459-461: B. Johnson, Sheriff of Union District, whereas by virtue of a writ of fieri facias from the court of common pleas held 23 April 1831 at the suit of William Sims and others to levy of the goods and chattels, lands and tenements of Christopher de Graffenried $150, sold 100 acres on Neals Creek adj. Thomas Pinckney, Jas Gasaway, William Sims, William Johnson, part of a tract of 500 acres granted to Isaac Bates 1 April 1791, purchased by David A. Mitchell for $59, 19 Nov 1832. B. Johnson, S. U. D. (Seal),Wit: B. G. Davis, G. D. A. Brandon. Proved by the oath of Benj. G. Davis 19 Nov 1832 before J. Rogers, Q.U. Recorded 19 Nov 1832.

V, 462-463: Christopher Young of Union District for $1105 to Thomas Sartor of same, tract on Tinker Creek, 276 acres adj. Gideon Steen, Thomas, Martha Bates, 1 Aug 1831. Christopher Young (LS), Wit: Robt Beaty, Jared Young. Proved by the oath of Robert Beaty 24 Nov 1832 before J. Rogers, Q. U. Recorded 24 Nov 1832.

V, 463-464: William R. Wilbourn of Union District for $300 to Hannah Brooks, 100 acres on both sides of Hainesworths Branch along the big road, 12 Jan 1832. W. R. Wilbourn (LS), Wit: R. W. Wallace, William Morgan. Proved by the oath of Robt W. Wallace 12 Nov 1832 before H. Gibbs, Q. U. Recorded 20 Nov 1832.

V, 465-467: Charner Saunders and John Saunders of Union District, whereas said Charner Saunders & John Saunders are indebted to John Hart, admr. of Thomas Hart Senr decd, by their single bill in sum of $506, mortgage of a negro woman named Celia and her two children Sarah & Jinny, 2 Jan 1832. Charner Saunders (LS), John Saunders (Seal), Wit: Wm. K. Clowney, Ellis Palmer. Proved by the oath of W. K. Clowney 13 Dec 1832 before J. Rogers, Q. U. Recorded 13 Dec 1832.

V, 467-468: John Anderson of Union District for $330 to David Beatenbough of Union District, tract on both sides of Morris branch, part of sundry grants resurveyed 16 Nov 1810, 200 acres adj. Christopher Young 6 Nov 1832. John Anderson (Seal), Wit: Michael Lee, J. Rogers. Proved by the oath of John Rogers 22 Nov 1832 before Saml Davis, J.P. Susannah Anderson, wife of John Anderson, relinquished dower 13 Nov 1832 before H. Gibbs, Q. U. Recorded 13 Dec 1832.

V, 469-470: Thomas Burns of Union District for love and affection for the children which my first wife bore to me to wit Jemima Fant who has intermarried with Lewis Fant, Elizabeth Owens who has intermarried with Thomas Owen, & Alvah Burns, tract whereon I now live on Brushy Creek, waters of Tinker Creek adj. John Keasler, Simon Croomer, John Gregory, Abram McJunkin, James Tate Senr, widow Hunt & others, 320 acres also the negroes Martin, Reason, Peter, Fortune, Isaac, Stephen, Julia Bet, Charles, Mary, Juno, Flora & her child Serena, 2 Jan 1833. Thos Burns (Seal), Wit: E. P. Porter, John Porter, W. Rountree. Proved by the oath of William Rountree 2 Jan 1833 before J. Rogers, Q. U. Recorded 2 Jan 1833.

V, 471: South Carolina, Union District. Thos Burns came personally and deposeth that certain negroes named in a deed of gift to Jemima Fant, Elisabeth Owen & Alvah Burns, are all the issue of Juno, who was willed by the will of Mary Thorne to her daughter Mary Thorne Jr., who intermarried with this deponent as his first wife, 2 Jan 1833 before J. Rogers, Q. U. Recorded 2 Jan 1833.

V, 471: South Carolina, Union District. Green S. Lee appeared and acknowledged himself guardian for Mary Runnels, a free woman of color, 10 Jan 1833. Green S. Lee (LS),Wit: J. Rogers, Clk. Recorded 20 Jan 1833.

V, 471-473: Jonathan Ashby of Union District for $76 to Joseph Evans of same, all my interest as a legatee in and to a certain tract belonging to the estate of John Ashby decd on Cane Creek, 355 acres, 12 Oct 1832. Nathan Ashbay (LS), Wit: Charner Stevens, Gideon McGraw. Proved by the oath of Charner Stephens and Gideon McGraw 12 Oct 1832 before E. McGraw, Q.U. Marenda Ashbay, wife of Nathan Ashbay, relinquished 12 Oct 1832 before E. McGraw, Q.U. Recorded 7 Jan 1833.

V, 473-474: South Carolina, Union District. Elisabeth Tucker of Union District for love, good will and affection to my son Willis Tucker of same, one sow & six pigs, one large pot, two shoats, 3 Jan 1833. Elisabeth Tucker (X) (Seal), Wit: Wooddy Tucker (X), Ripsey Tucker (X), Jas Greer. Proved by the oath of James Greer 7 Jan 1833 before Wm. Skelton, J. P. Recorded 7 Jan 1833.

V, 474-475: South Carolina, Union District. Elisabeth Tucker of Union District for love, good will and affection to my daughter Charlotte Tucker of same, two feathers beds, one sow & three shoats, one oven and skillet, one wheel cards, one half dozen of earthen plats, one water pail and two piggins & one table, two chairs & two bedsteads, 3 Jan 1833. Elisabeth Tucker (X) (Seal), Wit: Wooddy Tucker (X), Ripsey Tucker (X), Jas Greer. Proved by the oath of James Greer 7 Jan 1833 before Wm. Skelton, J. P. Recorded 7 Jan 1833.

V, 475-477: South Carolina, Union District. In the Court of Equity. Whereas William T. Crenshaw & others ex parte, heirs at law of James Crenshaw decd, filed their bill of complaint in the court of equity for Union District on 18 June 1832 shewing that James Crenshaw late of the aforesaid state & district died intestate seized of a tract on the waters of Tyger River, 1200 acres, and by decree, B. M. Pearson, Commissioner of said court, did sell 1 Dec 1832, said tract, whereas George Ashford became the purchaser for $1700, 325 acres, plat certified by Thomas Stribling, deputy surveyor, 1 Dec 1832. B. M. Pearson, C. E. U. D. (LS), Wit: P. W. Pearson, William Walker. Proved by the oath of P. W. Pearson before J. Rogers, Q. U. 7 Jan 1833. Recorded 7 Jan 1833.

V, 478-480: South Carolina, Union District. In the Court of Equity. Whereas William T. Crenshaw & others ex parte, heirs at law of James Crenshaw decd, filed their bill of complaint in the court of equity for Union District on 18

June 1832 shewing that James Crenshaw late of the aforesaid state & district died intestate seized of a tract on the waters of Tyger River, 1100 acres, and by decree, Bird M. Pearson, Commissioner of said court, did sell 1 Dec 1832, and Thomas C. Jeter became the purchaser for $2088, 209 acres, 1 Dec 1832. Bird M. Pearson, C. E. U. D. (LS), Wit: P. W. Pearson, George Ashford. Proved by the oath of George Ashford before J. Rogers, Q. U. 7 Jan 1833. Recorded 7 Jan 1833.

V, 481-482: Edward M. Bobo of the district of Union for $500 to Giles Sharp of same, tract whereon Hancock Porter now lives on both sides of the Road leading from Union Court House to Pinckney Ville adj. said Giles Sharp, estate of William Sharp, per a late survey made by Richard Thomson, 108 acres, 17 Jan 1833. E. M. Bobo (Seal), Wit: John Giles, William G. Faucett. Proved by the oath of William G. Faucett 22 Jan 1833 before J. Rogers, Q.U. Mrs. Elisabeth Bobo, wife of E. M. Bobo, relinquished dower 22 Jan 1833 before J. Rogers, Q. U. Recorded 22 Jan 1833.

V, 483-485: Bartholomew Johnson, Sheriff of Union District, by several writs of partition from the court of common pleas held 18 Oct 1830 at the suit of Richard Sharp and subject to a paper called a deed or mortgage of William Sharp decd, dated 4 Nov 1833, to levy of the goods and chattels, lands and tenements of Samuel Faucett $91, sells 371 acres on waters of Broad River & Hughes Creek adj. John Giles, John Savage, Jesse Savage, John Gist, Joseph Naugher, sold for $50 to Giles Sharp, 29 Dec 1831. Bartholomew Johnson (LS), Wit: Bird M. Pearson, Joseph S. Rogers. Cassy Faucett, wife of Saml Faucett, relinquished dower 17 Jan 1833. Cassy Faucett (X) (LS) before John Giles, Q. U. Proved by the oath of B. M. Pearson 18 Jan 1833 before J. Rogers, Q. U. Recorded 18 Jan 1833.

V, 485-488: South Carolina, Union District. In the Court of Equity. Whereas William T. Crenshaw & others ex parte, heirs at law of James Crenshaw decd, filed their bill of complaint in the court of equity for Union District on 18 June 1832 shewing that James Crenshaw late of the aforesaid state & district died intestate seized of a tract on the waters of Tyger River, 1100 acres, and by decree, Bird M. Pearson, Commissioner of said court, did sell 1 Dec 1832, and Thomas C. Jeter became the purchaser for $3520, 132 acres, 1 Dec 1832. Bird M. Pearson, C. E. U. D. (LS), Wit: P. W. Pearson, George Ashford. Proved by the oath of George Ashford before J. Rogers, Q. U. 7 Jan 1833. Recorded 7 Jan 1833.

V, 488-489: South Carolina, Union District. Fanny Sisson for natural love and affection to Charity Neal, one bed and furniture, bed stead, one pot, one oven, one skillet, and chest, 18 Jan 1833. Fanny Sisson (X) (LS), Wit: Isaac M. Going, Isaac Going. Proved by the oath of Isaac Going 24 Jan 1833 before J. Rogers, Q. U. Recorded 24 Jan 1833.

V, 489-491: South Carolina, Union District. Whereas John Wix, late of the district aforesaid died intestate and left several heirs, all of whom are of legal age, Elijah Wix, Sarah Wix who has intermarried with John Tate, Elisabeth Wix who has intermarried to Joseph Nix, Jane Wix who has intermarried with Marshall Barnett, Jeremiah Wix, Mary Wix who as intermarried with Bartholomew Grogan, Eleanor Wix who has intermarried with Silas Bishop, Anna Wix who has intermarried with Able Barnett, Emily Wix, heirs and legatees of said John Wix decd, appoint Marshall Barnett of Union District, our attorney to offer for sale, the real estate of John Wix decd, 450 acres, at public or private sale, 21 Jan 1833. John Tate (Seal), Sarah Tate (X) (LS), Able Barnett (Seal), Ann Barnett (X) (Seal), Emily Weeks (X) (Seal), Elijah Weeks (Seal), Jane Wix (Seal), Silas Bishop (Seal), Eleanor Bishop (X), Jeremiah Weeks (X) (Seal), Jiney Weeks (X) (Seal), Joseph Nix (Seal), Elisabeth Nix (X) (Seal), Barth Grogan (Seal), Mary Grogan (X) (Seal), Wit: Jason Greer, Darius Prince, Alfred Wilbourn, James Greer, James White, Wm. McClure, Benj. Page. Proved in Spartanburgh District by the oath of Benjamin Page 26 Jan 1833 before Thomas Grogan. Proved in Union District by the oath of Capt. Jason Greer 28 Jan 1833 before H. H. Holcomb, J.P. Recorded 28 Jan 1833.

V, 491-493: Handcock Porter Senr of District of Union for $450 to Edward M. Bobo of same, tract on waters of Browns Creek being the place where I now live, 108 acres, 15 March 1832. Handcock Porter (X) (LS), Wit: D. Wallace, Charles Meng. Proved by the oath of D. Wallace 26 Jan 1833 before J. Rogers, Q.U. Mary Porter (X), wife of Handcock Porter, relinquished dower 2 Jan 1833 before John Giles, Q. U. Recorded 26 Jan 1833.

V, 493-495: South Carolina, Union District. John V. Johnson of state aforesaid for $854 to Nathaniel Rochester of district aforesaid, 281 acres on a branch of Neals Creek adj. John Porter, Elisha Porter, on the north bank of little crowders creek, adj. William Savage, 30 Nov 1832. John V. Johnson (LS), Wit: John Porter, Handcock Porter. Proved by the oath of Hancock Porter 17 Dec 1832 before E. P. Porter, Q. U. Rebecca Stoks, wife of Benj. Stokes, relinquished dower to John V. Johnson 30 Nov 1832 before E. P. Porter, Q. U. Recorded 3 March 1833.

V, 495-497: B. Johnson, Sheriff of Union District, by virtue of a writ of fieri facias from the court of common pleas held 13 March 1829 at the suit of Ambros Ray to levy of the goods & chattels, lands and tenements of John White Junr, $100, sells 13 acres adj.lands of John Saunders, Mary Reeder & Geo S. Noland & Robert Beaty on the waters of Fairforest, sold for $16, 28 Jan 1833. B. Johnson, S. U. D. (LS), Wit: Jason M. Greer, Jas C. Kitchens. Proved by the oath of Jas C. Kitchens 5 March 1833 before J. Rogers, Q. U. Recorded 4 March 1833.

V, 498-499: Benjamin Bullington of Union District and James White of Gwinnett County, Georgia, for $254, paid by John Saunders of Union District, part of a tract formerly belonging to the estate of William Greer, decd, on the Charleston Road, leading by Hays Store at the head of a hollow leading to Capt. C. Greer's still house, to William Steen's old place, as pointed out by the will of Thomas Greer, decd, 30 Sept 1829. Benjamin Bullington (Seal), Jas White (Seal), Wit: Charner Saunders, Isaac Clark, Westly Saunders, Thos H. Steed, Jason M. Greer, John Hart. Proved by the oath of Jason M. Greer 4 March 1833 before J. Rogers, Q.U. Recorded 4 March 1833.

V, 500-501: Silas Bishop of Union District for $100 to Caleb Greer of same, my proportional share of a tract on north side of Tyger River, 313 acres adj. John Weeks, late of Union District, wherein I am a legal heir at law, 14 Nov 1832. Silas Bishop (Seal), Wit: D. A. Mitchell, Jason Greer, Abel Barnet. Eleanor Bishop (X), wife of Silas Bishop, relinquished dower 12 Feb 1833 before Jno Norman, J. Q. Proved by the oath of Abel Barnett 27 Nov 1832 before H. H. Holcomb, J.P. Recorded 4 March 1833.

V, 501-503: Elijah Weeks of Union District for $100 to Caleb Greer, my proportional share of a tract on north side of Tyger River, 313 acres adj. John Weeks, late of Union District, wherein I am a legal heir at law, 12 Sept 1832. Elijah Weeks (LS), Wit: Jason Greer, Young Bobo, Richard H. Hughes. Proved by the oath of Jason Greer 24 Sept 1832 before H. H. Holcomb, J.P. Jane Weeks [signed Wix], wife of Elijah Weeks, relinquished dower 24 Oct 1832 before Jno Norman, Q. U. Recorded 4 March 1833.

V, 503-505: Marshal Barnett, Agent for the legatees of John Wix decd, of Union District for $100 to Caleb Greer of same, tract, being a part of the real estate of the said John Wix deceased on the north side of Tyger River adj. Caleb Greer, Thos S. Greer, on Wixes branch, Mitchell Sparks, 100 acres, 6 Feb 1833. Marshal Barnett (LS), Wit: Thos Hart, Spencer Greer. Proved by the oath of Spencer Greer 19 Feb 1833 before Wm. Skelton, J. P. Janet Barnett (X), wife of Marshal Barnett, relinquished dower 1 March 1833 before John Norman, Q.U. Recorded 4 March 1833.

END OF DEED BOOK V

W, 1: South Carolina, Union District. John Blasingame of district aforesaid for $80 to Muckel B. Bogan of same, 38 acres, 10 Nov 1831. John Blasingame, Wit: John Murphy, Charles Bogan. Proved by the oath of Charles Bogan 25 March 1833 before J. Rogers. Recorded 25 March 1833.

W, 1-2: South Carolina, Union District. Daniel McHam of district aforesaid for $150 to Muckle B. Bogan of same, 56 acres on the dry branch of Sugar Creek, the powder spring branch, part of two tracts originally granted to philip Blasingame, 5 Nov 1830. Daniel Mackham (X), Wit: Charles Bogan. Benj. West. Proved by the oath of Charles Bogan 25 March 1833 before J. Rogers. Recorded 25 March 1833.

W, 2-3: South Carolina, Union District. Lemuel Lancaster of district aforesaid for $100 to Muckel B. Bogan of same, 73 acres on the dry fork of Sugar Creek, part of 252 acres. Lemuel Lancaster (Seal), Wit: Benjamin West, Charles Bogan. Proved by the oath of Charles Bogan 25 March 1833 before J. Rogers. Recorded 25 March 1833.

W, 3-4: South Carolina, Union District. Whereas Charles S. Sims of Chester District at the special instance and request of Charles Meng of Union District by obligation became bound with said Charles Meng unto the Commissioner in Equity for Union District for $___, for the guardianship of his minor brothers Edward & Waddy Meng, now to the end that the said Charles S. Sims and all the lands, goods & Chattels of said Charles S. Sims shall be clearly save and kept harmless of and on account of said bond, shall be discharged at or before the time when the minors above referred to shall each arrive at the age of 21 years, sell two negro men slaves named Tom and Nelson and 24, 5 or 6 years of age, 20 Nov 1832. Charles Meng (Seal), Wit: Clough S. Sims, W. A. Sims. Proved by the oath of Clough S. Sims 11 Feb 183 before B. M. Pearson, Q. U. Exoff. Recorded 11 March 1833.

W, 4: South Carolina, Union District. Amos Davis of York District for $11.18½ to John Jeffries Senr, one undivided part of a tract of land on the south side of Gilkies Creek, part of a tract granted to Alexander Martin in 1803, supposed to be 17.9 acres adj. Dowd, John Steen, said Jeffries, 4 Feb 1833. Amos Davis agent by power of atty for John Humphries & his wife Mary Humphries (Seal), Wit: Stephen Neal, Jacob Guyton. Proved by the oath of Jacob Guyton 18 March 1833 before S. A. Goodman, Q. U. Recorded 22 March 1833.

W, 5: South Carolina, Union District. Nathaniel Guyton of district aforesaid for $500 to John Jeffries Senr of same, 527½ acres by plat of land granted to Charles Harrington 3 Nov 1788 adj. Sejah Martin, on waters of Guilkies Creek, waters of Thicketty, waters of Broad River adj. Sejah Marton, John Jeffries, 17 Jan 1833. Nathaniel Guyton (Seal), Wit: William Mullinax, William Jeffries, Stephen Neal (X). Proved by the oath of Wm Jeffries 18 Jan 1833 before S. A. Goodman, Q. U. Recorded 22 March 1833.

W, 5-6: South Carolina, Union District. Foster Hooker of district aforesaid for $100 to William Malone of same, 50 acres on waters of Enoree River adj. Wm Malone, W. C. Pearson, David Spiva, Joseph Goswick, 19 Nov 1831. Foster Hooker, Wit: John Bates, Ann F. Malone, Robt G. Malone. Esther Hooker, wife of Foster Hooker, relinquished dower 15 Marhc 1833 before Jno Norman, J. Q. Proved by the oath of John Bates 15 March 1833 before Jno Norman, J. Q.

W, 7: South Carolina, Union District. Nathan Harlan for $60 to his father Samuel Harlan (both of said district), small piece of land on both sides of Fairforest, 12 Jan 1829. Nathan Harlan (Seal), Wit: Wm White, Eliza Harlan. Proved by the oathof Elisa Gibbs formerly Harlan, 26 Jan 1833.

W, 7-8: South Carolina, Union District. The heirs of Nathan Hawkins decd for $104 to Henry Hardy of distirc aforesaid, tract on waters of Tyger River on the north side, 33 acres granted to Nathan Hawkins decd, 8 Dec 1832. Jacob Hawkins (Seal), Wm Hawkins (Seal), John Hawkins (Seal), Elisha Hawkins (X) (Seal), Wit: T. A. Carlisle, Shadrick Wellseels (X). Proved by the oath of T. A. Carlisle 4 Feb 1833 before J. Rogers, Q. U.

W, 8: South Carolina, Union District. Thomas Crooks acknowledged himself guardian for John Thomas, a free person of color, 8 May 1833. Thomas C. Crooks (Seal).

W, 9-10: Agreement entered into between the Meansville Mining Co. who are Abram McArther, Wm. K. Clowney, A. W. Thomson, John Littlejohn, And William Norris, all of Union District, to R. G. Hazard of Providence, R. I., at Union Court House 13 April 1833, said Hazard does hereby sell the company a steam engine steading ina building near the Santee Canal being about 20 hor power with pumsp, pipe, iron fastenings, fixtures, etc., which said company agrees to pay seven and three quarter cents per pound for all the metal, paying in the folloiwn manner, $150 cash and the balance by depositing in the bank of Pennsylvania in Philadelphia. R. G. HAzsard (Seal), Wm. K. Clowney and A. W. Thomson for Company. PRoved by the oathof J. M. Gage 18 May 1833. Recorded 18 May 1833.

W, 10-11: South Carolina, Union District. William D. Corry for %600 to Thomas G. Bankhead, tact on waters of Thickety Creek on the south side of said creek, a part of tract being left by WIlliam to John C. Cotter & conveyed by him to William H. Cotter, the ballance bein a part of William H. Cotter's part of the estate, adj. William Baley Jr spring branch, William Sisson, 30 Jan 1833. Wm. D. Corry (Seal), Wit: Uriah Muller=ens, W. W. Carothers. Jane, wife of William D. Corry, relinquished dower 8 Feb 1833 before J. Carothers, Q. U. Proved by the oath of Uriah Mullins 8 Feb 1833 before J. Catoerhs, Q. U. Recorded 11 March 1833.

W, 11-12: Zachariah Belue Senr of Laurens County, Tennessee, appoints Zachariah Belew Jr & James Williams, both of County of Union, SC, attorney to dispose of a tract of land in Union County on which the said Zachariah Belew Senr formerly lived, 1 Oct 1832. Zachariah Belew Senr (Z) (Seal). Maximilian H. Buchanan, Clerk of Court for Laurence County, TN, certified that Zachariah Belew acknowledged the power of attorney, 1 Oct 1833. Recorded 4 Feb 1833.

W, 12-14: South Carolina, Union District. In the Court of Equity. Whereas Titus G. Farr and others on or about ___ filed their bill of complaint against William B. Farr on 10 June 1829 showing that James Farr departed this life sized and possessed of a tract on the waters of Broad River, 100 acres that partition remainder to be made of said land, court decreed that is should be sold at public auction by the said Commissioner of the court, now William K. Clowney, Commissioner, sells tract to William Kelly for $264, said tract adj. Nathan Glenn, James Farr, the widow Tranum, heirs of Nath Glenn, 13 May 1833. Wm. K. Clowney Commr (Seal), Wit: George Douglass, S. Beaty. Proved by the oath of Dr. George Douglass 13 May 1833 before J. Rogers, Q.U. Recorded 13 May 1833.

W, 14-15: South Carolina, Union District. Gabriel Lockhart of district aforesaid for $800 to Isabella Patrick, Gabriel Patrick Jr., Exors of Charles Patrick decd, tract on Abingdons Creek, Union District, adj. James Lockhart, Lydia Petty, 487 acres, 7 Nov 1832. Gabriel Lockhart (Seal), Wit: James Patrick, Jane[?] Patrick. Proved by the oath of James Patrick 1 Dec 1832 before G. A. Goodman, Q. U. Catharine Lockhart, wife of Gabriel Lockart, relinquished dower 15 Nov 1832 before S. A. Goodman, Q. U. Recorded 6 May 1833.

W, 15-16: South Carolina, Union District. John M. Moore of district aforesaid for $979 to Samuel Lowrey Senr, also of said district, two tracts on waters of Abingtons Creek, one at the south end of a tract sold by Gabriel Lockhart to John Patrick Jr. and by said Patrick to J. M. Moore; the other granted to said John M. Moore adj. Lockhart, Petty, 39 acres, 6 April 1833. John M. Moore (X) (LS), Wit: Saml J. Hoey, Wm. Reese. Proved by the oath of William Reese, 16 April 1833 before Jas. Dawkins, J. P. Recorded 13 May 1833.

W, 16-17: South Carolina, Union District. David Spiva of district aforesaid for $200 to Joseph Goswick of same, tract on branch of Hills Creek, waters of Enoree River adj. Henry Green, Gidson Tanner, part of a tract belonging to said Spiva, 100 acres, 12 Jan 1833. David Spiva (Seal), Wit: John Bates, Thos Goswick (X). Proved by the oath of Thos Goswick 15 Jan 1833 before Jno. Norman, Q. U. Mary Spiva, wife of David Spiva, relinquished dower 29 Jan 1833 before Jno Norman, Q. U. Recorded 12 March 1833.

W, 17-19: Whereas Daniel A. Mitchell stands indebted to William Sims Senr by note of hand for $500 payable two years from 3 Dec 1832, mortgage tract on waters of Broad River adj. J. K. R. Sims, Thos Jeter, Jordan Ashley, T. G. Farr, and said Daniel A. Mitchell, 150 acres, 24 Jan 1833. D. A. Mitchell (LS),

Wit: Z. Hooker, A. W. Thomson. Proved by the oath of Z. Hooker 6 May 1833 before J. Rogers, Q. U. Recorded 6 May 1833.

W, 19: South Carolina, Union District. Thomas Ezell and Nancy Ezell his wife of Union District for $140 to Thomas Hancock of same, 140 acres adj. Susannah Ezell, William Mitchell, Thomas Hancock, Nancy Shell, 29 Oct 1832. Thomas Ezell (X) (Seal), Nancy Ezell (LS), Wit: James Rountree, Amaza Ezell. Proved by the oath of James Rountree, Esqr., 6 May 1833 before Lem B. Askew, J. P. Recorded 6 May 1833.

W, 20-21: South Carolina, Union District. Whereas Gideon Steen and others exparte heirs at law of William Townsend decd filed their bill of complaint n the Court of Equity for Union District 24 March 1832 shewing that the said William Townsend died intestate seized of four several tracts of land on Tinker Creek, waters of Tyger River, and that partition remained to be made, B. M. Pearson, Commissioner of said court, by writ of partition at June Term 1832, one tract designed by letter D and according to the estimate of Stephen Johnson, Deputy Surveyor, 139 3/4 acres and valued at $489.12½, was assigned to Solomon Edwards in right of his wife Catherine who is one of the heirs t law of said William Townsend dec'd now, Bird M. Pearson, Commr, sells to said Solomon Edwards tract of 139 34 acres, 19 April 1833. Bird M. Pearson (LS), Wit: Ledford Rogers, John Wright. Proved by the oath of Ledford Rogers 6 May 1833 before J. Rogers, Q. U.

W, 21-23: South Carolina, Union District. Whereas Gideon Steen and others exparte heirs at law of William Townsend decd filed their bill of complaint n the Court of Equity for Union District 24 March 1832 shewing that the said William Townsend died intestate seized of four several tracts of land on Tinker Creek, waters of Tyger River, and that partition remained to be made, B. M. Pearson, Commissioner of said court, by writ of partition at June Term 1832, to be divided to Col. Saml Beaty, Jonathan Hawkins, John Voluntine, Arthur Lipsey & Isaac Gregory, one tract designed by letter D and according to the estimate of Stephen Johnson, Deputy Surveyor, 189½ acres and valued at $378.50, was assigned to Louisa Ann Townsend, widow of the said William Townsend, Bird M. Pearson, Commr, sells to said Louisa Ann Townsend said tract, 19 April 1833. Bird M. Pearson (LS), Wit: Ledford Rogers, John Wright. Proved by the oath of Ledford Rogers 6 May 1833 before J. Rogers, Q. U.

W, 23-24: South Carolina, Union District. Whereas Gideon Steen and others exparte heirs at law of William Townsend decd filed their bill of complaint n the Court of Equity for Union District 24 March 1832 shewing that the said William Townsend died intestate seized of four several tracts of land on Tinker Creek, waters of Tyger River, and that partition remained to be made, B. M. Pearson, Commissioner of said court, by writ of partition at June Term 1832, one tract designed by letter B and according to the estimate of Stephen Johnson, Deputy Surveyor, 156½ acres and valued at $430.37½, was assigned to Jane, one of the heirs of said William Townsend, deceased, Bird M. Pearson, Commr, sells to said Jane Townsend the said tract, 19 April 1833.

Bird M. Pearson (LS), Wit: Ledford Rogers, John Wright. Proved by the oath of Ledford Rogers 6 May 1833 before J. Rogers, Q. U.

W, 25: South Carolina, Newberry District. Thomas Clark of Union District stands indebted to the Bank of the State of South Carolina at Columbia about $300 which note was discounted for $600, my friends David & John Caldwell my security, now for the better securing my said friends D & J. Caldwell, mortgage tract on which I now live on waters of Enoree River adj. estate of Henry Gray, Mary Pruett, J. L. Edwards, 400 acres, 14 Nov 1832. Thos Clark (LS), Wit: Benj Lyles, J. L. Kenner. Proved by the oath of Jonas L. Kenner in Newberry District 19 Feb 1833 before Benj. Maybin, Q. U. Recorded 22 Feb 1833.

W, 25-26: South Carolina, Union District. Recd of Thos Beauchamp of the district aforesaid $585 for the purchase of a negro woman slave named Silvey and her infant, 4 Feb 1833. Hez Rice (Seal), Wit: Farr Bates. Proved by the oath of Farr Bates 4 Feb 1833 before J. Rogers, Q. U. Recorded 4 Feb 1833.

W, 26-27: South Carolina, Union District. We, the legatees and administrators of Clabourn Parr decd, for $200 in full of his part of his said estate, sell to Thos Parr, one of the legatees, tract north of the widow Woods branch adj. John Harris, 50 acres, 8 Jan 1833. Martha Parr executrix (X) (Seal), Thos Parr Exor (X) (Seal), Isham Vaughan in right of his wife Rebecca (Seal), James Parr (Seal), Jesse Parr (Seal), Thos Nance in right of his wife Elisabeth (Seal), Joel Adams in right of his wife Mary (Seal), Charlotte Parr (X) (Seal), William Motte in right of his wife Sally (Seal), Wit: Robt V. Harris, Charner Adams (X), John Harris. Proved by the oath of Robt V. Harris 4 Feb 1833 before J. Rogers, Q. U. Recorded 4 Feb 1833.

W, 27-28: South Carolina, Union District. We, the legatees and administrators of Clabourn Parr decd, for $200 in full of his part of his said estate, sell to Jesse Parr, one of the legatees, tract where said Jesse Parr now lives on Johnsons Creek, 50 acres, 8 Jan 1833. Martha Parr executrix (X) (Seal), Thos Parr Exor (X) (Seal), Isham Vaughan in right of his wife Rebecca (Seal), James Parr (Seal), Thos Parr (Seal), Thos Nance in right of his wife Elisabeth (Seal), Joel Adams in right of his wife Mary (Seal), Charlotte Parr (X) (Seal), William Motte in right of his wife Sally (Seal), Wit: Robt V. Harris, Charner Adams Jr. (mark), John Harris. Proved by the oath of Robt V. Harris 4 Feb 1833 before J. Rogers, Q. U. Recorded 4 Feb 1833.

W, 28-29: South Carolina, Union District. We, the legatees and administrators of Clabourn Parr decd, for $200 in full of his part of his said estate, sell to James Parr, one of the legatees, tract where said James Parr now lives adj. John Scales spring on Johnsons branch, 50 acres, 8 Jan 1833. Martha Parr executrix (X) (Seal), Thos Parr Exor (X) (Seal), Isham Vaughan in right of his wife Rebecca (Seal), Jesse Parr (Seal), Thos Parr (Seal), Thos Nance in right of his wife Elisabeth (Seal), Joel Adams in right of his wife Mary (Seal), Charlotte Parr (X) (Seal), William Motte in right of his wife Sally (Seal), Wit:

Robt V. Harris, Charner Adams Jr. (mark), John Harris. Proved by the oath of Robt V. Harris 4 Feb 1833 before J. Rogers, Q. U. Recorded 4 Feb 1833.

W, 29: South Carolina, Union District. Henry White of district of Spartanburgh for $27.29 to Andrew W. McBride of district aforesaid, 4.6 acres adj. Mrs. Black, 24 Oct 1832. Henry White, Wit: Wm. J. Gordon, Moses L. White. Proved in Spartanburgh District by the oath of W. J. Gordon 22 Feb 1833 before W. Reid, Q. U. Recorded 23 Feb 1833.

W, 30-31: Joseph Collins of Union District for $4600 to William Norris of same, tract on the south side of Packolett River adj. Nathl Gordon, William Littlejohn, Saml Hodge, William Wood, 520 acres, 15 Dec 1832. Joseph Collins (LS), Wit: John Littlejohn, Saml Mosley. Proved by the oath of John Littlejohn, Esqr., 1 April 1833 before J. Rogers, Q. U. Recorded 1 Apr 1833.

W, 31: South Carolina, Union District. Thomas Nance of district aforesaid for $650 to Lucey B. Reid of same, 25 acres adj. Putman, 10 Sept 1831. Thomas Nance (LS), Wit: James Lancaster, John Varner Jr. (X). Proved by the oath of James Lancaster 12 Sept 1831 before H. H. Means, J.P. Recorded 28 Jan 1833.

W, 31-32: South Carolina, Union District. Richard Faucett of district aforesaid for $460 to Saml Faucett Jr. of same, part of tract on the south side of Browns Creek adj. Ann Giles, 60 acres, 8 Aug 1827. Richard Faucett (X) (Seal), Wit: Thos G. Page, Thomas Jefferson Naugher, William White (X). Proved by the oath of Thomas G. Page 27 Feb 1833 before J. Rogers, Q. U. Recorded 17 Feb 1833.

W, 32-33: South Carolina, Union District. Saml Faucett Jr. of district aforesaid for a valuable consideration to Nancy Faucett & her trustee John Giles Jr., both of district aforesaid, tract on south side of Browns Creek where Richard Faucett's land crosses the said creek adj. Handcock Porter, Ann Giles, 60 acres, 8 Aug 1827. Samuel Faucett Jr (Seal), Wit: Thos G. Page, Thomas Jefferson Naugher, William White (X). Proved by the oath of Thomas G. Page 27 Feb 1833 before J. Rogers, Q. U. Recorded 17 Feb 1833.

W, 33-34: Philip Selby of Union District for $300 to Thomas A. Carlise of same, tract on south side of Tyger River being the same whereon Philip H. Selby formerly lived adj. Richard Teagle, Wm. C. Glenn decd, W. W. Glenn, Nathan Glenn, 60 acres, 2 Feb 1831. Philip Selby (Seal), Wit: W. W. Glenn, Jas. Selby. Mary Selby, wife of Philip Selby, relinquished dower 13 Dec 1832 before Thos Stribling, Q. U. Proved by the oath of W. W. Glenn 13 Dec 1832 before Thos Stribling, Q. U. Recorded 4 March 1833.

W, 34-35: Anny Humphries of Chester District for $50 to William Sims Junr of Union District, tract on the south side of Broad River on Browns Creek, 257 acres adj. Sims, agreeable to a grant to Thomas Brandon, 18 Sept 1832. Ann Humphris (X) (LS), Wit: Thomas Worthy, John Stokes. Proved by the oath of Thomas Worthy 15 Feb 1833 before John Giles, Q. U. Recorded 23 Feb 1833.

W, 35-36: South Carolina, Fairfield District. Adam Cooper of district aforesaid for $2400 to William Kelly of Union District, tract on the west side of Broad River in the District of Union, 330 acres originally granted to William Moore, part to Benjamin Johnson and part to Geo Bell and was a part of a legacy left by Benj. Johnson & George Bell decd to Saml Johnson & Elisabeth Johnson, 2 Nov 1829. A. Cooper (LS), Wit: James Meacham, Thos B. Cockrell. Proved by the oath of Jas Meacham 14 Feb 1833 before J. Rogers, Q. U. Jane Cooper (mark), wife of Adam Cooper, relinquished dower 23 Dec 1830 before D. R. Coleman, J. Quo. Recorded 14 Feb 1833.

W, 36-37: South Carolina, Union District. Perry Evans of district aforesaid for $200 to Davis Caldwell of Newberry District, plantation whereon I now live on the waters of Tyger River adj. John Rogers, Dr. B. Chick, Wm Wilson, Wm Selby, Joab Wells, 27 March 1833. Perry Evans (LS), Wit: J. R. Lyles, J. F. Owen, J. L. Kenner. Proved by the oath of Jas L. Kenner 4 April 1833 before V. Gordon, J. P. Recorded 6 April 1833.

W, 37-38: South Carolina, Union District. Nath Rochester of district aforesaid for $363 to Hancock Porter of same, 121 acres on the north bank of little Browns Creek, 30 Nov 1832. Nathaniel Rochester (LS), Wit: John Porter, John V. Johnson. Proved by the oath of John Porter 4 Feb 1833 before J. Rogers, Q. U. Recorded 4 Feb 1833.

W, 38: South Carolina, Union District. Mrs. Nancy H. Gregory, widow of Jeremiah Gregory, late of Union District, relinquished to John Porter all her interest in the tract of land of 99 acres, 20 Feb 1833. Ann H. Gregory (Seal) before J. Rogers, Clk. Recorded 20 Feb 1833.

W, 38-39: Elisabeth Brandon for ___ paid by Wm A. Sims of Union District, tract on the south side of Broad River on Browns Creek, 257 acres adj. Sims, granted to Thomas Brandon, ____ 1832. Elisabeth Brandon (LS), Wit: Z. Hooker, R. H. Hughes. Proved by the oath of Z. Hooker 24 Feb 1833 before J. Rogers, Q. U.

W, 39-40: South Carolina, Union District. Thos Brandon of district aforesaid for $10 to William A. Sims, tract on the south side of Broad River on Browns Creek, 257 acres adj. Sims, granted to Thomas Brandon, 19 Sept 1832. Thos Brandon (LS), Wit: Z. Hooker. Absalom Davis. Proved by the oath of Z. Hooker 24 Feb 1833 before J. Rogers, Q. U. Recorded 24 Feb 1833.

W, 40-41: John Haney of District of Union for $100 to Elisabeth Ivey, 60 acres on the north side of the north fork of little Browns Creek adj. Griffin, 18 Feb 1831. John Haney (Seal), Wit: John Giles, Lemuel Whitlock. Proved by the oath of John Giles Esqr 4 July 1833 before J. Rogers, Q. U. Recorded 4 Feb 1833.

W, 41-42: South Carolina, Union District. Nathan Hawkins of district aforesaid for $250 to John Jennings, 190 acres, part of two tracts: the one granted to James Spring in 1795 recorded in Grant Book No. 5, page 78, the other grand to Nicholas Skein 24 March 1793, recorded in Grant Bok G No. 5, page 133, and conveyed by said Nicholas Skein to James Spring 14 March 1803, conveyed by James Spring to Nathan Hawkins and John Hawkins in Co., adj. James Hall, on Cain Creek, 26 Aug 1818. Nathan Hawkins (Seal),Wit: I. J. Foster Senr, Thomas Highatt (X). Proved by the oath of Thomas Hyatt 4 Feb 1833 before E. P. Porter, Q. U. Recorded 19 Feb 1833.

W, 42-43: South Carolina, Union District. Argulous V. Jeter of district aforesaid to John Jennings for $1200, 400 acres on the branches of Brushy Creek, waters of Tinker Creek adj. A. DeGraffenreid, John Jennings, G. Trammel, John Gregory, Jehu Gregory, 4 Sept 1832. A. V. Jeter (LS), Wit: B. J. Gregory, W. H. Gregory. Proved by the oath of B. J. Gregory 28 Jan 1833 before E. P. Porter, Q. U. Matilda Jeter (X), wife of Argulous V. Jeter, relinquished dower 14 Nov 1832 before E. P. Porter, Q. U. Recorded 19 Feb 1833.

W, 43-44: Alabama, Fayette County. Whereas William Spears, late of Union District, South Carolina, deceased, by his will did bequeath unto me lawful heirs Delilah Steen formerly Delilah Spears of Fayette County, Alabama, a legacy to be paid unto me of which as in and by said will may appear, now I appoint James Steen of Fayette County, Alabama, my true and lawful attorney to receive the legacy, 21 Jan 1833. Delilah Steen (mark) (Seal), Test: Daniel Payton, Clk. Proved by the oath of Daniel Payton, Clerk of the county court of Fayette County, and acknowledged that he executed the power of attorney to James Steen, 21 Jan 1833. Walter Hawkins, Judge of the County Court of Fayette County, certifies that Daniel Payton was clerk, 21 Jan 1833. Recorded 11 March 1833.

W, 44: State of South Carolina, Union District. W. S. McBride acknowledged himself guardian for free Bill, 28 Jan 1833. John Rogers, Clerk. Recorded 28 Jan 1833.

W, 44: State of South Carolina, Union District. James McCreight acknowledged himself guardian for Elisabeth Prisock or Russell, who is a free woman of color, 7 Jan 1833. John Rogers, Clerk. Recorded 7 Jan 1833.

W, 44: State of South Carolina, Union District. Reuben Clifton acknowledged himself guardian for John Steel, a free boy of color, 23 March 1833. John Rogers, Clerk. Recorded 23 March 1833.

W, 44-45: South Carolina, Union District. Robert Davis of district aforesaid for $300 to James T. Galloway of York District, 100 acres granted to Abel Acrage, 200 acres the SW part of said tract adj. Daniel Holder, James Rountree, 1 Dec 1832. Robert Davis (LS), Wit: Patrick Williams, Robert G. Davis. Proved by the oath of Patrick Williams 1 Dec 1832 before James

Rountree. Jane Davis (X), wife of Robert Davis, relinquished dower 16 April 1833 before John Rogers, Q. U. Recorded 16 April 1833.

W, 45-46: South Carolina, Union District. Edward M. Bobo of district aforesaid for $652.50 to Daniel A. Mitchell of same, tract on both sides of Fair Forest, 261 acres, 13 Feb 1833. E. M. Bobo (Seal), Wit: D. Wallice, Saml P. Bailey. Proved by the oath of David Wallice 19 April 1833 before John Rogers, Q.U. Elizabeth Bobo, wife of E. M. Bobo, relinquished dower 19 April 1833 before John Rogers, Q.U. Recorded 19 April 1833.

W, 46-47: South Carolina, Union District. Edward M. Bobo of district aforesaid for $150 to Benjamin Landrum of same, tract on north side of Tiger River on the road from Martin Mills to Meansville adj. Robert Brownin, said Benjamin Landrum, John Lawson, 42 acres, 23 Jan 1833. E. M. Bobo (Seal), Wit: Z. Hooker, E. M. Glenn. Proved by the oath of E. M. Glenn 10 June 1833 before John Rogers, Q.U. Recorded 10 June 1833.

W, 47-48: South Carolina, Union District. Samuel Faucett & Cassy Faucett, both of the District of Union, for $2200 to Edward M. Bobo of same, tract on waters of Broad River and Hughes Creek adj. Jesse Savage, John Savage, James Hughs, Joseph Naugher, John Gist, Jno Giles, Levi Davis, 396 acres, 17 Jan 1833. Saml Faucett (Seal), Cassy Faucett (X) (Seal), Wit: John Giles, Giles Sharp. Proved by the oath of John Giles 10 June 1833 before John Rogers, Q. U. Recorded 10 June 1833.

W, 48: South Carolina, Union District. Daniel A. Mitchell of Union District for $1895 to Edward M. Bobo of same, tract near Union Village on both sides of the main road leading from Union Court House by Sharps old Tan yard to Pinkneyville adj. John Rogers, Fredrick Ison, John Gage Junr, lands formerly belonging to Giles and Sharps estate, Dr. Lemuel A. Askew, Daniel A. Mitchell, plat by Richard Thomson 28 Feb 1832, 366¼ acres, 13 Feb 1833. Daniel A. Mitchell (Seal), Wit: D. Wallice, Saml. P. Bailey. Proved by the oath of David Wallice 9 June 1833 before John Rogers, Q.U. Recorded 9 June 1833.

W, 49: South Carolina, Union District. B. Johnson, Sheriff of Union District, by virtue of a writ of fieri facias from the court of common pleas held for the District of Union tested 15 Sept 1831 at the suit of John J. Pratt to levy of the goods & chattles, lands and tenements of Wm. Bently $215.25, tract of 225 acres on waters of Browns Creek adj. Cluff S. Meng, Christopher Brandon, Patrick Williams and Judge David Johnson, sold to Samuel W. Bentley for $265, 22 March 1833. B. Johnson, S. U. D. (Seal), Wit: Henry Long. F. Ison. Proved by the oath of Henry Long and Fredrick Ison 22 March 1833 before John Giles, Q. U. Recorded 22 March 1833.

W, 50: South Carolina, Union District. Wm Prince of district aforesaid for $400 to Wm. H. Gist, tract on Tiger River, 300 acres adj. Wm. H. Gist, Isaac Prince, 13 Nov 1832. William Prince (Seal), wit: Richard R. Pickering, John

Garret (X). Amy Prince (mark), wife of William Prince, relinquished dower 7 Dec 1832 before Jno Norman, Q. U. Proved by the oath of Richard R. Pickering 2 Jan 1833 before John Rogers. Recorded 2 Jan 1833.

W, 50-51: South Carolina, Union District. John Anderson of Union District for $1500 to John J. Pratt of same, tract on a branch of Shoaly Creek, waters of Fair Forest on the north side of the road leading from Union Village to the Cross Keys adj. John Gage, 4 Oct 1835. John Anderson (Seal), Wit: E. J. Adicker, Wm. Rountree. Proved by the oath of william Rountree 2 Jan 1833 before Hiram Gibbs, Q. U. Susannah Anderson, wife of William Anderson, relinquished dower 2 Jan 1833 before H. Gibbs, Q. U. Recorded 30 Jan 1833.

W, 51-52: South Carolina, Union District. Philip H. Selby and Mary his wife of said district for $600 to Philip Selby of same, all that tract of land willed to Mary Selby the said P. H. Selby willed to her by Elijah Anderson her father on Fishing Creek, waters of Tiger River, 115 acres, 17 Jan 1831. Philip H. Selby (Seal), Mary Selby (Seal), Wit: James J. Selby, William W. Glenn, Silar Anderson. Proved by the oath of William W. Glenn 17 Jan 1831 before Thomas Stribling, Q.U. Mary Selby, wife of Philip Selby, relinquished dower 25 Jan 1831 before Thomas Stribling, Q. U. Recorded 4 March 1833.

W, 52-53: South Carolina, Union District. Anderson W. T. McBride of said district for $61.75 to Henry Kirby of same, 21.7 acres adj. Bolin Kirby, 29 Jan 1833. A. W. T. McBride (Seal), Wit: Samuel Harmon, Davis Harvey. Proved by the oath of Samuel Harmon 9 Feb 1833 before William Reid, J.P. Recorded 3 June 1833.

W, 53-54: South Carolina, Union District. B. Johnson, Sheriff of union District, pursuant to an order from the Court of Ordinary signed by J. J. Pratt, Esqr., ordinary for Union District 3 Dec 1832 at the suit of James Woodson & wife applicants vs Mrs. Sarah Harlan & others defendants, to sell a tract of land belonging to the estate of Samuel Harlan deceased on the waters of fair forest, 200 acres adj. J. Gregory, George Harlan, sold for $633 Sarah Harlan, 3 May 1833. B. Johnson, S. U. D. (Seal), Wit: D. G. W. Hopkins, O. Willburn. Proved by the oath of D. Geo. W. Hopkins 10 June 1833 before John Rogers, Q. U. Letter from William Rice requesting the sheriff to make titles, dated 22 April 1833. Recorded 10 June 1833.

W, 54-55: South Carolina, Union District. In the Court of Equity. Whereas James M. Whitten and others exhibited their bill of Complain in the court of equity for Union District against Mary Bobo and others on 11 May 1832 shewing that Kindred Bobo, late of said District, died intestate, seized and possession in his own right of considerable real estate and that partition remained to be made and at June Term 1832 the court did decree that said lands should be sold in separate tracts by the Commissioner of said court, now B. M. Pearson, Commissioner, did on 3 Dec 1832 at Union Court House open to public sale one tract of land whereat Mary Bobo became purchaser for $605, 246 acres known as Tract No. 1 the home place, adj. James Duncan, on

Tiger River, 3 Dec 1832. Bird M. Pearson (seal), Wit: J. S. Pearson, Isaac P. Murphy. Proved by the oath of Isaac P. Murphy 28 Jan 1833 before John Rogers, Q. U. Recorded 28 Jan 1833.

W, 55-57: South Carolina, Union District. In the Court of Equity. Whereas James M. Whitten and others exhibited their bill of Complain in the court of equity for Union District against Mary Bobo and others on 11 May 1832 shewing that Kindred Bobo, late of said District, died intestate, seized and possession in his own right of considerable real estate and that partition remained to be made and at June Term 1832 the court did decree that said lands should be sold in separate tracts by the Commissioner of said court, now B. M. Pearson, Commissioner, did on 3 Dec 1832 at Union Court House open to public sale one tract of land whereat Mary Bobo became purchaser for $181, 212 acres known as Tract No. 2, adj. James Duncan, on Tiger River, 3 Dec 1832. Bird M. Pearson (seal), Wit: J. S. Pearson, Isaac P. Murphy. Proved by the oath of Isaac P. Murphy 28 Jan 1833 before John Rogers, Q. U. Recorded 28 Jan 1833.

W, 57-58: South Carolina, Union District. Marriage settlement 30 Dec 1830 between Z. Hooker and Mary Hooker, wife of said Z. Hooker, late Mary A. Moorman, and whereas it was covenanted and agreed that William Rice was appointed for Mary Ann Hooker trustee, now we do empower the said William Rice without consent to purchase of Doc. Edwd M. Bobo, sundry negroes viz Patty a black woman and her six children Isaa, Elen, Elder, Sam, George & Rachell and one other family viz Billy, his wife Alsey, and their two daughters Betty & Patty, also Hager & her son Simpson, and also bonds on Charles S. Sims and Thomas Worthy of Chester and Nimrod Triplett and Samuel Morris, dated 11 Feb 1833. Z. Hooker (Seal), Mary A. Hooker (Seal), Wit: E. M. Glenn. Recorded 10 June 1833. Proved by the oath of E. M. Glenn 10 June 1833 before John Rogers, Q. U.

W, 58: South Carolina, Union District. Whereas I have this day sold to Wm. Rice by Z. Hooker a certain negro girl named Hager & her child Simpson, which said girl was some time since mortgaged to me by the said Zadock hooker for payment of sundry debts viz, Nathaniel Gists's claim against Edwd M. Bobo & others, 11 Feb 1833. E. M. Bobo (seal), Wit: Robt Moorman. Proved by the oath of Robt Moorman 20 June 1833 before John Rogers, Q.U. Recorded 10 June 1833.

W, 58-59: South Carolina, Union District. Edward M. Bobo for $3466 paid to me in bonds drawn by Chas. S. Sims and Thomas Worthy, Nimrod Triplett and Saml Morris of Chester in favor of Wm. Rice, trustee of Mrs. Mary Ann Hooker, negroes Patty and her six children Isaa, Elen, elder, Sam, George & Rachell also Billy and his wife Alsey and their two daughters Betty & Patty, also Hagar and boy child Simpson, 11 Feb 1833. E. M. Bobo (Seal), Wit: E. M. Glenn. Proved by the oath of E. M. Glenn 10 June 1833 before John Rogers, Q.U. Recorded 10 June 1833.

W, 59: South Carolina, Union District. Thomas Hart of state aforesaid for $1.50 per acre for my tract of land paid by Jesse Clark, tract on south side of Fairforest adj. John McBeth, Jesse Clark, Thomas Wright, Daniel A. Mitchell, 102½ acres, 21 Jan 1833. Thomas Hart (Seal), Wit: Thomas Sartor, Thomas Young. Mrs. Permelia Hart, wife of Thomas Hart, relinquished dower 25 Jan 1833 before John Rogers, Q.U. Proved by the oath of Thomas Young 1 April 1833 before John Rogers, Q.U. Recorded 1 April 1833.

W, 60-61: South Carolina. William Malone of Union District, greeting, where as the said William Malone is indebted to B. F. Bobo by note for $437.50, mortgage of 377 acres in Union District on Pagets Creek, waters of Tiger River on the road from Cross Keys to Columbia adj. Thomas Bishop, also a lot of black smith's & carpenter's tools, household & kitchen furniture, 4 March 1833. William Malone (Seal), Wit: J. J. Pratt, Robert Macbeth, H. W. Foote. Proved by the oath of H. W. Foote 12 June 1833 before John Rogers, Q. U. Recorded 12 June 1833.

W, 61: South Carolina. Thomas Lee and Green T. Lee of Union District for $2000 to Hezekiah Rice of same, tract where we now live on the north side of Tiger River adj. estate of Jesse Fincher decd, Rice, Farr Bates, Wm. Davis, 950 acres, 6 Feb 1833. Thomas Lee (X) (Seal), Wit: Wm. C. Pearson, C. B. A. Rice. Proved by the oath of C. B. A. Rice 16 Feb 1833 before John Norman, Q. U. Recorded 16 Feb 1833.

W, 62: South Carolina, Union District. Robert W. Wallice & Jannet Wallice, exrs., of the estate of William Wallice decd, and Mary Ann and Caroline Wallice, legatees if said estate, for $200 to Elizabeth W. Farrow, tract on waters of Sugar Creek known by the name of the Murrell Mill tract bought by wm. Wallice of H & William Means, exrs. of the estate of Hugh Means decd, and afterwards granted to Wm Wallice in 1827 adj. Z. Hooker, 4 Jan 1833. Robert W. Wallice exr (Seal), Jannet Wallice extx (Seal), Mary A. Wallice, Caroline Wallice. Wit: J. D. Harmoning, A. Delop, John P. Wallice. Proved by the oath of John D. Harmoning 14 Jan 1833 before H. Gibbs, Q. U. Recorded 14 Jan 1833.

W, 62-63: South Carolina, Union District. B. Johnson, Sheriff of Union District pursuant to an order from the court of ordinary directed to me by J. J. Pratt, ordinary, 28 Oct 1832 at the suit of Claybrooks, guardian to me directed to sell one tract of land belonging to the estate of Jemuel Brown decd, on Buffalow Creek, 87 acres adj. Carey Woodson, William Rice, Robert A. Claybrooks, and purchased by Robert A. Claybrooks for $250. B. Johnson, S. U. D. (Seal), Wit: Wm. C. Churchill, John Gage Junr. Proved by the oath of John Gage Junr 1 Feb 1833 before John Rogers, Q. U. Recorded 1 Feb 1833.

W, 63-64: Jeptha Ezell of Giles County, Tennessee, appoints his brother Timothy Ezell of said county his lawful agent and attorney to receive from the executors or administrators of my decd father's estate who lately departed this life in Union County, SC, 17 Sept 1832. Jepthah Ezell (Seal). Alexander Black, an acting justice in Giles County, Tennessee, certifies that Jeptha Ezel executed this power of attorney. German Lester, clerk of the court, certifies that Alexander Black was an acting justices of the pace, 19 Sept 1832. Arthur M. Upshaw, presiding justice, certifies that German Lester was clerk of said court. Recorded 4 Feb 1833.

W, 64-65: September 14, 1832. Jeremiah Ezell of Davidson County, Tennessee, appoints his Collathmims E. C. Ezell his lawful agent and attorney to receive what is due him from the will of William Ezell decd, late of Union District, SC, 17 Sept 1832. Jeremiah Ezell (Seal). Henry Ewing, clerk of the court of pleas and quarter sessions for said county, certified that Stephen Cantrel and R. W. Hill, Esquires, are two of the acting justices of the peace for said county, 21 Sept 1832. Stephen Cantrell and R. W. Hill certified that Jeremiah Ezell made this power of attorney, 21 Sept 1832. William Lytle, presiding magistrate, certified that Henry Ewing was clerk of court, 21 Sept 1832. Recorded 4 Feb 1833.

W, 65: Robert Buchanan of Giles County, Tennessee, appointed Timothy Ezell of said county his lawful agent and attorney to receive from the executors or administrators of his father in law's estate who lately departed this life in Union District, SC, 22 Sept 1832. Jepthah Ezell (Seal). Nathaniel G. Dye, an acting justice in Giles County, Tennessee, certifies that Robert Buchanan executed this power of attorney. German Lester, clerk of the court, certifies that Alexander Black was an acting justices of the pace, 19 Sept 1832. Arthur M. Upshaw, presiding justice, certifies that German Lester was clerk of said court. Recorded 4 Feb 1833.

W, 66: Abel Ezell of Giles County, Tennessee, appoints Amasa Ezell of said county his lawful agent and attorney to receive from James Newton, William Long and Ellis Palmer, all of Union District, SC, exrs., of the will of William Ezell decd, all sums of money, debts, demands, which may be coming to him, 25 Aug 1832. Abel Ezell (Seal), Test: L. W. Ezell, Gideon Ezell, Lucina[?] Ezell (X). Proved by the oath of Lamech W. Ezell Alexander Black before German Lester, clerk of the court, 5 Sept 1832. Arthur M. Upshaw, presiding justice, certifies that German Lester was clerk of said court. Recorded 4 Feb 1833.

W, 66-67: South Carolina, Union District. Sarah Savage of district aforesaid for love and affection to my daughter Mrs. Anna Johnson of same, one negro girl Peggy, during the life of Anna Johnson and then at her death to be divided between the surviving children of said Anna, the children and increase of said negro Peggy, 5 April 1833. Sarah Savage (mark), Wit: Robt F. H. Farr, William S. Savage. Proved by the oath of William S. Savage 6 April 1833 before John Rogers, Q. U. Recorded 6 April 1833.

W, 67-68: Wm Brown of Union District for $600 to Thomas & Warren Brown of same, two tracts containing in the whole 210 acres adj. Hodge, Harris[?],

Maybry, Cook, 9 Nov 1832. William Brown (X) (Seal), Wit: John Philips, Baptist H. Brown. Proved by the oath of John Philips 12 Dec 1832 before Saml Mosley, Q. U. Recorded 6 May 1833.

W, 68-69: South Carolina, York District. Jacob B. Moore of district aforesaid for $500 to Gordon Moore of same, tract in Union District adj. Goin Moore's old line, where John Moore's line on Broad River, Parker; another tract granted to said Jacob B. Moore 10 Sept 1828 adj. Daniel Smith, John Moore, said Gordon Moore, 28 March 1833. J. B. Moore (Seal), Wit: James M. McNeal, John Minter. Proved in York District by the oath of J. M. McNeal before Daniel Smith, J. Q. Recorded 21 June 1833.

W, 69-70: B. Johnson, Sheriff of Union District, pursuant to an order from the court of ordinary 10 Aug 1832 at the suit of Isaac Langston and wife applicants to sell a tract belonging to the estate of Anthony Leach, decd, on the waters of Broad River adj. L. B. Jeter, Leonard Baker, DeGraffenreid, sold for $20 to L. B. Jeter, 6 Feb 1833. B. Johnson, S. U. D. (Seal), Wit: E. Wilbourn, J. S. Cunningham. Proved by the oath of E. Wilbourn 13 June 1833 before J. Rogers, Q. U. Recorded 13 June 1833.

W, 70-71: South Carolina, Union District. Landlott Porter of district aforesaid for $83 to E. M. Bobo of same, tract on waters of Browns Creek adj.heirs of William Sharp decd, George Brandon Sr., lands now occupied by Dennis Miller, or the mill tract, Hartwell Jackson & owned by Hancock Porter Senr, 77½ acres 13 Feb 1832. Landlott Porter (LS), Wit: Z. Hooker. D. A. Mitchell. Susannah Porter (X), wife of Landlott Porter, relinquished dower 4 May 1833. Proved by the oath of Z. Hooker 13 June 1833 before J. Rogers, Q. U. Recorded 13 June 1833.

W, 71-72: South Carolina, Union District. William Walker of district aforesaid for $934 to Sarah Stevens of same, one negro man slave named Lewis about 34 years of age, one female slave named Penny about 35 years of age, 29 June 1833. William Walker (Seal), Wit: Wm. Epps. Proved by the oath of William Epps, J.Q., 29 June 1833. Recorded 1 July 1833.

W, 72-73: George Fant of Union District for $300 to James B. Fant of same, 100 acres on a branch of Tyger River, part of a larger tract sold by order of court as property of the heirs of Lovel Fant decd, and the said Geo Fant was purchaser, this tract surveyed 14 April 1832 by John T. McJunkin, D. Surveyor, dated 2 Jan 1833. George Fant (Seal), Wit: E. McGraw, David Harris Jr. Elizabeth Fant (X), wife of George Fant, relinquished dower 2 Jan 1833 before E. McGraw, Q.U. Proved by the oath of David Harris Jr., 1 July 1833 before R. Gilliam, J.P. Recorded 1 July 1833.

W, 73-74: South Carolina, Union District. John Reid Golding for love and affection to his step mother Sophianisba Golding and more particularly in consideration of the said Sophianesba having relinquished all her claim to the lands of my late father in the state of Georgia, sell all my right to any part of my father's estate which the said Sophionesba claims as an inheritance from her deceased infant the daughter of my father John Golding, 10 April 1833. John R. Golding (LS), Wit: J. S. Sims, R. A. Nott. Proved by the oath of R. A. Nott 2 July 1833 before J. Rogers, Q. U. Recorded 2 July 1833.

W, 74-75: Thomas Lee of Union District for love and affection to Mary Lee, Margaret Lee, Lovina Less, Massa Sally Lee & John Lee, four negroes Dice, Jim and Teener[?], and a small mare; to Margaret three negroes Luce, Dave & Adam & a sorrel. To Levina four negroes Ben, Priscila, Ellison & Bina and a little waggon & two horses Jack and Tom. To Massa A. four negroes Jack, Spence, Elisa, Carlisle & one black horse. To John three negroes Milly, Sally & George & one mule and the road waggon & geer. To Mary, Margaret & Levina, Massa & John two yoke of oxen & one cart, also $417 in notes & when collected to be equally divided between them. To William Lee, Green Lee & Cay Hopkins $10 each in notes, 14 Feb 1833. Thomas Lee (mark) (LS), Wit: J. T. McJunkin, Jas A. McJunkin. Proved by the oath of Jas A. McJunkin 29 June 1833 before J. T. McJunkin. Recorded 8 July 1833.

W, 75-76: South Carolina, Union District. Memorandum of an agreement entered into between William K. Clowney & Abram McArthur of the one part and A. W. Thomson of the other, the said A. W. Thomson is desirous of purchasing an interest in the Meansville Mine and as he has not had a sufficient opportunity of examining the same to his satisfaction and they are fully informed of its present apparent richness & William B. Means and Henry Harvey Means, two of the present owners of said mine, wishing to sell their shares which is two fifths in said mine, and said A. W. Thomson agrees to purchase said two fifths and pay said Means for the same & agrees to convey one of said shares to the said William K. Clowney and Abraham McArthur on their paying him for the same $3000 at the end of fifteen months from this date without interest... 23 Nov 1832. Wm. K. Clowney (Seal), A. McArthur (Seal), A. W. Thomson (Seal), Wit: W. Norris. Proved by the oath of William Norris 1 July 1833 before J. Rogers, Q. U. Recorded 18 Feb 1833 but not proven then.

W, 76-77: Henry Harvey Means & William B. Means by his attorney in fact Abram McArthur in the State of Tennessee, Tipton County, for $600 to Andrew W. Thomson of Union District, all our right, title and interest in a tract of land, being two fifths of the same, described in a deed from John Murphy to Saml Leitch, William B. Means, Harvey H. Means, Abram McArthur & William K. Clowney, dated 26 May 1831, also in the said lease dated 7 June 1831, 23 Nov 1832. H. H. Means (Seal), A. McArthur for Wm. B. Means (Seal), Wit: Wm. Norris, Joshua P. Dawkins. Proved by the oath of William Norris 1 July 1833 before J. Rogers, Q.U. Recorded 1 July 1833.

W, 77-78: South Carolina, Union District. Thomas Davis of district aforesaid for $100 to Peter P. Taylor and Malachi Keenan, tract of land [acreage not included], 25 April 1825. Thos Davis (LS), Wit: O. W. Cox, John Graham. Isabel Davis (X), wife of Thos Davis relinquished dower in Spartanburgh

District before Moses Casey, Q. U. Proved in Union District by the oath of John Graham 1 July 1833 before J. Rogers, Q. U. Recorded 1 July 1833.

W, 78-79: South Carolina, Union District. Laurel V. Nance and Mary Nance, exors of Zachariah Nance decd, late of Union District for $140 to Muckel Bogan of same, 100 acres on waters of Sugar Creek adj. land now conveyed to James Smith Esqr., Mills Sumner, Drury Sparks formerly granted to Solomon Span, 4 Dec 1830. L. V. Nance Exor (Seal), Mary Nance (X) Extx (LS), Wit: Aron Pruett, Danl Palmer. Proved by the oath of Aron Pruett 4 Dec 1830 before J. Palmer, J.P. Recorded 1 July 1833.

W, 79-80: South Carolina, Union District. Isaac Harlan of district aforesaid is indebted to Muckel Bogan in the sum of $472.63 upon settlement of our accounts up to this date, which is to be paid on 1 Jan next with interest, mortgage of two negro boys, one named Lewis aged about 25 years and Bill about 18 years of age, 21 Dec 1832. I. Harling (Seal), Wit: W. M. Thomson. Proved by the oath of William M. Thomson 1 July 1833 before J. Rogers, Q.U. Recorded 1 July 1833.

W, 80-81: South Carolina, Union District. Absolam Coleman of district of Union for $400 to Thomas Walker of same, 248 acres on waters of Mill Creek, the first tract of 115 acres and the other 15 acres adj. it, then 83 acres on the Gregory trail, 17 Aug 1832. Absolum Coleman (Seal), Wit: Bartley Coleman, Robert Coleman, Elisha Coleman. Proved by the oath of Bartley Coleman 17 Aug 1832 before Reuben Coleman, J.P. Recorded 1 July 1833.

W, 81-82: 26 Feb 1831, T. M. D. Coln bound to John J. Pratt, ordinary of Union District, whereas T. M. D. Coln stands indebted to said John J. Pratt in $150.59 by note, signed by T. M. D. Coln and John Lyles, 5 Jan 1831, mortgage of tract on waters of Fair Forest, 150 acres adj. Margt McDowald, Edward Mays, part of the real estate of James Doan decd, sold by order of the ordinary. T. M. D. Coln (Seal), J. J. Pratt (Seal), Wit: Bird M. Pearson. Proved by the oath of B. M. Pearson, Esqr., 13 June 1833 before John Rogers, Q.U. Recorded 13 June 1833.

W, 82-83: 26 Feb 1831, James Rogers to John J. Pratt, ordinary, bound in the sum of $100.67, mortgage of tract on waters of fair forest, 72 acres adj. James Means, Mrs. Mary Means, T. M. D. Coln, part of the real estate of James Doan decd, sold by order of the ordinary, James Rogers (Seal), J. J. Pratt (Seal), Wit: Bird M. Pearson. Proved by the oath of B. M. Pearson, Esqr., 13 June 1833 before John Rogers, Q.U. Recorded 13 June 1833.

W, 83-84: Edward M. Bobo of Union District for $500 to John Giles Junior, trustee for Mrs. Cassey Faucett, tract on waters of Browns Creek, known by the name of the Billy Wilson tract adj. James Turner, Mr. Cain, James Wilson, 134 acres, 17 Jan 1833. E. M. Bobo (Seal), Wit: Giles Sharp, Thos L. B. Hughs. Proved by the oath of Giles Sharp 26 Jan 1833. Elizabeth Bobo relinquished dower 1 Feb 1833 before John Rogers, Q. U. Recorded 1 Feb 1833.

W, 84-85: South Carolina, Union District. James M. Whitlow of district aforesaid for $800 to George S. Nowland of Newberry District, tract whereon I now live adj. John Anderson, Elizabeth Bogan, Chinor Humphries, John Sanders, William Rountree, which tract is composed of lands purchased by James. M. Whitlow of James Martin, 112 acres part of a tract formerly belonging to Robert Bullington supposed to contain 80 acres and also 13 acres belonging to William Rountree, and 13 acres bought of John White and eight acres bought from John Sanders, 16 acres taken up and granted to said Whitlow, 11 Aug 1831. James M. Whitlow (Seal), Wit: Thomas N. Dawkins, Wm. M. Thomson. Sarah M. Whitlow, wife of James M. Whitlow, relinquished dower 20 Oct 1832 before H. Gibbs, Q. U. Proved by the oath of Thomas N. Dawkins 11 July 1833 before John Rogers, Q.U. Recorded 11 July 1833.

W, 85-86: John Giles agreeable to the decree in the court of equity vesting in said John the tract No. 2 for $621.25 to Timothy Harvey of Union District, 178 acres on Pacolet River, 20 June 1833. John Giles (seal), Wit: Bird M. Pearson, John Rogers. Proved by the oath of Bird M. Pearson 20 June 1833 before John Rogers, Q. U. Recorded 20 June 1833.

W, 86-87: 7 Dec 1831, Charles Meng to Daniel A. Mitchell, whereas said Charles Meng stands indebted to said Daniel A. Mitchell in the sum of $2500 by his three notes, mortgage of tract of land on the west bank of Broad River, 120 acres adj William Sims, , and four negroes Jim, Peggy, Judy & Elias. Charles Meng (Seal), D. A. Mitchell (Seal), Wit: Charles Gowing, John Rogers. Proved by the oath of John Rogers 10 July 1833 before James Rountree, J. P. Recorded 13 July 1833.

W, 87-88: 9 Oct 1832, Jesse Gibson to John Rogers, whereas said Jesse Gibson stands indebted to said John Rogers by note for $238, mortgage of 81 acres on the waters of Fairforest adj. John Finchers[?], Jackson, Robinson, Sanders, Belew. Jesse Gibson (Seal), Wit: B. Johnson, Wm. Humphries. Proved by the oath of B. Johnson 11 July 1833 before D. Wallace, J. P. John Rogers acknowledged satisfaction 8 Aug 1836.

W, 88-89: B. Johnson, Sheriff of Union District, by virtue of a writ of fieri facias from the court of common pleas tested the third Monday of October 1830 at the suit of Thomas G. Danner to levy of the goods & chattles, lands & tenements of Thomas White of $83.73, sells 160 acres on waters of Fairforest adj. Jesse Clark, D. A. Mitchell, John Sanders, Benjamin Holcomb, Jane Brandon, sells for $151 to Robert McBeth, Maybry White and J. Kitchens, 5 March. B. Johnson, S. U. D. (Seal), Wit: H. W. Foote, James Greer. Proved by the oath of H. W. Foote 11 July 1833 before John Rogers, Q. U. Recorded 11 July 1833.

W, 89-90: 9 March 1812, Archelaus Kennedy for $128 to Reuben Lawson, part of tract of about 92 acres which was granted to Archelaus Kennedy in 1787 for 232 acres adj. Drucilla Lee, Daniel Norman, Saml Gilliam. Archelaus Kennedy (LS), Wit: William Dodd, Thos Huff. Proved by the oath of William Dodd 25 March 1826 before Robt Martin, J. Q. Recorded 11 July 1832.

W, 90-91: Marshal Barnett, agent for the legatees of the estate John Wix decd, of Union District, for $1000 to Mitchell Sparks of same, tract on the north side of Tyger River, 356 acres, part of the real estate of the said John Wix decd adj. James ____, Robert Greer, Benj. Holcomb, H. H. Holcomb, Sion Murphy, Carpenter Simonson[?] and Mitchell Sparks, 31 Jan 1833. Marshal Barnett (Seal), Wit: Caleb Greer, Wm. J. Sparks. Proved by the oath of Caleb Greer 12 July 1833 before Jno Norman, Q.U. Jane Barnett, wife of Marshal Barnett, relinquished dower 12 July 1833 before Jno Norman, Q.U. Recorded 25 July 1833.

W, 92: Mary Lee (M), wife of Thomas Lee, relinquished dower to Hezekiah Rice, 16 Feb 1833 before John Norman, Q.U. Recorded 25 Feb 1833.

W, 92-93: Jerome Miller, being one of the lawful heirs of Jonas Little Senr by marriage, and he made a supposed will of his plantation where he lived and died, the plantation is supposed to have 100 acres, that the above mentioned Jonas Little Senr willed to his wife during her natural life, then to be sold on twelve months credit and the money equally divided amongst his lawfull heirs, and there is eight legatees, my supposed part would be one eighth part after the death of the above mentioned widow, for $35 to Benjamin Little, sold my supposed claim, 27 Feb 1833. Jerome Miller (Seal), Mary Miller (X), (Seal), Wit: James Rountree, Richardson Rountree. Proved by the oath of James Rountree 19 Aug 1833 before J. Rogers, Q. U. Recorded 19 Aug 1833.

W, 93: So Carolina, Union District. Jonas Little for $35 to Benj Little of same, sell all my interest and right in a tract of 100 acres on Buffalow Creek in Union District, being one eighth part, 5 Aug 1833. Jonas Little (Seal), Wit: Thomas Bates, B. H. Rice. Proved by the oath of B. H. Rice 19 Aug 1833 before J. Rogers, Q. U.

W, 94: South Carolina, Union District. Lewis Smith and Hannah Swink for $35 to Benjamin Little of district aforesaid, all our interest and right in a tract of 100 acres on Buffalow Creek in Union District, being one eighth part of the land of Jonas Little decd, 5 Aug 1833. Lewis Swink (Seal), hannah Swink (X) (Seal), Wit: John Rogers, Thos M. Foote. Proved by the oath of Thos M. Foote 20 Aug 1833 before J. Rogers, Q.U.

W, 94-95: B. Johnson, Sheriff of Union District, by virtue of a writ of fieri facias from the court of common pleas held for Union District, tested 23 April 1831 at the suit of James A. Whitlow to levy of the goods and chattels, lands & tenements of Thos H. Steed $1084, sells tract of 340 acres on the waters of Tyger River adj. Littleton B. Clark, Robert Ray, James Johnson, Joseph

Prince and others, for $350, to John T. Murrell of Union District, 15 Aug 1832. Bartholomew Johnson S. U. D. (Seal), Wit: R. J. Gage, Jas G. Clowney. Proved by the oath of R. J. Gage 15 Aug 1833 before J. Rogers, Q. U. Recorded 16 Aug 1833.

W, 96-97: Timothy Haney and Betsey Haney his wife of the County of Jackson, State of Tennessee, appointed George McGipson of same our lawful attorney to ask, demand, settle for, receive and receipt for whatever property and other valuable things due to or to which the said Betsey may or is intitled to as heirs of Barney Woolbright deceased, late of Union County, South Carolina, 8 Feb 1830. Timothy Haney (LS), Betsey Haney (LS), Wit: Byor McGipson Jr., John Haney Jr.

State of Tennessee, Jackson County. February Sessions 1830. The power of attorney from Timothy Haney and Betsey Haney exhibited in court and acknowledged. Betsey examined by William Hamilton and Maurice Gore, Esquires, two members of the court, 8 Feb 1830. William Gailbreath. James W. Smith, Chairman of the court, certified that William Gilbraith, Esqr., is the acting clerk. William Gailbreath, Clerk of the court, certified that James W. Smith was chairman, 13 Feb 1830. Recoreed 12 Feb 1832.

W, 97: South Carolina, Anderson District. Mary Austin, Dickson M. Lumkins in behalf of his wife Sophia, Robert Hays in behalf of his wife Elisabeth, appoint our esteemed friend and brother in law John Nance our lawful agent and attorney to receive from John J. Pratt, Ordinary for Union District, and James F. Walker, admr. of the estate of Barney Woolbright decd our legacy, 11 Feb 1832. Mary Austin (X) (Seal), Dickison Lumpkins (Seal), Sophia Lumpkins (X) (Seal), Robt Hays (X), Lisebeth Hays (X). Wit: Ln. Wright, Lewis Bailey. Proved in Anderson County by the oath of Larkin Wright 13 Feb 1833 before Robt Holland, Q. U. Recoreed 12 Feb 1833.

W, 98: South Carolina, Union District. Davis Goudelock of district aforesaid for $125 to Samuel M. Gowdey & Co., 50 acres on the north side of Packolett River on the south side of Thicketty Creek adj. William Moorhead, 29 Feb 1828. Davis Goudelock (LS), Wit: John Phillips, Thos R. Gowdey. Proved by the oath of Thos R. Gowdey 11 March 1828 before W. H. Cotter, J. P. Recorded 1 April 1833.

W, 99-100: South Carolina, Union District. William H. Walton of the county of Rutherford, North Carolina, for $600 to Sarah E. Hendley & John W. Dais of district aforesaid, tract conveyed by Amos Davis to John Walton by deed and by John Walton to Richd McMillian by deed of trust for the use of said William H. Walton & John M. Walton on waters of Gilkies Creek, 8 Oct 1832. W. H. Walton (Seal), Wit: B. H. Bradley, Saml J. Hoey. Proved by the oath of ____ 25 Feb 1833 before J. Rogers, Q. U. Recorded 25 Feb 1833.

W, 100-101: South Carolina, Union District. Tripartite indenture, 23 Feb 1833, W. H. Steen of the first part, Elisabeth Lusk of the second part and Robt

Lusk and John V. Steen of the third part, whereas a marriage is intended between William H. Steen and Elisabeth Lusk, and said Elizabeth Lusk is possessed of a personal estate consisting of one negro girl named Sina and it is agreed the proceeds of the said personal estate at the death of either of them be at the disposal of the said Elisabeth Lusk. Wm. H. Steen (Seal), E. Lusk (LS), R. Lusk, (LS), John V. Steen (LS), Wit: Nancy Lusk, M. Lusk. Proved by the oath of Patsey Lusk (signed Martha Lusk), 20 Aug 1833 before S. A. Goodman, Q. U. Recorded 22 Aug 1833.

W, 101-102: South Carolina, Union District. James H. Becknell of said district for $210 to William B. Becknell, tract on waters of Browns Creek, tract adj. Joseph Jolly, Dabney Becknell, John Gregory, 31 Dec 1832. James H. Becknell (LS), Wit: G. D. A. Brandon, W. M. Brandon. Sarah Ann Becknell, wife of James H. Becknell, relinquished dower 3 Feb 1833 before J. Rogers, Q.U. Proved by the oath of Geo. D. A. Brandon 4 Feb 1833 before J. Rogers, Q.U.

W, 103: William Sims of Union District for love and affection to his son William A. Sims of same, tract on waters of Big and Little Browns Creek and Broad River, 700 acres at the mouth of the first branch making into the river below the mouth of Browns Creek, the old still house, adj. McCreight, widow Nancy Gregory, Rob Glenn, D. A. Mitchell, 24 Feb 1832. W. Sims (LS), Wit: J. S. Sims, Clough S. Sims, Proved by the oath of Clough S. Sims 6 May 1833 before J. Rogers, Q.U. Recorded 6 May 1833.

W, 104: State of Alabama, James L. Brandon of Lounds County, state aforesaid, for $10, to William Sims Jr. of Union District, SC, tract on south side of Broad River on Browns Creek, 257 acres, 12 March 1833. Jas L. Brandon (LS), Wit: John Varner, Z. Hooker. Proved by the oath of Z. Hooker 6 May 1833 before Z. Hooker, Q.U. Recorded 6 May 1833.

W, 105: Giles Sharp of Union District for $1500 to Dr. Edwd M. Bobo of same, tract on the waters of Broad River and Hughes Creek adj. Jesse & John Savage, Jas Hughes, Jas Nougher, John Gist, John Giles, Levi Davis, Wm. Sharp, Maj. Saml Faucett, and sold at Sheriffs sale at the suit of Richard Sharp subject to said mortgage and purchased by Giles Sharp, 396 acres, 17 Jan 1833. Giles Sharp (Seal), Wit: John Giles, Wm. G. Faucett. Proved by the oath of John Giles 24 Jan 1833 before J. Rogers, Q.U.

W, 106-107: Robt Stokes of Union District for $615 to Levi S. Holcomb of same, tract whereon I now live adj. estate of Jesse Fincher decd, estate of Duncan, Rice, 484 acres, 4 Feb 1833. Robt Stokes (LS), Wit: W. C. Pearson, Spencer Greer. Proved by the oath of William C. Pearson 4 Feb 1833 before Jas Greer, J.P. Ann Matilda Stokes, wife of Robert Stokes, relinquished dower 12 Feb 1833 before H. Gibbs, Q.U. Recorded 1 April 1833.

W, 107-108: South Carolina, Union District. Whereas Ferdinand McAshan and others exparte filed their Bill of complaint in the court of equity for Union District 9 May 1831 showing that Hendley McAshan died intestate possessed of four several tracts of land, three of which were situated in the district aforesaid and one in Fairfield District, which tracts are designated 1, 2, 3 and 4, and that partition remained to be made among the complainants who were the distributees of said Handley McAshan deceased and the cause was heard at June Term 1831 and the court did adjudge that the tracts should be sold at public auction separately, now Bird M. Pearson, Commissioner of the said court, did expose to sale 4 Dec 1831, and Nathan Coleman became the purchaser for $2861, 527 acres on Cane Creek, waters of Tyger River, granted to said Handley McAshan in 1818, tract number 3, 29 Dec 1831. Bird M. Pearson C. E. U. D. (LS), Wit: B. Johnson, G. S. Nolan. Proved by the oath of B. Johnson 12 Sept 1833 before J. Rogers, Q. U. Recorded 12 Sept 1833.

W, 109-110: South Carolina, Union District. Whereas Ferdinand McAshan and others exparte filed their Bill of complaint in the court of equity for Union District 9 May 1831 showing that Hendley McAshan died intestate possessed of four several tracts of land, three of which were situated in the district aforesaid and one in Fairfield District, which tracts are designated 1, 2, 3 and 4, and that partition remained to be made among the complainants who were the distributees of said Handley McAshan deceased and the cause was heard at June Term 1831 and the court did adjudge that the tracts should be sold at public auction separately, now Bird M. Pearson, Commissioner of the said court, did expose to sale 4 Dec 1831, and Nathan Coleman became the purchaser for $103, 103 acres on the north side of Cane Creek, waters of Tyger River, granted to said Reuben Gilliam, tract number 2, 29 Dec 1831. B. M. Pearson C. E. U. D. (LS), Wit: Bartholomew Johnson, G. S. Nolan. Proved by the oath of B. Johnson 12 Sept 1833 before J. Rogers, Q. U. Recorded 12 Sept 1833.

W, 110-112: South Carolina, Union District. Whereas Robert Tate and others filed their Bill of Complaint in the court of equity for Union District against Mary Tate and others on 11 May 1832 shewing that William Tate departed this life intestate seized of 700 acres on Minkhams Creek and subject to partition, said court did decree that two parcels of land be sold, designated in said proceedings as Tract C & D, at public auction, now Bird M. Pearson, Commissioner, did sell at auction 31 Aug 1833 to Edmond Blanton, for $805, tract of 291 acres on Minkhams Creek adj. J. Jeffries, Widow Tindal, Nat Tate, Saml Pearson, Littlejohn, tract numbered D, 13 Sept 1833. Bird M. Pearson C. E. U. D. (LS), Wit: J.Rogers, Wm. Rountree. Proved by the oath of Capt. William Rountree 13 Sept 1833 before J. Rogers, Q.U. Recorded 13 Sept 1833.

W, 112-114: South Carolina, Union District. Whereas Robert Tate and others filed their Bill of Complaint in the court of equity for Union District against Mary Tate and others on 11 May 1832 shewing that William Tate departed this life intestate seized of 700 acres on Minkhams Creek and subject to partition, said court did decree that two parcels of land be sold, designated in said proceedings as Tract C & D, at public auction, now Bird M. Pearson, Commissioner, did sell at auction 31 Aug 1833 to Henry Littlejohn, for $1060, tract of 255 acres on Minkhams Creek adj. John Jeffries, H. Littlejohn, E. Dawkins, tract numbered C, 9 Sept 1833. Bird M. Pearson C. E. U. D. (LS), Wit: John Parham, W. C. Pearson. Proved by the oath of Wm C. Pearson 12 Sept 1833 before J. Rogers, Q.U. Recorded 12 Sept 1833.

W, 114: South Carolina, Union District. Eleanor Walker, wife of Thomas Walker, relinquished dower to Thomas Belew, 9 Sept 1833 before J. Rogers, Q.U. Recorded 9 Sept 1833.

W, 114-115: State of Alabama, Pickens County. 10 May 1833 before Thomas Noland and John O. N. Love, Justices of the peace for said county, came Jesse Spencer and Elisabeth his wife and acknowledged the within indented to be her act and deed and desires that the same might be recorded, the said Elisabeth being of full age. Elisabeth Spencer (R) (Seal). Recorded 2 Sept 1833.

W, 115-116: South Carolina, Union District. J. S. White and Daniel White of Union District for $525 to Danizon Gault and Daniel Galman of same, tract of 100¼ acres on Little Sandy Run, waters of Packolett River, another tract of 12¼ acres adj. to mit. J. Smith White (LS), Danl White (LS), Wit: Jefferson White, Z. Johnson, J. Rogers. Henry Gault. Proved by the oath of Zachariah Johnson 26 Aug 1833 before Daniel White, J. Q. Isabella White, wife of Smith White, relinquished dower 26 Aug 1833 before Daniel White, Q. U. Proved by the oath of John Rogers 21 Sept 1833 before D. Wallace. Recorded 2 Sept 1833.

W, 116-117: James Leach by my attorney Charner Scaife of Union District for $1540 to John Jennings of same, tract whereon the said James Leach formerly lived on Cain Creek of Tiger River, 100 acres adj. John Jennings, Isaac Gregory, Hobkins Croker, John Boyd, Leonard Baker and others, 28 March 1831. James Leach by his attorney in fact Charner T. Scaife (Seal), Wit: James Glenn, F. H. McShan. Proved by the oath of Ferdinand H. McShan 21 Aug 1833 before E. P. Porter, Q.U. Ann H. Gregory, widow of the late Jeremiah Gregory, relinquished dower to John Jennings 3 July 1833 before E. P. Porter, Q.U. Recorded 3 July 1833.

W, 117: South Carolina, Union District. John Evans of district of Union for love, good will and affection to my daughter Mary Ison, who has intermarried with Thomas Ison, one negro woman named Rose and one negro girl named Martha, 28 Aug 1833. John Evans (X) (Seal), Wit: A. W. Thomson, John Rogers. Proved by the oath of John Rogers 12 Sept 1833 before D. Wallace, J.P. Recorded 28 Aug 1833.

W, 118: South Carolina, Union District. John Evans of district of Union for love, good will and affection to my daughter Rhody Possey, who has intermarried with James Possey, one negro woman named Sisley and her infant child name unknown and a negro girl Vestia, 28 Aug 1833. John Evans

(X) (Seal), Wit: A. W. Thomson, John Rogers. Proved by the oath of John Rogers 12 Sept 1833 before D. Wallace, J.P. Recorded 12 Sept 1833.

W, 118: South Carolina, Union District. John Evans of district of Union for love, good will and affection to my son Joseph Evans, a negro girl named Betty and the tract whereon he now lives, 112 acres adj. widow Ashby, James Hill & Toliver Farr, Col. Daniel Thomas, 28 Aug 1833. John Evans (X) (Seal), Wit: A. W. Thomson, John Rogers. Proved by the oath of John Rogers 12 Sept 1833 before D. Wallace, J.P. Recorded 12 Sept 1833.

W, 119: South Carolina, Union District. John Evans of district of Union for love, good will and affection to my son Zachariah Evans, a negro boy named Littleton, 28 Aug 1833. John Evans (X) (Seal), Wit: A. W. Thomson, John Rogers. Proved by the oath of John Rogers 12 Sept 1833 before D. Wallace, J.P. Recorded 12 Sept 1833.

W, 119-120: 2 Sept 1833, Abel Arnett & Zadoc Barnett to John T. Murrell, whereas said Abel Barnett and Z. Barnett stand indebted to the said John T. Murrell, by notes for $400, mortgage of tract on south side of Tiger River, 350 acres adj. Littleton B. Clark, Robt Ray, James Johnson, Joseph Prince. Abel Barnett (Seal), Zadock Barnett (X), Wit: J. Rogers, A. W. Thomson. Proved by the oath of 12 Sept 1833 before D. Wallace, J.P.

W, 120-121: South Carolina, Union District. Augustine Wood for $150 to Mark Wood, tract of land reserving to myself the dwelling house and fire wood which is to be furniture by the said Mark Wood, land being 50 acres adj. Golden, 3 May 1826. Augustine Wood, Wit: John P. Fowler, James Fowler. Proved by the oath of John P. Fowler, 6 March [*sic*] 1826 before Isaac Going, Q. U. Recorded 23 Sept 1833.

W, 121: South Carolina, Union District. John S. Crenshaw, now of Henry County, Georgia, appoint Z. Hooker of Union District, my true and lawful attorney in fact to received from all persons whatsoever all sums of money, debts, claims, etc., more particularly what may be due from the estate of my father James Crenshaw deceased, 26 June 1833. John S. Crenshaw (Seal), Wit: D. Wallace, E. M. Bobo, E. M. Glenn. Proved by the oath of Edward M. Glenn 26 June 1833 before D. Wallace, J. P. Recorded 19 Sept 1833.

W, 121-122: South Carolina, Union District. John Steen of Union District do lend unto William H. Steen my son of said district in consequence of natural love and affection, two negro girls named Ann & Lethy, one negro by Orange, until such time as I may think property to call for the property, 16 Aug 1833. John Steen, Wit: J. J. Pratt, J. Rogers. Proved by the oath of J. J. Pratt 16 Aug 1833 before John Rogers, Q. U. Recorded 16 Aug 1833.

W, 122: B. Johnson, Sheriff of Union District, pursuant to an order from the Court of Ordinary 4 April 1833 to sell one tract of land belonging to the estate of Robert Hilburn decd on waters of Rocky Creek, 60 acres adj. lands of Jackson, Benjamin G. Davis, James McDonald, sold to John Gage Senr for $70, 31 July 1833. B. Johnson, S. U. D. (Seal), Wit: E. Wilburn, H. W. Foote. Proved by the oath of H. W. Pratt 14 Aug 1833 before J. Rogers, Q. U.

W, 122-125: Whereas a marriage is agreed upon between Julia Ann Hix and John Joiner, both of Union District, and said Julia Ann Hix is possessed in her own right of sundry slaves and personal chattles, during her natural life only, and said Julia Ann has an expectancy in the real and personal estate of her mother Mrs. Meng, deeds in trust to John Rogers, Esqr., and if said John Joiner should die leaving the said Julia Ann Hix without issue of that marriage, the whole of the said estate, then to be sold and to go to James Edward Hix, son of said Julia Ann Hix, but if there should be issue, then to be divided between said Julia Ann and said child or children, 18 Sept 1833. John Joiner (Seal), Julia Ann Hix (Seal), John Rogers (Seal), Wit: C. S. Meng, J. W. S. Meng. Proved by the oath of John W. S. Meng, 24 Sept 1833 before D. Wallace. Schedule of property: three negroes Jane about 20 years of age, girl Fanny about three years of age, a child Saxon about ten or twelve months old, one bureau and table, two bedsteads, bed & furniture, stock of cattle, an interest in Mrs. Sarah Meng's estate real and persona, and an interest in the unsettled estate of Jesse S. Hix deceased, 18 Sept 1833. Recorded 24 Sept 1833.

W, 126: South Carolina, Union District. John Evans of district of Union for love, good will and affection to son Reuben Evans, one negro boy named Balam, and one filly named Doll, 28 Aug 1833. John Evans (X) (Seal), Wit: A. W. Thomson, John Rogers. Proved by the oath of John Rogers 12 Sept 1833 before D. Wallace, J.P. Recorded 28 Aug 1833.

W, 126: Mial Ezell of the District of Union for $240 to Jesse Gibson of same, tract of 81 acres on waters of Fair Forest adj. John Fincher, Jackson, Saunders & Z. Belew, 9 Oct 1832. Mial Ezell (Seal), Wit: B. Johnston, Wm. Humphries. Proved by the oath of B. Johnson 2 Oct 1833 before J. Rogers, Q. U. Recorded 2 Oct 1833.

W, 127: South Carolina, Union District. Robert McDaniel of Union District for $60 to Jesse Gordon of same, 58 acres per survey made by John T. McJunkin, Esqr., 21 Nov 1829, on the east side of Tiger River adj. John Smith, John Rogers, Lewis Fant, William Smith, 5 Aug 1833. Robert McDaniel (Seal), Wit: J. Rogers, A. V. Jeter. Proved by the oath of John Rogers before J. J. Pratt, Q. U. Recorded 2 Oct 1833.

W, 127-128: South Carolina, Union District. Henry Harvey Means of Union District who is about to remove to the State of Tennessee appoints William H. Clowney, Esqr. his lawful attorney to enjoy & exercise all the rights & privileges to which I am entitled as a member of the company composed of myself Wm. B. Means, Abram McCarthur, Henry H. Means, Samuel Leitch & Wm. H. Clowney, engaged in mining, 12 Oct 1831. Henry H. Means (Seal), Wit: Z. Holmes, Henry Oneill. Recoreed 12 Oct.

W, 128-129: B. Johnson, Sheriff of Union District, by virtue of a writ of fieri facias from the court of common pleas held 5 Nov 1832 at the suit of John Wright & Co. to levy of the goods & chattles, lands & tenements of James Cunningham $73.18, sells 118 acres adj. Thomas Howard, Alexander Akin, Herod Gipson, on the waters of Fairforest, sold for $115 to Absolum Wood, 5 June 1833. B. Johnson, S. U. D. (Seal), Wit: J. N. Hardy, Stith Hardy. Proved by the oath of J. N. Hardy 5 June 1832 before J. Rogers. Mary Cunningham (X) relinquished dower 27 July 1833 before Daniel White, Q. U.

W, 129-130: South Carolina, Union District. Jerome Miller of district aforesaid for $500 to John Miller, which by son John Miller by an agreement between his father Jerome Miller and himself is to account for the stipulated sum of $400 out of his part of my estate after my decease, 101½ acres on the waters of Buffalow Creek, 23 Nov 1831. Jerom Miller (Seal), Wit: Thomas Walker, Benjamin Little (X). Proved by the oath of Benjamin Little 16 July 1832 before J. Rogers, Q.U. Mary Miller (X), wife of Jerome Miller, relinquished dower 8 May 1832 before J. Rogers, Q.U.

W, 130-131: South Carolina, Union District. Jerome Miller of district aforesaid for $240 to John Miller, 60 acres on a branch of Buffaloe Creek, 10 Jan 1832. Jerom Miller (Seal), Wit: Avery Little, Thomas R. Miller. Proved by the oath of Avery Little 20 July 1832 before John Rogers, Q.U. Mary Miller (X), wife of Jerome Miller, relinquished dower 8 May 1832 before John Rogers, Q.U. Recorded 24 July 1833.

W, 131-132: 7 Jan 1833, Robert A. Claybrooks to Jno. J. Pratt, ordinary for the District of Union, whereas said Robert A. Claybrooks and William Rice Esqr stand indebted to said John J. Pratt, ordinary, in the sum of $157.72, by notes, mortgage of tract on Buffaloe Creek, a branch of Fairforest adj. Cary Woodson, Robert Claybrooks, Smith, William Rice, 87 acres, whereon Samuel Brown formerly lived and sold by order of the ordinary for division. R. A. Claybrooks (Seal), J. J. Pratt (Seal), Wit: Joseph H. Dogan, Wm. Rice. Proved by the oath of Dr. J. H. Dogan 3 Sept 1833 before John Rogers, Q. U. Recorded 3 Oct 833.

W, 132-133: South Carolina, Union District. Samuel Beaty of the District of Union for due regard for divine worship and the accommodation of the Baptist Denomination of Christians, convey to Elisha Eubanks, Mordecai Chandler & George Fant, in trust, tract on the east side of the main road leading to Cooks bridge & supposed to containing about 7½ acres adj. Wm. Skelton, with the priviledges of using the spring and said Samuel Beaty and his heirs are not to be deprived of the use of said spring, and said Saml Beaty reserve the school house and the priviledge of one whenever necessary, 2 Oct 1833. S. Beaty (Seal), Wit: John D. Wood, B. Johnson. Proved by the oath of B. Johnson 3 Oct 1833 before John Rogers, Q.U. Recorded 3 Oct 1833.

W, 133: South Carolina, Union District. Ex Parte. P. M. Huson, J. Huson & wife. In Equity June Term 1833. Petition for appointment of Trustee on the petition being heard in this case and by consent of the parties, it is ordered that the petitioner Peter M. Huson be appointed trustee of the petitioner Hanah Ann Flowers, wife of said John Flowers, and that the interest in legacies that may be due the said Hanah Ann Flowers under the will of her uncle John Huson and her distributive share of her mother Sarah T. Huson's estate is vested in said Peter M. Huson in trust. Job Johnston. A true copy from the minutes of June Term 1833. B. M. Pearson, C. E. U. D. Recorded 11 Oct 1833.

W, 133-134: South Carolina, Union District. Abraham King of district aforesaid for $101 to Margaret Willbright of same, tract of 50 acres on the north side of the road leading from Skull Shoals to Genl Dawkins, adj. R. Huckaby, John Haney, John Gubring [Seebring?], part of 300 acres granted by Wm. Bailey to Darnel Bradford, 16 Aug 1832. Abraham King (X) (Seal), Wit: J. B. Murphy, Hampton Huckabe. Proved by the oath of L. B. Murray 9 Oct 1833 before Isaac Going, Q. U. Recorded 9 Oct 1833.

W, 134: South Carolina, Union District. Jesse Sprouse of Pickens County, Alabama, for $71 to John Gee of district aforesaid, tract on waters of Pacolet River, 25 acres near the spring that John Wood formerly made use of, adj. John Henry, Haney, Samuel M. Gowdy, 18 Oct 1831. Joel Sprouse (Seal), Wit: Samuel M. Gowdy, James T. Bankhead. Proved by the oath of Samuel M. Gowdy 9 Oct 1833 before Isaac Going, Q. U. Recorded 9 Oct 1833.

W, 135: South Carolina, Union District. William W. Glenn of district aforesaid for $870 to John Vessels of same, 290 acres in Union District, part of a tract that formerly belonged to William C. Glenn decd, adj. B. Mitchell, George Fant, Thomas A. Glenn, 10 June 1833. William W. Glenn (Seal), Wit: John S. Sims, Charles P. Jenkins, T. A. Glenn. Proved by the oath of Thomas A. Glenn 20 Aug 1833 before Reuben Gilliam, J.P. Recorded 20 Aug 1833.

W, 135-136: 5 Oct 1833, Leonard B. Murray of Union District to William Russel Murray, for natural love and affection and for the better maintenance and support and livelihood of him the said Wm. R. Murray, all the estate, right, title, interest, claim and demand to tract of land, with stock of horses, hogs, cattle, sheep, waggon and harness, farming utensils. Leonard B. Murray (Seal), Wit: John Gee (mark), John B. Murray. Proved by the oath of John Gee 2 [*sic*] Oct 1833. Recorded 2 Oct 1833.

W, 136-137: South Carolina, Union District. William Gordon of district aforesaid for $587.50 to John Smith of same, 191 acres, part of a tract of 796 acres granted to John Smith in 1816 on waters of Otterson's Creek, waters of Tiger River, 6 Feb 1832. William Gordon (Seal), Wit: James Meacheam, Edward Stevens. Maria Gordon, wife of William Gordon, relinquished dower 5 Dec 1832 before E. McGraw, Q.U. Proved by the oath of James Meacheam 8 Oct 1833 before E. McGraw, Q.U. Recorded 9 Oct 1833.

W, 137-138: John Anderson of Union District for $768 to Peter P. Taylor of same, 384 acres on Shoaly Creek adj. Cary Woodson, Claybrook, Aaron Harlan, 9 Oct 1833. John Anderson (Seal), Wit: D. A. Mitchell, J. F. M. Taylor. Susannah Anderson, wife of John Anderson, relinquished dower 25 Oct 1833 before John Rogers, Q. U. Proved by the oath of D. A. Mitchell __ 1833 before John Rogers, Q. U. Recorded 30 Oct 1833.

W, 139-140: John Anderson of Union District for $4000 to Robert Beaty of same, 700 acres on both sides of Buffalo and a branch of Fair Forest, adj. Robert Woodson, estate of Robert Woodson, John Anderson, Aaron Harlan, Shoally Creek, Peter P. Taylor, on the road leading from Union Court House to McBeth, Wm. Rice, Esqr., John Sanders, 22 Oct 1833. John Anderson (Seal), Wit: Isaac Whitten, Rich'd Thomson. Susannah Anderson, wife of John Anderson, relinquished dower 25 Oct 1833 before John Rogers, Q.U. Proved by the oath of Rich'd Thomson 30 Oct 1833 before John Rogers, Q.U. Recorded 30 Oct 1833.

W, 140-141: B. Johnson, Sheriff of Union District, by virtue of a writ of fieri facias from the court of equity held for the District of Richland, 11 January 1882 [sic] at the suit of Abram D. Jones to levy of the goods and chattels, lands & tenements of William Corben & Martin Corbin $15,841.31, tract of 700 acres on Tiger River adj. Thomas C. Jeter, David Crenshaw, James A. Tucker, John Biddie, purchased by Abram D. Jones of Kershaw District for $325, 4 Nov 1833. B. Johnson, S. U. D. (Seal), Wit: W.R. Wilbourn, E. Wilbourn. Proved in Union District by the oath of E. Wilbourn 4 Nov 1833 before J. Rogers, Q.U. Recorded 3 Nov 1833.

W, 141-142: State of So Carolina, Union District. In the Court of Equity. Whereas James. M. Whitlow and others filed their bill of complaint in the court of equity against Mary Bobo and others 11 May 1832 showing sundry other things that Kindred Bobo died intestate seized and possessed in his own right in fee of several tracts of land in union District and that partition and division of the said remained to be made and the said cause being at issue came to be heard at June Term 1832, now B. M. Pearson, Commissioner of the said court, did on 32 December 1832 at Union Court House expose to public sale, and Edward M. Bobo became the purchaser of tract for $300, 122 acres on the waters of Tiger River adj. Hiram Gibs, Alexander Hays, Giddeon, and other lands of the estate of Kindred Bobo, 3 Dec 1832. Bird M. Pearson (Seal), Wit: E. Wilbourn. John H. Shelton. Proved by the oath of John H. Shelton 2 Nov 1833 before J. Rogers, Q. U. Recorded 20 Nov 1833.

W, 142-143: South Carolina, Union District. Alfred Gilkey of district aforesaid for $500 to William Lockhart Senr of Spartanburg District, tract on Gilkies Creek whereon Elisabeth Gilkey now lives, part of tract formerly belonging to Samuel Gilkey and by him given to me Alfred Gilkey in his will, adj. William Phillips, Isaac Peeler, 100 acres, 12 Nov 1833. Alfred Gilkey (Seal), Wit: Hiram Lockhart, Wm. Lipscomb. Proved by the oath of Hiram Lockhart 14 Nov 1833 before J. Camp, J.Q. Nov 12 1833. I have sold all my natural life estate in a tract of land that Saml Gilkey willed to his son Alfred Gilkey to William Lockhart Senr for value received. Elisabeth Gilkey (X) (LS), Wit: Hiram Lockhart. William Lipscomb.

W, 144: South Carolina, Union District. John Anderson for $350 to Thomas Humphris, tract formerly belonging to Henry Anderson adj. Charles Humphries Senr, Hooker, Bobo, Charles Humphries Junr, Sally Humphries, Thomas Humphries, 200 acres, 6 Feb 1832. John Anderson (LS), Wit: D. A. Mitchell, Edward Stevens. Proved by the oath of Daniel A. Mitchell 30 Oct 1833 before J. Rogers, Q. U. Recorded 30 Oct 1833.

W, 144-145: T. G. Farr of Union District for $534.91 to D. A. Mitchell of same, 109 acres on waters of Neals big creek, waters of Broad River, being a tract purchased of the said Danl A. Mitchell by said T. G. Farr, 2 Nov 1833. Titus G. Farr (LS), Wit: Uriah Porter, Rich'd Thompson. Proved by the oath of Rich'd Thompson 2 Dec 1833 before J. Rogers, Q.U. Recorded 2 Dec 1833.

W, 145-146: South Carolina, Union District. H. H. Holcombe for $500 to Clemmons Howard of said district, tract on waters of Fairforest and on both sides Dining Creek at Simmons' spring, A. Hays, Sarah Holcombe, to the old Fairforest Meeting House spring branch, with the Waggon Road to Benjamin Holcomb's line, 13 Nov 1833. H. H. Holcombe (LS), Wit: Wm. B. Murphy, Caleb Greer, Spencer Greer. Proved by the oath of Wm. B. Murphy 2 Dec 1833 before J. Rogers, Q.U. Recorded 2 Dec 1833.

W, 146-148: John T. Murrell of Union District for $600 to Able Barnet of same, 350 acres on the south side Tyger River adj. Littleton B. Clark, Robt Ray, Jas Johnston, Joseph Prince, Isaac Burnett, Marshal Boswell, 2 Sept 1833. John T. Murrell (Seal), Wit: A. W. Thompson, J. Rogers. Proved by the oath of John Rogers 2 Dec 182 before Jno Norman, Q. U. Sarah T. Murrell, wife of John T. Murrell, relinquished dower 23 Sept 1833 before H. Gibbs, Q. U. Recorded 13 Dec 1833.

W, 148-149: Wm Bentley of Union District bound to Freeman Bentley in the sum of $450, to make title to a tract of 76½ acres adj. Wm. Mitchell, D. Holder, Patrick Williams, James Newton, payment due @5 Dec 1833, dated 30 Aug 1832. Wm. Bentley (X) (LS), Wit: J. Rogers, Wm. Bentley Jnr (X). Polly Bentley (X), wife of Wm. Bentley, relinquished dower 4 Nov 1833 before J. Rogers, Q. U. Proved by the oath of John Rogers 10 Dec 1833 before J.Palmer, J. P. Recorded 10 Dec 1833.

W, 149-150: South Carolina, Union District. Zechariah P. Herndon of district aforesaid attorney in fact of Robert Caldwell of District of Orangeburgh, by virtue of a power of attorney from said Robert Caldwell dated 19 Feb 1831, sell for $800 to Reuben Lindsey of Union District, tract on Pacolet River by resurvey made by Richard Thompson, Esqr., 8 Aug 1827, 484 acres whereon John Pridmore and Thomas Pridmore formerly lived and sold by John Bates, late sheriff to said Robert Caldwell adj. Wm Brown, Z. holmes, Wm. Cotter,

Mr. Fitch, 11 July 1833. Z. P. Herndon atty for Robert Caldwell (LS), Wit: Levi Walker, Walter Farnandis. Proved by the oath of Levi Walker 6 Nov 1833 before D. Wallace, J.P. Recorded 6 Nov 1833.

W, 150-151: Elizabeth Sewell (formerly Elizabeth Sumner) of Maury County, Tennessee, appoint Gabriel Stone of said state and county my attorney to receive the amount of an estate or legacy coming to me by the will of my grandmother Roebuck (being the mother of my mother) who departed this life in the state of South Carolina al also to demand and receive the amount of my legacy which has descended to me from my father Miles Sumner who departed this life in Union District, SC, 9 Oct 1833. Elizabeth Sewell (X) (LS), Wit: Wile A. Johnson, Hugh Bradshaw. Proved in Maury County, Tennessee, before Thomas J. Porter, clerk of the court of pleas and quarter [sessions] for said county by William A. Johnston and Hugh Bradshaw, 9 Oct 1833. James Walker, chairman of the court of pleas and quarter session certified that Thos J. Porter is clerk of this court 9 Oct 1833. Recorded 9 Oct 1833.

W, 151-152: Lemuel B. Askew of Union District for $50 to Thomas N. Dawkins of same, tract on waters of Browns Creek, 34 acres adj. Danl A. Mitchell, Doct E. M. Bobo, Benjamin G. Davis, John Gage, Z. P. Herndon, tract of land whereon Doct. Askew lately resided adj. the village of union including two lots on the back grounds of lots No. 26 & 12, 6 May 1833. Lem B. Askew (LS), Wit: J. Rogers, Richd Thompson. Proved by the oath of John Rogers 4 Nov 1833 before James Rowntree, J.P. Recorded 4 Nov 1833.

W, 152-153: Anthony McElwain of District of Union for $500 to Joseph Davidson of same, 84 acres on both sides of McElwains Creek, part of tract granted to James McElwain Senr on an old line run between James McElwain and James McElwain Junr, 28 July 1818. Anthony McElwain (LS), Sally McElwain (X), Wit: Robert Simerville, Hanson Playman, William Patton. Sally State of Indiana, Dubois County. Sally McElaine, wife of Anthony McElwain, relinquished dower 5 Aug 1818 before Thomas Hope, J.P. Proved by the oath of Wm. Patton 5 Aug 1818 in Dubois County. Simon Morgan, clerk of the circuit court certified that Thomas Hope is a justice of the pace, 8 Aug 1818.

W, 153-154: John Anderson of the District of Union for $100 to Thomas Willard Jr of same, tract on waters of Maris[?] branch adj. Christopher Young, David Beatenbaugh, John W. Skelton, 67 acres, 23 Nov 1833. John Anderson (Seal), Wit: J. Rogers, Charles Gowing. Proved by the oath of John Rogers 13 Dec 1833 before Wm. Mitchell, J.P. Recorded 13 Dec 1833.

W, 154-155: South Carolina, Union District. David Johnson of the Town of Columbia for $5000 to John Anderson, Esquire, of Union, in the same state, tract of 867 acres on the branches of Buffalo Creek, waters of Fairforest, play certified by Richard Thompson, Esquire, 8 June 1819, also another tract of 80 acres adj. widow Bogan, lands lately owned by James M. Whitlow, said John Anderson, conveyed to me by John Bates, Esquire, then Sheriff of Union District, for partition among the heirs of Thomas Little, 29 Aug 1823, dated

29 Oct 1833. David Johnson (Seal),wit: J. Rogers, W. Farnandes. Proved by the oath of John Rogers 13 Dec 1833 before Wm. Mitchell, J.P. Recorded 13 Dec 1833.

W, 155-156: South Carolina, Union District. Edwd M. Bobo of district aforesaid for $2500 to William Rice, trustee for Mary Ann Hook[er], tract on Hughes Creek known as the lands formerly owned by Maj. Samuel Faucett adj. Jno Giles, Jno Gist, James Hughes Jos Naugher, John Savage, Jesse Savage, 411 acres, 9 Nov 1833. E. M. Bobo (LS), Wit: J. W. L. Meng, D. Wallace. Proved by the oath of John W. L. Meng 12 Dec 1833 before J. Rogers. Recorded 12 Dec 1833.

W, 156-158: Recd Union Ct. House 6 Nov 1833 of Wm. Rice, Trustee for Mary Ann Hooker $255 for seven negroes viz Sam a black man 24 years old known as Landrum's Sam, Tom a yellow complected fellow a Black smith by trade about 27 years old, Hannah a black woman about 26 years old and her four children (viz) Patsy, Eliza, Diley, Amy, 6 Nov 1833. E. M. Bobo (LS), Wit: John W. L. Meng, D. Wallace. Proved by the oath of John W. L. Meng 12 Dec 1833 before J. Rogers. Recorded 12 Dec 1833. A schedule of property sold by E. M. Bobo to Wm. Rice, trustee for Mrs. Mary Ann Hooker, 6 Nov 1833. [includes horses, cattle, hogs, tools, etc.]

W, 158: Recd Nov 6th 1833 of William Rice, Trustee for Mary Ann Hooker, $1600 for a family of negroes viz Billy, his wife Alcey and her two children Betsy & Patty, and Dick & Jim (two brothers (black men) about 26 and 22 years old, Louisa a Black girl about 12 years old, and Jeff a Black man about 22 years old, 6 Nov 1833. E. M. Bobo (LS), Wit: John W. L. Meng, D. Wallace. Proved by the oath of John W. L. Meng 12 Dec 1833 before J. Rogers. Recorded 12 Dec 1833.

W, 158-159: South Carolina, Union District. Claybourn D. Lawrence of district aforesaid for $200 to Aaron Wilkins of same, tract on waters of Gilkies Creek, 100 acres adj. Joseph B. Guyton's spring branch [not dated]. C. D. Lawrence (LS), Wit: J. R. Wilkins, John J. Wilkins. Proved by the oath of John J. Wilkins 2 Dec 1833 before S. A. Goodman, Q.U. Recorded 2 Dec 1833.

W, 159-161: South Carolina, Union District. Whereas by a deed of marriage contract 13 Dec 1830 between Z. Hooker and Mary Ann Hooker, wife of said Z. Hooker, late Mary Ann Moorman, William Rice was appointed trustee, schedule of property [see preceding documents, slaves, land, etc.], 6 Nov 1833. Z. Hooker (S), Mary A. Hooker (LS). Recorded 16 Dec 1833.

W, 161: South Carolina, Union District. John Rogers certifies that Susannah A. Mitchell, wife of D. A. Mitchell, relinquished dower to E. M. Bobo, 30 Nov 1833.

W, 161-162: South Carolina, Union District. Jason Boatman of Union District for $1500 to William Bailey of same, one acre on the north bank of Tyger

River on the west of Whites branch, 9 Nov 1833. Jason Boatman (mark) (LS), Wit: Fredk Jackson, Robt D. Gilliam. Proved by the oath of Robert Gilliam 9 Nov 1833 before Fredk Jackson, J.P. Recorded 14 Dec 1833.

W, 162-163: South Carolina, Union District. Daniel Chandler of district aforesaid for $150 to Absalom Langston of same, tract of land formerly belonging to John Gage Senr on the waters of Tinker Creek, a branch of Tyger River, 85 acres being surveyed for John Hawkins 28 May 1799 recoreed in Grant Book T No 5, page 277, adj. Isaac Hawkins, an Irish bounty, Wm. Goldsmith, Saml McJunkin, 5 Dec 1833. Daniel Chandler (LS), Wit S. Beaty, I. Edwards. Rhoda Chandler, wife of Daniel Chandler, 16 Dec 1833 before J. Rogers, Q.U. Proved by the oath of Isaac Edwards 16 Dec 1833 before J. Rogers, Q.U. Recorded 167 Dec 1833.

W, 163-164: B. Johnson, Sheriff of Union District, by virtue of a writ of fieri facias from the court of common pleas tested 10 April 1833 at the suit of Robert Malone to levy of the goods and chattels, lands and tenements of John T. McJunkin $205.30, sold 367 acres on both sides Tinker Creek, waters of Tyger River whereon John T. McJunkin now lives, adj. Abram McJunkin, heirs of James Dugan, Langston, Eubanks, Benj McJunkin, part of two grants, one to Henry Millhouse and the other to Thomas Furgason, one to John T. McJunkin, by deed from Henry Millhouse to Joseph McJunkin, recorded in Book B No. 2, page 418, purchased by Abram McJunkin, for $10, 11 Dec 1833. B. Johnson, S. U. D. (Seal), Wit: H. W. Foote, Farr Bates. Proved by the oath of Farr Bates 11 Dec 1833 before J. Rogers, Q. U. Recorded 11 Dec 1833.

W, 164-165: South Carolina, Union District. Robert Caldwell of the District of Orangeburgh appoints Zachariah P. Herndon of Union District my true and lawfull attorney to sell tract on Packolett River, 484 acres, being the tract of land I lately recovered from Thomas Pridmore in the court of common pleas & on which the said Thomas Pridmore lived this last year, 19 Feb 1831. Robt Caldwell (Seal), Wit: R. H. Spencer, E. M. Glenn. Proved in Union District by the oath of E. M. Glenn 28 Dec 1833 before J. Rogers, Q.U. Recorded 28 Dec 1833.

W, 165-167: South Carolina, Union District. Robert Boatman Senr of district aforesaid for $450 to William Sparks (son of John), part of tract originally granted to Ambrose Yarborough on the NE side of Tyger River adj. said Sparks, 98½ acres, 4 May 1832. Robert Boatman (X) (LS), Wit: James White, John Boatman, Jesse Boatman (X). Martha Boatman (X), wife of Robert Boatman, relinquished dower 18 May 1822 before Mark Murphy, J.Q. Proved by the oath of John Boatman 24 May 1823 before Mark Murphy, J.Q. Recorded 14 Dec 1833.

W, 167-168: South Carolina, Union District. Joseph McJunkin of Union District for $1200 to Abram McJunkin of same, 370 acres on Tinker Creek, waters of Tiger River, part of two tracts, one granted to Henry Millhouse the other to Thomas Ferguson and a small part granted to John T. McJunkin, adj. James Dugan, Langston, Eubanks, Benjn McJunkin, said Abram McJunkin, 11 Dec 1833. Joseph McJunkin (Seal), Wit: John Kesler, James McJunkin. Margaret McJunkin, wife of John T. McJunkin, and mother of the within named Joseph McJunkin, relinquished dower 19 Dec 1833 before Edwd McGraw, Q.U. Proved by the oath of James McJunkin 19 Dec 1833 before Edwd McGraw, Q. U. Recorded 19 Dec 1833.

W, 168-169: South Carolina, Union District. 8 Jan 1834, Clough S. Meng to Joseph H. Dogan, whereas said Clough Meng stands indebted to said Joseph H. Dogan in the sum of $200 by two notes of hand, mortgage of lot in Union Village on the north side of the Mane Street whereon said Clough S. Meng now lives adj. Samuel T. Bailey, by Bachelor Street. C. S. Meng (Seal), Jos H. Dogan (Seal), Wit: E. M. Glenn, J. Rogers. Proved by the oath of E. M. Glenn 8 Jan 1834 before John Rogers, Q. U. Recorded 8 Jan 1834. Mortgage satisfied 11 Jan 1837.

W, 169: John Rogers of Union Village for $250 to Lewis Fant of Union District, tract on Swift run a water of Tinker Creek, 116 acres adj. said Lewis Fant, John Keisler, Jesse Jeter & others, 3 Jan 1834. John Rogers (Seal), Wit: Wm. Adams, D. Duncan. Proved by the oath of William Adams 3 Jan 1834 before John Rogers, Q.U. Recorded 3 Jan 1834.

W, 170: Mary Rice, William Rice and Charles B. N. Rice of Union District for $10 to Thomas Sartor of Union District, tract on waters of Fair forest Creek, 20 acres at the old well near the house occupied by James Foote, 20 Jan 1834. Mary Rice (Seal), Wm. Rice (Seal), C. B. N. Rice (Seal), Wit: Solomon Clark, H. B. Foote. Proved by the oath of Solomon Clark 6 Jan 1834 before John Rogers, Q. U. Recorded 6 Jan 1834.

W, 170-171: South Carolina, Union District. B. Johnson, Sheriff of said district, pursuant to an order from the court of ordinary, 8 Oct 1833 at the suit of Michael [*sic*, for Mitchell] Sparks applicant directed to sell one tract of land belonging to the estate of Jesse Boatman deceased, on waters of Tiger River adj. Fredk Jackson Senr, Jesse Holcomb, Robt Boatman, Jason Boatman, about 100 acres, purchased by William Sparks, 14 Dec 1833. B. Johnson (Seal) S. U. D. Wit: H. W. Foote, Charles Gowing. Proved by the oath of H. W. Foote 14 Jan 1834 before John Rogers, Q. U.

W, 171-172: South Carolina, Union District. William W. Glenn of district aforesaid for $2200 to Thomas A. Glenn of same, 558 acres on Tiger River, and one tract of land of 162 acres, being a part of two tracts of land granted to John Hughy, in all 620 acres adj. William Humphries, Thomas C.Brooks, George Fant, John Vessells, William W. Glenn, 4 June 1833. William W. Glenn (Seal), Wit: John S. Sims, Charles P. Jenkins, John Vessels. Received of Thomas A. Glenn $1008 in full of my interest in the first mentioned tract of 458 acres, part of the real estate of William C. Glenn deceased, 4 June 1833. Wit: John S. Sims, Charles P. Jenkins. Proved by the oaths of C. P.

Jenkins, John Vessels, 20 Aug 1833 before Reuben Gilliam, J.P. Recorded 13 Jan 1834.

W, 172-173: South Carolina, Union District. Job Hammond of Union District for $100 to Zachariah Belew of same, tract on waters of Fairforest supposed to contain 116 acres reserving the grave yard adj. Zechariah Belew Junr, estate of Benjn Saunders, Jesse Gibson, Joseph Robinson, William Rice, 27 Sept 1833. Job Hammond (Seal), Wit: Joseph Greer, John Fincher. Proved by the oath of John Fincher 6 Jan 1834 before John Rogers, Q.U. Recorded 6 Jan 1834.

W, 173-174: South Carolina, Union District. Zach'r Belew Sen for $116 to Zachariah Belew Junr, tract on branches of Fair forest, 47 acres adj. Wm Rice, said Zachariah Belew, part of two surveys, 7 March 1826. Zachariah Belew (Seal), Wit: Wm. White, Mial Ezell. Proved by the oath of John Rogers who attested to the handwriting of William White 6 Jan 1834. Recorded 3 Jan 1834.

W, 174-175: South Carolina, Union District. Zachariah Belew Junr and James M. Williams, both of district aforesaid, and through a power of attorney from Zachariah Belew Senr, sell 116 acres on waters of fairforest belonging to Z. belew Senr of Lawrence County, Tennessee, to Job Hammond for $100 [see deed above W, 172-173], 27 Sept 1833. Zachariah Belew (Seal), James M. Williams (Seal), Wit: Joseph Greer, John Fincher. Proved by the oath of John Fincher 6 Jan 1834 before John Rogers, Q.U. Recorded 6 Jan 1834.

W, 175: South Carolina, Union District. James B. Harrison of said district for $294.50 to Jno Blair of Yorkville, one of the late firm of Blair & Harrison, all my interest or undivided share of a certain lot in Union District near Pinckneyville adj. Daniel McMahon Senr, on the main road adj. Col. Jos Gist, Daniel McMahon Junr, 13 June 1833. J. B. Harrison (Seal), Wit: J. W. Faires, James H. Alexander. Proved in Union district by Justice James H. Alexander & J. W. Faires 29 Oct 1833 before Isaac Going, Q. U. Recorded 13 Dec 1833.

W, 176-177: South Carolina, Union District. Whereas John H. Adams filed his bill of complaint in the court of equity for Union District against William Adams, Robert Adams, Susan M. S. Adams, Jane M. Adams, Margaret E. M. Adams and James W. Adams 21 June 1833, shewing that by the will of Mrs. Jane Hope deceased, the said complainants were entitled to partition and division of certain lands and mills on Thickety Creek in Union District, after the determination of the wife's estate therein of their father the deceased William Adams, and heard at a special court at York Court House 29 June 1833 and the said court did order that the lands and mills should be sold at public auction by the commissioner in equity for Union District, now B. M. Pearson, commissioner of said court, on 1 January 1834 did expose to public sale tract of land whereat Richard Thomson became the purchaser for $4511, 276 acres on Thickety Creek at Carothers field, 3 Jan 1834. Bird M. Pearson (Seal), Wit: James W. Thomson, Thos B. Cockrell. Proved by the oath of

James W. Thomson 3 Jan 1834 before John Rogers, Q.U. Recorded 3 Jan 1834.

W, 177-178: South Carolina, Union District. William M. Thomson of Union District for $213 to William Rice Senr of same, all my right and interest in a tract of land known by the name of the Ivy Tract which Land was sold by John Anderson, Sheriff, and purchased by Wm Rice and Wm. M. Thomson, 20 Sept 1828, deed dated 4 June 1832. William M. Thomson (Seal), Wit: A. W. Thomson, Job Hammond. Proved by the oath of A. W. Thomson 16 Jan 1834 before J. Rogers, Q.U. Recorded 16 Jan 1834.

W, 178-179: South Carolina, Union District. Joseph R. Howard of Union District for $1500 to William Rice of same, tract whereon I now live adj. James Mays, Stephen Jones, Elias High, Capt. William Wirt, and Meansville Mining Company, 430 acres, being a tract granted to Samuel Patten with a part of a tract granted to Mark Jackson, 9 Sept 1833. Joseph R. Howard (Seal), Wit: J. Harlan, John Littlejohn. Elenor Howard, wife of Joseph R. Howard, relinquished dower 31 Oct 1833 before H. Gibbs, Q.U. Proved by the oath of James Harlan 16 Jan 1834 before John Rogers, Q.U. Recorded 16 Jan 1834.

W, 179-180: South Carolina, Union District. ___ 1833, Thomas Mitchell of the one part and Frances Mitchell his wife of the other part, both of district aforesaid, whereas Thomas Mitchell (tanner) hath given the notice by law required for the future to trade as a feme sole, 16 Jan 1833. R. B. Mitchell (Seal), F. F. Mitchell (Seal), Wit: John Harris, R. V. Harris. Proved by the oath of Robt V. Harris 16 Jan 1833 before J. Rogers, Q. U. Recorded 16 Jan 1833.

W, 180-181: South Carolina, Union District. Joel Bentley of Union District for $100 to Wm Bentley of same, 148 acres on waters of Browns Creek, 17 Jan 1834. Joel Bentley (Seal), Wit: John Rogers, Sherwood W. Nance. The above tract on a small branch of Fannans Creek, part of tract granted to William Sims, 10 Jan 1816. Richard Thomson, D. S. George & James Ennis, Chain Carriers. Proved by the oath of Sherwood W. Nance 17 Jan 1834 before J. Rogers, Q.U. Recorded 17 Jan 1834.

W, 181: William M. Thomson of Union District for $180.70 to Joseph A. McJunkin, 100 acres on Tinker Creek, by deed from John Anderson, Sheriff, 4 March 1828 and recorded in the proper office 23 April 1828, dated 17 June 1830. Wm. M. Thomson (Seal), Wit: R. H. Spencer, Benjn. McJunkin. Proved by the oath of Benjn McJunkin 18 Jan 1834 before J. Rogers, Q.U. Recorded 18 Jan 1834.

W, 182: South Carolina, Union District. Patrick Williams of Union District quit claims to John Forbes, tract on Buffalo Creek, 332 acres, 18 Jan 1834. Patrick Williams (Seal), Wit: B. Johnson, J. Rogers. Proved by the oath of John Rogers 21 Jan 1834 before D. Wallace, J.P. Recorded 21 Jan 1834.

W, 182-184: South Carolina, Union District. In the Court of Equity. Whereas Gideon Steen and others exparte, heirs at law of William Townsend, deceased, filed their bill of complaint in the court of Equity for Union District 24 March 1832 shewing that the said William Townsend died intestate seized and possessed of four several tracts of land on tinker Creek, a branch of Tiger River and that partition remained to be made of the same, a writ of partition should issue. The tract marked C according to the estimate of Stephen Johnson, Deputy Surveyor, 79½ acres, tract marked E according to the estimate, 92 acres, valued by the said Commissioner at $138 was assigned to Elisha Eubanks in right of his wife Elizabeth who is one of the heirs. Said Commissioner makes deed to Elisha Eubanks, 19 April 1833. Bird M. Pearson, C. E. U. D. (Seal), Wit: Daniel Malone, Jesse Gordon. Proved by the oath of Jesse Gordon 17 Jan 1834 before J. Rogers, Q. U. Recorded 17 Jan 1834.

W, 184: South Carolina, Union District. George Foster for $100 to Robert Foster of district aforesaid, tract which James Foster is now living & which formerly belonged to our father Francis Foster and deeded from him to William Foster on the Pinckney Road on waters of Pacolet, 93 acres, adj. Henry George, Jonah Foster Jr., 14 Dec 1833. George Foster (X) (Seal), Wit: G. W. Plaxco, Marshal Dupree. Proved by the oath of F. W. Plaxco 23 Dec 1833 before Isaac Going, Q.U. Recorded 27 Jan 1834.

W, 184-185: South Carolina, Union District. Polly S. Handley of said district for $850 to Robert Jones of same, part of a tract granted to Merryman McGuire adj. John B. Bailey, J. Foster, William Foster, 212½ acres, 19 Nov 1830. Polly S. Handley (Seal), Wit: I. J. Foster, W. D. Hendley. Proved by the oath of William D. Hendley 19 Nov 1830 before A. Foster, J.P. Recorded 27 Jan 1834.

W, 185-186: South Carolina, Union District. W. W. E. Moreland for $50 to Isaac Going of said district, part of tract on which I now live on the waters of Pacolet, 25 acres adj. said Going, 3 Jan 1834. W. W. E. Moreland (Seal), Wit: J. Moreland, O. K. Moreland. Mariah Moreland, wife of W. W. E. Moreland, relinquished dower 16 Jan 1834 before Daniel White, Q.U. Proved by the oath of J. Moreland 16 Jan 1834 before Daniel White, Q.U. Recorded 27 Jan 1834.

W, 186-187: South Carolina, Union District. 27 Jan 1834, James Savage to John Rogers, whereas the said James Savage stands indebted to Samuel Brooks in the sum of $230 by his note of hand, and said John Rogers is security for the said note, mortgage of 270 acres on Hughs Creek, being the land whereon the said James Savage now lives adj. Hiram Davis, Daniel Reynolds, John Ennis, John Parr, Walter Wisher, and Mr. Hughs & others. James Savage (Seal), J. Rogers (Seal), Wit: John Gage Junr, John Smith. Proved by the oath of John Gage Junr 28 Jan 1834 before E. P. Porter, Q.U. Satisfied in full August 8th 1837.

W, 187-188: Plat of 54 3/4 acres on Shoal Creek, a branch of Fairforest, waters of Tyger River, 27 Feb 1833 by Richd Thomson, D.S. H. T. Davis, Jonas

Little, Ch. Carriers. Shows adjacent land owners Jacob Paulk, H. T. Davis, Mrs. Howard, Crenshaw, J. J. Pratt.

Recd 21 Feb 1833 of P. P. Taylor $200 in part of the purchase of tract of land whereon I now live adj. Mrs. Howard, Capt. Saml Davis, on Shoal Creek, at Six dollars pr acre, 22 Fe 1833. Jacob Paulk (LS), Wit: E. J. Adicks, J. J. Pratt. Proved by the oath of J.J. Pratt 28 Jan 1834 before J. Rogers, Q.U. Elizabeth Polk, wife of Jacob Polk, relinquished dower 28 Jan 1834 before J. Rogers, Q. U. Recorded 28 Jan 1834.

W, 188-189: South Carolina, Union District. James Becknell of district aforesaid for $101 to Joseph M. Dogan, tract on waters of Browns Creek adj. Absolum Barnett, Edward Bobo, Dabney Becknell, James McBride, 50 acres, 28 Dec 1833. James H. Becknell (Seal), Wit: C. Young, G. N. Smith. Sarah Ann Becknell, wife of James H. Becknell, relinquished dower 30 Dec 1833 before B. M. Pearson, Q.U. Ex off. Proved by the oath of Giles N. Smith 28 Jan 1834 before J. Rogers, Q.U. Recorded 28 Jan 1834.

W, 189-190: South Carolina, Union District. E. M. Bobo of district aforesaid for $150 to Dabney Becknell of same, tract on the side of the main road, 34 acres, 24 Jan 1834. E. M. Bobo (Seal),Wit: J. W. L. Meng, D. Wallace. Proved by the oath of J. W. Meng 17 Jan 1834 before J. Rogers, Q.U. Mrs. Elizabeth Bobo relinquished dower 31 Jan 1834 before J. Rogers, Q.U. Recorded 31 Jan 1834.

W, 190-193: Olive Hawkins, widow of Benjamin Hawkins deceased, and former widow of John Cook, late of Union District, SC, deceased, and William Hollingsworth and Mary his wife formerly Mary Cook of the County of Tipacanoe & state of Indiana & Jesse Green and Charity Green his wife, formerly Charity Cook, of the county of Preble and state of Ohio, the said Mary and Charity being children & heirs at law of the said John Cook deceased, appoint Robert Kenworthy of the county of Tipacanoe, Indiana, our true and lawful attorney to sell and convey all and any tract or tracts of land which may have descended to us from said John Cook deceased, 3 Oct 1833. Olive Hawkins (Seal), William Hollingsworth (Seal), Mary Hollingsworth (Seal), Jesse Green (Seal), Charity Green (Seal), Wit: John Lovejoy, Abert S. White, John Odell, A. Mack. Tipacanoe County, Indiana 3 Oct 1833 Olive Hawkins, William Hollingsworth and Mary Hollingsworth acknowledged before John Lovejoy, J.P. Samuel Hoover, clerk of said County certified that John Lovejoy was a justice of the peace. John R. Porter, judge, certified that Samuel Hoover was clerk.

Preble County, Ohio. Alexander Mack, J. P., certified that Jesse Green & Charity his wife acknowledged the letter of attorney, 15 Oct 1833, F. A. Cunningham, Clerk Pro Tem. Geo H. Ball, presiding judge, certified that Francis Cunningham was clerk pro tem. Recorded 3 Feb 1834.

W, 193: South Carolina, Union District. Celia Lancaster (X), wife of Lemual Lancaster, relinquished dower 8 Feb 1834 before H. Gibbs, Q.U. Recorded 10 Feb 1834.

W, 194: South Carolina, Spartanburgh District. Richard Starns for $75 to Thomas Layton, 105 acres on waters of Elisha Creek, waters of Enoree River, it being part of Lot No 3, sold by order of court for partition among the representatives of S. Farrow decd, 11 Oct 1833. Rich'd Starns (Seal), Wit: D. Wallace, John W. L. Meng. Joel Dean, D.S., certified that he resurveyed a tract for Richard Starns, 26 Sept 1833. Proved by the oath of Justice D. Wallace 3 Feb 1834 before John Norman, Q. U. Recorded 3 Feb 1834.

W, 194-195: South Carolina, Union District. Thomas Layton in one part and Polly Layton on the other part and Betty Layton in the other part and Susanah Layton on the other part of district aforesaid for natural love and affection which we have and do bear one to the other and towards the better support and maintenance of each other, have agreed and give one to the other the whole of the property both real and personal that is possessed by the parties so dieing before they marry is to be bonafide property of the surviving parties, and should the whole of these parties above mentioned die and leave only one survivor them the whole of the property both real and personal that is possessed by the parties shall be the bonafide property of the last surviving party, if either of the parties Thomas Layton, Betty Layton, Polly Layton, or Susannah Layton, should marry, the parties so marrying shall draw their full distributive share of the estate of Stephen Layton decd, 3 March 1830. Thomas Layton (Seal), Betty Layton (X) (Seal), Polly Layton (X) (Seal), Susannah Layton (X) (Seal), Wit: Jeffery Palmer, Drury Sparks, Stephen Taylor. Proved by the oath of Stephen Taylor 2 Sept 1830 before Fredk Jackson, J.P.

W, 195-196: Thomas Howard of Union District for $20 to Benjamin W. Arrowood, tract of land on waters of Mitchells Creek, being a tract granted to myself 23 Feb 1807 adj. Wm Thomson, John Davidson, James Farris, 31 Oct 1833. Thomas Howard (Seal), Wit: Wm. Trammell, James Means. Proved by the oath of William Trammell 3 Feb 1834 before J. Rogers, Q.U. Recorded 3 Feb 1834.

W, 196: G. S. Noland of Union District for $75 to Charner Humphries of same, tract on a branch of Shoal creek, waters of Fair forest, 16 acres, agreeable to a grant made to J. M. Whitlow 4 Jan 1818, dated 3 Feb 1834. G. S. Noland (Seal), Wit: J. Rogers, Thos Humphries. Proved by the oath of Thomas Humphries 3 Feb 1834 before J. Rogers, Q.U. Recorded 3 Feb 1834.

W, 197: John Howard of Union District for $400 to Benjamin W. Arrowood, tract of land on both sides of Mitchells Creek, adj. Dr. McGowan, James Means, Thomas Howard, George Thomson, at the corner of an old survey granted to Thomas Armstrong, adj. George Thomson, on the Pinckney Road, 184 acres ______ 1833. John Howard (Seal), Wit: W. S. Means, Wm.

Trammell. Proved by the oath of William Trammell 3 Feb 1834 before J. Rogers, Q.U. Recorded 3 Feb 1834.

W, 197-198: W. W. E. Moreland of the District of Union for $615 to Henry George of same, tract on Tesseners Branch, waters of Broad River, 140 acres on the Spartanburgh Road, adj. McMahen's line, 20 July 1833. W. W. E. Moreland (Seal), Wit J. Moreland, John Haney. Maria Moreland, wife of W. W. E. Moreland, relinquished dower 9 Nov 1833 before Isaac Going, Q. U. Proved by the oath of Jeremiah Moreland 9 Nov 1833 before Isaac Going, Q.U. Recorded 3 Fe 1834.

W, 199: South Carolina, Union District. John McPherson of Union District for $700 to Wm. Rice of same, 100 acres on both sides of the south fork of Mitchells Creek, part of a grant to John Wood and the other to John Putman, and conveyed by Stephen McPherson to John McPherson in said Stephen's last will and testament, adj. Widow Mayhew, widow McPherson, Amos Lee, John Parham, 8 Feb 1834. John McPherson (Seal), Wit: H. W. Foote, John McIlwain, B. H. Rice. Lucy McPherson, wife of John McPherson, relinquished dower 8 Feb 1834 before J. J. Pratt, Q. U. Ex off. Proved by the oath of H. W. Foote 22 Feb 1834 fore J. Rogers, Q.U. Recorded 22 Feb 1834.

W, 200-201: 6 Jan 1845, B. M. Pearson, Commissioner of the court of equity, to Henry D. Vanlew, whereas the said Henry D. Vanlew stands indebted to the said B. M. Pearson, by his bond in the sum of $500 for the payment of $267.27, mortgage of tract about one mile below Goshen Hill on the Charleston Road adj. James Hunter, James Hughs, widow Pruet, John Burwell, James Hunter, Thomas Davis, estate of Randolph Jenkins decd. H. D. Vanlew (Seal), Bird M. Pearson (Seal), Wit: B. Johnson, W. H. Gist. Proved by the oath of B. Johnson 20 Feb 1834 before J. Rogers, Q.U. Recorded 20 Feb 1834.

W, 201: South Carolina, Union District. Joseph Gist of district aforesaid for $200 to Dr. William McGowan of same, 25 acres adj. Blair & Harris, on the road leading from Pinckney to Union Court House and by the margin of my old field in the rut separating the woods from the clear ground, 15 Nov 1831. Jos Gist (Seal), Wit: G. W. Plaxco, J. Farr. Proved by the oath of James Farr 20 Dec 1831 before Isaac Going, Q.U. Sarah Gist, wife of Joseph Gist, relinquished dower 20 Dec 1833 before Isaac Going, Q.U. Recorded 22 Feb 1834.

W, 202: South Carolina, Union District. Reuben Gilliam of said district for 4150 to Handley McShan of same, 100 acres on the north side of Cain Creek on the main road adj. N. Sims, according to a deed from Maulevin [*sic*] to Freeman of 100 acres and another deed from said Mauldin to Freeman for 50 acres, 13 Jan 1830. Reuben Gilliam (Seal), Wit: Saml C. Gordon, Ferdinand H. McShan. Proved by the oath of Ferdinand H. McShan 22 Feb 1834 before J. Rogers, Q. U. Recorded 22 Feb 1834.

W, 202-203: South Carolina, Union District. Christopher L. Vaughan of Union District for $250 to Nevil Smith of same, 80 acres on the waters of Browns Creek adj. Samuel P. Harris, 16 Dec 1833. C. L. Vaughan (Seal), Wit: Robert V. Harris, Samuel Vaughan. Proved by the oath of Samuel Vaughan 21 Dec 1833 before Daniel White, Q. U. Ginny Vaughan (X), wife of Christopher Vaughan, relinquished dower 21 Dec 1833 before Daniel White. Recorded 8 Dec 1834.

W, 203-204: South Carolina, Union District. 10 Feb 1834, Benjn G. Davis to John Rogers, whereas said Benj G. Davis stands indebted to Doctor Jos Dogan in the sum of $458.66 by two notes of hand and said John Rogers is security, mortgage of tract whereon said B. G. Davis now lives, on the main road from Union C. H. to Pinckneyville, four acres. B. G. Davis (LS), John Rogers (LS), Wit: B. Johnson, J. H. Dogan. Proved by the oath of B. Johnson 22 Feb 1834 before Jos Greer, J. P. Recorded 27 Feb 1834.

W, 205: South Carolina, Union District. Netty Howard (X), wife of Thomas Howard, relinquished dower to Jas Jackson 27 Feb 1834 before J. Rogers, Q.U.

W, 205-206: Robert Kenworthy attorney in fact in part for the heirs of Jno Cook and J. Eli Cooper for $1100 to Moses Cooper of Union District, tract on east side of Tiger River, 179 acres adj. A. V. Jeter, 27 Feb 1834. Charity Green by Robert Kenworthy (LS), Eli Cooper (X) (LS), John Hawkins (LS), Wm. Holingsworth (LS), Mary Holingsworth (LS), Jesse Greer (LS), Wit: N. Dawkins, R. J. Gage. Proved by the oath of Robert J. Gage 27 Feb 1834 before J. Rogers, Q. U. Recorded 27 Feb 1834.

W, 206-207: South Carolina, Union District. Agreeable to orders received from Joseph S. Shelton, Brig. Gen. of the Ninety Brigade of South Carolina Militia, we the under signed Commissioners appointed to divide the south battalion in the 34th Regiment into four beat companies have met this date and have laid off the boundaries of said companys as follows (viz No 1 or otherwise called the Santuck Company beginning at the ford of Tinker Creek where the fish dam Road crosses said creek thence running up the said creek to the fork of said creek thence a straight line to Trevellers old place then a straight on the old line that divided the south & north battalions to the widow Savages old place thence a straight line to the mouth of Browns Creek on Broad River thence down said river to Lyles ferry thence a road to Benjamin Ellis then a long a road leading to Cain Creek Meeting House by Mrs. Sorters thence to Wilsons Store by A. V. Jeters to the ford of Tinker Creek at the beginning. No. 2 or otherwise called the Fork Company beginning at the fork of Tinker Creek at or near A.V. Jeters on the fishdam Road thence along said road by Wilsons Store by Cain Cree Meeting House to the widow Sorters then to Benjn Ellis then the road to Lyles Ferry on Broad River thence down said river to the mouth of Tiger thence up Tiger river to the mouth of Tinker Creek thence up said creek to the ford where the road leading from Cooks Bridge leading to Fish Dam crosses said Creek. No. 3 or otherwise called

Goshen Hill Company begining at Adams ford on Tiger River along the Charleston road a small distance past Col. Wm Gist House thence taking the road leading to the widow Stephens & thence a strait line to Enoree River at or just below Thos G. Danners thence down said river to Averes ford on said river along the old county road to Crenshaws old Ford on Tiger River then up said river to Adams old ford on said river. No. 4. or otherwise called the Cross Keys Company beginning at Adams old ford on Tiger River and running up said River to the Spartanburg line or the uper boundary of said company thence along said boundary to Enoree River thence down said river to or just below Thos G. Danners, thence a straight line to the widow Stevens, then the main road leading into the Charleston Road at or near Col. Wm. Gist, thence along said road to Adams old ford on Tiger River, 30 Jan 1834. B. Johnson, S. Beaty, Jno K. B. Sims, Jesse Wilson. Recorded 27 Feb 1834.

W, 207: Col. Bradley's, Feb 8th 1834. Brg'a Genl Jos. S. Shelton. Sir, in pursuant or order from you to us as Commissioners to lay off the beat companies in the 34th Ridgment North Battalion & 9th Brigade, we have met and agreed upon the following lines (viz) by dividing J. F. Walkers old Company betwixt Capt Bevel & Kimberly by a line running with the road from Pinckney ferry to Esqr Lipsey and also by dividing Capt. Jason Greer's company betwixt Capt. Jos. Greer & Charles Rice by a line from McBeths bridge with the road to Holcombs store thence by the lower Brick meeting house to Nixes ford on Tiger River. Js. F. Walker, Saml Mosely, Elias Michael, Joseph Greer. Recorded 27 Feb 1834.

W, 207-208: Evans Williams of Union District for $200 to John Forbes of same, 135 acres on Buffalo Creek, a branch of Fair forest adj. John Forbes, McDugles, Butler, Permenus Palmore, Abram Jones, 28 Jan 1833. Evans Williams (LS), Wit: Thos Williams, David Howard, Christr Steen. Proved by the oath of Christr Steen 3 Feb 1834 before J. Rogers, Q. U.

W, 208-209: South Carolina, Union District. Bird Murphy of district aforesaid for $460 to John Gibbs of same, 80 acres near Lea White's fence, on new cut road, Baily Road, McGarity, part of tract deed by Robert White to said Bird Murphy, second 40 acres near Elizabeth White's spring, John Gibbs, Wilson's old field, estate of Kindred Bobo decd, estate of Frederick Jackson decd, by the waggon road, Thos Wilson, estate of William White decd, part of tract deeded by Gideon to said Bird Murphy, 28 Dec 1833. Bird Murphy (LS), Wit: Jesse Holcomb (X), Robert D. Gilliam (X). Charlotte Murphy (X), wife of Bird Murphy, relinquished dower 2 Jan 1834 before H. Gibbes, Q.U. Proved by the oath of Robert D. Gilliam 2 Jan 1834 before H. Gibbs, Q.U. Recorded 3 Feb 1834.

W, 209-210: John Anderson of Newton County, Georgia, for $1000 to Bartholomew Johnson of Union Village, lot whereon Mag'r B. Johnson now lives by Grog Street, J. J. Pratt, John Graham, Main Street, four acres 28 Dec 1833. John Anderson (LS), Wit: Thos Anderson, John Rogers. Proved by the oath of J. Rogers, 28 Feb 1834 before D. Wallace, J.P. Susannah Anderson, wife of John Anderson, relinquished dower 28 Dec 1833 before J. Rogers, Q.U.

W, 210-211: Clough S. Meng of Union Village for $650 to John Porter of Union District, tract on Browns Creek adj. Robert Davis, George Brandon, Patrick Williams, Saml Bentley, Mrs. Brandon, Mrs. Kenedy, 317 acres, being the land whereon John Norvell lived, 15 Jan 1834. C. S. Meng (LS), Wit: D. Wallace, John Rogers. Proved by the oath of John Rogers, Q. U., before D. Wallace, J. P. Mary Meng, wife of C. S. Meng, relinquished dower 27 Feb 1834 before J. Rogers, Q. U. Recorded 27 Feb 1834.

W, 211-212: South Carolina, Union District. Isaac Harlin for $250 to M. Bogan, both of said district, 100 acres on waters of Durhams[?] Creek, 16 March 1827. I. Harlin (LS), Wit: Caswell Bogan, Thos Nance. Proved by the oath of Thomas Nance 18 March 1834 before J. Rogers, Q. U. Recoreed 18 March 1834.

W, 212-213: Thos Craven of Union District for $2000 to McCluny Bogan of same, tract on south side of fair forest creek and both sides of Michael Creek adj. Francis Parham, heirs of John Parham decd, heirs of Thos Brooks, Nathan Harlin, being the tract whereon I now live, 729 acres by granted to Thomas Craven dated 6 April 1829, 22 Jan 1833. Thos Craven (LS), Wit: Thos N. Dawkins, D. A. Mitchael. Proved by the oath of D. A. Mitchael 22 Jan 1833 before J. Rogers, Q.U. Recorded 18 March 1834.

W, 213-214: South Carolina, Union District. William R. Wilbourn of district aforesaid for $1800 to Henry Forguson of District of Spartinburg, tract whereon I formerly lived on both sides of Black stock Road and on the north of Tiger River at the mouth of a drean, 462 acres, 14 Nov 1833. W. R. Wilbourn (LS), Wit: George Nickles, John McGarity. Proved by the oath of John McGarity 19 Nov 1833 before H. Gibbs, Q.U. Chloe Wilbourn, wife of Wm. R. Wilbourn, relinquished dower 19 Nov 1833 before H. Gibbs, Q.U. Recorded 18 March 1834.

W, 214-215: Barnabas Woolbright of Union District for $321 to Thos Armstrong, 71 acres on the waters of Thickety Creek on the south side of said Creek, being part of a tract formerly belonging to Zacariah Mabery decd, near Herbert[?] Archer's gate, Dickson Corry's line, 31 Jan 1833. Barnabas Woolbright (LS), Wit: Leonard B. Murry, Malesa R. Murray. Proved by the oath of Leonard B. Murry 10 March 1834 before Isaac Going, Q.U. Recorded 10 March 1834.

W, 215-216: William Adams of York District for $86 to Richard Thomson of Spartinburg District, tract in Union District originally granted to Richard Winn, being part of a tract on both sides Thickety Creek adj. the mill tract, near the mouth of said creek, King's corner, Good's line, 11½ acres, 31 Jan 1834. W. M. Adams (LS), Wit: Wm. Brown, Thos N. Black. Proved in Union

District by the oath of William C. Brown 13 Feb 1834 before Danl White, Q.U. Recorded 12 March 1834.

W, 216-217: South Carolina, Union District. John Miller of Laurens and Martha [*sic*] Miller of Union District for $1100 to Lewis Jones of Laurens District, 317 acres on or near River, adj. Mays, Rees, Stevens, on said Enoree River, 24 Sept 1832. John Miller (LS), Mathew Miller (LS), Wit: Reuben Anderson, John Whitmore. Proved by the oath of Reuben Anderson 10 March 1834 before D. Wallace, J.P. Margaret Miller (mark), wife of John Miller, and Melinda Ann Miller (mark), wife of Mathew Miller, relinquished dower 26 Sept 1832 before Robert Long, Q.J. Recorded 20 March 1834.

W, 217: South Carolina, Union District. John C. Voluntine of the District of Union for $810 to Phebe Paulk of same, tract on waters of Tinkers Creek & Browns Creek on Franks branch, 270 acres, 31 Oct 1833. John C. Voluntine (LS), Wit: Johnathan Hawkins, Nathan Hawkins, John Savage. Proved by the oath of Johnathan Hawkins 11 March 1834 before John Rogers, Q.U. Recorded 11 March 1834.

W, 218: John Anderson of Union District for $160 to Thomas Young of same, 80 acres on the south side of Mudy Branch, waters of Morrises Branch of fair forest adj. Christopher Young, John H. Skelton, 24 Oct 1832. John Anderson (LS), Wit: Isaac Whitten, George M. Young. Proved by the oath of George M. Young 18 March 1834 before J. Rogers, Q. U. Recorded 18 March 1834.

W, 218-219: 11 Feb 1834, Z. P. Herndon to J. T. Murrell, whereas J. T. Murrell stands indebted to said Z. P. Herndon in the sum of $1500 by a single bill, mortgage of lot in the village of Union now in the possession of B. M. Pearson, for or five acres adj. lot occupied by John Joiner[?], on Cross Street, C. S. Meng, and Main Street. John T. Murrell (LS), Z. P. Herndon (LS), Wit: H. W. Foot, John N. Herndon. Proved by the oath of H. W. Fort 28 March 1834 before J. Rogers, Q. U. Recorded 26 March 1834. Satisfied Feby 5 1835.

W, 220: John Parham of the District of Union for $65 to William Rice of same, 136 acres on the south side of fair forest Creek on the branches of the same, waters of Tiger River adj. heirs of John Parham decd, Wm Rice, Col. N. Gist, originally granted to Elisabeth McCullough 5 July 1830, plat drawn by Richard Thomson, 21 June 1830, dated 1 April 1834. John Parham (LS), Wit: B. Johnson, J. H. Skelton. Proved by the oath of B. Johnson 1 April 1384 before J. Rogers, Q. U. Recorded 1 April 1834.

W, 220-221: George Myers of Union District for $400 to Hezekiah Rice of Union District, land whereon Wm Davis now lives in the fork of Tiger River and fair forest... dated 28 Dec 1833. George Myers (X) (LS), Wit: C. B. Rice, Wm. Davis. Rachel Myers, wife of George, relinquished dower 3 Jan 1834.

W, 222: South Carolina, Union District. Walter Gilky of Alabama, Pickens County, and Saml Gilkey of State of Arkansas for $200 to Isaac Peeler of

South Carolina, district aforesaid, all our right and title teo a parcel of land on Gilkeys Creek, 100 acres, adj. Curry, on which Elisabeth Gilkey did live, 7 Dec 1833. Walter Gilkey (LS), Saml Gilkey (LS), Wit: Anderson J.Peeler, William Gee. Proved by the oath of Anderson J. Peeler who swore that he saw Alfred Gilkey as agent for Walter Gilkey and Samuel Gilkey acknowledged the within deed to Isaac Peeler, Esqr., 17 March 1834 before J. Rogers, Q.U. Recorded 17 March 1834.

W, 222-223: Danl Peeler of York District for $225 to David Malcomson of Union District, tract on main Broad River immediately above the mouth of London Bridge Creek on which Moses Dun now lives, 69 acres, 4 Feb 1832. Daniel Peeler (Seal), Wit: James Black, Emmor Graham. Proved in York District by the oath of James A. Black 21 Dec 1833 before Abraham Hardin, J.Q. Lucy Peeler (S), wife of Danl Peeler, relinquished dower 28 Dec 1833 before Abr. Hardin, J. Q. Recorded 28 Dec 1833. Recorded 17 March 1834.

W, 223-225: Henry Hardy of Union District for $4500 to James A. Tucker of same, tract on north side Tiger River on west side of McDuffies Road adj. Henry Richards, Moses Mardis, Nathan Glover, widow Glenn, John Biddy, heirs of Tucker, 3 Sept 1833. Henry Hardy (LS), Wit: Henry Richards, Jeremiah Kingsley, George Ashford. Proved by the oath of George Ashford 12 Nov 1383 before Reuben Gilam, J.P. Elisabeth, wife of Henry Hardy relinquished dower of 988 acres on north side Tyger River, 19 Dec 1833 before E. McGraw. Recorded 17 March 1834.

W, 225-226: 3 March 1834, James Meacham to Zacheriah Evans, whereas said Zacheriah stands indebted to said James Meacham in the sum of $500 by a single note, mortgage of tract whereon said Zacheriah Evans now lives, 200 acres being the land lately purchased of Jordon Ashley. Zacheriah Evans (LS), James Meacham (LS), Wit: Amasa T. Parks, E. R. Finch. Proved by the oath of E. R. Finch 2 April 1834 before J. Rogers, Q. U. Recorded 2 April 1834.

W, 226-227: South Carolina, Union District. Lot Porter of Union District for $150 to Edward M. Bobo of same, tract on waters of Browns Creek adj. JAmes Turner, ladn formerly Wilsons, E. M. Bobo, 50 acres, 21 Jan 1834. L. Porter (LS), Wit: E. M. Glenn, Z. P. Herndon. Susan Porter (X), wife of Lot Porter, relinquished dower 5 Feb 1834 before John Giles, Q. U. Proved by the oath of E. M. Glenn 7 April 1834 before J. Rogers, Q. U. Recorded 7 April 1834.

W, 227-228: James Jeter Junr of Union District for $300 to William Beaver of same, 162 acres on Lye branch, waters of Broad River whereon I now live, part of a large tract granted to Bartholomew Baker by Gov. William Moultrie, adj. Leonard Baker, Dr. Graffenreid, 6 Aug 1833. James Jeter (LS), Wit: C. [Charner] T. Scaife, E. A. Jackson. Proved by the oath of Edward A. Jackson 2 Sept 1833 before E. McGraw, Q. U. Elisabeth Jeter, wife of James Jeter, relinquished dower 29 Oct 1833 before E. McGraw, Q.U. Recorded 7 April 1834.

W, 228-229: William Beaver of Union District for $420 to David A. Thomas of same, 162 acres on Lye branch, waters of Broad River whereon I now live, part of a large tract granted to Bartholomew Baker by Gov. William Moultrie, adj. Leonard Baker, Dr. Graffenreid, 6 Aug 1833. William Beaver (B) (LS), Wit: C. [Charner] T. Scaife, T. A. Carlile. Proved by the oath of Charner T. Scaife 14 Dec 1833 before James Mcashan, Q. U. Recorded 7 April 1834.

W, 229-230: Independence L. Pearson of Union District for $3340.75 to Doc'r Hezekiah Rice of same, 581 acres bequeathed to me by the will of my father Isaac Pearson on Padgets Creek and the head of Finchers branch, waters of Tyger River adj. H. Rice, estate of James Mayes decd, Lewis Pressly, Wm. Turpin, reserving the grave yard which contains one acre square, 19 June 1834. I. L. Pearson (Seal), Wit: E. M. Glenn, J. Rogers. Proved by the oath of E. M. Glenn 19 June 1834. Recorded 19 June 1834.

W, 230: South Carolina, Union District. Elizabeth Hight of Union District for love and affection to my son Elisha Palmer of same, tract of land to which I am entitled as the widow of Thomas Palmer my first husband decd, on both sides of Shugar Creek adj. John Pruett, Jeffrey Palmer, Mills Sumner, Aaron Pruitt, James Smith, Levi Smith, the one third part of the said land above described, 4 Jan 1834. Elizabeth Hight (X) (Seal), Wit: J. S. Jones. Sally Burrel (O). Proved by the oath of James S. Jones 21 June 1834 before J. Palmer, J.P. Recorded 24 June 1834.

W, 230-231: South Carolina, Union District. Nathan Vinson of district aforesaid for love and good will to my son James Vinson, tract of land whereon I now live, 50 acres, 8 May 1834. Nathan Vinson (Seal), Wit: Daniel White, Thos B. Going. Proved by the oath of Daniel White 8 May 1834 before Isaac Going, Q. U. Recorded 26 May 1834.

W, 231-232: John P. Thomson of Union District for $400 to Joseph Mayes and William F. Reynolds, 154 acres in Union District on both sides of Mill Creek, a branch of Fairforrest adj. Joseph Mayes, John Eisin, Benjamin Boyce, also a tract of 3 acres which the said Thomson purchased of Sarah Boyd on the north side of Harris Creek adj. said Joseph Mays, 20 Aug 1832. John P. Thomson (Seal), Wit: Elijah Gossett, Solomon Crocker. Proved by the oath of Elijah Gossett 22 June 1833 before Nathan Gist, Q.U. Recorded 16 June 1834.

W, 232: William F. Reynolds and Joseph Mayes, both of Union District have recently purchased 137 acres rom John P. Thomson, late of said district, now we have mutually agreed to divide the land between us adj. John Wright, 19 Nov 1833. Wm. F. Reynolds (Seal), Joseph Mayes (Seal), Wit: Robert Cunningham Junr, D. White. Proved by the oath of Robert Cunningham 19 Nov 1833 before D. White, Q.U. Recorded 16 June 1834.

W, 232-233: B. Johnson, Sheriff of Union District pursuant to an order from the court or ordinary 16 Aug 1833 at the suit of the heirs and legatees of

William Jones deceased, to divide one tract of land belonging to the estate of William Jones deceased on waters of Fannans Creek adj. Samuel Cole, William Vinson, R. Lipsey, Esq., 87½ acres, sold for $80 to Willy Vinson, 13 Dec 1833. B. Johnson (Seal), Wit: H. W. Foote, Charles Gowing. Proved by the oath of H. W. Foote 26 May 1834 before J. Rogers, Q.U. Recorded 26 May 1834.

W, 233-234: South Carolina, Union District. William Rountree bound to Robert McBeth of said state in the penal sum of $2400 for the payment I bind myself, 1 Oct 1833, to make title to tract where the said Rountree now lives and for the sum of $600 in United bills now or before 1 Oct 1834 adj. John McBeth. Wm Rountree (Seal), Levi S. Holcomb, John Saunders. Proved by the oath of John Saunders (Sanders) 18 June 1834 before J. Rogers, Q. U. Recorded 18 June 1834.

W, 234-235: Ruth Hail of Union District for $390 to John Hames of same, 130 acres on branches of Fairforest on the road from Union village to Spartanburgh Village adj. Charles Cunningham, Alexander Akin, 14 April 1834. Ruth Hale (Seal), Wit: Frances Hail (a), Richard Thomson. Proved by the oath of Richard Thomson 7 June 1834 before Isaac Going, Q. U. Recorded 7 June 1834.

W, 235: South Carolina, Spartenburgh District. John Buchler and Eugine Buchler for $250 to A. G. Gordon, tract of 100 acres in the districts of Union and Spartanburgh on the waters of Elisha creek, 31 Jan 1834. John Buchler (X) (Seal), Eugine Buchler (X) (Seal), Wit: Bird Hill, Wm. Starnes. Proved by the oath of Bird Hill 1 Jan 1834 before Joel Dean, J.P. Recorded 16 June 1834.

W, 235-236: South Carolina, Spartenburgh District. John Buchler and Eugine Buchler for $250 to A. G. Gordon, all our interest in a tract of 500 acres in the districts which interest is two thirds thereof it being the land decreed by the court of chancery held in said District to the heirs of Eugene Buchler whereof we are two of the said heirs & Washington Buchler the third heir, 31 Jan 1834. John Buchler (X) (Seal), Eugine Buchler (X) (Seal), Wit: Bird Hill, Wm. Starnes. Proved by the oath of Bird Hill 1 Jan 1834 before Joel Dean, J.P. Recorded 16 June 1834.

W, 236: South Carolina, Union District. Henry Green of district aforesaid to my son Lorenzo Dow Boyd, tract of 60 acres on the waters of Enoree River adj. William Malone, Wm. C. Pearson, Joseph Goswick, 22 Nov 1 833. Henry Green (Seal), Wit: John Bates, Mary Bates. Proved by the oath of John Bates 7 April 1834. Proved by the oath of John Bates before Fredk Jackson, J. P. Recorded 16 June 1834.

W, 237: Maybry White & Robert McBeth of Union District for $266 to James C. Kitchens of chester District, tract on the south side of Fairforest adj. Jesse Clark, D. A. Mitchell, John Saunders, Benj. Holcomb and Jason greer and

Robert McBeth, being the tract purchased from the Sheriff as the property of Thomson White, 160 acres, 5 March 1834. Mabry White (Seal)l Robert McBeth (Seal), Wit: Levi S. Holcomb, Philip Holcomb. Proved by the oath of Levi S. Holcomb 28 April 1834.

W, 237-238: Francis McKown of Union District to George McKown of same, all my lawful right & title in a tract on both sides of McKowns[?] Creek, adj. William McKowns old line, 12 Nov 1833. Francis McKown (Seal), Wit: Morgan Martin, William Porter. Proved by the oath of William Porter 26 Nov 1833 before Isaac Peeler, J.P.

W, 238-239: Robert Kenworthy attorney in fact for the heirs of John Cook decd of the state of Indiana and County of Tippecanoe for $323 to Isaac Gregory of Union District, tract on waters of Swift run creek and Smith branch, waters of Tyger River, 323 acres adj. John Smith, John Gordon, Lewis Fant, A. V. Jeter, R. McDaniel, 26 Feb 1834. Robert Kenworthy (B) attorney in fact for Oliver Hawkins (LS), William Hollingsworth (LS), Mary Hollingsworth (LS), Jesse Green (LS), Charity Green (LS), Wit: Stephen Johnson, Levi Gregory. Proved by the oath of Stephen Johnson 7 April 1834 before J. Rogers, Q.U. Recorded 7 April 1834.

W, 239-240: Isaac McKissick of Union District for $207 to Joseph McKissick of same, tract whereon Joseph McKissick now lives on waters of Pacolet River near the Cedar Rock, 91 acres, 26 June 1820. Isaac McKissick (Seal), Wit: W/ W. E. Moreland, Wm. S. Palmer. Proved by the oath of W. W. E. Moreland 29 Dec 1821 before Isaac Going, J.Q. Recorded 5 May 1834.

W, 240-241: South Carolina, Union District. Thomas Glass for $250 to John McKissick and Rhoda McKissick of same, tract on which I now live, 100 acres on the waters of Fannans Creek, adj. V. Davis, 1 Jan 1834. Thomas Glass (Seal), Wit: W. W. E. Moreland, O. K. Moreland. Proved by the oath of O. K. Moreland 16 Jan 1834 before Isaac Going, Q.U. Jane Glass (X), wife of Thomas Glass, relinquished dower 6 Feb 1834 before Isaac Going, Q. U. Recorded 5 May 1834.

W, 241-242: South Carolina, Union District. Coleman Fowler of Union District for $173 to Joseph McKissick of same, 86½ acres on waters of Pacolet River adj. Isaac McKissick, 5 Feb 1829. Coleman Fowler (Seal), Wit: Isaac McKissick, John W. P. McKissick. Proved by the oath of Isaac McKissick 18 Aug 1829 before Isaac Going. Q. U. Ellender Fowler (X), wife of Coleman Fowler, relinquished dower 23 Aug 1829 before Isaac Going, Q. U. Recorded 5 May 1834.

W, 242: Ferdinand Hopkins of Chester District for $320 to Isaac McKissick of Union District, 99 acres, part of 627 acres granted to said Ferdinand Hopkins 1 March 1790, on waters of Pacolet River, adj. said Isaac McKissick and including the tract whereon Joseph McKissick now lives, 12 March 1819. Ferd

Hopkins (Seal), Wit: James Moreland, Joseph McKissick. Proved by the oath of Joseph McKissick 7 April 1819 before Isaac Going. Recorded 5 May 1834.

W, 243-244: South Carolina, Union District. Whereas Agnes Boyce and others ex parte heirs at law of David Boyce decd filed their [bill] of complaint in the Court of Equity for Union District 54 June 1833 showing that David Boyce died intestate possessed of several tracts of land and that partition remained to be made, and at June Term 1833 the said court did order that the said land be sold at public auction, now B. M. Pearson, commissioner, did on 2 Dec 1833 sell to Mathias Myers for $303, 188 acres on Pagets Creek on the Charleston road, known as tract No. 3 in the partition, 6 June 1834. Bird M. Pearson (Seal), Wit: J. Rogers, W. T. Bobo. Proved by the oath of John Rogers 27 June 1834 before D. Wallace, J. P. Recorded 27 June 1834.

W, 244: South Carolina, Union District. Telitha Jackson, wife of Frederick Jackson, relinquished dower to tract deeded by Gideon Jackson to Bird Murphy, 9 June 1834 before Hiram Gibbs, Q. U. Recorded 12 July 1834.

W, 244-246: 16 Nov 1833, Capt. John Thomas of Union District to Abram D. Jones, David Hopkins, William Weston & James R. Tucker, whereas said John Thomas stands indebted to the said Abram D. Jones, David Hopkins, William Weston & James R. Tucker by three notes for $2000, mortgage of 700 acres on Tyger River, waters of Broad River formerly belonging to Wm. R. Tucker, adj. John Biddie, David Crenshaw, Jas A. Tucker and Thomas C. Jeter. John Thomas (Seal), Wit: Alexander Marks, Thos Hogar[?]. Proved in Richland District by the oath of Thomas M. Hogar[?] before Jesse Debruehl, Q. U. Recorded 12 July 1834.

W, 246: South Carolina, Union District. Stephen Jordan Ashly of district aforesaid for $2000 to Zachariah P. Evans of same, tract on NW side Broad River adj. Wm. P. Thomson, David S. Jeter, Jas B. Glenn, T. G. Farr, David Johnson, 202 acres, 28 Nov 1833. S. J. Ashley (Seal), Wit: James Meacham, Nathan Nelson. Proved by the oath of Nathan Nelson 27 Nov 1833 before Jas Meacham, Q. U. Recorded 7 July 1834.

W, 247: South Carolina, Union District. William Lawson in right of my wife Telitha, Jason Boatman, Susannah Lawson wife of Jeremiah Lawson decd, and Thomas Lawson in right of my wife Elizabeth, heirs and legatees of john Boatman Senr decd, for $20 to Robert Boatman of same, all our right, title and interest in the tract whereon Robt Boatman now lives on Tyger River adj. Jesse Holcomb, Wm Sparks, said Jason Boatman, 12 April 1834. Thomas Lawson (X) (LS), Jason Boatman (mark) (LS), Susannah Lawson (mark) (LS), Elisabeth Lawson (X) (LS), Telitha Lawson (X) (LS), William Lawson (LS), Wit: W. S. Murphy, H. H. Holcombe. Proved by the oath of H. H. Holcombe 4 Aug 1834 before J. Rogers, Recorded 4 Aug 1834.

W, 247-248: Nathaniel Gordon of Union District for $690 to Andrew W. Gordon of same, 230 acres on the north side of Mill Creek on the road from

Grindle Shoals to Spartanburgh Court House adj. William Littlejohn, Norris, Wm. Reid, Richard Gordon, 11 Dec 1833. Nathaniel Gordon, Wit: Richard Thomson, William Norris. Proved by the oath of William Norris 4 Aug 1834 before R. Coleman, J.P. Recorded 6 Aug 1834.

W, 248-249: South Carolina, Union District. Coleman Fowler of district aforesaid for $280 to James Briggs of same, tract on Portmans Creek, waters of Packolet River, 130 acres adj. said Briggs, Polly Fowler, including the Walker spring, Martin Fowler, Ibby George, 25 Dec 1832. Coleman Fowler (LS), Wit: E. Hames, Mark Hames. Proved by the oath of Edmond Hames 11 Jan 1834 before Isaac Going, Q. U. Recorded 4 Aug 1834.

W, 249: South Carolina, Union District. Ibby George, wife of Thomas George, to James Briggs, all her interest, right and claim of dower, 22 April 1830 before Isaac Going, Q.U. Recorded 4 Aug 1834.

W, 249-250: B. Johnson, Sheriff of Union District, by virtue of a writ of fieri facias from the court of common pleas tested 5 Nov 1833 at the suit of William Rice to levy of the goods and chattels, lands and tenements of Zachariah Sparks $25.50, sells tract of 125 acres whereon John Vaughan now lives, waters of Tiger River adj. Robert Martin, Jerry Lawson, Daniel Oshields, purchased by Spencer Bobo for $30, 8 March 1834. B. Johnson, S. U. D. (LS), Wit: James Rountree, H. W. Foote. Proved by the oath of H. W. Foote 7 Aug 1834 before John Rogers, Q. U. Recorded 7 Aug 1834.

W, 250-251: South Carolina, Chester District. Allen DeGraffenreid of Chester District for $4224.80¼ to Benjamin J. Gregory and L. B. Jeter of Union District, 1304 acres in Union District on branches of Neals Creek, 23 July 1834. Allen DeGraffenreid (LS), Wit: George P. Hussey, A. Gordon. Proved by the oath of A. Gordon 4 Aug 1834. Plat certified 4 Aug 1834.

W, 251-252: Charles Meng of Union District for $200 to Joseph Hughes of same, 81 acres, it being the lot of land laid off to Samuel Sharp as one of the heirs of William Sharp on waters of Browns Creek adj. James Sharp, Flemming Harris, Zach Ivy, Robert Savage, 24 Jan 1833. Charles Meng (LS), Wit: Thomas G. Page, John Giles. Proved by the oath of John Giles 4 Aug 1834 before J. Rogers, Q. U. Recorded __ Aug 1834.

W, 252-253: Giles N. Smith of Union District for $600 to Doct Samuel Otterson, 143 acres on the south side of Pacolet, 4 Aug 1834. Giles N. Smith (LS), Delivered to William Norris as agent for Saml Otterson. Wit: Clinton Wilson, John Skain. Elisabeth M. Smith, wife of Giles N. Smith, relinquished dower 7 Aug 1834 before J. Rogers, Q.U. Proved by the oath of Clinton Wilson 8 Aug 1834 before J. Rogers, Q.U. Recorded 8 Aug 1834.

W, 253-254: William Evans and Solomon Evans of Union District for $20 to John Evans of same, tract on the Ninety Six Road adj. John P. Fair, William Rice, and Dr. John C. Jeter, whereon Thomas E. Ison now lives, 90 acres, deed made by William Evans to John Evans 26 Jan 1829, dated 20 May 1834. William Evans (X) (LS), Solomon Evans (LS), Wit: Charner T. Scaife, John P. Sartor, Jos. E. Ison. Proved by the oath of Charner T. Scaife 8 June 1834 before James Meacham, Q. U. Recorded 4 Aug 1834.

W, 254-255: Thomas Woodson of Union District for $360 to Robert M. Roberson of same, part of tract on Fairforest Creek, 130 acres adj. Elizabeth Minell, John Murrell, above the mouth of Smiths spring branch, 25 Jan 1834. Thomas Woodson (LS), Wit: Levi Smith Jun, William Smith Jun. Delila Woodson (X), wife of Thomas Woodson, relinquished dower 14 Feb 1834 before Hiram Gibbs, Q.U. Proved by the oath of William Smith Junr 14 Feb 1834 before Hiram Gibbs, Q.U. Recorded 4 Aug 1834.

W, 255-257: Thomas Woodson of Union District for $440 to Churchell Gibbs of same, part of tract on Shugar Creek, 140 acres, 25 Jan 1834. Thomas Woodson (LS), Wit: Levi Smith Jun, William Smith Jun. Delila Woodson (X), wife of Thomas Woodson, relinquished dower 14 Feb 1834 before Hiram Gibbs, Q.U. Proved by the oath of William Smith Junr 14 Feb 1834 before Hiram Gibbs, Q.U. Recorded 4 Aug 1834.

W, 257: South Carolina, Union District. Absolom Davis of said district for $225 to Wm Willson of same, tract on waters of Tyger River, part of tract that I purchased of Edward M. Bobo adj. Thos Brandon, at the mouth of my spring branch, 50 acres, 10 July 1834. Absalom Davis (LS), Wit: Wm. B. Murphy, H. H. Holcombe. Proved by the oath of H. H. Holcomb 4 Aug 1834 before J. Rogers, Q.U. Recorded 4 Aug 1834.

W, 257-258: South Carolina, Union District. Johnson Goswick of district aforesaid appoint Levi G. Danner of said district my lawful attorney to a recovery and to a just & settle accompts with all persons in the state of North Carolina, Franklin County, 12 Feb 1834. Johnson Goswick (X), Wit: Asa Dodd, Thos G. Danner. Proved by the oath of Asa Dodd 12 Feb 1834 before Jno Norman, J. Q. Certified by John Norman 12 Feb 1834

W, 258-259: South Carolina, Union District. Zachariah P. Evans of district aforesaid for $1000 to Titus G. Farr of same, tract on west side of Broad River adj. Christopher Degraffenreid now Doct Wm P. Thomson, Titus G. Farr, 202 acres, 29 July 1834. Zac P. Evans (Seal), Wit: D. A. Thomas, S. J. Ashly, J. W. Perry. Augustian Evans, wife of Zachariah P.Evans, relinquished dower 29 July 1834 before E. P. Porter, Q.U. Proved by the oath of James W. Perry 29 July 1834 before E. P. Porter, Q.U. Recorded 31 July 1834.

W, 260-261: Isaac Gregory of District of Union for $430 to William Beaver of same, tract on waters of Swift run Creek, and a small branch, waters of Tyger River and on both sides of Cooks Mill Road adj. John Gordon, Lewis Fant, A. V. Jeter, Robert McDaniel, John D. Wood, 215 acres, 5 March 1834. Isaac Gregory (LS), Wit: Stephen Johnson, T. A. Glenn. Proved by the oath of Thomas A. Glenn 5 March 1834 before Stephen Johnson, J.P. Elizabeth, wife of Isaac Gregory, relinquished dower 6 July 1834 before Edward McGraw, Q.U. Recorded 11 Aug 1834.

W, 261-262: Hearod Gibson of Union District for $68 to Absalum Ward of same, 19 acres adj. Absalum Ward, Clowney, 22 May 1834. Herod Gibson (H), Wit: Thomas N. Williams, James Jackson. Proved by the oath of Thomas Williams 5 July 1834 before Daniel White, Q. U. Marthey Gibson (X), wife of Herod Gibson, relinquished dower 5 July 1834 before Daniel White, Q. U. Recorded 7 July 1834.

W, 263: South Carolina, Union District. Whereas I have conveyed to my daughter Kitty P. F. Carlisle all my right, title, claim, or interest to the tract of land whereon I now live on Tiger River adj. William C.Glenn Senr deceased and others, which conveyance is not in force until my death & having made her a deed to one other tract of land adj. the same also having conveyed to her one negro woman named Abby & her increase which negro & her children were to remain in my possession during my life & whereas I being desirous of putting her in immediate possession of the aforesaid property, therefore I, Richard Teagle, for natural love and affection to my said daughter, have given and confirmed to Thomas A. Carlisle in right of his wife Kitty all the property aforesaid, 11 April 1834. Richard Teagle (Seal), Wit: N. Glenn, John Hawkins, William Rogers. Proved by the oath of William Rogers 23 July 1834 before Tho Stribling, Q.U. Recorded 4 Aug 1834.

W, 263-265: South Carolina, Union District. John Hainey, James Taylor, Henry George & James Hainey, all of district aforesaid for $825 to Timothy Hainey of same, tract on south side Packolet River whereon Anny Hainey widow of James Hainey, Goddfer, decd now lives, 313 acres, 2 Jan 1830. John Hainey (LS), James Taylor (LS), Henry George (X) (LS), James Haney, Wit: I. J. Foster, William Palmer. Proved by the oath of Isaac J. Foster 22 April 1830 before Isaac Going, Q.U. Nancy Hainey, Elisabeth Taylor, and Nancy George, wives of John Hainey, James Taylor & Henry George, relinquished dower 22 April 1830 before Isaac Going, Q.U. Recorded 7 July 1834.

W, 265-266: South Carolina, Union District. Thomas George of district aforesaid for natural love and affection to my son in law Timothy Hainey, quit claim to part of tract of land granted to John Portman, 50 acres on the south bank of Packolet River, 4 Feb 1820. Thomas George (LS), Wit: I. J. Foster, James Briggs. Proved by the oath of James Briggs 22 April 1830 before Isaac Going, Q.U. Ibby George (X), wife of Thomas George, relinquished dower 22 April 1830 before Isaac Going. Recorded 7 July 1834.

W, 266-267: South Carolina, Union District. James Briggs of district aforesaid for $650 to Timothy Hainey of same, tract whereon I now live on Packolet River, 50 acres originally granted to John Portman, 16 Nov 1824. James Briggs (LS), Wit: I. J. Foster, John Haney. Proved by the oath of Isaac J. Foster 22 April 1830 before Isaac Going, Q.U. Rebekah Briggs (X), wife of James

Briggs, relinquished dower 22 April 1830 before Isaac Going, Q.U. Recorded 7 July 1834.

W, 267-268: South Carolina, Union District. George Garner for $36 to Robert Foster, part of tract I bought of the estate of John Hainey, Goodfellow, decd, 12 acres adj. I. J. Foster, 20 Nov 1833. G. Garner (LS), Wit: I. J. Foster, Isaac Hope. Proved by the oath of Isaac J. Foster 23 Nov 1833 before Isaac Going, Q.U. Recorded 7 July 1834.

W, 268-269: South Carolina, Union District. Robert Foster of district aforesaid for $600 to Timothy Hainey, Goffee, tract on south side of Pacolet River, 171 acres adj. I. J. Foster, Spears, at the mouth of a branch being a corner of land formerly belonging to James Hainey (Goffee), 20 Nov 1833. Robert Foster (mark) (LS), Wit: I. J. Foster, Isaac Hope. Proved by the oath of Isaac J. Foster 23 Nov 1833 before Isaac Going, Q.U. Sarah Foster (X), wife of Robert Foster, relinquished dower 20 Nov 1833 before Isaac Going, Q.U. Recorded 7 July 1834.

W, 269-270: South Carolina, Union District. Polley Bailey, James Hainey, John Hainey, Josiah Hainey, & Timothy Hainey, Elizabeth Hainey, Edy Hainey & Sibby Hainey & Mary Hainey widdow sd decd, legatees of John Hainey, F. G., decd, for $926.50 to Robert Foster of said district, tract on Pacolet River, the south side, 59 acres adj. H. Spears, 3 Nov 1817. Polly Bailey (X) (LS), James Hainey (X) (LS), john Hainey (X) (LS), Josiah Hainey (X) (LS), Timmothy Hainey (X) (LS), Edy Hainey (X) (LS), Elizabeth Hainey (LS), Sibby Haney (X) (LS), Mary Hainey (X) (LS), Wit: Ferdinand Bailey, John Hainey son gf (X), John Bailey (X). Proved by the oath of Ferdinan Bailey 22 Oct 1819 before Isaac Going, J.P. Recorded 7 July 1834.

W, 270-271: 30 Nov 1796, Jonathan Cud of County of Union to William Spears of same, for £90 sterling, part of tract surveyed and granted to Abel Kindrick by the Governor of this State, 100 acres also 10 acres adj. said tract granted to Turner Kindrick adj. Abel Kindrick and John Spears, John Hainey, to the mouth of a branch that emptys into Pacolet River, Wm. Spears. Jonathan Cud (mark) (LS), Cathron Cud (X) (Seal), John Bailey (EB), Wit: John Hainy gu, Luice Turner (mark). Proved by the oath of John Hainey 4 April 1797 before Thos Vance, J. P. Recorded 7 July 1834.

W, 271: South Carolina, Union District. Ibby George, wife of Thomas George, relinquished dower to Timothy Hainey, 22 April 1830 before Isaac Going, Q.U. Recorded 7 July 1834.

W, 272-273: William McCafferty & Anna his wife, Nancy Gregory wife & widow of William Gregory decd, for $198.75 to William A. Sims, all of Union District, tract on both sides of Little Browns Creek, south west side of Broad River adj. said William A. Sims, Robert Glenn, Thos Moore, McCreight, Moses Mathews, originally granted to Isaac Gregory 26 Oct 1767 for 219 3/4 acres, 9 May 1834. William McCafferty (X) (LS), Anna McCafferty (X) (LS),

Nancy Gregory (mark) (Seal). Anna McCafferty relinquished dower 4 June 1834 before John Giles. Proved by the oath of James T. Johnson who made oath that he and Benjamin F. Kirk were witnesses 9 May 1834 before John Giles, Q. U. Recorded 7 July 1834.

W, 273-275: South Carolina, Union District. John F. Glenn of district aforesaid for $200 to William Kelly, tract of 29¼ acres on a small branch of Broad River, it being small parts of a tract granted to David Hopkins by the state and by David Hopkins conveyed to Nathan Glenn and from Glenn to his son Alexr Glenn conveyed by Alex Glenn to Spilsby Glenn and from Spilsby Glenn to John F. Glenn, adj. John F. Glenn, John P. Sorter, James Macham, 14 May 1833. William F. Glenn (LS), Wit: Elijah Hawkins, Andrew Lusk. Proved by the oath of Elijah Hawkins 9 Aug 1833 before James Macham, J.Q. Jane S. C. Glenn, wife of John H. Glenn, relinquished dower 9 Aug 1833 before James Macham, Q. U. Recorded 7 July 1834.

W, 275-276: South Carolina, Union District. James Macham of district aforesaid for $170 to William Kelly of same, 128 acres on the road leading from the Fish dam for on Broad River to Crenshaws fork on Tiger River, it being only part of a tract of land conveyed to William B. Farr by William Williams and granted also to William B. Farr 4 March 1822 and conveyed to said J. Macham 12 Feb 1825 by said William B. Farr, adj. James Macham, William Kelley, and another tract of 86 acres on waters of Broad River, part of a tract granted to David Hopkins and conveyed by said Hopkins to Nathan Glenn from said Nathan Glenn to his son Alexander Glenn by will, said Alexander Glenn to Spilsby Glenn and by Spilsby Glenn to Jincy P. Glenn adj. Kelley and Macham, on the Carlisle Branch, 7 Aug 1833. James Macham (LS), Wit: Amasa T. Park, Saml P. Gordon. Proved by the oath of Amasa T. Park 5 July 1834 before James Meacham. Lucy C. Macham, wife of James Macham, relinquished dower 5 July 1834. Recorded 7 July 1834.

W, 277-278: William McCafferty & Anna his wife & Nancy Gregory wife and widow of William Gregory decd for $1098 to William A. Sims, all of Union District, tract on both sides of Little Browns Creek, south west side of Broad River adj. said William A. Sims, Robert Glenn, Thos Moore, James McCright, Moses Mathews, originally granted to Isaac Gregory 26 Oct 1767 for 219 3/4 acres, 9 May 1834. William McCafferty (X) (LS), Anna McCafferty (X) (LS), Nancy Gregory (mark) (Seal), Wit: James T. Johnson, Benjamin F. Kirk. Anna McCafferty relinquished dower 4 June 1834 before John Giles. Proved by the oath of James D. Johnson who made oath that he and Benjamin F. Kirk were witnesses 9 May 1834 before John Giles, Q. U. Recorded 7 July 1834.

W, 278-280: South Carolina, Union District. James Meacham of district aforesaid for $1070 to William Kelly of same, two separate tracts: 120 acres on the road leading from the fish dam ford on Broad River to Crenshaws ford on Tiger River, part of tract conveyed to William B. Farr by William Williams and granted to said William B. Farr 4 March 1822, and conveyed to James Meacham 12 Feb 1825 by said William B. Farr adj. William Kelly, John P.

Sarter, and another tract of 86 acres on the waters of Broad river, part of tract granted to David Hopkins and conveyed by him to Nathan Glenn and from Glenn to his son Alexr Glenn conveyed by Alex Glenn to Spilsby Glenn and from Spilsby Glenn to Jincy P. Glenn, adj. John F. Glenn, John P. Sorter, James Mackam, 7 Aug 1833. James Meacham (LS), Wit: Amasa T. Park, Samuel O. Gordon. Proved by the oath of Amasa T. Park 5 July 1834 before James Meacham, Q.U. Lucy C. Meacham, wife of James Meacham, relinquished dower 5 July 1834 before James Meacham, Q. U.

W, 280-281: South Carolina, Union District. Henry Hardy of Union District for $228.53 to George M. Sarter of same, tract on north side of Tiger River, 70 acres adj. John P. Sarter, Thomas Sarter, Linam, 31 Dec 1833. Henry Hardy (Seal), Wit: T. A. Carlisle, Redden Morgan. Recorded 1 Sept 1834.

W, 281-282: 11 April 1834, John Ennis of Union District to Acquilla Powers, John Powers, Fleming Harris, Mathew Harris, Joseph H. Dogan, Arthur Lipsey, Caswell Bogin, Thomas A. Glenn & William May, trustees, for $5, a lot in Union District near a place known by the five forks, to erect a house of worship for the use of the Methodist Episcopal Church. John Ennis (LS), Wit: Hezekiah Palmer, Isam Vaughn. Proved by the oath of Isam Vaughn 1 Sept 1834 before Daniel White, Q.U. Recorded 1 Sept 1834.

W, 282-283: South Carolina, Union District. Henry Hardy of Union District for $228.53 to George M. Sarter of same, tract on north side of Tiger River, 70 acres adj. John P. Sarter, Thomas Sarter, Linam, 31 Dec 1833. Henry Hardy (Seal), Wit: T. A. Carlisle, Redden Morgan. Proved by the oath of Reddin Morgan 27 Jan 1834. Elizabeth Hardy (X), wife of Henry Hardy, relinquished dower 27 Jan 1834 before James Meacham, Q.U. Recorded 1 Sept 1834.

W, 283-284: Bird M. Pearson, Trustee under the will of Isaac Pearson deceased, for Mary Bates and the heirs of her body of Union District, for $500 to Dr. Thomas Young of Union District, 275 acres on the waters of Enoree River adj. David Spiva, heirs of Edward Stephens deceased, and land sold for partition among the heirs of David Boyce deceased, ____ 1834. B. M. Pearson trustee for Mary Bates (LS), Wit: Levi S. Holcombe, Thomas Humphries. Proved by the oath of Thomas Humphries 1 Sept 1834 before J. Rogers, Q. U. Recorded 1 Sept 1834.

W, 285: Clough S. Sims of Union District for $161 to William A. Sims of Union District, 41¼ acres adj. William Sims Senr, 11 April 1834. Clough S. Sims (LS), Wit: Benjamin F. Kirk. George Wise. Proved by the oath of Benjamin F. Kirk 6 May 1834 before John Giles, Q.U. Recorded 1 July 1834.

W, 286-287: South Carolina, Union District. Winny Porter of Union District for the support and maintenance by Absalem Barnet to me during the remainder of my life, on the main road to the fish dam Ford on Broad River, about one and a half or two miles from Union Village, 100 acres being willed to me by my father William Porter deceased, adj. Epp Porter, on the waggon Road, James Becknall, Smith, 8 May 1832. Winny Porter (X) (LS), Wit: John Hubanks, Lucy Porter. Proved by the oath of John Eubanks 1 ___ 1832 before John Rogers, Q. U. Recorded 27 Aug 1834.

W, 287-288: South Carolina, Laurens District. William Young of district aforesaid for $400 to George Young of Union District, all my part & claim in all that tract in the district of Union, 325 acres adj. Joseph McJunkin, Chesley Canant, Chandlers & Humphries, John Clark, Caleb Frazer, 27 Dec 1828. William Young (LS), Wit: Thomas Young, Joshua Whitmore. Elizabeth Young, wife of William Young, relinquished dower in Laurens District 13 Jan 1829 before David Mason, Q. U. Proved by the oath of Dr. Thomas Young 1 Sept 1834 before John Rogers, Q.U. Recorded 1 Sept 1834.

W, 288-289: J. B. Johnson, Sheriff of Union District, by virtue of a writ of Fieri Facias from the court of common pleas held 15 June 1831 at the suit of Thomas Gannon to levy of the goods and chattels, lands and tenements of Silas Anderson, Executor of Elijah Anderson, deceased, $363.07, sells 273 acres on the waters of Tiger and Enoree Rivers and on both sides of the main Charleston Road adj. estate of William Glenn, James Huey, Mary E. Pruett, Joshua Wadkins, Samuel Welby deceased, plat made by Stephen Johnson, D.S., 13 Aug 1834, purchased by Wm. W. Glenn for $256, 18 Aug 1834. B. Johnson, S. U. D. (LS), Wit: P. P. Taylor, T. A. Glenn. Proved by the oath of Thos A. Glenn 18 Aug 1834 before John Rogers, Q.U. Recorded 18 Aug 1834.

W, 289-290: B. J. Gregory of Union District in consideration of a certain purchase by myself to L. B. Jeter made of Allen deGraffenreid of Chester District will show and on a reference to the plat of Richard Thompson dated 25 Jan 1824 diving & laying off the same, now B. J. Gregory of Union District, on of the purchasers of Allen deGraffenreid do quit claim to L. B. Jeter to tract of 770½ acres, and B. J. Gregory & L. B. Jeter purchased of Allen de Graffenreid of Chester District, one survey 1293 acres but conveyed by said deGraffenreid for 1304 acres, to sell to L. B. Jeter 770½ acres, 18 Aug 1834. B. J. Gregory (LS), Wit: Giles Sharp, J. Rogers. Proved by the oath of Giles Sharp 18 Aug 1834 before John Rogers. Recorded 18 Aug 1834.

W, 291: L. B. Jeter of Union District in consideration of a certain purchase by myself to B. J. Gregory and myself made of Allen deGraffenreid of Chester District will show and on a reference to the plat of Richard Thompson dated 25 Jan 1824 diving & laying off the same, now L. B. Jeter of Union District, on of the purchasers of Allen deGraffenreid do quit claim to B. J. Gregory to tract of 522½ acres, 18 Aug 1834. L. B. Jeter (LS), Wit: Giles Sharp, J. Rogers. Proved by the oath of Giles Sharp 18 Aug 1834 before John Rogers. Recorded 18 Aug 1834.

W, 292: South Carolina, Union District. John G. Woodson and Mary Ann Woodson of State of Georgia, County of Hall, legatees of the estate of John

Woodson, late of Union District for $106 to John Gibbes of Union District, he being the administrator of the estate of Nathan Harland of said district decd, the bargain being made with said Harland before his death, our parts of a tract of land in Union District on waters of Fairforest Creek adj. said Harland, F. Smith, 140 acres, ____ 1834. John C.Woodson (LS), Mary Ann Woodson (LS), Wit: R. G. Shackelford, E. M. Johnson, J. P. John B. Nichols, clerk of the inferior court of Hall County, Georgia, certified that Ephraim M. Johnson is an acting justices of the peace 17 July 1834. John McAfee, one of the justices of the inferior court certified that J. B. Nichols is clerk of the court 17 July 1834. Recorded 4 Sept 1834.

W, 293-294: South Carolina, Union District. James Plaxco of Union District for $600 to James H. Alexander of same, tract whereon I now live on Pacolette River in Union District adj. Joseph Gist, William Gault, and others, 209 acres, 21 Feb 1834. James Plaxico (LS), Wit :John T. Plaxco, T. G. Wylie. Margaret Plaxico, wife of James Plaxico, relinquished dower 26 June 1834 before Isaac Going, Q.U. Proved by the oath of Thomas Wylie 9 July 1834 before Isaac Going, Q.U.

W, 294-295: 27 May 1834, Joseph S. Shelton to the President and directors of the Bank of South Carolina, whereas said Joseph S. Shelton stands indebted to the said President & directors in the penal sum of $18,400 by note, mortgage of tract of land adj. Doctor Burrell, Chick and James Hunter on Enoree Rivers, 700 acres. Jos S. Shelton (Seal), Wit: Jno Fisher, N. Ramsey. Proved in Richland District by the oath of Nathaniel Ramsay 25 June 1834 before W. J. Myddleton, Notary Public & Q. U. exofficio. Recorded 11 Sept 1834. Satisfied.

W, 295-296: William Ownby for $500 to Herod Blanton, tract on Gilkeys Creek including the plantation whereon the said Blanton now lives, 267 acres, 16 Nov 1833. W.Ownby (LS), Wit: Edmond Blanton, John McLean. Agness Owenby, wife of William Owenby, relinquished dower 26 Nov 1833 before David Putman, J.P. Also, Judith Whelchel relinquished all her right title & interest to a tract of land conveyed by William Owenby to Herrod Blanton, 28 Nov 1833 before David Putman, J.P. Proved by the oath of Edmond Blanton 29 Aug 1834 before Wm. Goudlock, J.P. Recorded 1 Sept 1834.

W, 297: South Carolina, Union District. Jared Young, 21 May 1834, for $5 paid by Christopher Young and natural love and affection to my daughter Eleanor Martin, wife of Samuel L. Martin, a negro woman named Clarissa and her child Rachael. Jared Young (LS), C. Young (LS), Wit: Thomas Young, Elizabeth Young. Proved by the oath of Thomas Young 12 Aug 1834 before John Rogers, Q. U. Recorded 12 Aug 1834.

W, 297-299: B. Johnson, Sheriff of Union District, by virtue of a writ of fieri facias from the court of common pleas tested 9 March 1833 at the suit of Samuel Brooks to levy of the goods and chattels, lands and tenements of Samuel G. Martin $474.56, sells tract of 147 acres adj. Dr. Christopher Young,

Jared Young, Christopher Young Senr, Charles Humphries, on the waters of fairforest and on the head of Mulkeys branch, purchased by Dr. Christopher young for $214, 10 May 1834. B. Johnson, S. U. D. (LS), Wit: Joseph H. Dogan, Jared Young. Proved by the oath of Joseph H. Dogan 11 Sept 1834 before J. Rogers, Q.U. Recorded 11 Sept 1834.

W, 299-300: South Carolina, Union District. Robert Moorhead for $5 to Jos Bankhead and Cynthia his wife, with natural love and affection, quit claim to all my rights, interest & claim on account of my decd wife Cynthia, tract on the south west side of Thicketty known as John Martin's land, adj. Williamson Howel, Wm Sisson, Robert Lusk, 314 acres, 21 March 1834. Robert Morehead (LS), Wit: John Stone, R. Lusk. Proved by the oath of John Stone 23 Sept 1834 before J. Rogers, Q. U. Recorded 23 Sept 1834. We the undersigned being called upon to appraise the real estate of John Martin decd formerly of this district do appraise the same at $1800 or $5.73 per acre, 31 March 1834. Samuel Davidson, R. Lusk, W. C. Brown.

W, 300: William S. Hendley and Charlott his wife of Union District for $50 to Henry Gibbs, all our right, title and claim to a certain legacy in a tract belonging to the estate of John Ashby decd on Cane Creek, not yet divided between the legal heirs, of which the said Charlott is one who is intermarried with William S. Henly, 28 June 1834. William S. Hendley (LS), Charlott Hendley (X) (LS), Wit: W. N. McGraw, Thos Brodrick. Proved by the oath of William N. McGraw 28 June 1834 before E. W. McGraw, Q. U. Charlotte Hendley (X), wife of William S. Hendley, relinquished dower 8 July 1834 before E. W. McGraw, J. Q. Recorded 22 Sept 1834.

W, 301-302: South Carolina, Union District. Whereas Martha Simpson, wife of Washington Simpson, has given due notice of her intention to become a free & sole trader, with the approbation of the said Washington Simpson, a planter residing near the Cross Key in Union District, Benjamin Lamb and Mitchell Lawson appointed trustees, 10 Sept 1833. Martha Simpson (X) (LS), Washington Simpson (LS), Benj Lamb (LS), Mitchell Lawson (LS), Wit: John H. Whitlock. Recorded 11 March 1834.

W, 302: South Carolina, Union District. Joseph B. Guyton acknowledged himself guardian of Betsy Laney, a free woman of color, 6 Oct 1834, before J. Rogers, Clk. s/ Joseph B. Guyton.

W, 302-303: State of Alabama, Butler County. Amos Little of said county as one of the heirs of Jonas Little, late of Union District, SC, and legally entitled to a portion of a tract of land formerly owned by said Jonas Little, said Amos Little have appointed Goodwin Woodson attorney to sell his said portion, 22 Sept 1834. Amos Little (LS), Wit: Jno Herbert, Starling Baldwin. Proved in Butler County, Alabama, by the oath of Henry T. Jones, justice of the peace, 22 Sept 1834. Benjamin Newton, clerk of court, certified that Henry T. Jones was a justice of the peace. David Gafford, Judge of the County Court, certified that the transaction was legal, 23 Sept 1834. Recorded 27 Oct 1834.

W, 304: Aaron Harlan of Union District for $165 to Abram G. Davis of same, tract on Dining Creek, waters of Fairforest, 200 acres adj. David Holcomb, Clemons Howard, Benja Holcomb, Olman Howard, known by the Philip Holcomb place near the Brick Church [this is the Lower Fairforest Baptist Church-- BHH], 4 Nov 1834. Aaron Harlan (X) (Seal), Wit: J. Rogers, Q.U., H. H. Holcomb. Charlotte Harlan, wife of Aaron Harlan, relinquished dower 8 Nov 1834 before J. Rogers, clk. Proved by the oath of H. H. Holcomb 4 Nov 1834 before J. Rogers, Q.U. Recorded 4 Nov 1834.

W, 305-306: Aaron Harlan of Union District for $1165 to Thomas Danner of same, tract on both sides Buffalo Creek, waters of Fairforest, on Forresters branch, 335 acres adj. Robert Claybrook, 3 Nov 1834. Aaron Harlan (X) (Seal), Wit: J. Rogers, Q.U., Giles Sharp. Charlotte Harlan, wife of Aaron Harlan, relinquished dower 8 Nov 1834 before J. Rogers, clk. Proved by the oath of Giles Sharp 3 Nov 1834 before J. Rogers, Q.U. Recorded 5 Nov 1834.

W, 306: South Carolina, Union District. James Rountree of Union District for $65 to Giles N. Smith of same, tract on waters of Brown Creek, 66 acres, 11 Nov 1834. James Rountree (Seal), Wit: J. Rogers, Samuel L. Martin. Proved by the oath of S. L. Martin 11 Nov 1834 before J. Rogers, Q.U. Recorded 11 Nov 1834.

W, 307-308: 10 Nov 1834, Spencer A. Bobo to Clough S. Meng, whereas Spencer A. Bobo stands indebted to Clough S. Meng by two notes for $1250, mortgage of lot in Union village on the south side of Main Street, two acres, three roods and eleven perches, Lot #17, being the lot formerly owned by Jesse S. Hix. Spencer A. Bobo (Seal), C. S. Meng (Seal), Wit: T. J. Hughs, J. Rogers. Proved by the oath of T. J. Hughs 11 Nov 1834 before J. Rogers, Q. U. Recorded 11 Nov 1834.

W, 308-309: William Hodge Senr of Union District for $400 to Henry Farnandis of same, 69 acres, part of tract granted to Joab Mitchell, 23 Oct 1820. William Hodge Senr (A) (Seal), Wit: Saml Reid, William Hodge. Proved by the oath of Saml Reid 5 Jan 1824 before J. Rogers, Q. U. Recorded 5 Jan 1824 [*sic*].

W, 309: South Carolina, Union District. Elizabeth Farnandis of district aforesaid for $500 to Nancy Little of same, 60 acres, part of a tract granted to Joab Mitchell, 8 Nov 1834. Elizabeth Farnandis (Seal), Wit: J. S. Sims, Adam Little. Proved by the oath of Adam Little 10 Nov 1834 before J. Rogers, Q.U. Recorded 10 Nov 1834.

W, 310: Caroline H. Farnandis of Union District for $1000 to Elizabeth Farnandis of same, two tracts on waters of Pacolet adj. Doctor Wm Notts, J. S. Sims, Mrs. Farnandis, 155 acres, and the other on both sides of the road from Grindel Shoals to Spartanburgh Court House adj. Thomas Hawkins, William Norris, Mr. Gordon, Mrs. Little, Saml Otterson, 69 acres, 14 Oct 1834. Caroline Farnandis (Seal), Wit: J. S. Sims, William Norris. Proved by the oath of Adam Little 14 Oct 1834 before J. Rogers, Q.U. Recorded 14 Oct 1834

W, 310-311: W. W. E. Moreland of the District of Union for $203 to Jeremiah Moreland of same, tract on Reedy branch, waters of Pacolet, 62½ acres adj. Mark Wood, on the Skull Shoal Road, with free access to the spring & waters thereof and with the liberty of a spring of milk house at the spring, 24 March 1834. W. W. E. Moreland (Seal), Wit: O. H. Moreland, Lemuel Mosley. Maria Moreland, wife of W. W. E. Moreland, relinquished dower 5 April 1834 before Isaac Going, Q.U. Proved by the oath of O. H. Moreland 5 April 1834 before Isaac Going, Q.U. Recorded 9 Oct 1834.

W, 312: South Carolina, Union District. James Guthrie for natural love and affection to my daughters Morning P. and Nancy C. Guthrie; to Morning one feather bed and furniture, one bedstead, one pine chest, one side saddle, one cow and her increase, one pine table; to Nancy one stand of curtains, one feather bed and furniture, one bedstead, one cow & Calf, one wallnut chest, one loom and one flat skillet, one lot of earthen ware, 1 Oct 1834. James Guthrie (mark (Seal), Wit: William M. B. Stribling, F. A. Carlisle. Proved by the oath of Thos A. Carlisle 7 Oct 1834 before J. Rogers, Q. U. Recorded 7 Oct 1834.

W, 312-313: South Carolina, Union District. John Park of district aforesaid for $88 to William A. Rogers of same, tract on the east side of Fairforest Creek, 12.06 acres adj. John Park, William A. Rogers, 7 Jan 1829. John Park (Seal), Wit: H. H. Means, John Murphy. Proved by the oath of John Murphy 6 Oct 1834 before J. Palmer, J.P. Recorded 6 Oct 1834.

W, 313-314: Clough S. Meng of Union District for $2100 to William Rice of same, 431 acres on the west side of Fairforest in Union District adj. William Rice, Doc. Rogers, heirs of John Parham, by reference to two deeds, one from Joseph Harland to myself 29 Nov 1833 the other from Robert & Elizabeth McCullough to myself 25 Nov 1833, dated 23 Oct 1834. C. S. Meng (Seal), Wit: J. Rogers, Joseph H. Dogan. Mary Meng, wife of C. S. Meng, relinquished dower 23 Oct 1834 before J. Rogers, Q.U. Proved by the oath of 23 Oct 1834 before J. Rogers, Q. U. Recorded 23 Oct 1834.

W, 314-315: South Carolina, Union District. John Jeffries Senr of district aforesaid for $1750 to William Jeffries of same, 320 acres on Gilkeys Creek, waters of Thickety, waters of Broad River, adj. John Jeffries, Philip Petty, R. S. Rice, James Dawkins, 31 May 1834. John Jeffries Senior (Seal), Wit: Drury Harrington, Wm. H. Neal, James Smith. Proved by the oath of Drury Harrington 13 Sept 1843 before Isaac Peeler. Recorded 13 Sept 1834.

W, 315-316: Jesse Gordon, admr. cum test. annex't of Edward Stevens decd of Union District, by virtue of the power and authority in me vested by the will of said Edwards Stevens and for $2900 to Sarah W. Stevens of Union District, tract on Pagets Creek, waters of Tyger River & branches of Enoree

River, one tract of 1000 acres conveyed by Spencer A. Bobo to said Edwards Stevens by deed 19 July 1830 and the other 35 acres conveyed by James Hollis to said Edwards Stevens 23 June 1832, in the whole 1035 acres adj. Doc. Rice, Wm. H. Gist, Mrs. Agnes Boyce, Thomas Young, Asa Dodd, T. G. Danner, Mathew Miller, 29 Oct 1834. Jesse Gordon (Seal), Wit: Wm. C. Pearson, R. Starnes. Proved by the oath of Richard Starnes 28 Oct 1834 before J. Rogers, Q.U.

W, 316-317: Robert McCollough and Elizabeth McCollough of Edgefield, to Clough S. Meng of Union District, for $500, tract on the west side of Fairforest, 103 acres, 25 Nov 1833. Robt McCollough (Seal), Elizabeth McCollough (Seal), Wit: J. Richardson, M. Frazier. Elizabeth McCollough, wife of Robert McCullough relinquished dower in Edgefield District 12 Dec 1833 before A. B. Addison. Proved in Edgefield District by the oath of Jefferson Richardson 12 Dec 1833 before A. B. Addison, Q.U. Recorded 22 Nov 1834.

W, 317-318: Malachi Keenan of the village of Union for $100 to John J. Pratt of same, parcel of land adjoining the village known by the name of the tan yard place conveyed to said Keenan by William Rice, Esqr., by two separate deeds, the first dated 30 Oct 1822 and the second 21 Nov 1829, on the south side of the main road leading from the cross keys to Union village adj. Mr. Graham, on Tush's branch, 28 Oct 1834. M. Keenan (Seal), Wit: Newton Anderson, A. Barnett. Rachel Keenan (X), wife of Malachi Keenan, relinquished dower 1 Nov 1834 before J. Rogers, Q.U. Proved by the oath of Newton Anderson 1 Nov 1834 before J. Rogers, Q.U. Recorded 1 Nov 1834.

W, 319: Joseph Davidson of Union District for $350 to Anthony W. Bates of same, 84 acres on both sides of Mcelwains Creek, part of tract granted to James McElwain Senr, adj. J. McElwain Senr & J. McElwain Junr, 6 Nov 1833. Joseph Davidson (Seal), Wit: Elisha Poole, Uriah M. Bates. Proved by the oath of Uriah M. Bates 14 Oct 1834 before J. Rogers, Q. U. Recorded 14 Oct 1834.

W, 319-320: Joseph Harlan of Union District for $1600 to Clough S. Meng of same, tract on west side of Fairforest, 328 acres, 29 Nov 1833. Jos Harlan (Seal), Wit: Thos Craven, J. Rogers. Charlotte C. Harlan, wife of Joseph Harlan, relinquished dower 4 Nov 1834 before J. Rogers, Q.U. Proved by the oath of John Rogers 24 Nov 1834 before J. J. Pratt, Q.U. ex off. Recorded 24 Nov 1834.

W, 320-321: South Carolina, Union District. Elizabeth Askew, wife of Lemuel B. Askew, relinquished dower to Thomas N. Dawkins, 17 Feb 1834 before J. Rogers, Q.U. Recorded 17 Feb 1834.

W, 321-322: Reuben S. Rice and Stephen McCollum of Union District for $500 to Thomas Hiott of same, tract on north west side of Rocky Creek, a water course of Fairforest, 125 acres where the Union road leading to

Spartanburgh crosses said creek, on the road to Linnens Meeting House, 6 March 1828. R. S. Rice (Seal), S. McCollum (Seal), Wit: John T. Murrell, Wm. Rice. Proved in York District by the oath of John T. Murrell 243 Nov 1834 before J. Rogers, Q.U.

W, 322: South Carolina, Union District. Thomas McCaferty and Hanah McCaferty of district aforesaid for good will and affection to our daughter Elenor McCaferty of said district, 100 acres of land on which we now reside and all and every the crop of corn & fodder and cotton and five cows and three calves, one bed, five head of hog and one gray horse, 4 Oct 1834. Thos McCaferty (X) (Seal), Hannah McCaferty (X) (Seal), Wit: John H. Skelton. A. Barnett. Proved by the oath of John H. Skelton 24 Nov 1834 before J. Rogers, Q.U.

W, 322-323: South Carolina, Union District. James Wilson of district aforesaid for $410 to Lott Porter of same, tract on branches of Browns Creek, part of a tract formerly granted to Elenor Wilson of 92 acres, 14 Jan 1834. James Wilson (Seal), Wit: James morris, Wm. McCreight. Proved by the oath of Wm McCreight 14 Nov 1834 before J. Rogers, Q.U. Recorded 14 Nov 1834.

W, 323-324: South Carolina, Union District. James McCreight of the first part, Nancy Gregory of the second part, William McCaferty of the third part, whereas the said James McCreight has a small daughter by the name of Mary Ann Catherine McCreight that his sister Nancy Gregory has raised from the breast & whereas the said Nancy Gregory is about to leave the state for the state of Alabama and in as much as she has raised the said Mary Ann Catherine to the age (say eleven years old the 13th day of April next) and wishing yet to keep and raise her from this until she shall marry or arrive at full age from affection, that she the said Nancy now entertains for the said Mary Ann Catherine it is agreed by the said James McCreight that his sister shall keep and have the raising of his daughter and shall pay said Mary Ann Catherine $100 on her marriage or arrival at full age and said Nancy have the full management and control of his said daughter and said William McCaferty does on his page also agree to pay to the said Mary Ann Catherine $100, 26 Nov 1834. James McCreight (Seal), Nancy Gregory (X) (Seal), Wm. McCaferty (X) (Seal), Wit: Jacob Ison, J. Nelson, Jas Wilson. Proved by the oath of James Nelson 26 Nov 1834 before J. Rogers, Q.U. Recorded 26 Nov 1834.

W, 324-325: South Carolina, Union District. Goodon Woodson of State of Alabama, County of Butler, the agent of Amos Little of same, by power of attorney dated 22 Sept 1834, for $35 paid by Benjamin Little of district first written, all interest in a tract of land formerly owned by Jones Little now deceased, 100 acres, the one eighth part, 25 Oct 1834. Goodin Woodson agent (Seal), Wit: John Barham, C. S. Meng. Proved by the oath of John Parham 24 Nov 1834 before J. Rogers, Q.U. Recorded 24 Nov 1834.

W, 325: South Carolina, Union District. Wm Rice of district of Union for $30 to Malachi Keenan of same, 2 acres near said Keenen bark[?] mill, on Tanyard branch including the same, to the main road leading through the village of Union, 21 Nov 1829. Wm. Rice (Seal), Wit: P. P. Taylor, Wm. H. Glenn. Proved by the oath of P. P. Taylor 29 Nov 1834 before J. Rogers, Q.U. Recorded 24 Nov 1834.

W, 326: B. Johnson, Sheriff of Union District, pursuant to an order from the court of ordinary directed to me as sheriff, signed by J. J. Pratt, Esqr., 7 July 1834 at the suit of Hezekiah Mullinax and wife applicants against Francis Peters and others, to sell the real estate of Peter Peterson deceased on both sides of Abington's Creek, waters of Broad River, adj. James Lockhart, widow Patrick, Gabriel Patrick, 530 acres, purchased by Hezekiah Mullinax for $894, 1 Nov 1834. B. Johnson S. U. D. (Seal), Wit: E. Wilbourn, James Philips. Proved by the oath of E. Wilbourn 24 Nov 1834. Recorded 24 Nov 1834.

W, 327: South Carolina, Union District. Levi Gregory of district aforesaid for $750 to Elisha P. Porter of same, 216 acres on the north fork of Neels Creek, waters of Broad River adj. heirs of Samuel Astell, Thomas Pinckney, Benjn. Gregory, 24 Sept 1834. Levi Gregory (Seal), Wit: Isaac Gregory, Joseph Tate, Thos Y. Gregory. Dorcas Gregory (X), wife of Levi Gregory, relinquished dower 26 Nov 1834 before J. Rogers, Q.U. Proved by the oath of Isaac Gregory 27 Nov 1834 before J. Rogers, Q.U. Recorded 27 Nov 1834.

W, 328: South Carolina, Union District. Hezekiah Johnson of said district for $65 to Adam Cromer, 20 acres granted to G. W. Sartor 3 Jan 1820, 25 Oct 1834. Hezekiah Johnson (X) (LS), Wit: Hugh M. Hunt, James B. Hunt. Proved by the oath of James B. Hunt 29 Nov 1834 before Stephen Johnson, J.P. Recorded 29 Nov 1834.

W, 328-329: South Carolina, Union District. B. J. Gregory of district aforesaid for $700 to Gideon Steen of same, 150 acres on the waters of Tinker and Brushy Creeks, part of a tract granted to John Savage and now the property of B. J. Gregory adj. John Steen, J. B. Gregory, Vanlew, 26 Nov 1834. B. J. Gregory (Seal), Wit: Edw'd Porter, John T. Parnell, A. S. Gregory. Proved by the oath of E. P. Porter 5 Jan 1835 before J. Rogers, Q.U. Elizabeth C. Gregory (X), wife of B. J. Gregory, relinquished dower 26 Nov 1834 before E. P. Porter, Q.U. Recorded 5 Jan 1835.

W, 329-330: South Carolina, Union District. Herrod Gipson of district aforesaid for $24 to James Ward of same, 6 acres, 25 Oct 1834. Herod Gipson (X) (Seal), Wit: N. Word, Willis Ward. Proved by the oath of Nathan Ward 5 Jan 1835 before James Rountree, J.P. Recorded 5 Jan 1835.

W, 330: South Carolina, Union District. Elizabeth Ivy and Zachariah Ivy, husband of said Elizabeth, for $200 to Flemming M. Harris of said district, tract whereon we no live on waters of Little Browns Cree, 60 acres, adj. said Fleming Harris, 29 Oct 1834. Elizabeth Ivy (X) (Seal), Zachariah Ivy (Seal),

Wit: William Prince, F. Horry [*sic*]. Proved by the oath of F. Harris 5 Jan 1835 before John Rogers, Q.U. Recorded 5 Jan 1835.

W, 331: Thomas Young of Lawrence District, SC, for $750 to Robert Easters of Union District, 274 acres on waters of Enoree River adj. Spivy, heirs of Edward Stevens decd, adj. land sold for partition among the heirs of Daniel Boyd decd, 12 Jan 1834. Thomas Young (Seal), Wit: William Malone, Simon P. Murphy. Proved by the oath of William Malone 5 Jan 1835. Recorded 5 Jan 1834.

W, 331-332: South Carolina, Union District. Samuel Moseley of said district for $1100 to Edmond Hames of same, 206 acres on the south side of Pacolet River adj. said Hames, James Moseley, 28 Nov 1834. James Moseley (Seal), Wit: Edmond Hames Jun, William G. Fowler. Proved by the oath of Edmond Hames Junr 6 Dec 1834 before Daniel White, Q.U. Winney Moseley (X), wife of Samuel Moseley, relinquished dower 6 Dec 1834 before Daniel White, Q. U. Recorded 5 Jan 1835.

W, 332-333: South Carolina, Union District. Samuel W. Bentley of district aforesaid for $700 to Samuel Newberry of same, 315 acres on the waters of Browns Creek adj. Christopher Brandon, Thomas Handcock, William Cowson, Patrick Williams, John Peters, 19 Sept 1834. S. W. Bentley (Seal), Wit: B. H. Bradley, Robert V. Harris. Proved by the oath of B. H. Bradley 3 Dec 1834 before Daniel White, Q.U. Marthy Bentley (X), wife of Samuel W. Bentley, relinquished dower 5 Dec 1834 before Daniel White, Q.U. Recorded 3 __ 1834.

W, 334: South Carolina, Union District. John Boyce of District of Lawrence for $2349 to William A. Wilbourn of Union District, tract which I claim in right of my wife the late Martha Saunders, which is composed of several tracts and contains 840 acres in the district of Spartanburgh and Union adj. Mr. Ferguson, on Tiger River, Tilman Bobo, Fanny Bobo, across Dutchmans Creek, Thomas Layton, 10 Nov 1835, John Boyce (Seal), Wit: John F. Kern, R. W. Saunders. Proved by the oath of R. W. Saunders 5 Jan 1835 before H. Gibbs, Q. U. Recorded 5 Jan 1835.

W, 334-335: South Carolina, Union District. November 10th 1834. Received of W. R. Wilbourn $2078 balance in full for the purchase money of the under named property viz Jenny and her six children Enoch, thine[?], Sally, Nerre, Irene, Daniel, the said negroes deed to Charlotte Harling by Martha Saunders to Martha Boyce, also six other negroes Mary, and her five children Jones, Fanny, Jutel, Prince, Sam deeded to Chloe Wilbourn by said Martha also three other negroes Violet, Jim, Tom, deeded to Reuben & John Saunders by said Martha also my right to negro man Jess, 11 head of horses, one waggon, carriage, plantation tools, stock of cattle, household and kitchen furniture. John Boyce (Seal), Wit: John F. Kern, R. W. Saunders. Proved by the oath of R. W. Saunders 5 Jan 1835 before H. Gibbs, Q. U. Recorded 5 Jan 1835.

W, 335: South Carolina, Union District. Joseph Davis of Abbeville District for $250 to John Buford of district aforesaid, 107 acres on the north side of Enoree River and on one of the branches of said river adj. James Flanagan, 10 Jan 1815. Joseph Davis (Seal), Wit: Thos Valentine, Benjamin Valentine. Proved by the oath of Thomas Valentine 19 July 1815 before Wm Selby, J.P., Union District. Recorded 5 Jan 1835.

W, 336: South Carolina, Union District. John Buford of district aforesaid for $600 to William Selby of same, 107 acres in Union District on the north side of Enoree River adj. Jonathan Bird, John Bearden, heir of Davis, 21 Nov 1817. John Buford (Seal), Wit: Terry Evans, George Summers. Proved by the oath of Perry Evans 11 June 1819 before Thos Davis, J.P. Recorded 5 Jan 1835.

W, 336-337: South Carolina, Newberry District. Smith Lester, now of Union District, and lately of Newberry District, for $200, to Benjamin B. Gains of Newberry District, mortgage of tract in Union District adj. James Mayhu decd, on reedy branch, 28 Jan 1834. Smith T. Lester (Seal), Wit: Berry J. Jones, Isaac M. Jones. Proved in Union District by the oath of Isaac Jones 14 Feb 1834 before J. Palmer, J.P. Recorded 11 Jan 1835.

W, 337-338: Mary Browning of Union District for $245 to Hiram Gibbs, Esqr., of same, plantation whereon I now live on the bigg branch, waters of Sugar Creek, waters of Fairforest, 68½ acres, 15 Dec 1834. Mary Browning (X) (Seal), Wit: John Rogers, Wych Goodin. Proved by the oath of Wych Goodin 15 Dec 1834 before John Rogers, Q.U. Recorded 15 Dec 1834.

W, 338-339: South Carolina, Union District. Henry Rogers of district aforesaid for $3000 to William R. B. Farr of same, tract on waters of Tiger River and Pagets Creek, part of a tract granted to Jacob Hoyle, part of a tract willed by William Rogers decd to Ledford Rogers, part of a tract willed by said WM Rogers decd to me the said Henry Rogers, and part of a tract formerly owned by Doctor T. Casell, and a tract deeded from James Hunter to Ledford Rogers and from Ledford Roberts to Olias[?] Norman and from Norman to said Henry with a deed from John Bates, Sheriff adj. Daniel Myers, Isaac Whitton, William Turpin, Thos Stribling, Jesse Rogers, Thos Buchanan, 16 Aug 1834. Henry Rogers (Seal), Wit: T. A. Glenn, Samuel Vance, James Rogers. Proved by the oath of Samuel Vance 10 Aug 1834 before Thos Stribling, Q. U. Mary Rogers (mark), wife of Henry Rogers, relinquished dower 24 Nov 1834. Recorded 28 Nov 1834.

W, 339-341: Fleming Harris & Fleming M. Harris, both of Union District for $500 to Doctor Edwd M. Bobo of same, tracts of land known as the lands of Henry & Polly Rogers, being the lands laid off to Polly Rogers wife of Henry of her fathers estate, of the estate of William Sharp decd, also on other tract known as the Rebecca Hampton tract or the tract laid off to Robert Hampton wife of Jonathan Hampton, 170 acres and 90 acres in the Rogers tract, adj. Robt Savage, Handock Porter Senior, Andrew Hampton, land laid off to

Andrew Hampton's wife, one of the heirs of William Sharp decd, 6 Nov 1834. F. Harris (Seal) F. M. Harris (Seal), Wit: Thomas Jones, Charles D. Bobo. Augusta Ann Harris (X), wife of F.M. Harris, relinquished dower 1 Dec 1834 before Daniel White, Q. U. Jane Harris (X), wife of Fleming Harris, relinquished dower 1 Dec 1834 before Daniel White, Q.U. Proved by the oath of Charles D. Bobo 19 Jan 1835 before John Rogers, Q.U. Recorded 6 Dec 1834.

W, 341-342: 6 June 1794, John Kinsland of Union County, SC, planter, and Rebecca his wife, for £20 sterling, to John Campbell of same, shoemaker, by a grant dated 5 March 1793 to John Kingsland 100 acres adj. Zachariah Estys, James Hohking, Thomas Biddy. John Kinsland (Seal), Wit: Philip Hinton (mark), Henry Campbell, Samuel Campbell. Assigned to John Biddie Wit: Samuel Campbell, John Campbell, Hester Campbell, William Rogers. Proved by the oath of Henry Campbell 21 May 1799 before Samuel Hardy, J. P. Recorded 2 Jan 1835.

W, 342-343: South Carolina, Union District. William Read of Spartanburgh District for $430 to William Littlejohn of Union District, 83 acres on Mill Creek, waters of Pacolet River, 31 March 1834. William Reid (Seal), Wit: David Reid, Richard Littlejohn. Proved by the oath of Richard Littlejohn 11 July 1834.

W, 343-344: William Rice of Union District for $100 to Malachi Keenan of same, tract adj. the village of Union, six acres, near the Tan yard at the Bark mill house, adj. Peter P. Taylor, the land on which Samuel Sherman lately lived and upon which the tan yard is erected, 13 Oct 1822. Wm Rice (Seal), Wit: William M. Thomson, Benjn Saunders. Proved by the oath of William M. Thomson 27 Jan 1833 before John Rogers, Q.U.

W, 344-345: South Carolina, Union District. Washing Backher for $385 to Wm. A. Young, 200 acres on the branches of Elisha Creek, waters of Enoree River where the lower line of fence joins it of the plantation whereon M. N. Musgrove now lives, adj. P. W. Head, Dorah Daker, Jesse Dodd, Wm Simpson, 26 July 1834. W. Bachler (Seal), Wit: Joel Dean, W. H. Milbanks. Proved in Spartanburgh District by the oath of W. H. Milbanks 26 Feb 1834 before Joel Dean, J.Q. Recorded 31 Dec 1834.

W, 345: South Carolina, Spartenburgh District. Eugenie Bachler for $300 to Washington Bachler, all my interest in 500 acres conveyed this day to A. G. Gordon, 13 Jan 1834. Eugene Bachler (Seal), Wit: Joel Dean, Bird hill. Proved in Spartanburgh District by the oath of Bird Hill 1 Dec 1833 before Joel Dean, J.P. Assigned to William A. Young till I make him a good title, 2 Aug 1834. Washington Bachler. Test: Emanuel Boh. Recorded 31 Dec 1834.

W, 345-347 [page number 346 was skipped in numbering]: South Carolina, Union District. Leonard Smith of district aforesaid for $500 to Levi Smith of same, 100 acres 22 May 1819. Leonard Smith (Seal), Wit: James Smith, Philip

Littlefield, Wm. Smith. Proved by the oath of Wm Smith 12 Jan 1835 before H. Gibbs, Q.U. Recorded 12 Jan 1835.

W, 347-348: William Huckaby of Union District for $200 to William Brown of same, two tracts of land, one granted to John McWhirter 3 May 1790 and containing by resurvey 95 acres, and other part anciently deeded to Joseph Mitchell, 25 acres adj. James Sprouse, John George, 9 Aug 1834. William Huckaby (Seal), Wit: William Kent, S. Jeffries. Proved by the oath of Wm Kent 27 Dec 1834 before John Rogers, Q.U. Elizabeth Huckaby (X), wife of Wm Huckaby, relinquished dower 5 Dec 1834 before Saml Mosley, Q.U. Recorded 3 Dec 1834.

W, 348-349: South Carolina, Union District. Wm Reid Sen of district aforesaid for $1300 to J. F. Walker of same, 325 acres, being the upper part of the tract which contains in all 525 acres, the lower part contains 200 acres which 200 acres, I make over to the said J. F. Walker as by deed of gift , on the north side of Pacolet River, a small part on the south side adj. Kendrick, Wm. Reid, John Bailey decd, John Howel, H. Spears, Gibbs' branch, 8 Sept 1827. William Reid (Seal), Wit: Wm. Reid Junr, John Reid, James Reid. Proved by the oath of John Reid 5 Jan 1835 before John Rogers, Q.U. Recorded 5 Jan 1835.

W, 349-350: South Carolina, Union District. Martha Norman of district aforesaid for $600 to Dicy Norman of same, a negro woman Vine Fielder and Jack, 26 Dec 1829. Martha Norman (O) (Seal), Wit: Jason Norman, Jno Norman. Proved by the oath of Jason Norman 13 Oct 1834. Recorded 1 Dec 1834.

W, 350: South Carolina, Union District. Wm Mitchell of the district aforesaid for $30 to Thomas Handcock of same, tract adj. Coursin, said Handcock, 9 Nov 1833. Wm. Mitchel (Seal), Wit: S. W. Beatty, Thomas N. W. Williams, Alfred W. Davis. Proved by the oath of Samuel W. Bentley 1 Dec 1834 before Daniel White, Q.U. Recorded 1 Dec 1834.

W, 351: South Carolina, York District. John Blair of district above mentioned for $589 to Samuel H. Alexander of Pinckneyville, South Carolina, lot in the village of Pinckneyville adj. Daniel McMahon, McGowan, Col. Joseph Gist, Daniel McMahon Junr, 22 Oct 1834. John Blair (Seal), Wit: William Jameson, Thos Patricks. Proved in Union District by the oath of Thomas Patrick 22 Oct 1834 before William Jamieson, Q.U. Recorded 5 Jan 1835.

W, 351-352: South Carolina, Union District. Bennet Whitlock of said district for $600 to John Harris of same, 182 acres on the waters of Browns Creek adj. Newil Smith, 20 Sept 1834. Bennet Whitlock (Seal), Wit: Robert V. Harris, T. J. Whitlock, James C. Harris. Nancy Whitlock (X), wife of Bennet Whitlock, relinquished dower 29 Nov 1834 before Daniel White, Q. U. Proved by the oath of James C. Harris 24 Nov 1834 before Daniel White, Q.U. Recorded 5 Jan 1835.

W, 352-353: Andrew Story Jr. of the State of Illinois, White County, for $12 to Thos P. Story of Spartanburgh District, all my right, interest, and claim in the tract in Union District, 52 acres, part of a tract formerly belonging to Samuel Pateron and willed to Jane Pateron during her life and at her death to be equally divided between the surviving legatees, on the sell branches of McLures Creek adj. James Mayes, the company of Gold Digers, Joseph Howard, 29 May 1833. Andrew Story (Seal), Wit: John White, Sarah C. Shands. Proved by the oath of John White 5 Jan 1835 before John Rogers, Q.U. Recorded 5 Jan 1834.

W, 353-354: Samuel P. Harris of Union District for $200 to Delaston Holder of same, 130 acres on waters of Big Browns Creek, on the Scull Shoal Road, conveyed by James Newton to Samuel P. Harris by deed 21 Oct 1833, 10 Nov 1834. Samuel P. Harris (Seal), Wit: Isaac Gregory, John Rogers. Sophiah Harris, wife of Samuel P. Harris, relinquished dower 29 Nov 1834 before Daniel White, Q.U. Proved by the oath of John Rogers 1 Dec 1834 before Daniel White, Q.U. Recorded 1 Dec 1834.

W, 354-355: South Carolina, Union District. Orman R. Moreland for $424 to Timothy Hainey of district aforesaid, tract formerly belonging to James Moreland decd on Pacolet River, 122 acres adj. James Foster Jun, George Foster,Robert Foster, James Foster, Josiah Foster Junr and Josiah Foster Senr, 6 Dec 1823. O. H. Moreland (Seal), Wit: J. Moreland, John Garner. Jane V. Moreland, wife of O. H. Moreland, relinquished dower 13 Dec 1834 before Isaac Going, Q. U. Proved by the oath of J. Moreland 6 Dec 1834 before Isaac Going, Q.U.

W, 355-356: Samuel Otterson of Spartenburgh District for $925 to Thomson B. Collins of Union District, tract conveyed to me by Powel Ormbey adj. William Blakely, on Pacolet River, John Littlejohn, plat by Zachariah Bullock, Deputy Surveyor, adj. Jacob Mitchell's old original lines, 150 acres, 1 Jan 1835. Samuel Otterson (Seal), Wit: William Norris, James Scott. Proved by the oath of William Norris 5 Jan 1835 before John Rogers, Q.U. Recorded 5 Jan 1835.

W, 356-357: South Carolina, Union District. Joshua Wilbourn for $210 to Silas Bishop, both of said district, tract on south side of Pagets Creek, waters of Tiger River, adj. Mrs. Boyce, William Malone, Shiryard Duke, Alfred Wilborn, 28 Nov 1834. Joshua Wilbourn (Seal), Wit: William Malone, Elijah Weeks. Proved by the oath of William Malone 3 Dec 1834 before John Norman, Q.U. Recorded 6 Dec 1834.

W, 357: Samuel Otterson of Spartenburgh District for $600 to Thomson B. Collins of Union District, 143 acres on the south side of Pacolet River, 1 Jan 1835. Samuel Otterson (Seal), Wit: William Norris, James Scott. Proved by the oath of William Norris 5 Jan 1835 before John Rogers, Q.U. Recorded 5 Jan 1835.

W, 358-359: Georgia, Habersham County. 17 Dec 1829, George Philips and state & county aforesaid to John Mitchell of Union District, for $600, tract on waters of Browns Creek adj. widow White, Johnston. George Philips (Seal), Wit: Joseph Philips, Andrew Dorsey, J.P. Fanny Philips (X)w, wife of George Philips, relinquished dower 19 Dec 1829 before Andrew Dorsey, J.P. John T. Carter, Deputy Clerk of the inferior court, certified that Andrew Dorsey was a justice of the peace. Fanny Philips also relinquished dower in Union District before Daniel White, 17 Aug 1830. Recorded 5 Jan 1835.

W, 359-360: South Carolina, Union District. William Wilson of district aforesaid for $325 to William W. Glenn (trustee for Lucy Ivey) of same, tract on waters of Enoree River, 161 ares, per plat made by Steven Johnson, D. S., 12 Aug 1834, 30 Sept 1834. William Wilson (X) (Seal), Wit: Thomas Davis, Silas Anderson. Proved by the oath of Silas Anderson 25 Oct 1834 before Thos Stribling, Q.U. Elizabeth Wilson, (X), wife of William Wilson, relinquished dower 25 Oct 1834 before Thomas Stribling, Q.U. Recorded 5 Jan 1835.

W, 360-361: South Carolina, Union District. Jeremiah Gregory of Union District for $150 to Hugh Gregory of same, tract of 50 acres on south side of Little Browns Creek, waters of Broad River, adj. Rochester, E. P. Porter, Hancock Porter [not dated]. Jeremiah Gregory (X) (Seal), Wit: Thomas Gregory (X), Isaac Gregory. Naomy Gregory (X), wife of Jeremiah Gregory, relinquished dower 24 Dec 1834 before E. P. Porter, Q.U. Proved by the oath of Isaac Gregory 26 Jan 1835 before John Rogers, Q.U. Recorded 25 Jan 1835.

W, 361-363: B. Johnson, Sheriff of Union District, by virtue of several writs of fieri facias from the court of common pleas held for Union District 9 Feb 1834 at the suit of Wm. Rice indorsee to levy of the goods and chattles, lands and tenements of Fleming Harris $335.71, tracts of land on the north side of Browns Creek, waters of Broad River one tract known as the Mrs. Griffy tract, 50 acres adj. James Vandiford, Sam Sharp, Zach Ivey, James Pair and a tract sold in February 1833 known as the land apportioned to the said Fleming Harris' wife adj. James Vandiford, Saml Sharp, Mrs. Griffen, 80 acres, and two other tracts known as the Rebecca Hampton and Henry Rogers tracts, each about 90 acres adj. Hancock Porter Senior, Robert Savage, and lands laid off Mrs. Hampton, being in North Carolina, purchased by Edmd M. Bobo of Union for $181 for the whole four tracts, 5 Nov 1834. B. Johnson, S. U. D. (Seal), Wit: John Murrell, Charles Going. June Harris (X), wife of Fleming Harris, relinquished dower 1 Dec 1834 before Daniel White, Q.U. Augusta Ann Harris, wife of Fleming M. Harris, relinquished dower 1 Dec 1834 before Daniel White, Q.U. Proved by the oath of John T. Murrell 29 Jan 1835 before John Rogers, Q.U. Recorded 29 Jan 1835.

W, 363: South Carolina, Union District. Aron Pruett acknowledged himself guardian for Aggy Bailey, a free woman of color, 29 Jan 1835 before J. Rogers, Clk. Recorded 29 Jan 1835.

W, 363-364: Fleming Harris and Jane Harris, wife of Fleming Harris, of Union District, for $300 to Doct. Edw'd M. Bobo of same, two tracts of land known as the Mrs. Griffy tracts including 20 acres which F. Harris bought of Saml Sharp and the other tract adj. the Griffy tract known as the lands apportioned to the wife ____ Harris, wife of Fleming Harris, as one of the heirs of Wm. Sharp decd, 80 acres, in the whole 150 acres, adj. Saml and James Sharp, Z. Ivey, James Pair, James Vandiford, Wm. Reynolds or Runnels, 6 Nov 1834. F. Harris (Seal), Jane Harris (X) (Seal), Wit: Thomas Johns, Charles D. Bobo. Jane Harris (X), wife of Fleming Harris, relinquished dower 1 Dec 1834 before Daniel White, Q.U. Proved by the oath of Charles D. Bobo 29 Jan 1835 before John Rogers, Q.U. Recorded 29 Jan 1835.

W, 364: on examining the within deed I find that in reading the NW corner of the smoke house the deed is in error. It should read NE corner & the lot is so conveyed to me, 17 Jan 1835. Nath Gist (Seal), Wit: D. Wallace, J. W. L. Meng. Recorded 6 Feb 1835. [see following deed]

W, 365-366: John T. Murrell of Union District for $2925 to Levi Walker, lot in Union Village adj. Virgin & Main Streets adj. Nathaniel Gist, at the NE corner of the smoke house, 24 Dec 1834. John T. Murrell (Seal), Wit: John McLure, W. E. Cotten. Sarah F. B. Murrell, wife of John T. Murrell, relinquished dower 27 Dec 1834 before Jno Norman, Q. U. Proved by the oath of William E. Cotten 6 Feb 1835 before J. Rogers, Q.U. Recorded 6 Feb 1835.

W, 366-367: South Carolina, Union District. Thomas Black Senr of district aforesaid for $1000 to Thomas Black Junr of same, tract adj. Joseph Howell, Thomas Black Senr, 200 acres, 30 Jan 1835. Thos Black (Seal), Wit: John G. Davidson, Robt G. Davidson. Proved by the oath of John Davidson before John Carothers, Q.U. Recorded 2 Feb 1835.

W, 367-368: South Carolina, Union District. Joseph Jolly of said district for $350 to Arthur Lipsey of same, tract on waters of Browns & Tinkers Creeks & on both sides of the Charleston Road, 200 acres adj. James Turner, Asbery Rochester, 7 Jan 1835. Joseph Jolly (Seal), Wit: Stephen Johnson, Uriah Paulk, James McBride. Cloe Jolly (X), wife of Joseph Jolly, relinquished dower 22 Jan 1835 before E. P. Porter, Q.U. Proved by the oath of James McBride 2 Feb 1835 before J. Rogers, Q.U. Recorded 2 Feb 1835.

W, 368: North Carolina, Rowan County. James Smith & Oney Smith his wife of county aforesaid for $200 to Levi Smith of Union District, 104 acres, 8 Nov 1834. James Smith (Seal), Oney Smith (X) (Seal), Wit: James Cavender, Mary Callicott. Proved in Rowan County 8 Nov 1834 by the oath of James Cavender before E. A. Foster, J.P. Recorded 14 Feb 1835.

W, 369-370: South Carolina, Union District. Joseph Phillips of district aforesaid for $900 to Joseph Woodward & Randal Woodward Jr. both of same, tract on waters of Enoree River on the waggon Road, 317 acres, 10 Sept

1834. Joseph Phillips (Seal), Wit: Isaac P. Murphy, Peter Davis. Jane Phillips, wife of Joseph Phillips, relinquished dower 13 Feb 1835 before Thomas Stribling, Q.U. Proved by the oath of Isaac P. Murphy 19 Feb 1835 before Thos Stribling, Q.U. Recorded 26 Feb 1835.

W, 370-371: Isaac Langston of Union District for $621.25 to James B. Fant of same, tract on waters of Tinkers & Fairforest Creek, waters of Tyger River, adj. David Cooper, Abram McJunkin, E. Eubanks, 252½ acres, 3 Dec 1834. Isaac Langston (LS), Wit: Stephen Johnson, Thos Sartor. Sarah Langston (X), wife of Isaac Langston, relinquished dower 8 Dec 1834 before E. McGraw, Q.U. Proved by the oath of Thomas Sartor 2 Feb 1835 before J. Rogers, Q.U. Recorded 2 Feb 1835.

W, 371-372: Isaac Gregory of Union District for $216 to John D. Word of same, tract on waters of Smiths Branch, waters of Tyger River, adj. John Smith, 108 acres, 5 March 1834. Isaac Gregory (Seal), Wit: Stephen Johnson, T. A. Glenn. Proved by the oath of T. A. Glenn 5 March 1834 before Stephen Johnson, J.P. Elisabeth Gregory, wife of Isaac Gregory, relinquished dower 12 Feb 1835 before E. P. Porter, Q. U. Recorded 14 Feb 1835.

W, 372-373: South Carolina, Union District. Hancock Porter of district above written for $100 to Elisa Coomer of same, 50 acres, 16 Feb 1831. Hancock Porter (LS), Wit: E.P. Porter, Isaac Gregory, J. S. Turner. Proved by the oath of Isaac Gregory 16 Feb 1831 before E. P. Porter, Q.U. Recorded 19 Feb 1835.

W, 373-374: South Carolina, Union District. Thomas Hyatt of Union District for $350 to Wyley Ward of same, tract whereon the said Wiley Ward now lives on Rocky Creek, waters of Fairforest, 100 acres adj. James Orr, Samuel Harlan, William Jeter, Aron McCollum, 12 Jan 1835. Thomas Hyatt (X) (LS), Wit: Aron McCollum, Thos Scott. Martha Hyatt (X), wife of Thomas Hyatt, relinquished dower 20 Jan 1835 before Daniel White, Q.U. Proved by the oath of Aron McCollum 17 Jan 1835 before Danl White, Q.U. Recorded 1 Feb 1835.

W, 374-375: South Carolina, Union District. Edmond Lipford of said district for $500 to Isaac S. Kimberly of same, 135 acres on the head of Rocky Creek, a branch of Fairforest adj. McBeth, Belew, Tolison, 13 Sept 1834. Edmond Lipford (O), (LS), Wit: H. Gault, D. S. F. Gault. Proved by the oath of Henry Gault 15 Dec 1834 before Danl White, Q.U. Catharine Lipford (X), wife of Edmond Lipford, relinquished dower 15 Dec 1835 before Daniel White, Q.U. Recorded 2 March 1835.

W, 375-377: South Carolina, Union District. Zachariah Johnson and Easther his wife of district aforesaid for $920.09 to William Davis of same, tract on the beaver dam Creek, a branch of Tyger River, adj. Jas. B. Fant, James Johnson, Jeter, 200 acres, 27 Aug 1834. Zachariah Johnson (LS), Esther Johnson (LS), Wit: John S. Sims. Thos McCollough. Elisabeth Johnson, wife of Sam O.

Johnson, relinquished dower 29 Sept 1834 before Thos Stribling, Q.U. Esther Johnson, wife of Zachariah Johnson, relinquished dower 29 Sept 1834 before Thos Stribling, Q.U. Proved by the oath of Thos McCollough 28 Sept 1834 before Thos Stribling, Q.U. Recorded 2 March 1834.

W, 377: Commission to John Rogers as clerk of the court of common pleas & Genl Sessions for Union District, 5 Feb 1835. John Rogers took the necessary oath 19 Feb 1835.

W, 378-379: South Carolina, Union District. Henry Rogers & Polly Rogers his wife of said district for $275 to Fleming M. Harris of same, 90 acres, lot laid off Pollly Rogers wife of Henry Rogers as one of the heirs of William Sharp decd, 10 March 1832. Polly Rogers (X) (Seal), Henry Rogers (Seal), Wit: P. A. Davis, Robt Black. Polly Rogers (X), wife of Henry Rogers, relinquished dower 14 April 1832 before Thos Stribling, Q.U. Proved by the oath of Philip A. Davis 10 March 1832 before Thos Stribling, Q.U. Recorded 10 Feb 1835.

W, 379-380: South Carolina, Union District. Joseph Tate of Union District for $600 to John Man of same, tract whereon I now live, 227 acres on Browns Creek 9 Dec 1834. Joseph Tate (LS), Wit: B. Johnson, J. Rogers. Lucinda Tate, wife of Joseph Tate, relinquished dower 8 Jan 1835 before E. P. Porter, Q.U. Proved by the oath of John Rogers 5 March 1835 before D. Wallace, Q.U. Recorded 5 March 1835.

W, 380-381: B. Johnson, Sheriff of Union District, by vbirtue of a writ of fieri facias from the court of common pleas tested 15 April 1831 at the suit of Joseph Rice to levy of the goods & chattels, lands and tenements of Allen Foster Jr., $58.40, sells 71 acres adj. McNeil Bevil & Sterling Powers, Jas H. Green, B. Tracey, John Ennis, this being the tract sold by Aquilla Powerse to said Allen Foster, purchased by Zadock Hooker for $32, 18 Feb 1835. B. Johnson S. U. D., Wit: E. Wilbourn, W. M. Thommson. Proved by the oath of E. Wilbourn 9 March 1835 before J. Rogers, Q.U. Recorded 9 March 1835.

W, 381-382: Thomas Bowker of Union District for $6350 to Jas B. Davis of Fairfield District, trcat in the fork of Broad & Tyger Rivers in Union District, 500 acres,also six acres granted to Wm Rogers in Jan 1791, dated 14 May 1834. Thomas Bowker (Seal), Wit: Joel Cartan, Wm. K. Davis. Proved in Fairfield District by the oath of W. K. Davis before J. W. Nelson, J.P. Margaret K. Bowker relinquished dower 27 May 1834 before JAmes Meacham, J. Q. Recorded 9 March 1835.

W, 382-384: Jas. W. Gray, Commissioner of the court of Equity for the District of Charleston, whereas Thaddeus Street in his own & admiinstrator of Timothy Street's estate on or about 17 May 1834 did exhibit his bill in the court of Equity at Charleston against Mrs. Angelina Street, Saml. M. Gowdy, Henry T. Street, Emeline Cecillia Street, Gustavus Street, Saul Ally Street, and Stptimus Street, in which it was stated that hitherto a copartnership existed in Union District consisting of the said Thaddues Street, Timothy

Street & Samuel M. Gowdy & was continued under the management of said Samuel M. Gowdy until the dissolution of the said copartnership, that among the property of the said copartnership are thre tracts of land hereinafter mentioned, that the said Saml M. Gowdy has agreed to become the purchase of the same for $2000 provided good titles can be given him, that Timothy Street has departed this life & administration of his estate has been granted to complainant S. D. Boinest & the bill prays that the cause would sanction the said agreement of sale, now for $2000 paid by Saml M. Gowdy, sells tract of 152 acres on waters of Thickety Creek adj. Robt Moorhead, Anna Cotter, and tract of 50 acres on north side of Packolett River and south side of Thickety Creek adj. William Moorhead, Saml M. Gowdy, L. B. Murry, Wm. Huckaby, Wm. H. Cotter, Samuel Otterson, 23 May 1834. Jas W. Gray Com. in Eq. (LS), Wit: Edward Frost, Henry Y. Gray. Proved in Charleston District by the oath of Henry Y. Gray 7 April 1835 before Geo W. Egleston, Not. Pub. Recorded 4 May 1835.

W, 384-385: Jas. W. Gray, Commissioner of the court of Equity for the Equity of Charleston District [similar deed as preceding] for the sale of negro slaves named will, Hannah, Nancy, Grace, John, Elleck, Francis Jim, Matilda, Charles, Sandy, Betsy, Mary, Prince, Lafayette, Lafleur, Carolina, Rose, Archy, Fillis, Paula, and hoses, cattle, sold by Saml M. Gowdy for $7000, 23 May 1834. Jas W. Gray Com. in Eq. (LS), Wit: Edward Frost. Recorded 4 May 1835.

W, 385-386: James N. Hardy of Union District for $65 to Joseph Evans of same, all my right, title, claim, or interest to a tract belonging to the estate of John Ashley decd, on Cain Creek, 355 acres as yet undivided, and being the same which I purchased of William Ashly 12 Oct 1832, dated 24 March 1834. Jas. N. Hardy, Wit: A. W. Dubois, John T. Hill. Proved by the oath of A. W. Dubois 14 April 1835 before Reuben Gilliam, J. Q. Recorded 4 May 1835.

W, 386: South Carolina, Union District. Mary E. Pruett of district aforesaid for $800 to James N. Hardy of same, 210 acres on waters of Enoree River adj. W. W. Glenn, Thomas K. Cofield, Elijah Anderson, on which Jesse Evans now lives, 10 April 1835. Mary E. Pruett (X) (LS), Wit: Geo Douglass, W. E. Hardy. Proved by the oath of Geo Douglass 28 April 1835 before W. Gordan, J.P. Recorded 10 May 1835.

W, 387: South Carolina, Union District. James McCluney of York District for $12.75 to John Jeffries Senr, one undivided part of a tract on the south side Gilkeys Creek, part of a tract granted to Alexander Martin in 1803, supposed to be 17.9 acres adj. Dowd, said Jeffries, 23 Nov 1833. J. McCluney agent by power of attorney for Saml D. & Hancock Alexander (LS), Wit: John Patrick Snr, Anderson Petty. Proved by the oath of Anderson Petty 23 Aug 1834 before Daniel Smith, J.Q. Recorded 4 May 1835.

W, 387-388: South Carolina, Union District. Nathan Coleman of district aforesaid for $200 to Thomas Sartor of same, 140 acres, part of a tract originally granted to Easen & Braselman, adj. John Hawkins, P. R. Pearson, Thomas D. Johnson, Thomas Linam, 12 Aug 1834. Nathan Coleman (LS), Wit: John P. Sartor, Geo W. Sartor. Proved by the oath of John P. Sartor and Geo W. Sartor 12 Aug 1834 before E. McGraw, Q.U. Elizabeth G. Coleman, wife of Nathan Coleman relinquished dower 19 Feb 1835 before Reuben Gilliam, Q.U. Recorded 6 April 1835.

W, 388-389: South Carolina, Union District. Jesse Gordon of Union District for $95 to Thos H. Word of same, 58 acres agreeable to a survey of John T. McJunkin, Esqr., made 21 Nov 1829, on the east side of Tyger River adj. John Smith, Lewis Fant[?], and William Brown, 6 Jan 1835. Jesse Gordon (LS), Wit: Stephen Johnson, Gideon Steen. Proved by the oath of Gideon Steen 6 April 1835 before Wm. Skelton, J.P. Recorded 6 April 1835.

W, 389-390: South Carolina, Union District. Britton Mitchell of district aforesaid for $150 to John D. Word of same, 100 acres on a small branch on the north side of Tyger River, 100 acres ranted to Nathan Hawkins adj. Eli Cook, Wm. Smith, 7 March 1832. Britton Mitchell (X) (LS), Wit: James M. Dillard, Robert Young. Nancy Mitchell (X), wife of Britton Mitchell, relinquished dower 1 Jan 1834 before W. McGraw, J. Q. Proved by the oath of Robert Young 8 July 1832 before J. t. McJunkin. Recorded 6 April 1835.

W, 390-391: South Carolina, Union District. Nathan Coleman of district aforesaid for $600 to Thomas Sartor of same, 650 acres on Deals Creek, waters of Tyger River and willed by Geo Linam to Frances Lucas, 12 Aug 1834. Nathan Coleman (Seal), Wit: John P. Sartor, George w. Sartor. Proved by the oaths of both wit 12 Aug 1834 before E. McGraw, Q. U. Elizabeth G. Coleman, wife of Nathan Coleman, relinquished dower 19 Feb 1835 before Reuben Gilliam, J.Q. Recorded 6 April 1835.

W, 391-392: South Carolina, Union District. Saml J. Mays and Elisabeth B. Mayes his wife of district aforesaid for $85.56 to Mary Black and also Isabella Black for $85.56 to Mary Black, all our shares, titles and interest in the tracts of land belonging to the estate of William Black, late of district aforesaid deceased, the share of the said Samuel J. Mayes & Elizabeth B. his wife being one ninth part of two third parts thereof, and the share of said Isabella Black being one ninth part of the two third parts thereof, being all the real estate which belonged to said deceased at the time of his death, viz, one tract of 72 acres in Spartanburgh District on waters of Harris branch, conveyed to said William Black by Elijah Gossett adj. Henry White, Geo Kennett & others, also 244 acres in Union District and partly in Spartanburgh District on harris branch being the same which was conveyed by one Joseph Hays to said William Black' also tract partly in Union and partly in Spartanburgh District on both sides of Harris's Creek adj. last mentioned tract conveyed to William Black by one David R. Burns, 9 Aug 1834. Samuel J. Mayes (Seal), Elisabeth B. Mayes (Seal), Isabella Black (Seal), Wit: David McDowal, John McDowell. Elizabeth B. Mayes, wife of Samuel J. Mayes, relinquished dower 13 Dec 1834 before Nathl Gist, Q.U. Proved by the oath of John McDowell 13 Dec 1834 before Nathl Gist, Q.U. Recorded 6 April 1835.

W, 393: South Carolina, Union District. John Puckett, Richard Page, John Mosely, Lemuel Moseley, Daniel Moseley, James G. Fowler, Absalom Hyde, Henrietta Mosley & Mary Mosley, of Union District and Pickens District, for $40 to each of us to Samuel Mosley of Union District, all our right, title, or claim to a tract of land deeded by James Mosley to Baxter Mosley, and which the said Baxter Mosley died possessed of, on waters of Packolett, 206 acres adj. Hames, Foster, Jas Mosley, 6 Dec 1834. Rich'd Page (X) (LS), Mary Mosley (X) (LS), Henrietta Mosley (X) (LS), John Mosley (LS), Jas Fowler (X) (LS), Danl Mosley (LS), John Puckett (LS), Leml Mosley (LS), Wit: John B. Mosley, Miles Puckett. Proved by the oath of John B. Mosley 12 Jan 1835 before Wm. Goudelock, J.P. Recorded 25 April 1835.

W, 394-395: John Wilkins. March 25th 1835. In obedience to a general order, we the undersigned commissioners appointed to divide the Regiment north of the Packolett River into two Battalions and Eight companys, have met and taken the matter into consideration and now offer the following report.

1st. We have divided the regiment into two Battalions by a line from Maj'r John Kerby's on Packolett River where the District line crosses the River along the road by Jesse Griffins to John Wilkins to the mouth of the blue branch on Thickety Creek, then up the creek by the forge to Green River Road & with that road to the Coulter ford Road at the Battle Ground.

2nd. We have also laid off the first Battallion commanded by Lt. Col. Robert G. Davidson in four beat companies. Beat No. 1 commanded by Capt. A. Bonner included by a line running from the battle ground with the Island ford Road to the North Carolina line along the state line to Broad River down the river to Gafney's ferry thence to Capt Gafney's ferry running with the line of No. 1 to Thickety Creek thence down the creek to the Smith ford Road, thence along the road to Smiths ford & up the river to the beginning.

Also Beat No. 3 beginning at Smiths ford &running the grindal Shoal Road to Thickety Creek thence down the creek to William Moorheads, thence to Gowdeys store and thence down Bennet Mill Creek to Packolett River thence down Packolett to Pinkney & up Broad River to the beginning.

Also Beat No. 4 Beginning at John Kerby's where the District line crosses the river & runs with the road by Jesse Griffin's to John Wilkies to the mouth of the blue branch on Thickety Creek down that creek to the Smith ford road & to William Moorhead & by Gowdeys & Bennett Mill Creek to Packolett & up Packolett to the beginning.

The second Battallion we have also divided into four beat companies.

Beat No. 1 is included by a line from Ralph Smith's with the Road by James Sea's to Spartanburgh Ct. House then the Coulter ford Road to Lawsons fork at Harris's Mills, thence down the Creek to the upper ford on said Creek at the old iron works then the road by Richard Thomson's old place & Cedar Springs to the Court House Road then down the road by Col. J. Smith by Golightly's mills & with the road to the fork of Gibbs mountain then over the top of that mountain then to the road leading to Ralph Smith's then up that road.

Beat No. 2 of the second battalion commencing at Kelly's aforesaid & running up to Hammetts ford on that river then with the road to the old iron works aforesaid, then with the road by Rich'd Thomson's old place to the Cedar Springs to the Court House Road down that road by Co. J. Smith's to the road to McDaniels mills then down teat road to McDaniel mil on Fairforest Creek, then down that creek to the District line then northerly with that line to the beginning.

Beat No. 3 beginning where the line crosses Packolett at Kerby's thence along the road by Jesse Griffins, John Wilkins & to the mouth of the blue branch on Thicketty Creek, then up the creek to the Forge, then a direct line to the Rolling Mill on Packolett, then down the Road to the beginning.

Beat No. 4 beginning where the Coulter's ford Road crosses Lawsons fork at Harris's Mills thence down that creek to the old Iron Works upper ford, then the road at Hammetts ford on Packolett River, then up the river to the Rolling mill, then a direct line to the forge on Thickety Creek, then up that creek to the Green River Road, & then with that road to the Coulter Road, then along the Coulter ford Road to the beginning. Together with the inclosed list of managers of Elections & places of Elections all of which is respectfully submitted. We also would submit the propriety of the meeting of the managers of Elections at Dr. Otterson's as a most central point to count the votes for field officers of the regiment. If known it should be more advisable to examine & count the votes for Major of the second battalion we are of opinion that Nath Tracey's would be a central spot. John Littlejohn, Sectry. D. White, Ch. Recorded 16 April 1835.

W, 395-397: South Carolina, Union District. We the undersigned commissioners who were appointed by Daniel Wallace Brigade major of the 9th Brigade, SC Militia, to divide the Regiment having the following boundaries. Beginning at Rice's mills on Enoree River then a straight line to McBeth's mills on Fairforest then up Fairforest to the District line thence with said line to Packolett River, thence down Packolett River to Broad River, thence down Broad River to the mouth of Tyger, thence with the district line to the beginning, into two battalions & each Battalion into four companies. We established as a dividing line between the two Battalions the Road leading from McBeths mills on Fairforest by Union Court House to Shelton Sims ferry on Broad River, designating the Battalion below said road the south Battalion & the Battalion above said road by the name of the north Battalion.

2nd. We proceeded to divide the South Battalion into four beat companies, giving to each the same extent of territory as near as the locality would admit.

The first company commencing at Rices Mills on Enoree River thence with the regiment line to Tyger River then down said road to the district line & then with the district line to the beginning.

The second company to commence at Cook's bridge on Tyger River then to the mouth of Swift Run Creek then up said creek to Henry Koons, from Henry Koons to Leonard Baker then to Gilliam Hobsons, then to Johnson Mills on Broad River, then down said river to the mouth of Tyger, thence up Tyger to Cook's bridge.

The third commencing at Cook's bridge up said river to the regiment line then a straight line to McBeths mills on Fairforest, then the Union Road to Union Court House, then on the main road to Benj. J. Gregories, then to John Jennings, then to Union Court House then to Pinckney Road below Lucy Porter's then on said road to Sims's ferry on Broad River, then down said river to Johnson mills, then to Gilliam Hobson's then to Leonard Bakers then to John Jennings the beginning.

3d. We also divide the north Battalion into four companies. The first at the road leading to Henry Gaults & up said road to Gault's store, then down the Pinckney Road to Bradley's store, then to Hughes saw mill on Broad River then down the river to Shelton Sims ferry, then on the road to Union Court House, the beginning.

The second to commence at Henry Gaults store then on the line of the first company to Hughes saw mill on Broad River, then up the river to the mouth of Packolett, then up Packolett River to the Grindal Shoals then down the main road to Henry Gault's store, the beginning.

The third beginning at the road which leads to Henry Gault's at Union Court House, then on the road to McBeth's mills, then up Fairforest Creek to the Spartanburgh line, then on the district line to the road leading from Spartanburgh Court House to Union Court House where McBride lives, then down the said road to B. Culps, then on Pinckney Road to Henry Gaults, thence on the road to Union Court House, the beginning.

The fourth to commence at McBrides on the Spartanburgh line then on district line to Packolett River, thence down said road to the Grindal Shoals then on the main road to Henry Gault's, then up the Spartanburgh Road to B. Culps, then on said road to the Spartanburgh line, the beginning. 18 March 1835. T. N. Dawkins, B. J. Gregory, Jesse Wilson, Gideon Steen. Recorded 26 April 1835.

W, 397: South Carolina, Union District. James Alexander of Union District for obligations made to me by Lindsey Alexander for the maintenance of myself and daughter Malinda Alexander during our lifetime & for the maintenance of Anna Alexander & Solomon Alexander children of said Malinda Alexander until they shall become of age, 100 acres of land, part of a tract of 200 ares granted to William Skelton under the hand of William Bull, conveyed by Skelton to James Ray and from James Ray to Robt Lamb & Robt Lamb to James Putman and on a branch of John's Creek, waters of Enoree River, adj. Skelton, Holcomb, 5 Dec 1834. Jas Alexander (X), Wit: Hosea Ray, E. Ray. Proved by the oath of Hosea Ray 2 March 1835 before Fredk Jackson, J.P. Recorded 28 April 1835.

W, 398: March 29, 1835, James A. Stevenson to James Vinson Senr, both of Union District, whereas James Vinson stands indebted to said James A. Stephenson in the sum of $214, mortgage of tract on waters of Fannans Creek, 150 acres being the land conveyed to said James Vinson by Lott Whitlock, Esqr. James Vinson (Seal), Wit: Elias Smith, Levi Davis. Proved by the oath of Levi Davis 11 April 1835 before Isaac Going, J.Q. Recorded 16 April 1835.

W, 399: South Carolina, Union District. David Cooper of district aforesaid for $150 to Nathan Whilby Cooper of same, 100 acres, part of a tract granted to Jeremiah Cooper and conveyed from him to David Cooper on the NW side of the road leading to Union Court House adj. Langston, Bates, Malone, 7 Dec 1834. David Cooper (Seal), Wit: David Spiva, Nathan Cooper. Proved by the oath of Nathan Cooper 28 April 1834 before J. Rogers, Q. U. Recorded 28 April 1835.

W, 399-401: Whereas Jesse Fincher, late of the District of Union, did by his will bequeath to his wife Ann Fincher, all that tract on the north side of Tyger River during her life or widowhood & at her death or marriage, one half of the said tract to be equally divided between John Fincher & Sarah Malone and the heirs of their bodies, and said William Malone and Sarah his wife is willing to sell the one fourth of the said tract or all the right, title and interest that they may have in the same, now William Malone & Sarah Malone for $500 to Ann Fincher, one fourth part of tract on north side of Tyger River, the whole of said tract containing 490 acres, 13 Jan 1835. William Malone (Seal), Sarah Malone (X) (Seal), Wit: Joseph Goswick, Levi G. Danner. Proved by the oath of Joseph Goswick 21 Jan 1835 before John Norman, Q.U. Sarah Malone (X), wife of William Malone, relinquished dower 21 Jan 1835 before Jno Norman, Q.U.

W, 401-402: South Carolina, Union District. E. M. Bobo and Z. Hooker for $10 to Sarah Porter of Union District, all our right, title, and interest in a tract on the south side of the Pinckney Road on the north fork of Browns Creek, 30 acres, being the land whereon the said Sarah Porter now lives adj. said Sarah Porter, Robert Savage, being the land conveyed by Fleming Harris to said Sarah, 1 May 1835. Z. Hooker (LS), E. M. Bobo (LS), Wit: J. Rogers, Lewallen Gladden. Proved by the oath of John Rogers, 17 May 1835 before Wm. Mitchell, J.P. Recorded 27 May 1835.

W, 402-403: Thomas Woodson & James Hogarth of Union District for $170 to Robert Macbeth of same, all our right, title in a tract belonging to the estate of Thomson Browning decd on Sugar Creek, waters of Fairforest adj. Elisabeth Murrell, Alexander Hay, Hiram Gibbs, Wm. R. Wilbourn, Churchill Gibbs, Monroe Robinson, 20 Feb 1835. Thomas Woodson (LS), James Hogarth (LS), Wit: Robt J. Gage, G. S. Noland. Proved by the oath of R. J. Gage 6 April 1853 before John Norman, J.Q. Clary Woodson (X), wife of Thomas Woodson relinquished dower 6 April 1835 before Jno Norman, Q.U. Huldah Hogarth (X), wife of James Hogarth relinquished dower 5 April 1835 before Jno Norman, Q.U. Recorded 20 April 1835.

W, 403-404: South Carolina, Union District. James N. Hardy of district aforesaid for $400 to Stith Hardy of same, tract on waters of Cane Creek between Broad and Tyger Rivers, part of two tracts originally granted to James Hawkins 1 Aug 1785, a part being conveyed from John Hawkins to Edward McGraw and from Edward McGraw to Dr. James Meacham and from Jas Meacham to Peter & J. C. Tucker, the other part conveyed from said James Hawkins to John Hawkins by the will of James Hawkins and conveyed from John Hawkins to Geo Lucas and from Lucas to James Meacham, and from Jas Meacham to Peter & J. C. Tucker, 100 acres adj. Ashley, John Jennings, 4 Nov 1833. James N. Hardy, Wit: John Jennings, P. K. Jennings. Proved by the oath of John Jennings 4 Nov 1833 before E. McGraw, Q.U. Recorded 29 May 1835.

W, 404-405: South Carolina, Union District. John Boyd Jr. of district aforesaid for $13 to Edward McGraw of same, 25 acres of land that my father purchased of John Boyd Senr which title now made to me by consent of the contracting parties, part of a tract formerly belonging to John Boyd Senr known by the name of the ___ tract that was in a grant to said McGraw, 29 Nov 1834. John Boyd (X) (LS), Wit: W. N. McGraw, Gideon McGraw. Proved by the oath of W. N. McGraw 6 May 1835 before Reuben Gilliam, J. Q. Recorded 29 May 1835.

W, 405-406: Mary Lee of Union District for and in consideration of blood & of my natural love and affection for my beloved daughter Sarah Ann M. Lee of same, all my right, title, and interest in two negroes, a negro boy named James & a negro girl named Milly, 21 April 1835. Mary Lee (X) (LS), Wit: William Walker, Green F.Lee, Harriett C. Lee. Acknowledged by Mary Lee 21 April 1835 before Fredk Jackson, J.P. Proved by the oath of William Walker 21 April 1835 before Fredk Jackson, J.P.

W, 406: South Carolina, Union District. J. A. Stephenson of Union District for $375 to Levi Davis, tract now deeded to me by William Stripling, 150 acres adj. Aron Davis, Saml Smith, Jordan Bailey, 11 Nov 1834. Jas A. Stephenson (LS), Wit: L. Whitlock, F. W. Spears. Proved by the oath of F. W. Spears 20 May 1835 before Isaac Going, Q.U. Recorded 1 June 1835.

W, 406-407: South Carolina, Union District. Nathaniel Rogers of said district for love, good will & affection to my grandson John Rogers, son of John Rogers, one third part of my tract of land whereon I now live, being the first deeded to my grandson John Rogers, 100 acres, 22 Feb 1830. Nathaniel Rogers (mark), Wit: James Greer, Mary Rogers. Proved by the oath of James Greer 1 June 1835 before J. Rogers, Q.U. Recorded 1 June 1835.

W, 407-408: South Carolina, Union District. Nathaniel Rogers of said district for love, good will & affection to my grandson Jeremiah Rogers, son of Elijah Rogers, one third part of my tract of land whereon I now live, being the second deeded to my grandson John Rogers, 100 acres, 22 Feb 1830. Nathaniel Rogers (mark), Wit: James Greer, J. F. Crosley. Proved by the oath of James Greer 31 May 1835 before J. Rogers, Q.U. Recorded 30 May 1835.

W, 408: Giles Sharp of Union District for $36.95 to Absalom Ivey of same, tract on waters of Browns Creek, 7.39 acres adj. said Ivey, 30 May 1835. Giles Sharp (LS), Wit: John Gage Jr., J. Rogers Proved by the oath of John Gage Jr. 30 May 1835 before J. Rogers, Q.U. Recorded 30 May 1835.

W, 409-410: James M. Whitton [Whitlow?] of Union District for $2000 to Ambros Ray, 500 acres on waters of Tyger adj. Jesse Whitmire, Col. Robt Martin, Thomas Brandon, Mary Bobo, Jas Dunn, Bailey Lawson, Delilah Jackson, Ambros Gibbs, 22 Dec 1834. James M. Whitton (Seal), Wit: William Ray Jr., Thos Ray, John Gibbs. Proved by the oath of John Gibbs 9 Jan 1835 before Jno Norman, Q.U. Sarah M. Whitton, wife of James M. Whitton, relinquished dower 8 Jan 1835 before Jno Norman, Q.U. Recorded 29 May 1835.

W, 410-411: South Carolina, Union District. John T. Murrell of district aforesaid for $2500 to Clough S. Meng of same, three lots in Union Village, numbers 49, 63, and 77 on Union Street adj. Z. P. Herndon, the race paths, Bachelor Street, 24 Dec 1834. John T. Murrell (Seal), Wit: R. W. Saunders, Wm. T. Roberts. Sarah F. B. Murrell, wife of John T. Murrell, relinquished dower 27 Dec 1834 before Jno Norman, Q.U. Proved by the oath of Wm. T. Roberts 3 June 1835 before J. Rogers, Q. U. Recorded 3 June 1835.

W, 411-412: South Carolina, Union District. Thomas Sartor of Union District for $2000 to Daniel Coleman of Union District, tract of land except one acre which is reserved as a burying ground, on the fish dam Creek, 270 acres adj. Thomas Bowker, Sytha Bowles, 1 Feb 1826. Thomas Sartor (Seal), Wit: Daniel Thomas, Farr Bates, Richd Thomson. Proved by the oath of Richd Thomson 6 Feb 1826 before G. Gregory, J.P. Ann Sartor, wife of Thomas Sartor, relinquished dower 2 Feb 1835 before Reuben Gilliam, J. Q. Recorded 13 March 1835.

W, 412-413: James Glenn of Union District for $132.75 to Daniel Coleman of same, all my right to the claim and interest which I may have to a tract of land on the west side of Broad River originally belonging to James Glenn Senr now deceased by the will of said James Glenn Senr he lends the said tract to his wife Elisabeth Glenn during her life and at her death to be equally divided amongst his children and on the 18 October 1837 the said Elisabeth Glenn relinquished all her right and title to the said land to the heirs of the said James Glenn Senr decd and by their consent was sold 3 January 1831 and purchased by the said Daniel Coleman, said tract containing 150 acres adj. lands of Thomas Bowker and others, 7 May 1831. James Glenn (LS), Wit: C.T. Scaife, John S. Sims. Proved by the oath of Charner T. Scaife 20 Sept 1831 before James Meacham, J. Q. Recorded 13 March 1835.

W, 413-415: John F. Glenn of Union District for $44.25 to Daniel Coleman of same, all my right, title and claim to a tract on the west side of Broad River originally belonging to James Glenn Senr decd [see preceding deed], 7 May 1831. Jno F. Glenn (LS), Wit: C. T. Scaife, John A. Willey. Proved by the oath of Charner T. Scaife 20 Sept 1831 before James Meacham, J. Q. Jane S. C. Glenn, wife of John F. Glenn, relinquished dower 9 Aug 1833 before James Meacham, J. Q. Recorded 13 March 1835.

W, 415-416: Gideon N. Carlisle of Sumter District for $31.67 to Daniel Coleman of Union District, all my right, title, interest in a tract on the west side of Broad River originally belonging to James Glenn Senr now deceased [see preceding deed], 18 Feb 1832. Gideon N. Carlisle (LS), Wit: C. T. Scaife, John T. Hill. Proved by the oath of Charner T. Scaife 18 Sept 1831 before James Meacham, J. Q. Recorded 13 March 1835.

W, 416-417: James B. Glenn of Union District for $44.25 to Daniel Coleman of same, all my right, title, interest in a tract on the west side of Broad River originally belonging to James Glenn Senr now deceased [see preceding deed], 7 May 1831. J. B. Glenn (LS), Wit: C. T. Scaife, John A. Willey. Proved by the oath of Charner T. Scaife 20 Sept 1831 before James Meacham, J. Q. Recorded 13 March 1835.

W, 417-418: Thomas A. Carlisle of Union District for $142.42 to Daniel Coleman of same, all my right, title, interest in a tract on the west side of Broad River originally belonging to James Glenn Senr now deceased [see preceding deeds], 7 May 1831. Thomas A. Carlisle (LS), Wit: C. T. Scaife, John S. Sims. Proved by the oath of Charner T. Scaife 20 Sept 1831 before James Meacham, J.Q. Kitty F. P. Carlisle, wife of Thomas A. Carlisle, relinquished dower 20 Sept 1831 before James Meacham, J.Q. Recorded 13 March 1835.

W, 418-419: James Hill & Susan Hill his wife of Union District for $132.75 to Daniel Coleman of same, all our right, title, interest in a tract on the west side of Broad River originally belonging to James Glenn Senr now deceased [see preceding deeds], 7 May 1831. James Hill (LS), Susannah Hill (LS), Wit: C. T. Scaife, G. Roseman. Proved by the oath of Charner T. Scaife 20 Sept 1831 before James Meacham, J.Q. Susanna Hill, wife of James Hill, relinquished dower 14 Aug 1833 before James Meacham, J.Q. Recorded 13 March 1835.

W, 420: John Bankhead of Union District for $146 to Daniel Coleman of Union District, tract on Broad River adj. Mrs. Sytha Bowles, Capt. Thomas Bowker, John F. Glenn, 140 acres, part of the real estate of James Glenn Senr decd, 16 June 1834. John Bankhead (LS), Wit: Thos N. Glenn, Edward Mayes. Proved by the oath of Thomas A. Glenn 16 June 1834. Recorded 13 March 1835.

W, 420-421: South Carolina, Union District. Geo Fant for $175 to Nathan Coleman of said district, 140 acres, part of a tract deeded by William Turpin Jr. to the said George Fant, 3 Oct 1829. George Fant (Seal), Wit: Tho Linam, Thos Stribling, N. Glenn. Elisabeth Fant (mark), wife of George Fant, relinquished dower 25 Feb 1835 before Reuben Gilliam, J. Q. Proved by the oath of Nathan Glenn 10 March 1835 before Reuben Gilliam, J. Q. Recorded 1 June 1835.

W, 421-422: James Jackson of Union District for $445 to Hobson Thomson of same, tract on Rocky Creek, 147½ acres in two separate tracts adj. said Hobson Thomson, estate of Benjamin Saunders decd, John Fincher or Gibson, Joseph Greer, Job Hammond, B. G. Davis, reference to the deed of Rolly Horton and Thomas Howard, 13 Jan 1835. James Jackson (LS), Wit: J. Rogers, Christopher Steen. Proved by the oath of Christopher Steen 13 Jan 1835 before J. Rogers, Q. U. Recorded 13 Jan 1835.

W, 422-423: South Carolina, Union District. Thomas Black Senr of district aforesaid for $400 to Robt G. Davidson & John G. Davidson of same, tract on the north side of Thickety & Gilkeys Creeks, waters of Broad River, on Howeys line, 150 acres, 8 Jan 1835. Thos Black (LS), Wit: Saml J. Hoey, J. W. Davis. Proved by the oath of Sam. J. Hoey 12 Jan 1835 before John Carothers, Q.U. Recorded 16 March 1835.

W, 423-424: South Carolina, Union District. Jesse Briggs & Mary An Briggs of district aforesaid for $74.44 to Reuben S. Rice of same, all our right and title in a tract in Union & Laurens Districts on both sides of Enoree River adj. Eli Odle, Thomas Hendricks, Horace Lee, Jeremiah Phillips, William Presley, Geo Hogan, part of the real estate of Bernard Glenn decd, and our portion of the same being the one eighth of the one seventh part, 24 Oct 1834. Jesse Briggs (LS), Mary A. Briggs (LS), Wit: B. H. Rice, John N. Herndon. Proved by the oath of B. H. Rice 11 March 1835 before J. Rogers, Q. U. Recorded 11 March 1835.

W, 424-425: South Carolina, Union District. Nathan Glenn and Permelia Glenn for $84.46 to Reuben S. Rice of same, all our right and title in a tract in Union & Laurens Districts on both sides of Enoree River adj. Eli Odle, Thomas Hendricks, Horace Lee, Jeremiah Phillips, William Presley, Geo Hogan, part of the real estate of Bernard Glenn decd, and our portion of the same being the one eighth and the one tenth of two sevenths parts, 16 Aug 1834. Jesse Briggs (LS), Mary A. Briggs (LS), Wit: T. A. Carlisle, W. W.

Glenn. Proved by the oath of T. A. Carlisle 11 March 1835 before J. Rogers, Q. U. Recorded 11 March 1835.

W, 425-426: South Carolina, Union District. Mary Coleman of Union District for $51.70 to Reuben S. Rice of same, a tract in Union & Lawrence Districts, adj. Eli Odle, Thomas Hendricks, Horace Lee, Jeremiah Phillips, William Presley, Geo Hogan, part of the real estate of Bernard Glenn decd, 13 Aug 1834. Mary Coleman (LS), Wit: N. Glenn, Daniel Coleman. Proved by the oath of Daniel Coleman 14 Aug 1834 before James Meacham, Q.U. Recorded 11 March 1835.

W, 426-427: South Carolina, Union District. Nathan Coleman of Union District for $51.67 to Reuben S. Rice of same, all the right, title and interest that John Crosby & Elisabeth Crosby his wife have in a tract in Union & Laurence Districts, adj. Eli Odle, Thomas Hendricks, Horace Lee, Jeremiah Phillips, Wm Presley, Geo Hogan, part of the real estate of Bernard Glenn decd, and the part of John Crosby & Elisabeth his wife being the one eleventh of the one seventh part, 13 Aug 1834. Nathan Coleman (LS), Wit: A. T. Park, James Meacham. Proved by the oath of Amasa T. Park 12 [*sic*] Aug 1834 before James Meacham, Q.U. Recorded 11 March 1835.

W, 427-428: South Carolina, Union District. John Triplet and Patience Triplet his wife of Chester District for $51.70 to Reuben S. Rice of Union District, all our right and title in a tract in Union & Laurens Districts on both sides of Enoree River adj. Eli Odle, Thomas Hendricks, Horace Lee, Jeremiah Phillips, William Presley, Geo Hogan, part of the real estate of Bernard Glenn decd, and our portion of the same being the one eleventh of one seventh part, 12 Aug 1834. John Triplett (LS), Patience Triplett (LS), Wit: Thomson Johnson, Richard Wood. Proved by the oath of Thompson Johnson 12 Aug 1834 before Wm. Wood, Q. U. Recorded 11 March 1835.

W, 428-429: South Carolina, Union District. William W. Glenn of district aforesaid for $46.96 to Reuben S. Rice of same, all the right interest and title that I have in a tract in Union & Lawrence Districts, adj. Eli Odle, Thomas Hendricks, Horace Lee, Jeremiah Phillips, William Presley, Geo Hogan, part of the real estate of Bernard Glenn decd, my portion being one eighth of one seventh part, 13 Aug 1834. Wm. W. Glenn (LS), Wit: T. A. Carlisle, John Hawkins. Proved by the oath of T. A. Carlisle 13 Aug 1834 before Stephen Johnson, J.P. Recorded 11 March 1835.

W, 429: South Carolina, Union District. William W. Glenn of district aforesaid for $46.96 to Reuben S. Rice of same, all the right interest and title that Lucy Ivey may have in a tract in Union & Lawrence Districts, adj. Eli Odle, Thomas Hendricks, Horace Lee, Jeremiah Phillips, William Presley, Geo Hogan, part of the real estate of Bernard Glenn decd, her portion being one eighth of one seventh part, 13 Aug 1834. Wm. W. Glenn (LS), Wit: T. A. Carlisle, John Hawkins. Proved by the oath of T. A. Carlisle 13 Aug 1834 before Stephen Johnson, J.P. Recorded 11 March 1835.

W, 430: James Morrow of Union District to Obadiah Tate, for $300 tract of 107 acres (except nineteen acres Wm. Phillips claims & that I warrant from me), 88 acres, 9 Dec 1833. James Morrow. Wit: Stephen Pearson ,James Tate. Proved by the oath of Stephen Pearson 30 June 1835 before Wm Goudelock, J.P. Recorded 6 July 1835.

W, 430-431: South Carolina, Union District. James B. Fant of district aforesid for $400 to Geo Fant of same, 100 acres on a branch of Tyger River, part of a tract that was formerly sold by orer of court as the property of the heirs of Love Fant decd and the said Geo Fant was purchaser & by said Geo Fatn sold to said James B. Fant, 20 Dec 1834. J. B. Fant, Wit: John P. Duncan, THos C. Crooks, James D. S. Kain. Proved by the oath of Thomas C. Crooks 25 Feb 1835 before Reuben Gilliam, J. Q. Elisabeth Fant, wife of James B. Fant, relinquished dower 11 March 1835 before Reuben Gilliam, J.Q. Recorded 15 March 1835.

W, 431-432: South Carolina, Union District. John F. Glenn & Jane Glenn his wife for $260 to Reuben S. Rice of same, all our right, title and interest in a tract in Union & Laurens Districts, adj. Eli Odle, Thomas Hendricks, Horace Lee, Jeremiah Phillips, William Presley, Geo Hogan, part of the real estate of Bernard Glenn decd, John F. Glenn's portion being one third of one seventh part and Jane Glenn his wife's part being the one eight part of the one seventh, 31 July 1834. John F. Glenn (LS), Jane F. C. Glenn (LS) Wit: Amasa T. Park, John Johns. Proved by the oath of Amasa T. Park 31 July 1834 before James Meacham, J.Q. Recorded 11 March 1835.

W, 433: John B. Glenn & Patsey Glenn his wife of Spartanburgh District for $80 to Reuben S. Rice of Union District, all our right of one seventh of a tract in on both sides Enoree River, by late survey 1500 acres, adj. Eli Odle, Thomas Hendricks, Horace Lee, Jeremiah Phillips, William Presley, Geo Hogan, 4 Aug 1834. John B. Glenn (LS), Patsey Glenn (LS) Wit: Jno K. B. Sims, Saml Shelton. Proved by the oath of Jno K. B. Sims 4 Aug 1834 before James Meacham, J.Q. Recorded 11 March 1835.

W, 433-434: Augustin Shands and Sarah C. Shands his wife of Spartanburgh District for $71 to Reuben S. Rice of Union District, all our right, title and interest in a tract on both sides Enoree River in Union & Laurens Districts, adj. Eli Odle, Thomas Hendricks, Horace Lee, Jeremiah Phillips, William Presley, Geo Hogan, part of the real estate of Capt. Bernard Glenn decd, ______ 1834. Augustin Shands (LS), Sarah C. Shands (LS) Wit: Jno K. B. Sims, John B. Glenn. Proved by the oath of Jno K. B. Sims 4 Aug 1834 before James Meacham, J.Q. Recorded 11 March 1835.

W, 434-435: South Carolina, Union District. Nathan Coleman of district aforesaid for $51 to Reuben S. Rice of same, all my right, title and interest in a tract in Union & Laurens Districts, adj. Eli Odle, Thomas Hendricks, Horace Lee, Jeremiah Phillips, William Presley, George Hogan, part of the real estate of Bernard Glenn decd, my portion being one eleventh part of one seventh part, ____ Aug 1834. Nathan Coleman (LS), Wit: Joshua Darnal, Amasa T. Park. Proved by the oath of Dr. Amasa T. Park 2 Aug 1834 before James Meacham, J.Q. Recorded 11 March 1835.

W, 435-436: South Carolina, Union District. John Johns & Mary B. Johns his wife of district aforesaid for $89.48 to Reuben S. Rice of same, all our right, title and interest in a tract in Union & Laurens Districts, adj. Eli Odle, Thomas Hendricks, Horace Lee, Jeremiah Phillips, William Presley, Geo Hogan, part of the real estate of Bernard Glenn decd, our portion being one third part of one seventh part, 31 July 1834. John Johns (LS), Mary B. Johns (LS), Wit: Amasa T. Park, John F. Glenn. Proved by the oath of Amasa T. Park 31 July 1834 before James Meacham, J.Q. Recorded 11 March 1835.

W, 436-437: South Carolina, Union District. Mason Crosby of Union District for $51.70 to Reuben S. Rice of same, all my right, title and interest in a tract in Union & Laurence Districts, adj. Eli Odle, Thomas Hendricks, Horace Lee, Jeremiah Phillips, William Presley, Geo Hogan, part of the real estate of Bernard Glenn decd, ___ Aug 1834. Mason Crosby (LS), Wit: Richard Crosby, Ferdinand A. McAshan. Proved by the oath of Ferdinand H. McAshan 13 Aug 1834 before James Meacham, J.Q. Recorded 11 March 1835.

W, 437-438: James B. Glenn for $189.58 to Reuben S. Rice, all my right in a tract in on both sides Enoree River, by late survey 1500 acres, adj. Eli Odle, Thomas Hendricks, Horace Lee, Jeremiah Phillips, William Presley, George Hogan, being one third part of one seventh part, 4 Aug 1834. James B. Glenn (LS), Wit: J. E. Ellis, Clinton Wilson. Proved by the oath of James E. Ellis 4 Aug 1834 before James Meacham, J.Q. Recorded 11 March 1835.

W, 438-439: South Carolina, Union District. Thomas A. Glenn of district aforesaid for $71 to Reuben S. Rice of same, all my right, title and interest in a tract in Union & Laurence Districts, adj. Eli Odle, Thomas Hendricks, Horace Lee, Jeremiah Phillips, William Presley, and Hogan, my part of the real estate of Bernard Glenn decd, being one eighth part of the one seventh, 17 Jan 1834. T. A. Glenn (LS), Wit: John T. Hill, A. W. Dubois. Proved by the oath of John T. Hill 17 Jan 1834 before James Meacham, J.Q. Recorded 11 March 1835.

W, 439-440: South Carolina, Union District. Thomas Bowler of district aforesaid for $142 to Reuben S. Rice of same, all my right, title and interest in a tract in Union & Laurence Districts, adj. Eli Odle, Thomas Hendricks, Horace Lee, Jeremiah Phillips, William Presley, Geo. Hogan, part of the real estate of Bernard Glenn decd, my part being one fourth of one seventh, 4 Aug 1834. Thomas Bowker (LS), Wit: J. B. Glenn, J. E. Ellis. Proved by the oath of J. B. Glenn 4 Aug 1834 before James Meacham, J.Q. Recorded 11 March 1835.

W, 440: South Carolina, Union District. Daniel Coleman of district aforesaid for $51.70 to Reuben S. Rice of same, all my right, title and interest in a tract in Union & Laurence Districts, adj. Eli Odle, Thomas Hendricks, Horace Lee, Jeremiah Phillips, William Presley, Geo. Hogan, part of the real estate of Bernard Glenn decd, my part being one eleventh of one seventh, 14 Aug 1834. Daniel Coleman (LS), Wit: A. T. Park, James Meacham. Proved by the oath of Dr. A. T. Park 14 Aug 1834 before James Meacham, J.Q. Recorded 11 March 1835.

W, 441: South Carolina, Union District. Margaret Lee of district aforesaid for $280 to Mary Lee, one negro boy named Dave, 28 Jan 1835. Margarett Lee (X) (LS), Wit: Mathias Myers, Wm. Bailey. Proved by the oath of William Baley 14 July 1835 before Fredk Jackson, J.P. Recorded 15 July 1835.

W, 441: South Carolina, Union District. Margaret Lee of district aforesaid for $400 to Levina Lee, one negro boy named Adam, 28 Jan 1835. Margarett Lee (X) (LS), Wit: Mathias Myers, Wm. Bailey. Proved by the oath of William Baley 14 July 1835 before Fredk Jackson, J.P. Recorded 15 July 1835.

W, 442: South Carolina, Union District. Margaret Lee of district aforesaid for $500 to John Lee, one negro woman named Lucey, 28 Jan 1835. Margarett Lee (X) (LS), Wit: Mathias Myers, Wm. Bailey. Proved by the oath of William Baley 14 July 1835 before Fredk Jackson, J.P. Recorded 15 July 1835.

W, 442-444: Territory of Florida, Gadsden County. William Wright and Mary Wright, both of county and territory aforesaid, for $142 to Reuben Rice, all our interest in a tract, late the property of Bernard Glenn decd, in Union and Laurence Districts, adj. Eli Odle, Thomas Hendricks, Horace Lee, Jeremiah Phillips, William Presley, George Hogan, part of the real estate of Bernard Glenn decd, 25 Sept 1833. William Wright (LS), Mary Wright (LS), Wit: J. M. Gilchrist, B. Meacham. Proved in Gadsden County, Florida, by the oath of Banks Meacham before D. L. Kenan, J.P. Mary Wright, wife of William Wright, relinquished dower 15 Nov 1833 before B. Meacham, J. P. Robert Lester, clerk of the county court, certified that D. L. Kenan and Banks Meacham were justices of the peace, 10 Dec 1833. Jas McBride, Judge of the County Court, certified that Robt C. Leslie was clerk of court, 31 Dec 1833. Recorded 11 March 1835.

W, 444-446: Territory of Florida, Gadsden County. Ann Bowker of county and territory aforesaid, for $142 to Reuben Rice, all my interest in a tract, late the property of Bernard Glenn decd, in Union and Laurence Districts, adj. Eli Odle, Thomas Hendricks, Horace Lee, Jeremiah Phillips, William Presley, George Hogan, part of the real estate of Bernard Glenn decd, 21 Oct 1833. Ann Bowker (LS), Wit: S. T. Houston, Owen Fillyou Jr. Proved in Gadsden County, Florida, by the oath of S. T. Houston before B. Meacham, J.P. Robert Lester, clerk of the county court, certified that D. L. Kenan and Banks Meacham were justices of the peace, 10 Dec 1833. Jas McBride, Judge of the County Court, certified that Robt C. Leslie was clerk of court, 31 Dec 1833. Recorded 11 March 1835.

W, 446-447: Territory of Florida, Gadsden County. Banks Meacham and Sarah Meacham his wife, both of county and territory aforesaid, for $142 to Reuben Rice, all my interest in a tract, late the property of Bernard Glenn decd, in Union and Laurence Districts, adj. Eli Odle, Thomas Hendricks, Horace Lee, Jeremiah Phillips, William Presley, George Hogan, part of the real estate of Bernard Glenn decd, 21 Oct 1833. Ann Bowker (LS), Wit: S. T. Houston, Owen Fillyou Jr. Proved in Gadsden County, Florida, by the oath of S. T. Houston before John C. Love, J.P. Sarah Meacham, wife of Banks Meacham, relinquished dower 6 Dec 1833 before D. L. Kenan, J.P. Robert Lester, clerk of the county court, certified that D. L. Kenan was a justice of the peace, 10 Dec 1833. Jas McBride, Judge of the County Court, certified that Robt C. Leslie was clerk of court, 31 Dec 1833. Recorded 11 March 1835.

W, 447-448: South Carolina, Union District. E. Bobo of Union District for $160 to John St. Clair Senr of same, tract on waters of Browns Creek, being the place whereon John Jolly Sr. formerly lived adj. estate of Jas Meng, Absalom Ivey, Charner Adams decd, and a small moiety of land which Drury Walls lives upon, 70 acres, 1 June 1835. E. M. Bobo (LS), Wit: J. W. Meng, D. Wallace. Elisabeth Bobo, wife of E. M. Bobo, relinquished dower 21 July 1835 before J. Rogers, Q.U. Proved by the oath of J. W. Meng 23 July 1835 before J. Rogers, Q.U. Recorded 12 July 1835.

W, 449: South Carolina, Union District. Thomas Peterson of district aforesaid appoints Abram J. Smith of same, lawful attorney to receive from the ordinary of Union District my distributive share of the real estate of my father Peter Peterson decd & pay over to Aron Wilkins & John Phillips exrs of Peter Peterson decd, what my share of the personal estate should lack in paying my debts due the estate, and due Aron & also one note due to Charles Patrick, 15 Nov 1834. Thos Peterson (X) (LS), Wit: Aron Wilkins, Peter Mulinax. Proved by the oath of Capt. Aron Wilkins 6 July 1835 before J. Rogers, Q.U. Recorded 6 July 1835.

W, 449-450: South Carolina, Union District. Spencer A. Bobo of district aforesaid for $486.50 to Asa Dodd of same, 139 acres on Bills Creek, waters of Enoree River adj. Edward Stevens, Thos. G. Danner, per plat by Wm. White 20 Jan 1825, dated 12 June 1834. Spencer A. Bobo (LS), Wit: T. J. Hughes, John Bates. Louisa S. Bobo, wife of Spencer A. Bobo, relinquished dower 2 Feb 1835 before Jno Norman, J. Q. Proved by the oath of T. J. Hughes 10 Oct 1834 before Jno Norman, Q.U. Recorded 6 July 1835.

W, 450-451: South Carolina, Union District. John Parker of district aforesaid for $650 to Gordon Moore of York District, tract whereon I now live in Union District on Abingtons Creek, waters of Broad River adj. Joseph Guyton, 21 Feb 1835. John Parker (LS), Wit: John Moore, A. J. Guyton. Elisabeth Parker (X), wife of John Parker, relinquished dower 3 March 1835 before John Carothers. Proved by the oath of John Moore 28 Feb 1835 before John Carothers, Q.U. Recorded 10 March 1835.

W, 452: South Carolina, Union District. Jepthah Harrington of aforesaid district for $94 to Saml A. Goodman of same, tract between Thickety and Guilkeys Creek, 8.6 acres, part of a tract granted to J. McNitt Alexandria [*sic*, for Alexander], 10 Nov 1834. Jepthah Harrington (LS), Wit: Wm. H. Steen, Wm. D. Robertson. Nancy Harrington, wife of Jepthah Harrington, relinquished dower 11 Nov 1834 before John Carothers, Q.U. Proved by the oath of Wm. D. Robertson 19 Nov 1834 before J. Rogers, Q.U. Recorded 10 March 1835.

W, 453 & 455: John Steen of District of Union for $606.80 to Samuel A. Goodmam of same, tract on waters of Thickety and Guilkies Creeks, waters of Broad River, 151.7 acres, part of 400 acres granted to John Steen 15 Oct 1784 and from John Steen descended to the present grantor, adj. John Jeffries Sr., Drury Harrington, John Littlejohn & William Jeffries, 15 Nov 1834. John Steen (LS), Wit: Wm. H. Steen, Richd Thomson. Proved by the oath of Richard Thomson 10 March 1835 before James Rowntree, J.P. Margaret Steen (X), wife of John Steen, relinquished dower 19 Nov 1834 before John Carothers, Q.U. Recorded 10 March 1835.

W, 454: South Carolina, Union District. Hancock Porter (X) acknowledged himself guardian for Isaac Salmon, a free negro, 17 Sept 1835 before J. Rogers, Clk. Recorded 17 Sept 1835.

W, 455: South Carolina, Union District. Jepthah Harrington of aforesaid district for $300 to Nathaniel Jeffries of same, tract between Thickety and Gilkeys Creek, 90 acres, adj. Alexander, 19 Dec 1834. Jepthah Harrington (LS), Wit: Saml A. Goodman, Wm. H. Steen. Proved by the oath of Saml. A. Goodman 19 Jan 1835 before John Carothers, Q.U. Nancy Harrington, wife of Jepthah Harrington, relinquished dower 19 Jan 1835 before John Carothers, Q.U. Recorded 10 March 1835.

W, 456: This agreement in partition made and agreed to 31 March 1834 betwixt Robt Moorehead for his decd wife Cynthia, John Stone for his wife Melinda and John S. Hamilton for his wife Mary, the heirs at law of John Martin decd, and Mary Martin, admx., sheweth that we do agree and bind ourselves to abide the division of the real estate of said decd. Robt Moorhead (LS), John Stone (LS), J. T. Hamilton (LS), Mary Martin (LS), Wit: R. Lusk, W. C. Brown. Proved by the oath of Robt Lusk 22 May 1835 before Saml A. Goodman, Q. U. Recorded 6 July 1835.

W, 457: Jane Boyd of Union District for love and affection for my daughter Nancy Keisler, a female negro child named Jane, 20 Feb 1830. Jane Boyd (mark) (LS), Wit: John O. Tate, Jos A. McJunkin, Benj McJunkin. Proved by the oath of Benj. McJunkin 14 May 1830 before J. T. McJunkin, J.P. Recorded 5 Aug 1835.

W, 457-458: Bartholomew Johnson, Sheriff of Union District, by virtue of several writs of Fieri facias from the court of common pleas tested 28 March

1831 at the suit of D. A. Mitchell & others to levy of the goods and chattels, lands & tenements of Joseph Mulligan $25.82, sells tract of 107 acres adj. Leonard Baker, James Jeter Senr, Nathan Cooper, estate of Nicholas Skein, purchased by Daniel Thomas of Union District for $51, 29 Dec 1831. Bartholomew Johnson (LS), Wit: B. M Pearson, J. S. Rogers. Proved by the oath of Bird M. Pearson 8 March 1835 before D. Wallace, Q.U. Recorded 21 May 1835.

W, 458-460: Thomas Hyatt of Union District for $500 to John Galman of same, tract on north side of Rocky Creek, a water course of Fair Forrest, 125 acres where the Union Road leading to Spartanburgh crosses said creek, 12 Jan 1835. Thomas Hyatt (X), Wit: Aron McCollum, Thomas Scott. Martha Hyatt (X), wife of Thomas Hyatt, relinquished dower 20 Jan 1835 before Daniel White, Q.U. Proved by the oath of Aron McCollum 17 Jan 1835 before Daniel White, Q. U. Recorded 10 March 1835.

W, 460-461: John Johns & Mary B. Johns his wife of Chester District for $45.25 to Daniel Coleman, all our right, title, claim or interest in a tract on the west side of Broad River originally belonging to James Glenn Senr now decd, and by the will of said James Glenn Senr he lends the said tract to his wife Elisabeth Glenn and at her death to be equally divided amongst his children, and ont he 18 October 1827 the said Elizabeth Glenn relinquished all her right to said land to the heirs of said James Glenn Senr, decd, and by their consent was sold 3 Jan 1831 and purchased by said Daniel Coleman, 150 acres, adj. Thomas Bowker, 21 May 1830. John Johns (LS), Mary B. Johns (LS), Wit: Nathan Coleman, G. Roseman. Mary B. Johns, wife of John Johns, relinquished dower 4 July 1835 before Reuben Gilliam, J. Q. Proved by the oath of Nathan Coleman 5 Dec 1831 before T. A. Glenn, J.P. Recorded 6 July 1835.

W, 461-462: South Carolina, Union District. Mary Howard of district above mentioned for love and affection to my daughter Sally Nix, do give in trust to her for her support and assistance in rearing her six small children, one negro girl named Hetty and a negro boy Milton about four years of age, 18 Sept 1835. Mary Howard (X) (Seal), Wit: J. J. Pratt, P. P. Taylor. Proved by the oath of J. J. Pratt 18 Sept 1835 before J. Rogers, Q. U. Recoreed 18 Sept 1835.

W, 462-463: John Powers of Union District for $1000 to Joshua Palmer of same, tract on waters of Hughes Creek adj. Savage, J. Palmer, John Powers, Mrs. Bird, 246 acres, 20 Oct 1834. John Powers (Seal), Wit: Z. Reid, James Bailey, P. Palmer. Lettice Powers, wife of John Powers, relinquished dower 25 Oct 1834 before Isaac Going, Q.U. Proved by the oath of Z. Reid 25 Oct 1834 before Isaac Going, Q.U. Recorded 19 Sept 1835.

W, 463-464: South Carolina, Union District. Starling Garner of district aforesaid for $325 to Henry Gault of same, tract on waters of Browns Creek, 100 acres on the Spartanburg road adj. Isaac White, 8 Dec 1834. Starling

Garner (LS), Wit: D. S. F. Gault, John Rountree. Proved by the oath of Daverson Gault 15 Dec 1834 before Daniel White, Q.U. Sarah Garner (X), wife of Starling Garner, relinquished dower 15 Dec 1834 before Daniel White, Q.U. Recorded 17 Sept 1835.

W, 464-465: Brigade Orders. Newberry C. H. May 10th 1835. The Commissioners of the Forty Regiment of the Tenth Brigade of the South Carolina Militia having made their report by which they have divided the said Regiment into two Battalions and each battalion into four beat companies... The Battalion line beginning at Fosters Mills on Fairforest, thence to Smith's store on Dutchmans Creek, thence to the mouth of James Creek, thence to Gideon Woodruff's on the Musgrove road, thence to Ben Rhode's Canoe landing on Enoree River.

Eastern Battalion. No. 1. McCarters beat company as follows, beginning at Fosters mill on Fairforest to E. P. Smith's store thence to the mouth of James Creek thence on Tiger River thence down said river to Davis's Bridge, thence to Mills Sumner's dec'd by Aaron Pruett's to Putman's meeting House, thence to the mouth of Rocky Creek on Fairforest, thence up the Forest to the beginning.

No. 2. Anchor beat or Yarborough's beginning at the mouth of James Creek, thence with the Battalion line to Rhode's canoe landing on Enoree, thence down said river to the mouth of Cedar Shoal Creek thence with the District line to Buncombe Road, to Anchor, thence with the burnt factory road to Hacker's Creek down the creek to Tiger River, thence up said creek to the beginning.

No. 3. Waters. Beginning at the mouth of Hackers Creek on Tiger thence with the line of Beat Company No. 2 to Enoree, the mouth of Cedar Shoal, thence down said river to Rice's mills, thence with the regimental line to Tiger river, thence up Tiger river to the beginning.

No. 4. McBeths. Beginning at the mouth of Rocky Creek on Fairforest, thence with the beat company No. 1 to Putman's meeting House thence by Aaron Pruett's to Davis's bridge on Tiger, thence down said river to the regimental line, thence to McBeth's up the forest to the beginning.

Western Battallion. No. 1. Hoys. Beginning at Rogers's bridge, Tiger, thence to the Brick House to Cottrell's on Enoree, down the river to the Battalion line, thence with the Battalion line to the mouth of James Creek on Tiger river, thence up said river to the beginning.

No. 2. Glenns. Beginning at Dr. Moore's, thence with the Regimental line to McDaniel's mills, thence down Fairforest to Foster's mill, thence with the Battalion line to Dutchman's Creek, thence up said creek to the Pinckney Ford on said Creek, thence burnt shop with Pinckney road, thence up

Blackstock take left hand by Widow Rogers's to Moore's to the Beginning Dr. Moore's.

No. 3. Woodruffs. Beginning at Price's, thence to Woodruff's thence with the Regimental line to Wofford's mill on Enoree, thence down said river to Richard Eitrols[?] thence to Crow's brick house,thence to Rogers's bridge Tiger, up said river to the fork, thence to Rice's ford the beginning.

No. 4. Woffords. Beginning at Dr. Moore's thence with the Regimental line to Prince's thence down said river to Rogers's bridge, thence to the mouth of James's Creek, thence with the Battalion line to Dutchman's Creek, thence up said creek with Beat No. 2 to the Beginning, Dr. Moore's. James J. Caldwell, Brigadier General 10 Brigade. 4th Division of the South Carolina Militia. Recorded 7 Sept 1835.

W, 465-466: South Carolina, Union District. Thomas Clary & Anna Clary his wife and Charlotte Dupree, Griffin Dupree (for himself & Drury Dupree & Jno Dupree), William D. Gault & james H. Alexander heirs by inheritance & by purchase to a tract of land the property of or belonging to the estate of John Dupree Senr decd, for $175 to Marshal Dupree of said district, tract whereon said John Dupree Senr decd formerly lived on Pacolet River in Union District adj. Wm. D. Gault, James H. Alexander, estate of Thomas C. Taylor, Danl McMahan & Josiah Foster, 130 acres, 31 Aug 1835. Thomas Clary (X) (LS), Anna Clary (X) (LS), Charity Dupree (LS), Griffin Dupree (LS), William Gault (LS), James H. Alexander (LS), Wit: T. G. Wylie, George Foster (X). Proved by the oath of George Foster 14 Sept 1835 before Isaac Going, Q. U. Judea Dupree (X), wife of Griffin Dupree, relinquished dower 14 Sept 1835 before Isaac Going, Q. U. Recorded 17 Sept 1835.

W, 466-467: John Comer of Union District for $149 to Robt Walker of same, tract on waters of Rocky Creek adj. Robert Walker, Thos Howard, Joseph Greer, Susannah Coomer, 67 acres, lately sold to Joseph Greer, 6 April 1835. John Coomer (X) (LS), Wit: J. Rogers, Joseph H. Dogan. Proved by the oath of John Rogers 3 June 1835 before D. Wallace, J.P. Lucy Coomer (X), wife of John Coomer, relinquished dower 7 Sept 1835 before J. Rogers, Q. U. Recorded 3 June 1835.

W, 467-468: South Carolina, Union District. Thomas Foster, Stiller, for $300 to Henry Gault, 70 acres adj. Baxter Mosely's and James Mosely's land, also transferred for John Foster, Stiller, to said Thomas Foster, to hold the said land to him the said Henry Gault, 5 Oct 1833. Thomas Foster (X) (LS), Wit: James Petty (X), D. S. F. Gault. Proved by the oath of Danison Gault 17 Sept 1835 before J. Rogers, Q.U. Recorded 17 Sept 1835.

W, 468-469: South Carolina, Union District. 2 Feb 1829, William K. Clowney, Esquire, Commissioner of the Court of Equity for Union District, to Joseph Mayes of same, whereas Henry Harvey Means, guardian of Mary W. Boyd, Jane H. Boyd & Louis C. Boyd, minor children of Benjanin Boyd decd, on or about 5 Jan did exhibit their bill of complaint against Sarah Boyd, shewing that Benjamin Boyd departed this life about ____ 1819 intestate, leaving a tract of land of 208 acres conveyed to Benjamin Boyd by James Park Senr, and that it is to the benefit and interest of all parties concerned that partition, division or sale of the above premises should take place, and said court did decree that said parcel should be sold at public auction, sold to said Joseph Mayes for $479, said tract adj. Col. Nathl Gist, John Wright, widow McBride, James Parks, plat number 2. Wm. K. Clowney, C. E. U. D. (LS), Wit: Saml Beaty, Saml Otterson Proved by the oath of Col. S. Beaty 28 Aug 1835 before J. Rogers, Q.U. Recorded 28 Aug 1835.

W, 470: South Carolina, Union District. Reuben S. Rice of district aforesaid for $400 to Nathaniel Ward, 100 acres on waters of Rockey Creek adj. Gallman, Rockey Creek, Samuel Ward, Stephen McCollum, John Lyles, 18 Aug 1835. R. S. Rice (LS), Wit: Thos Belue, J. H. Rountree. Proved by the oath of J. H. Rountree 23 Sept 1835 before Jno Norman, Q.U. Recoreed 23 Sept 1835.

W, 470-472: South Carolina, Union District. This agreement of three parties made 22 July 1834, by and between Jared Young of the first part, and Nancy holder of the second part, and Deastin Holder of the third part, whereas a marriage is intended to be had between the said Jared Young and Nancy Holder, and said Nancy Holder is possessed of personal property of bedding, household furniture, and some amount of cash, and said Jared Young is possessed of considerable real and personal estate, that the property of the said Jared Young shall not be liable for the payment of the debts which may have heretofore or may hereafter be contracted by the said Nancy Holder, nor shall any of the property of the said Nancy Holder be liable for the payment of any contracts or legal liabilities which may have heretofore or may hereafter be entered into by said Jared Young. Jared Young (LS), Nancy Holder (LS), D. W. Holder (LS), Wit: Hezekiah McDougal, Martha C. Holder, C. Young. Proved by the oath of Hezekiah McDougal 18 Aug 1835 before J. Rogers, Q. U. Recorded 18 Aug 1835.

W, 472: South Carolina, Union District. John Ennis for love, good will and affection to my loving grandson John Jackson Ennis, one negro man named Peter, 2 May 1835. John Ennis (LS), Wit: Thomas Nance, Isom Vaughan. Proved by the oath of Thomas Nance 3 Aug 1835 before J. Rogers, Q. U. Recorded 3 Aug 1835.

W, 472-473: South Carolina, Union District. John Ennis for love, good will and affection to my loving grandson George Ware Ennis, one mulatto man named Aliab, 2 May 1835. John Ennis (LS), Wit: Thomas Nance, Isom Vaughan. Proved by the oath of Thomas Nance 3 Aug 1835 before J. Rogers, Q. U. Recorded 3 Aug 1835.

W, 473: South Carolina, Union District. Thomas L. B. Hughes of the district aforesaid for $600 to Mary Nougher, tract on the Sims Ferry Road, 100 acres adj. Judge Johnson, James Nougher, Widow Taylor, Z. Hooker, 6 July 1835. Thos L. B. Hughes (LS), Wit: William McGowen, J. Rogers. Proved by the oath of William McGowen 6 July 1835 before J. Rogers, Q.U. Recorded 6 July 1835.

W, 473-474: John Carothers of Union District for $40 to Dudley Mullins of same, 10 acres and thirty rood taken off the west end of a certain tract conveyed to Jane Hope by James Jinnings, adj. Dudley Mullins, William Adams, 25 March 1830. J. Carothers (LS), Wit: Frs. McCulloch. Uriah Mullins. Proved by the oath of Uriah Mullins 4 Dec 1834 before Isaac Going, Q. U. Recorded 22 Sept 1835.

W, 474-475: South Carolina, Union District. Robert Martin of said district for $450 to Robert McBeth of same, 134 acres, it being the land given by James White to Isaac White, on the waters of Sugar Creek and Fairforest, adj. Wm. Rountree, Alexander Hay, Goodwin, Free Tom, Polly Gibbs, 2 Feb 1835. Robert Martin (LS), Wit: John C. Jeter, James Hay. Jane L. Martin, wife of Robert Martin, relinquished dower 1 May 1835 before Jno Norman, Q.U. Proved by the oath of James Hay 6 April 1835 before Jno Norman, Q.U. Recorded 5 Aug 1835.

W, 475-476: South Carolina, Union District. Jesse Browning of district aforesaid for $275 to Jesse Estridge of same, part of an original survey granted to Edward Prince (Long), adj. Prince, Wilbanks, 138½ acres on Sparks Creek, waters of Tiger River adj. Johnston, Martin Gambling, John Alexander, Alexander Boyce, James Johnston, 25 Oct 1834. Jesse Browning (LS), Wit: James Johnson Jr., James Johnson Sr. Casa Browning (X), wife of Jesse Browning, relinquished dower 10 Jan 1835 before Jno Norman, Q.U. Proved by the oath of James Johnson Sr., 12 Jan 1835 before Jno Norman, Q.U. Recorded 5 Aug 1835.

W, 476-477: South Carolina, Union District. Edmund Simpson of district aforesaid for $6 to William Simpson of same, 50 acres, part of a tract that was laid out for John Head on waters of Elisha Creek adj. Kever, Thomas Hill, said Simpson, 6 Feb 1833. Edmond Simpson Sen (X), Wit: Wm. Huff, James Campbell. Proved by the oath of Wm. Huff 12 Jan 1835 before Jno Norman, Q.U. Recorded 26 March 1835.

W, 477: South Carolina, Union District. Edmund Simpson of district aforesaid for $62.50[?] to William Simson of same, 50 acres, part of a tract on waters of Elisha Creek adj. Jesse Dodd Senr, James Willard, 14 Aug 1834. Edmund Simpson (X), Wit: Jason Norman, Sam Simpson. Proved by the oath of Jason Norman 12 Jan 1835 before Jno Norman, Q.U. Recorded 25 March 1835.

W, 478: Whereas Robert Harris, late of the District of Union, deceased, duly made and executed his will which has been proved and now remains of record in the Office of the Ordinary in the said district of Union by which he nominated and appoint Ephraim Harris and Richard Thomson, exrs., who have qualified as such and take upon the execution thereof, and said Robert Harris devised and bequeathed that all his land not otherwise disposed of be sold by executors, and partitioned among his legatees, on 9 Sept 1809, said Ephraim Harris became the purchaser for $820 but has not received titles, now Ephraim Harris and Richard Thomson do grant to Benjamin Boyd for $900, tract of 358 acres, being a part of a tract granted to said Robert Harris on both sides of Harris Creek, adj. Ephraim Harris, John Ison, Capt. Nathaniel Gist, James Park now Benjamin Boyd, Joseph Mayes, 12 Sept 1816. Ephraim G. Harris (LS), Rich'd Thomson (LS), Wit: Wm. White, Jos. Mayes. Proved by the oath of Capt. Jos. Mayes 11 Aug 1835 before J. Rogers, Q.U. Recorded 11 Aug 1835.

W, 479A [there are two pages numbered 479]: South Carolina, Union District. Isaac Gregory of district aforesaid, for $92.50 to Gideon Steen of same, tract on waters of Brushy Creek, a branch of Tiger River, 38½ adj. Isaac Gregory, said Gideon Steen, 18 July 1835. Isaac Gregory (LS), Wit: Campbell Vance, Stephen Johnson. Proved by the oath of Campbell Vance 3 Aug 1835 before J. Rogers, Q. U. Recorded 3 Aug 1835.

W, 479A-479B: Ephraim Harris of District of Union for $300 to Benjamin Boyd of same, 100 acres on both sides of harris Creek, part of tract granted to Robert Harris, devised to said Ephraim Harris by the will of Robert Harris, late of Union District, deceased, adj. John P. Thomson, Jos. Mayes, John Ison, said Benjamin Boyd, 11 April 1817. Ephraim G. Harris (LS), Wit: Joseph Blassingham, H. Means. Proved by the oath of Capt. Joseph Mayes 11 Aug 1835 before J. Rogers, Q. U. Recorded 11 Aug 1835.

W, 479B: South Carolina, Union District. Thomas Nance of district of Union for $200 to Isom Vaughan of same, 57 acres on waters of Hughes Creek [not dated]. Thomas Nance (LS), Wit: James Ennis, George Ennes. Proved by the oath of George Ennis 43 Nov 1834 before Elias Mitchell, J.P. Recorded 28 March 1835.

W, 480: South Carolina, Union District. William White of district aforesaid for $600 to George Wofford of Spartanburgh District, part of the tract whereon I now live on the south side of Fairforest Creek and both sides of McElwains Creek, adj. Lancaster, Mayes, 71½ acres, 4 Oct 1834. Wm White (Seal), Wit: Isaac Wofford Jr., Perry West, Wm. Wofford. Mary D. White, wife of William White, relinquished dower in Spartanburgh District 9 Oct 1833 before James Hamm, J. Q. Proved by the oath of Isaac Wofford Jr. in Union District 21 Aug 1835 before J. Rogers, Q.U. Recorded 21 Aug 1845.

END OF DEED BOOK W

In Volume IV, the abstracts of the following deeds contained some errors. Correct abstracts follow.

R, 229: Sarah Steen, Nancy Steen, Nelly Steen, Thos Steen, James Steen, John Greer, William Steen, Katy Steen, Robert Steen, James Steen, William Steen, Nathaniel Steen, Sarah Enix, John Enix, James Nobles, Elias Steen, Silas Steen, James Steen, Richard Steen of Union District for $500 to John Steen Jr., all our rights or title to any tract of land belonging to us heirs of John Steen Senr, 12 Oct 1822. Nancy Steen (X) (LS), John Greer (LS), William Steen (LS), Catherine Steen (LS), Sarah Steen (X) (LS), Wit: Cs D. Jenkins, James Steen. Proved by the oath of James Steen 4 March 1823 before Saml Jeffries, J.P. Recorded 31 March 1823.

R, 405-406: State of Georgia, Henry County. Saml Houston & Patsey Houston his wife for $30 to William Steen of Union District, SC, tract on both sides of a branch of Guilkies Creek of Thickety of the waters of Broad River, adj. John Steen, 400 acres, also to all other lands to which we have nay right title or claim accruing from John Steen deceased, 21 June 1823. Saml Houston (LS), Patsey Houston (X) (Seal), Wit: Carter Houston, John Steen. Proved by the oath of John Steen 5 Feb 1824 before S. Jeffries, J.P. Recorded 5 Feb 1824.